Lecture Notes in Computer Science   10446

Commenced Publication in 1973
Founding and Former Series Editors:
Gerhard Goos, Juris Hartmanis, and Jan van Leeuwen

More information about this series at http://www.springer.com/series/7411

Jacek Rak · John Bay · Igor Kotenko
Leonard Popyack · Victor Skormin
Krzysztof Szczypiorski (Eds.)

Computer Network Security

7th International Conference
on Mathematical Methods, Models, and Architectures
for Computer Network Security, MMM-ACNS 2017
Warsaw, Poland, August 28–30, 2017
Proceedings

 Springer

Editors
Jacek Rak
Gdansk University of Technology
Gdansk
Poland

John Bay
Binghamton University
Binghamton, NY
USA

Igor Kotenko
St. Petersburg Institute
  for Informatics and Automation
St. Petersburg
Russia

Leonard Popyack
Utica College
Utica, NY
USA

Victor Skormin
Binghamton University
Binghamton, NY
USA

Krzysztof Szczypiorski
Warsaw University of Technology
Warsaw
Poland

ISSN 0302-9743   ISSN 1611-3349 (electronic)
Lecture Notes in Computer Science
ISBN 978-3-319-65126-2   ISBN 978-3-319-65127-9 (eBook)
DOI 10.1007/978-3-319-65127-9

Library of Congress Control Number: 2017948184

LNCS Sublibrary: SL5 – Computer Communication Networks and Telecommunications

Printed on acid-free paper

This Springer imprint is published by Springer Nature
The registered company is Springer International Publishing AG
The registered company address is: Gewerbestrasse 11, 6330 Cham, Switzerland

Preface

This volume contains papers presented at the 7th International Conference on Mathematical Methods, Models, and Architectures for Computer Network Security (MMM-ACNS 2017) held in Warsaw, Poland during August 28–30, 2017. The conference was organized by Gdansk University of Technology, in cooperation with Binghamton University (State University of New York), USA, and the Polish Association of Telecommunication Engineers (SIT), Poland.

MMM-ACNS 2017 followed six former editions of MMM-ACNS all hosted by St. Petersburg Institute for Informatics and Automation of the Russian Academy of Sciences (SPIIRAS), RU. MMM-ACNS 2017 provided an international forum for sharing the original results referring to fundamental as well as applied problems in the context of computer network security. Special focus was put on mathematical aspects of information and computer network security.

In all, 40 regular papers submitted to the conference were subject to extensive reviews. Each paper received at least three reviews (and some of them as many as five reviews). Finally, 12 papers were accepted as full papers, and 13 papers as short papers. Approved regular papers were organized into seven technical sessions, namely:

- Critical Infrastructure Protection and Visualization
- Security and Resilience of Network Systems
- Adaptive Security
- Anti-malware Techniques: Detection, Analysis, Prevention
- Security of Emerging Technologies
- Applied Cryptography
- New Ideas and Paradigms for Security

The conference program was enhanced by three invited talks and two keynote speeches (by Dipankar Dasgupta from USA, and Antanas Cenys from Lithuania, accordingly).

The success of the conference was undoubtedly due to the team effort of the organizers, reviewers, and participants. In particular, we would like to acknowledge the individual contributions of the Technical Program Committee members and reviewers. Our sincere gratitude goes to all the participants of the conference as well as to Polish Association of Telecommunication Engineers, SIT, Poland (in particular to Ewa Woroszyło and Mirosław Stando), for their great help in solving the local arrangement issues.

August 2017

Jacek Rak
John Bay
Igor Kotenko
Leonard Popyack
Victor Skormin
Krzysztof Szczypiorski

Organization

General Co-chairs

Jacek Rak   Gdansk University of Technology, Poland
John Bay   Binghamton University
     (State University of New York), USA

Steering Committee

John Bay   Binghamton University
     (State University of New York), USA
Igor Kotenko   St. Petersburg Institute for Informatics
     and Automation of the Russian Academy
     of Sciences, SPIIRAS, Russia
Leonard Popyack   Utica College, USA
Jacek Rak   Gdansk University of Technology, Poland
Victor Skormin   Binghamton University
     (State University of New York), USA

Publication Chair

Krzysztof Szczypiorski   Warsaw University of Technology, Poland

Local Organizing Committee

Andrzej Dulka   Polish Association of Telecommunication Engineers,
     Poland
Wojciech Halka   Polish Association of Telecommunication Engineers,
     Poland
Miroslaw Stando   Polish Association of Telecommunication Engineers,
     Poland
Ewa Woroszylo   Polish Association of Telecommunication Engineers,
     Poland

Program Committee

Ryszard Antkiewicz   Military University of Technology, Poland
Cataldo Basile   Politecnico di Torino, Italy
Fabrizio Bayardi   University of Pisa, Italy
Nataliia Bielova   Inria, France
Elias Bou-Harb   Florida Atlantic University, USA
Julien Bourgeois   University of Franche-Comté/FEMTO-ST, France

Douglas Summerville   Binghamton University
                                (State University of New York), USA
Jerzy Surma   Warsaw School of Economics, Poland
Nadia Tawabi   Laval University, Canada
Bhavani Thuraisingham   The University of Texas at Dallas, USA
Arnur Tokhtabayev   T&T Security LLP, Kazakhstan
Shambhu Upadhyaya   University at Buffalo, USA
Janusz Zalewski   Florida Gulf Coast University, USA

Additional Reviewers

Marios Anagnostopoulos   Singapore University of Technology and Design,
                                Singapore
Spyros Kokolakis   University of the Aegean, Greece
Michał Misztal   Military University of Technology, Poland
Francesco Mercaldo   Consiglio Nazionale delle Ricerche, Italy
Christos Kalloniatis   University of the Aegean, Greece
Nael Abu-Ghazaleh   University of California, Riverside, USA

Contents

Invited Papers

Meeting Requirements Imposed by Secure Software Development
Standards and Still Remaining Agile 3
   Janusz Górski and Katarzyna Łukasiewicz

Adapting Enterprise Security Approaches for Evolving Cloud Processing
and Networking Models. 16
   Andrew Hutchison

Data Mining and Information Security. 28
   Alexander Grusho

Critical Infrastructure Protection and Visualization

Extending FAST-CPS for the Analysis of Data Flows
in Cyber-Physical Systems. 37
   Laurens Lemaire, Jan Vossaert, Bart De Decker, and Vincent Naessens

Visualization-Driven Approach to Anomaly Detection in the Movement
of Critical Infrastructure. 50
   Evgenia Novikova and Ivan Murenin

Detection and Mitigation of Time Delay Injection Attacks on Industrial
Control Systems with PLCs 62
   Emrah Korkmaz, Matthew Davis, Andrey Dolgikh, and Victor Skormin

Choosing Models for Security Metrics Visualization 75
   Maxim Kolomeec, Gustavo Gonzalez-Granadillo, Elena Doynikova,
   Andrey Chechulin, Igor Kotenko, and Hervé Debar

Security and Resilience of Network Systems

iCrawl: A Visual High Interaction Web Crawler 91
   Deeraj Nagothu and Andrey Dolgikh

Race Condition Faults in Multi-core Systems 104
   Leonard Popyack and Jay Biernat

Security Requirements for the Deployment of Services
Across Tactical SOA. 115
   Vasileios Gkioulos and Stephen D. Wolthusen

Adaptive Security

Nodal Cooperation Equilibrium Analysis in Multi-hop Wireless
Ad Hoc Networks with a Reputation System   131
   Jerzy Konorski and Karol Rydzewski

Network Anomaly Detection Based on an Ensemble of Adaptive Binary
Classifiers   143
   Alexander Branitskiy and Igor Kotenko

Cardholder's Reputation System for Contextual Risk Management
in Payment Transactions   158
   Albert Sitek and Zbigniew Kotulski

Towards Self-aware Approach for Mobile Devices Security   171
   Nanda Kumar Thanigaivelan, Ethiopia Nigussie,
   Seppo Virtanen, and Jouni Isoaho

Anti-malware Techniques: Detection, Analysis, Prevention

Resident Security System for Government/Industry Owned Computers   185
   Matthew Davis, Emrah Korkmaz, Andrey Dolgikh, and Victor Skormin

tLab: A System Enabling Malware Clustering Based on Suspicious
Activity Trees.   195
   Anton Kopeikin, Arnur Tokhtabayev, Nurlan Tashatov,
   and Dina Satybaldina

Malware Analysis and Detection via Activity Trees
in User-Dependent Environment   211
   Arnur Tokhtabayev, Anton Kopeikin, Nurlan Tashatov,
   and Dina Satybaldina

A Concept of Clustering-Based Method for Botnet Detection   223
   Hubert Ostap and Ryszard Antkiewicz

Security of Emerging Technologies

Easy 4G/LTE IMSI Catchers for Non-Programmers.   235
   Stig F. Mjølsnes and Ruxandra F. Olimid

Anomaly Detection in Cognitive Radio Networks Exploiting Singular
Spectrum Analysis   247
   Qi Dong, Zekun Yang, Yu Chen, Xiaohua Li, and Kai Zeng

HEPPA: Highly Efficient Privacy Preserving Authentication for ITS   260
   An Braeken, Sergey Bezzateev, Abdellah Touhafi, and Natalia Voloshina

Applied Cryptography

Automated Cryptographic Analysis of the Pedersen Commitment Scheme . . .   275
    Roberto Metere and Changyu Dong

Steganalysis Based on Statistical Properties of the Encrypted Messages   288
    *Valery Korzhik, Ivan Fedyanin, Artur Godlewski,
    and Guillermo Morales-Luna*

Security Assessment of Cryptographic Algorithms.   299
    Marcin Niemiec and Maciej Francikiewicz

Quick Response Code Secure: A Cryptographically Secure Anti-Phishing
Tool for QR Code Attacks   313
    Vasileios Mavroeidis and Mathew Nicho

New Ideas and Paradigms for Security

A Novel and Unifying View of Trustworthiness in Cyberphysical Systems . . .   327
    Steven Drager and Janusz Zalewski

Information Security of SDN on the Basis of Meta Data   339
    *Alexander Grusho, Nick Grusho, Michael Zabezhailo,
    Alexander Zatsarinny, and Elena Timonina*

Toward Third-Party Immune Applications   348
    Omar Iraqi and Hanan El Bakkali

Author Index   361

Invited Papers

Meeting Requirements Imposed by Secure Software Development Standards and Still Remaining Agile

Janusz Górski and Katarzyna Łukasiewicz[✉]

Department of Software Engineering,
Gdańsk University of Technology, Gdańsk, Poland
janusz.gorski@eti.pg.gda.pl,
katarzyna.lukasiewicz@pg.gda.pl

Abstract. The paper introduces the AgileSafe method of selecting agile practices for software development projects that are constrained by assurance requirements resulting from safety and/or security related standards. Such requirements are represented by argumentation templates which explain how the evidence collected during agile practices implementation will support the conformity with the requirements. Application of the method is demonstrated by referring to a case study of development of a medical domain related application that is supposed to meet the requirements imposed by the IEC 62443-4.1 standard.

1 Introduction

In the last years, several initiatives have been undertaken to address security in the software development lifecycle. These include prescriptive models like Microsoft Security Development Lifecycle (SDL) [1], descriptive surveys like Building Security In Maturity Model (BSIMM) [2], and recent standards, like ISO/IEC 27034 [3] and IEC 62443-4.1 [4].

Implementing a full-fledged security into software development lifecycle may be expensive. Smaller software vendors like small and medium enterprises may not afford to have enough resources for full-scale security software initiatives however, they still need to compete in the market. Typically companies start with reactive security risk management, and then, if their business context presses for this, possibly consider moving towards a more proactive approach to security. In many cases however, this move is being initiated after a company gets hit by the first serious security incident. A reason for this can be that customers do not often require evidence of software security, and ignore (possible) negative events that are rare and often not publicly shared. However, the significant change in the threats landscape together with the growing proliferation of ICT technologies into critical application domains lead to the situation of rapidly growing awareness that insufficient software security may result in unacceptable losses. As the result, we can observe emerging standards which attempt to provide the up to date reference to the recommended practices, mechanisms and controls with the intention to close the gap through which security risks can sneak into

© Springer International Publishing AG 2017
J. Rak et al. (Eds.): MMM-ACNS 2017, LNCS 10446, pp. 3–15, 2017.
DOI: 10.1007/978-3-319-65127-9_1

critical software applications. Examples can be general standards like ISO/IEC 27034, the leading company standards like Microsoft SDL and others.

The increasing concern for security issues has coincided with a growth of agile methods. Since the announcement of Agile Manifesto [5] more and more companies are adopting this approach in some form. Scrum [6], eXtreme Programming [7] and other methodologies have evolved to cater for more complex, less naturally agile environments involving larger teams (for instance SAFe [8] and Scrum of Scrums [9]) or corporate structures (for instance, DevOps [10]). Presently, an increasing number of the companies concerned about secure software development are at the same time using and appreciating different forms of agility. Traditional guidelines applicable to the rigid, plan-driven software development processes do not appeal to these companies, which often appreciate the benefits of following the lightweight processes and do not want to give them up. This opens a room for researching towards a solution which enables to meet the recommendations and to follow the related best practices of secure software development processes while still not backing down from being agile unless it is necessary. A framework, which would allow to find a right balance between the security assurance constraints and the agile approach to software development might be of a great value to present software vendors.

The allure of agile methods and their potential benefits have also influenced domains assumed to be home grounds for a disciplined approach. Evolution of new personal use devices that might have safety implications along with a shift from hardware to more software intensive solutions intensified the pace of product development and invigorated user expectations. As a result, more companies along with researchers have become interested in introducing agile practices into the safety-critical software development process [11, 12, 13, 14]. To this end, we have introduced AgileSafe method [15] to help to define such hybrid agile approach customized for a safety-critical software project and to maintain conformity with relevant safety standards and norms at the same time. In its essence, AgileSafe is a tool for collecting and suggesting, for a given development project, the most suitable agile practices as well as the means for managing and monitoring conformance with the relevant assurance requirements.

In this paper we demonstrate how AgileSafe could be adapted to support agile approach to secure software development in a way that provides for assessment and demonstration to which extent the security recommendations of a given normative document (like a standard) are met by the agile practices incorporated into the software development process. The expected result is achieving two important goals: (1) selecting a set of agile software development practices which do not violate secure software development recommendations, and (2) demonstrating (e.g. to the third party) that the implemented software development process meets the requirements imposed by the secure software development standards and/or guidelines.

The paper is structured as follows. First, we give an overview of AgileSafe explaining its process model and the knowledge base component. Then we explain how the assurance requirements resulting from the selected standards are represented in a form of assurance argument patterns and how they are linked with the software development practices being selected from the knowledge base. This is followed be a case study illustrating AgileSafe application to a system from the medical domain constrained by the IEC 62443-4.1 standard. At the end we present the conclusions resulting from this research.

2 Overview of AgileSafe

An overview of AgileSafe applied to a software development project (the Project) is presented in the Fig. 1. The main end products of AgileSafe are: *Project Practices Set* and *Assurance Arguments.*

The software development project under consideration (the Project) is constrained by its *Project Characteristics* and the relevant *Regulatory Requirements*. Project Characteristics are obtained by assessing different aspects (called *Factors*) of the Project. Factors describe Project environment and infrastructure. Regulatory Requirements represent selected standards and/or guidelines the Project is supposed to be conformant with.

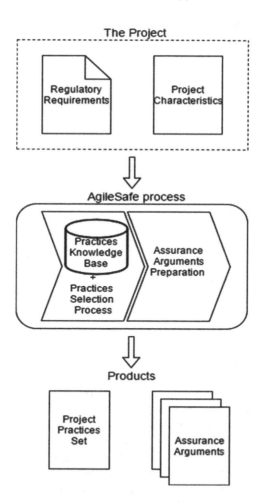

Fig. 1. AgileSafe applied to a software development project

To characterize projects, we follow the approach of [16] for scaling agile, focusing on the following seven factors: Team Size, Geographical Distribution, Domain Complexity, Organizational Distribution, Technical Complexity, Organizational Complexity, Enterprise Discipline. The influence of each Factor on a project can then be evaluated on a five-point scale (multiple selection is allowed):

1. *Team Size* (based on the survey in [17])

A – Under 10 developers; B – From 10 to 50 developers; C – From 50 to 100 developers; D – 100's of developers; E – 1000's of developers

2. *Geographical Distribution* (based on the survey in [17])

A – Co-located; B – Same building; C – Within driving distance; D – some working from home; E – Globally distributed

3. *Domain Complexity*

A – Straightforward; B - Predictable; C – Quickly changing; D – Complicated; E – Intricate/Emerging

4. *Organizational Distribution*

A – Collaborative; B – Different teams; C – Different departments; D – Different partner companies; E – Contractual

5. *Technical Complexity*

A – Homogenous; B - Multiple technologies; C – New technology; D - System/embedded solutions; E – Heterogeneous/Legacy

6. *Organizational Complexity*

A – Flexible, intuitive; B – Flexible, structured; C – Stable, evolutionary; D – Stable, planned; E – Rigid

7. *Enterprise Discipline*

A – Project focus; B – Mostly project focused; C – Balanced; D – Mostly enterprise focused; E – Enterprise focus

A user of AgileSafe is guided through the *Practices Knowledge Base* (PKB) which contains descriptions of software development practices. The user selects from PKB the practices suitable for the Project. Selection of these practices is based on the Project Factors and the assurance requirements (derived from Regulatory Requirements) the Project needs to comply with. The resulting *Project Practices Set* is to be implemented in the software development process of the Project. The assurance requirements derived from Regulatory Requirements are reflected in *Assurance Arguments*. These arguments help the user to collect, during the software development process, the evidence sufficient to demonstrate that the assurance requirements have been met.

PKB is populated, along with general software development practices, with practices focused on security issues. And if security is the primary concern, the Regulatory Requirements would represent the requirements imposed by the security-oriented standards and/or guidelines (like ISO/IEC 27034, IEC 62443-4.1 and others).

3 Practices Knowledge Base (PKB)

The intention behind PKB is to assemble these agile practices for software development which provide a base for the custom-made approach. Additionally, PKB stores information about the elements vital to the practices selection as well as the rules, which determine the suggested Project Practices Set.

Each practice stored in PKB is described following the same pattern: (1) name of the practice, (2) description details of the practice, (3) discipline the practice belongs to, (4) practice's *Environment Characteristics* in which the practice performs the best and (5) *Assurance Context* which identifies the security assurance requirements the practice is able to meet.

Project environment characteristics provide information about the Factors where the practice fits the best.

The assurance context describes the relationship between a given practice and the specific security assurance requirements. For each requirement belonging to the assurance context of a given practice, the practice, if implemented, has a potential to deliver acceptable evidence to demonstrate the compliance with the requirement. The purpose of the practice (in relation to the security requirement) and the results delivered by the practice are given explicitly.

In Fig. 2 we present an example description of the Abuser Stories practice relevant to IEC 62443 4.1, section 7.3 SR2-*Threat model*.

The AgileSafe practices selection process shown in Fig. 1 implements the algorithm that takes as its input the Project Characteristics as well as the Regulatory Requirements of the Project and then searches PKB for the practices which match the Project. The practices which correspond the best are included in the Project Practices Set that is being suggested to the user.

4 Meeting Requirements of Security Related Standards

An assurance argument (called *assurance* case) is a structure of claims supported by explicitly provided evidence. In its application context, an assurance case demonstrates that a product, process or system achieves a specified goal (like the safety of a patient using a medical device, security of a product in its application environment and so on). Recommendation on the structure of assurance arguments can be found in ISO/IEC 15026 [19]. Figure 3 presents a generic model of assurance argument implemented in the Argevide NOR-STA tool [20] (the icons show how the model elements are represented graphically).

The goal is represented by the *Claim* node. In order to demonstrate this goal the *Argumentation strategy* is used and it can be further justified by expressing its *Rationale*. The argumentation is then supported by *Sub-claims* (more specific goals), *Facts* and/or *Assumptions*. The sub-claims can be then further decomposed by giving their argumentation strategies. Facts and Assumptions are demonstrated by *evidence* which is collected and integrated with the assurance argument by using *references*.

The idea of *safety cases* (a specific assurance argument, focusing on safety) was initiated in relation to nuclear safety several decades ago and then proliferated to other

Id	1.1
Name	Abuser Stories
Description	Abuser stories describe likely threats to critical assets in the form and language familiar to XP (eXtreme Programming) developers and customers. Like User stories, they are documented on index cards in a language understandable by the customer and developers. An abuser story is a textual description of such a malicious interaction of a threat agent with the system that, if successful, results in the increase of risk to the asset(s) valued by the owner or user(s) of the system. An example of a simplified abuser story is: *A participant could modify another competitor participant's proposal to make it look bad.* Abuser stories are discussed with the customer team to ensure their relevance and importance. Finding good Abuser stories is a brainstorming activity. However, using resources such as attack patterns can be helpful here. Abuser stories are the basis for security testing of the system [18].

Discipline		
	Architecture	No
	Deployment	No
	Development	No
	Environment	No
	Project Management	Yes
	Requirements	Yes
	Test	Yes

Environment Characteristics:	Factor	Values
	Team Size	A – Under 10 developers; B – From 10 to 50 developers; C – From 50 to 100 developers
	Geographical Distribution	A – Co-located; B – Same building; C – Some working from home; D – Within driving distance; E – Globally distributed
	Domain Complexity	A – Straightforward; B - Predictable; C – Quickly changing; D – Complicated
	Organisational Distribution	A – Collaborative; B – Different teams; C – Different departments; D – Different partner companies; E – Contractual
	Technical Complexity	A – Homogenous; B - Multiple technologies; C – New technology; D - System/embedded solutions
	Organisational Complexity	A – Flexible, intuitive; B – Flexible, structured; C – Stable, evolutionary; D – Stable, planned
	Enterprise Discipline	A – Project focus; B – Mostly project focused; C – Balanced

Assurance context:	Name of the Regulation and regulatory requirement	Purpose	Results
	IEC 62443 4.1 Section 7.3 SR2- Threat model	Security threats can be identified and documented using stories written in natural language and managed in a backlog form	Abuser stories describe likely threats to critical assets using natural language and can be managed in a backlog form.

Fig. 2. Example practice description in PKB

domains. Presently, under a more general name *assurance case* is being used in many application domains like railway, medical devices, automotive and others. For instance,

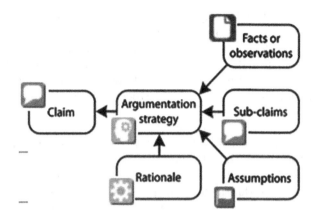

Fig. 3. The generic structure of assurance argument in NOR-STA.

a series of documents describe the application of assurance cases in US FDA certification process [21, 22]. Assurance cases also have gained attention in relation to security. In 2007 SEI issued a paper with general advice on creating security assurance cases [23], which was followed by a more detailed guidance [24]. A growing body of researchers acknowledge potential benefits of using assurance cases in security context [25–27].

In AgileSafe, the Regulatory Requirements (see Fig. 1) are the requirements imposed by the applicable standards, guidelines and other normative documents. The relationship between these requirements and the practices maintained in PKB is represented in separate Assurance Arguments (see Fig. 4).

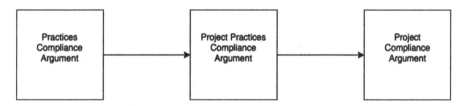

Fig. 4. Assurance arguments in AgileSafe

As illustrated in Fig. 4, AgileSafe distinguishes three types of assurance arguments: Practices Compliance Argument (PCA), Project Practices Compliance Argument (PPCA) and Project Compliance Argument (PrCA).

PCA is an argumentation template, which is developed separately for each relevant standard (belonging to Regulatory Requirements). The structure of PCA follows the structure of the standard. PCA focuses on the conformance of the practices from PKB with the requirements of the standard. For each such requirement, PCA proposes an argumentation strategy that refers to selected practices of PKB and suggests the evidence to be collected while applying such practices to demonstrate the compliance. PCA is standard specific and is independent of the Project.

PPCA is PCA adapted to a specific Project and constrained by the Project Practices Set specific to this Project. PPCA refers only to the Practices used in the Project along with the description of evidence they are able to provide. The practices that do not belong to the Project Practices Set are not considered in PPCA. Therefore, PPCA is standard specific and project specific.

PPCA serves as a template to create PrCA for the Project. PrCA is an assurance argument collecting the required evidence sufficient to demonstrate conformance with Regulatory Requirement associated with the Project. While PPCA proposes an argumentation structure that refers to the practices selected for the Project and indicates the evidence to be collected while implementing the practices, PrCA integrates the actual evidence in the argumentation structure in a way which makes the evidence accessible to the assessor of the argument. Then the assessor, after examining the evidence, can decide if the argument is acceptable and consequently the Project conforms with its Regulatory Requirements.

5   Case Study

A real project was conducted by a group of students of Informatics and lasted for 2 semesters, from February 2015 till January 2016. It concerned a health-related mobile application. The project team cooperated with a software company Bright Inventions [28] which was a stakeholder as well as offered a technical support. The task assigned to the students was to implement an iBeacon [29] based clinic appointment and queue management system for iOS.

Three students with work experience in iOS were assigned for this project. The project was called DocBeacon, which was also the name of the resulting product [30]. DocBeacon was supposed to integrate with Apple Watch, the device that contains four sensors which monitor heart rate and an accelerometer [31]. The data stored in the application were classified as confidential. Because of its functionality and privacy/safety constraints, DocBeacon could be placed somewhere between fitness-tracking/wellness-related applications and the applications used for diagnosis, treatment and prevention.

As the first step, project analysis was carried out and resulted in DocBeacon description and characteristics. It could also be assumed that DocBeacon is to be constrained by selected security requirements of IEC 62443-4.1, as presented in Fig. 5.

A selection of software engineering practices might be added to the AgileSafe PKB (including the security-oriented practices) which were referred to while building the PCA for IEC 62443 4.1. Figure 6 presents an excerpt of PCA represented in the Argevide NOR-STA tool:

Id	1
Name	DocBeacon
Description	*The product is a full-featured system supporting work of medical clinics. There are two main problems addressed and solved by this project. The first one is really earthbound: queues. Many medical clinics allow for online signup, yet clients are compelled to confirm their presence at the registration desk right before the visit. This usually means waiting in a long queue. This is particularly a problem during rush hours such as before 9 am or after 5 pm.* *DocBeacon solves this issue through automating the whole process by connecting beacons in the medical clinic and iOS devices in clients' pockets. This simple idea and seamless implementation allow for „no hassle" experience for the users.* *The second issue with medical clinics is the reliability of patients' medical history interview. People are often confused about what and when is exactly happening to them. They exaggerate or, even worse, ignore some symptoms, which makes doctors' work to identify health problems often a very painful experience. This product makes an attempt to fix that. DocBeacon utilizes HealthKit API which makes medical reports and interviews much more reliable and partially independent from patients' sensations and emotions.* *Potential users of the product: All people and all medical clinics around the world! For starters, we target only iOS users but the iBeacon® technology used allows for communication with all kinds of different devices.*
Regulatory Requirements	IEC 62443-4.1;

Project Characteristics	Factor	Values
	Team Size	A – Under 10 developers;
	Geographical Distribution	C – Some working from home
	Domain Complexity	C – Quickly changing; D – Complicated;
	Organisational Distribution	A – Collaborative
	Technical Complexity	B - Multiple technologies; C – New technology; D - System/embedded solutions;
	Organisational Complexity	B – Flexible, structured
	Enterprise Discipline	A – Project focus

Fig. 5. *DocBeacon* project description and characteristics.

The structure of PCA and the labels of the argumentation elements follow the organization of the standard, with specific Security Requirements (SR) of IEC 62443-4.1 being explicitly represented in PCA (Fig. 7 presents a fragment of IEC 62443 4.1 contents table related to Fig. 6).

☐ 7. Practice 2 - Specification of security requirements
⊟ ⧄ Argument by the standard requirements
　 ⧉ Decomposition by the standard requirements
⊞ ☐ SR-1 Product security context
⊟ ☐ SR-2 Threat model
　 ⊟ ⧄ Argument by artefacts providing evidence for compliance with the specific standard requirement
　 　 ⧉ Each of the following types of artefacts provide enough evidence to support the compliance with a given standard requirement.
　 ⊟ ☐ Security threats can be identified and documented using stories written in natural language and managed in a backlog form
　 　 ⊟ ⧄ Argument by providing a description of the practices generating given evidence material
　 　 　 ⧉ By following given practices a satisfying evidence should be obtained
　 　 ⊟ ☐ Abuser stories describe likely threats to critical assets using natural language and can be managed in a backlog form.
　 　 　 ⧉ Abuser Stories [DESCRIPTION]
　 　 ⊞ ☐ Risk Backlog collates stories and decision concerning risk in a backlog form
　 　 ⊞ ☐ SAFECode Security-focused stories address most common issues in a natural language form
　 　 ⊞ ☐ Generic Security User Stories reflect commonly found security needs in a user story form
　 ⊟ ☐ Security threats can be pictured and analysed using a tree structure
　 　 ⊟ ⧄ Argument by providing a description of the practices generating given evidence material
　 　 　 ⧉ By following given practices a satisfying evidence should be obtained
　 　 ⊞ ☐ Attack trees provide a formal way of describing the security of a system in a tree structure
⊞ ☐ SR-3 Product security requirements

Fig. 6. A fragment of PCA for IEC 62443 4.1

7   Practice 2 – Specification of security requirements ..
7.1   Purpose...
7.2   SR-1 – Product security context ....
　7.2.1   Requirement....................................
　7.2.2   Rationale and supplemental guidance.
　7.2.3   Requirement enhancements ....
7.3   SR-2 –Threat model ....
　7.3.1   Requirement....................................
　7.3.2   Rationale and supplemental guidance.
　7.3.3   Requirement enhancements ....
7.4   SR-3 – Product security requirements ....

Fig. 7. A fragment of IEC 62443 4.1 contents table

Based on DocBeacon characteristics a Project Practices Set would be then selected from PKB. As DocBeacon was a 'small' project, the selected practices would be mostly agile oriented.

In the next step, PPCA was derived from PCA focusing on the practices that could be included in the Project Practices Set. An excerpt of PPCA is given in Fig. 8.

As illustrated in Fig. 8, one of the practices chosen for use in DocBeacon is Abuser Stories – the stories that describe potential threats in an agile way, following the user stories style but focused on security (a description of Abuser Stories practice is given in Fig. 2). Note that only Abuser stories and Risk Backlog remained in PPCA whereas SAFECode Security-focused Used Stories and Generic Security User Stories were not included.

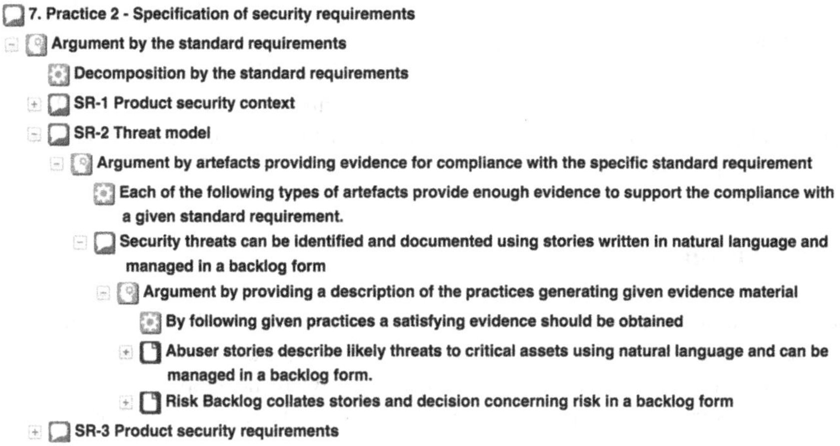

📄 **7. Practice 2 - Specification of security requirements**

  ⊟ 🔲 **Argument by the standard requirements**

     ⚙ Decomposition by the standard requirements

  ⊞ 📄 SR-1 Product security context

  ⊟ 📄 SR-2 Threat model

    ⊟ 🔲 Argument by artefacts providing evidence for compliance with the specific standard requirement

      ⚙ Each of the following types of artefacts provide enough evidence to support the compliance with a given standard requirement.

     ⊟ 📄 Security threats can be identified and documented using stories written in natural language and managed in a backlog form

      ⊟ 🔲 Argument by providing a description of the practices generating given evidence material

       ⚙ By following given practices a satisfying evidence should be obtained

       ⊞ 📄 Abuser stories describe likely threats to critical assets using natural language and can be managed in a backlog form.

      ⊞ 📄 Risk Backlog collates stories and decision concerning risk in a backlog form

  ⊞ 📄 SR-3 Product security requirements

Fig. 8. A fragment of PPCA for DocBeacon

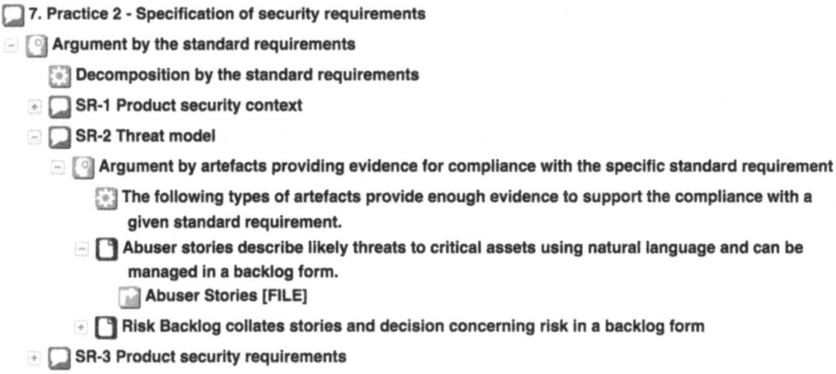

📄 **7. Practice 2 - Specification of security requirements**

  ⊟ 🔲 **Argument by the standard requirements**

     ⚙ Decomposition by the standard requirements

  ⊞ 📄 SR-1 Product security context

  ⊟ 📄 SR-2 Threat model

    ⊟ 🔲 Argument by artefacts providing evidence for compliance with the specific standard requirement

      ⚙ The following types of artefacts provide enough evidence to support the compliance with a given standard requirement.

     ⊟ 📄 Abuser stories describe likely threats to critical assets using natural language and can be managed in a backlog form.

      🔗 Abuser Stories [FILE]

     ⊞ 📄 Risk Backlog collates stories and decision concerning risk in a backlog form

  ⊞ 📄 SR-3 Product security requirements

Fig. 9. A fragment of PrCA for DocBeacon

From PPCA the DocBeacon developers would know that in order to demonstrate conformity with SR-2 Threat Model it is necessary to follow the Abuser Stories practice. In effect Abuser Stories application, a set of different abuser stories would be created and stored in a dedicated file. Below is an example of an abuser story for DocBeacon:

As a Malicious Hacker, I will take advantage of unencrypted connection,
so I could get unauthorized access to data, and pick up patient's private medical information.

Based on PPCA, the PrCA argument can be developed by collecting the evidence 'produced' by the implemented practices and integrating this evidence with PPCA. An example of such evidence is Abuser Stories [FILE] resulting from the implementation of Abuser Stories practice. An excerpt from the resulting PrCA is shown in 🔗 Fig. 9. The icon represents the link integrating the file containing abuser stories with the argument.

The assessor can easily follow this link and evaluate if the Abuser Stories [FILE] contains enough evidence to support the compliance with SR-2 Threat Model requirement.

PrCA can be a subject of evaluation to assess if the collected evidence provides a satisfactory support to the claims included in the argumentation. Argevide NOR-STA supports different argument evaluation mechanisms that can be used to this end, an example can be found in [32].

6   Conclusion

In this article we presented an overview of AgileSafe, a method supporting agile software development while still being able to demonstrate and assess conformity with selected standards. The method is dedicated to software development projects constrained by assurance requirements resulting from regulations and standards, in particular in safety and security critical applications.

Most of the elements of the method once elaborated, can be reused for different projects (it concerns the practices represented in PKB and PCA argumentation templates). While applied to a specific software development project, AgileSafe helps to custom-tailor the set of practices and the set assurance arguments in a way which provides for meeting the assurance requirements while still remaining agile.

We have been validating AgileSafe using real life data in safety-critical context and presently we expand the effort to cover the security aspects as well. To this end, the basic result of the presented case study is that it demonstrates the applicability of AgileSafe to the security-related constraints imposed by an emerging international standard. Presently we are also looking into complementarity between AgileSafe and SafeScrum [33] to see if and how both methods can mutually benefit.

References

1. Microsoft Security Development Lifecycle (SDL). https://www.microsoft.com/en-us/sdl/
2. Building Security in Maturity Model (BSIMM). https://www.bsimm.com/
3. ISO/IEC 27034 series Application security. http://www.iso27001security.com/html/27034.html
4. IEC 62443-4-1 4-1: Secure product development life-cycle requirements
5. Manifesto for Agile Software Development. http://agilemanifesto.org
6. Schwaber, K., Beedle, M.: Agile Software Development with Scrum. Prentice Hall, Upper Saddle River (2002)
7. Beck, K., Andres, C.: Extreme Programming Explained. Addison-Wesley Professional, Boston (2004)
8. Knaster, R., Leffingwell, D.: SAFe Distilled: Applying the Scaled Agile Framework for Lean Software and Systems Engineering. Addison-Wesley Professional (2017)
9. Scrum of Scrums | Agile Alliance. https://www.agilealliance.org/glossary/scrum-of-scrums/
10. Kim, G., Willis, J., Debois, P., Humble, J., Allspaw, J.: The DevOps Handbook. Trade Select (2016)

11. Paige, R.F., Charalambous, R., Ge, X., Brooke, P.J.: Towards agile engineering of high-integrity systems. In: Harrison, M.D., Sujan, M.-A. (eds.) SAFECOMP 2008. LNCS, vol. 5219, pp. 30–43. Springer, Heidelberg (2008). doi:10.1007/978-3-540-87698-4_6
12. Rasmussen, R., Hughes, T., Jenks, J., Skach, J.: Adopting agile in an FDA regulated environment. In: Proceedings of the 2009 Agile Conference, pp. 151–155 (2009)
13. McHugh, M., McCaffery, F., Coady, G.: An agile implementation within a medical device software organisation. Commun. Comput. Inf. Sci. **477**, 190–201 (2014)
14. Myklebust, T., Stålhane, T., Hanssen, G.: Use of agile practices when developing safety-critical software. In: Proceeding of International System Safety Conference (2016)
15. Łukasiewicz, K., Górski, J.: AgileSafe – a method of introducing agile practices into safety-critical software development processes. In: Proceedings of the 2016 Federated Conference on Computer Science and Information Systems (2016)
16. Ambler, S.: IBM agility@scale™: Become as Agile as You Can Be. IBM (2010)
17. Ambler, S.: Agility at Scale: Results from the Summer 2012 DDJ State of the IT Union Survey. http://www.ambysoft.com/surveys/stateOfITUnion201209.html
18. Boström, G., Wäyrynen, J., Bodén, M., Beznosov, K., Kruchten, P.: Extending XP practices to support security requirements engineering. In: Proceedings of the 2006 International Workshop on Software Engineering for Secure Systems - SESS 2006, pp. 11–18 (2006)
19. ISO/IEC 15026 Systems and software engineering – Systems and software assurance
20. NOR-STA tool. www.argevide.com
21. Weinstock, C., Goodenough, J.: Towards an assurance case practice for medical devices. Technical Note Software Engineering Institute (2009)
22. FDA: Guidance – Total Product Life Cycle: Infusion Pump-Premarket Notification Submissions [510 (k)] (2010)
23. Weinstock, C.B., Lipson, H.F., Goodenough J.: Arguing security – creating security assurance cases. In: Software Engineering Institute Report (2007). http://resources.sei.cmu.edu/asset_files/WhitePaper/2013_019_001_293637.pdf
24. Weinstock, C.B, Lipson, H.F.: Evidence of assurance: laying the foundation for a credible security case. In: Software Engineering Institute Report (2013), https://resources.sei.cmu.edu/asset_files/WhitePaper/2013_019_001_295685.pdf
25. Alexander, R., Hawkins, R., Kelly, T.: Security assurance cases: motivation and the state of the art. In: University of York Report Number: CESG/TR/2011/1 (2011)
26. Finnegan, A., McCaffery, F.: A Security argument pattern for medical device assurance cases. In: 2014 IEEE International Symposium on Software Reliability Engineering Workshops (2014)
27. Ray, A., Cleaveland, R.: Security assurance cases for medical cyber and physical systems. IEEE Des. Test **32**, 56–65 (2015)
28. Bright Inventions. http://brightinventions.pl/
29. iBeacon - Apple Developer. https://developer.apple.com/ibeacon/
30. Łukasiewicz, K.: Method of selecting programming practices for the safety-critical software development projects – a case study. Technical report n. 02/2017. Gdańsk University of Technology (2017)
31. Your heart rate. What it means, and where on Apple Watch you'll find it. https://support.apple.com/en-us/HT204666
32. Cyra, L., Górski, J.: Support for argument structures review and assessment. Reliab. Eng. Syst. Safety **96**, 26–37 (2011)
33. Stalhane, T., Hanssen, G., Myklebust, T.: The Application of SafeScrum to IEC 61508 certifiable Software, January 2014

Adapting Enterprise Security Approaches for Evolving Cloud Processing and Networking Models

Andrew Hutchison[(✉)]

Department of Computer Science, University of Cape Town,
Cape Town 7700, Republic of South Africa
hutch@cs.uct.ac.za

Abstract. With the advent of public cloud services, enterprise are moving to adopt the lower cost, more flexible, scalable public cloud offerings like OTC, AWS and Azure. Simultaneously they are adapting their network models to move away from centralized enterprise QoS networks (with internet break out from a single or few large enterprise gateways) in favor of lower cost, direct offloading of corporate traffic from company locations via local and distributed Internet service providers. Using this model enterprises are also accessing cloud services from multiple entry points, and this completely changes the enterprise security deployment landscape. As an additional ongoing trend, the networking of physical devices is bringing a whole new 'operational technology' domain to the enterprise space, and a new approach to enterprise security is therefore required. In this paper the drivers of change in approaches to security for public cloud computing are presented, considering also the responsibilities of the customer and of the cloud service provider and the component which enterprises still need to focus on. In addition, the network model for security is explained and considered, with the new distributed deployment zone for security as described. Cyber physical/IoT type systems are also then discussed as an additional security landscape over which enterprises increasingly need to take special care.

Keywords: Enterprise security · Hybrid cloud · Local internet breakout

1 Introduction

1.1 The Changing World

It is clear that there is a large momentum in enterprises to embrace cloud based processing models, in contrast to having their own infrastructure. With different layers being virtualized, organizations are embracing software, platforms and infrastructure as services from various providers. Since many of these cloud services are accessed via Internet paths, often with multiple entry points, there is increasingly less imperative to route all corporate traffic back to main data center locations, or processing hubs of the organization, since increasing parts of the workload are serviced directly to distributed locations. In this sense there is a trend to 'offloading' corporate traffic from more expensive, Quality of Service based MPLS networks and instead to route some of the processing requirement directly to cloud providers and services via local Internet links.

© Springer International Publishing AG 2017
J. Rak et al. (Eds.): MMM-ACNS 2017, LNCS 10446, pp. 16–27, 2017.
DOI: 10.1007/978-3-319-65127-9_2

Another trend which is growing is the digitization of processes, and the connecting of all sorts of devices and sensors into the enterprise landscape. This introduces a further class of traffic and processing requirement, which is also typically in line with the processing and network model described.

From an enterprise security point of view, this evolving picture changes the enterprise security landscape quite considerably. Current centralization of processing has meant that most enterprise traffic has been routed to few processing locations, and large security hubs have typically also been co-located to ensure that incoming and outgoing traffic is inspected and marshalled in various ways to achieve security objectives and organizational integrity. The emerging situation described means that traffic is likely to depart (and enter) the enterprise from many different points – and this changes the way that security needs to be considered in this vastly expanded and distributed landscape.

In terms of the actual migration of processing to cloud based services, there are also additional and new security requirements for organizations. Cloud providers do not necessarily, for example, provide secure Operating System images or basic security management beyond the raw virtual machines which are provided. Organizations also need to link the cloud processing models into their application architecture, so topics like identity management, access control and confidentiality/integrity still need to be realized in a holistic way across these new landscapes as well.

With the addition of new types of device (increasingly including cyber-physical systems, likely representing the operation technology areas of an organization) there is a whole new class of device and connected entities to consider in the security space too.

This paper is structured such that each of the considerations (processing model/network model and expanded processing components) is discussed further and considered in terms of security implications.

2   The New Cloud World

2.1   Hybrid Cloud

With local virtualization having existed for some time, the next step in our computing evolution has been remote virtualization through private, and increasingly public, cloud services. The implicit security and availability of cloud services is increasingly considered adequate by enterprises for their processing requirements. With regard to private cloud services, there have been service providers who over the last decade or more have already been providing shared services accessed by open networks – although often for closed user communities. These so called private clouds have the advantage that customers can to some extent tailor the requirements, and have more participation in the configuration, establishment and operation of the cloud service. With public clouds becoming more scalable, flexible and cheaper than private clouds, organizations have started to embrace this model of 'market services' as opposed to having their own cloud communities or customized environments. On the one hand this is understandable, as it provides endless scalability and dynamic addition or removal of capacity based on the large economies of scale of the cloud providers. But on the other hand it introduces a new and de-coupled architecture for cloud based applications. It is widely acknowledged that to really achieve the benefit of cloud based applications there should be a (re-)architecture to support this and generally just 'migrating' applications to the cloud is not the most effective approach for leveraging the full benefits of cloud processing.

It is not the intention of this paper to focus on the security of clouds *per se*, but rather to consider the technological and organizational implications on enterprises which may be moving towards this mode of processing.

In Fig. 1 the AWS cloud service is used as an example to illustrate processing responsibilities which are provided in the cloud service – in contrast to those which need to be addressed by customers. It is clear that there is an extensive customer responsibility for dealing with different aspects of customer data, platform & application management, OS/network/firewall configuration and both client and server side encryption, integrity and authentication. In addition, network traffic protection needs to be incorporated, as applicable. And in terms of identity and access management, this task still needs to be managed by customers of the cloud service as well.

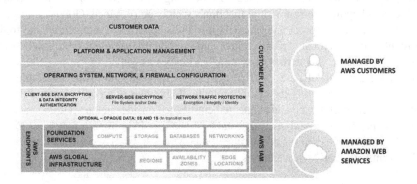

Fig. 1. AWS cloud service areas of customer and provider responsibility (Source: Amazon).

The intention here is not to provide answers or approaches for each of these items in particular, but rather to reinforce the point that enterprise responsibilities for security do not just vanish with the adoption of cloud processing – particularly at the level of Infrastructure as a Service (IaaS). With Platform- and Software as a service solutions there may be more consideration of the security concepts and built in mechanisms, but at an infrastructure and processing level there is still a lot of augmentation and integration which is required. It is considered to be the case that most current cyber-attacks are against the "blue" boxes and not the "orange" boxes of Fig. 1 – which is in fact the area which is *not* under the cloud service provider's responsibility.

In [1], for example, the situation regarding "AWS Customer Security Responsibilities" is made very clear in the following important text (italics added for emphasis of key points): "With the AWS cloud, you can provision virtual servers, storage, databases, and desktops in minutes instead of weeks. You can also use cloud-based analytics and workflow tools to process your data as you need it, and then store it in the cloud or in your own data centers. Which AWS services you use will determine how much configuration work you have to perform as part of your security responsibilities.

AWS products that fall into the well-understood category of Infrastructure as a Service (IaaS), such as Amazon EC2 and Amazon VPC, are completely under your control and *require you to perform all of the necessary security configuration and management tasks*. For example, for EC2 instances, you're responsible for *management of the guest OS* (including *updates* and *security patches*), any application software or utilities you install on the instances, and the *configuration of the AWS-provided firewall (called a security group) on each instance*. These are basically the same security tasks that you're used to performing no matter where your servers are located.

AWS managed services like Amazon RDS or Amazon Redshift provide all of the resources you need in order to perform a specific task, but without the configuration work that can come with them. With managed services, you don't have to worry about launching and maintaining instances, patching the guest OS or database, or replicating databases - AWS handles that for you. However, as with all services, *you should protect your AWS Account credentials and set up individual user accounts with Amazon Identity and Access Management (IAM) so that each of your users has their own credentials and you can implement segregation of duties*. We also *recommend using multi-factor authentication (MFA) with each account, requiring the use of SSL/TLS to communicate with your AWS resources, and setting up API/user activity logging with AWS Cloud-Trail*. For more information about additional measures you can take, refer to the AWS Security Resources webpage".

In the above guidance to AWS cloud customers, it is made very clear that there are still many security tasks and activities to fulfil.

The picture becomes even more complex in the case that multiple, or hybrid, clouds are used. In this case there also needs to be a harmonized view to ensure that organizational security policies, requirements and architecture are preserved by the arms-length processing, storage and access approach.

In Fig. 2 a target hybrid architecture is depicted, while the list of security services on the right hand side shows some of the security aspects which need to be extrapolated and integrated for a multi-cloud, hybrid processing model.

Seeing enterprises confronted with this complexity, service provider organizations are advocating models such as shown in Fig. 3 whereby a common security framework is achieved across a collective of Cloud Provider specific security frameworks. Offerings such as a "Cloud Integration Center" show the evolving role of current outsource and private cloud providers, who are showing flexibility in fulfilling the potentially tricky customer requirements and heterogeneous integration tasks which the new world requires.

Overall, organizations embarking on a cloud based strategy need to do a careful business case to ensure that they are not missing important tasks and responsibilities within a cloud eco-system. Simultaneously, technical solutions for the identified tasks need to be defined and the cloud approach established within the identity, authentication, encryption and integrity regimes which are applicable. The Common Security Framework of the enterprise has to be expanded to include the approaches of the different cloud providers, and an assessment should be done on whether the hybrid approach is still consistent with the organizational security objectives and requirements.

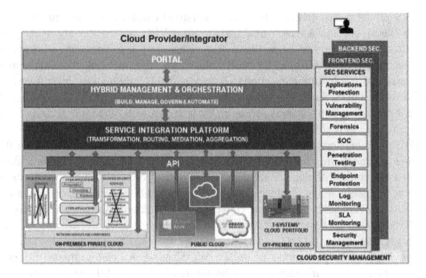

Fig. 2. Cloud security management issues across multiple cloud providers

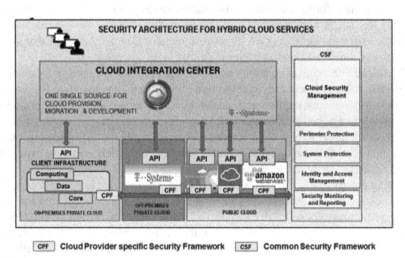

Fig. 3. Security architecture and services to enable a hybrid architecture

3   Pathway to the Clouds

3.1   Offloading and Going Direct

While enterprise Global Area Networks (GANs) and Wide Area Networks (WANs) have existed for many years, the associated requirements of: getting traffic to a central processing point; and ensuring quality of service have resulted in any-to-any type MPLS and other QoS networks being the typical enterprise connectivity model.

With the changing processing landscape, whereby distributed access points to cloud based services become the norm, there is potentially less traffic which needs to go to a central location. It is attractive to 'offload' traffic from a corporate QoS/MPLS network, since lower cost local network access can be obtained at each business location with relevant traffic being directed immediately to the (cloud) service access point.

It is clear that the 'site' for security shifts from a single, highly centralized concentration of traffic to multiple, decentralized Internet access points. This suggests that an associated security model is required, to ensure that Internet bound (and originating) traffic is inspected and filtered/managed in the same way that it would have been had the centralized single breakout model been implemented.

In Fig. 4 a hybrid IP WAN architecture is reflected, categorizing source locations in terms of criticality. While high and medium criticality locations are connected via both Internet and MPLS, the low criticality locations connect only via best-effort Internet. The paths to cloud providers are also reflected on the right hand side of the figure showing how connections can either be made directly from source locations to cloud providers (and the enterprise data center), or the cloud provider could also be invoked as a processing and storage engine from the enterprise data center.

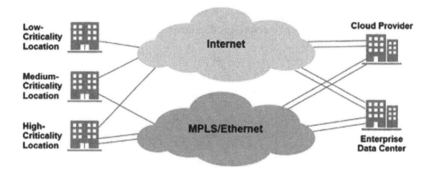

Fig. 4. Typical hybrid IP WAN architecture [2]

In the Figs. 5 and 6 more details of a typical large, global enterprise are shown with respect to their connectivity models. In Fig. 5 there is a strong emphasis on primary and secondary sites – in line with a centralized processing model, but Fig. 6 reflects how a more direct access to cloud based services can occur – with the associated security elements being identified. These are typically the services which can also be 'virtualized' and provided as cloud services to organizations so that the communication paths are filtered and secured.

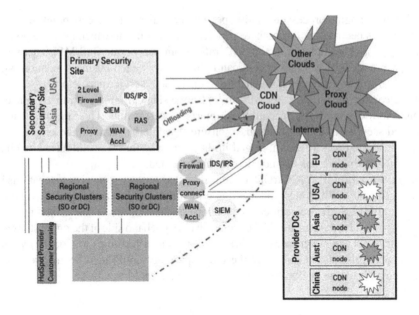

Fig. 5. Typical large enterprise with primary site and regional sites

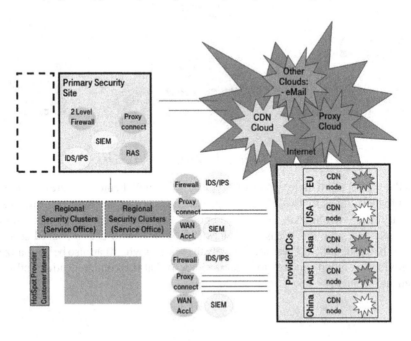

Fig. 6. Example large enterprise with primary site and regional access to cloud services

Content Distribution Networks (CDNs) are also shown in Figs. 5 and 6 and it also worth mentioning the role which these can play in optimizing and caching content with a great performance enhancement impact. This approach can further reduce the actual amount of unique processing which may be required of processing systems – ensuring that content which is used frequently and widely is accessible directly from local points.

In Fig. 4 it should be evident that the location of the security services has moved from the primary and secondary sites in Fig. 4 to a model whereby security becomes more localized. This situation lends itself well to a cloud based security service, whereby the distributed network paths are secured via a distributed (possibly cloud based) security service which is then 'inline' with the revised connectivity and communication model. It is this model which enterprises need to embrace and support as they move toward cloud based processing with associated 'local' breakout connectivity.

4   More Things to Deal with

4.1   IoT

The mega-trend to digitization of businesses introduces a whole new class of components into the enterprise landscape. In additional to the typical 'information technology' (IT) there is now an additional frontier of 'operational technology' (OT) which is either directly or indirectly part of the technology landscape. By direct and indirect is meant the distinction between those organizations which operate specific machinery, vehicles, equipment or processes with physical entities (and therefore process control and other automation activities are implicit) and those organizations which may indirectly monitor physical aspects of their buildings, equipment, supply chains etc. Those organizations with direct machinery and OT environments have the opportunity to manage and monitor these areas in increasingly connected ways. With respect to supporting the indirect business environment, many organizations are deploying sensors and using control software to perform smart management of buildings, vehicles, assets (for example stock, temperature, power, refrigerators, furnaces etc.). With both direct and indirect modes of OT, management and efficiency possibilities are enhanced. Unfortunately a side-effect of this increasingly connected mode is that security consequences are also introduced.

In very many cases physical systems and machines have been designed as standalone, autonomous systems. With hyper connectivity and networking of numerous new types of device the possibility is introduced for external connection to the physical systems. Although this can be very useful for monitoring and managing systems, it introduces the possibility that systems could also be manipulated if an unintended party is able to connect to, and communicate with/control, the physical system. Security principles of authentication, access control, confidentiality and integrity of system interaction are all required – but not necessarily provided – in the inter-connected mode.

The challenge for enterprises is to look very carefully at the landscape of IT and OT environments, and to isolate these via zoning mechanisms which at least ensure a reduced locus of control [3].

Protection of specific cyber-physical communication channels is an emerging area of activity and, for example, SCADA interaction is one particular area of investigation.

But the plethora of sensors and access channels to all manner of devices from cameras to display screens to doors to elevators to medical equipment mean that there is a chance for these devices to be interrogated or controlled by adversaries. Botnet attacks from unexpected sources like security cameras have already been observed.

4.2 End-to-End Cyber-Physical Security

One of the key challenges of security is to provide an end-to-end scope for transactions and interactions which occur. In Fig. 7 the IoT landscape of a large service provider is shown as a sample approach. Different layers from connectivity to service are shown as components of the IoT approach. What is most relevant for this discussion is the positioning of security, which is shown as an end-to-end theme spanning all the other layers of enablement. From the figure it should be evident that the cloud processing and network model discussions of the preceding sections of this paper are also building blocks of this emerging IoT world, and therefore this domain brings together all of the issues and requirements which we have discussed in the previous deliberations on evolving enterprise requirements for cloud and network.

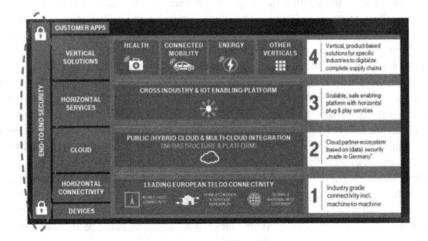

Fig. 7. Example IoT approach and organization (Source: Deutsche Telekom)

With many organizations utilizing Security Information and Event Management (SIEM) platforms to monitor and manage their overall security landscape, it is essential that IoT devices can also be managed within such SIEM approaches. In Fig. 8, the integration of SCADA devices using the SIEM platform AlienVault is illustrated. The general security challenge of such sources and cyber-physical systems in general has been discussed in [4].

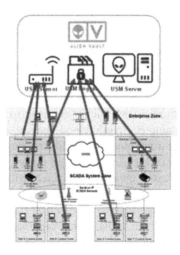

Fig. 8. Example of use of AlienVault SIEM to monitor SCADA system input feeds

Some of the key SCADA security requirements with respect to SIEM integration of events include:

- Asset discovery and management
- Vulnerability Management
- Network and Host intrusion detection
- Log collection, aggregation, correlation and storage

Collection and tracking of these attributes supports the implementation of selected ISA99/IEC62443 requirements as shown in Table 1.

Table 1. Supporting the implementation of ISA99/IEC62443 requirements:

FR 2 – Use Control, including	SR 2.8 – Auditable events
	SR 2.9 – Audit storage capacity
	SR 2.10 – Response to audit processing failures
	SR 2.11 – Timestamps
FR 3 – System Integrity, including	SR 3.2 – Malicious code protection
	SR 3.3 – Security functionality verification
FR 5 – Restricted data flow, including	SR 5.2 – Zone boundary protection
FR 6 – Timely response to events, including	SR 6.1 – Audit Log accessibility
	SR 6.2 – Continous Monitoring

5   Conclusion

5.1   Key Findings

It is evident that to achieve a high level of security in a hybrid cloud environment, the aspects of People, Processes and Technology need to be re-visited and re-defined.

While additional options like next generation firewalling/IDS/IPS/dDOS protection/data encryption/log correlation/enhanced incident management with escalation, etc., can be obtained via the 'marketplaces of services such as AWS and Azure, they typically require acceptance of expensive extended SLAs or purchase of third-party options from their marketplace. And even in this case, many such options are self-managed, i.e. the enterprise still needs to fulfil various aspects or functions.

Based on some infrastructure analyses, it has been approximated that for some large enterprise environments, a complete hybrid cloud landscape - with the same level of security as the current on-premises solution - would cost roughly the same in the public cloud. In addition, many virtual security appliances do not scale as well as hardware appliances, which in some cases may further increase the costs. Many enterprise customers are not really aware of this situation and are attracted by the cheap VM unit costs and basic services without perhaps looking at the full picture.

Another area which is cost driven, is that of the corporate network approach of many enterprises. Instead of long-hauling all traffic to centralized data centers, where processing is done, it is in many instances possible to 'offload' traffic from the enterprise Global Area Network to local, direct links to cloud service providers and platforms. Since the opportunity for central policy and rule management is lost, alternative solutions for the local break out traffic are required. Various security service providers have cloud based security solutions which are can be used to take over the functions which the central firewall and gateway infrastructure may have been providing in the past. The network strategy of enterprises should be consistent with their evolving processing model, and consider that the "frontier" for security may well be widely distributed across their branches or enterprise locations.

Internet of Things (IoT) devices introduce a whole new security dimension to organizations, since now cyber-physical systems become components of the security landscape. For enterprises involved in any kind of manufacturing, monitoring, production, automation, transport activity etc. there are an increasing number of devices and sensors which are being "connected" and this introduces new attack paths and threat vectors. Enterprises should ensure that systems are adequately protected, and integrated from the outset, for example into the Security Information and Event Management (SIEM) and other Security Operation Centre (SOC) monitoring functions.

5.2   Future Work

More work needs to be done on the identification and development of suitable solutions and approaches for the processing, networking and smart-connection of cyber-physical devices. In this paper we provided a motivation and problem statement, and in this context organizations need to assess specific solutions to see how a distributed, but harmonized, security solution can be implemented to harness the benefits within an orderly and well planned security context.

5.3   Closing Remarks

It is likely that organizations will obtain an increasing proportion of their services from generic infrastructure engines such as AWS, and via myriad networking paths as described. With numerous devices and sensors being incorporated, the landscape has the potential to grow and become even more complex and sophisticated. Considerations such as 'jurisdiction of processing and storage' can also play a role in which public cloud provider to select, and this should be yet another consideration when selecting a security partner.

References

1. Amazon Web Services, Inc.: Overview of Security Processes (2016)
2. Munch, B., Rickard, N.: Cloud Adoption is Driving Hybrid WAN Architectures. Gartner (2017)
3. ENISA: Ad-hoc and sensor networking for M2 M Communications – Threat Landscape and Good Practice Guide (2017)
4. Hutchison, A., Rieke, R.: Management of security information and events in future internet. In: Proceedings of Cyber Security and Global Affairs, Conference on Cyber Security, Budapest (2011)

Data Mining and Information Security

Alexander Grusho[(✉)]

Institute of Informatics Problems of Federal Research Center,
"Informatics and Control" of the Russian Academy of Sciences,
Vavilova 44-2, 119333 Moscow, Russia
grusho@yandex.ru

Abstract. Analysis of information security monitoring data is based on detection of anomalies causalities in "normal" process of an information system operation.

In the paper the JSM-method of data mining in the solution of this task is considered. For this purpose in identical situations the objects generated by "normal" data and anomalies are built. Further these objects are researched by JSM-method as the positive and negative examples of anomalies appearance.

The causalities of anomalies appearance found by JSM-method can be used as signatures for fast determination of information security violations.

Keywords: Data mining · Information security · Anomaly · JSM-method

1 Introduction

There are about 70 definitions of an intelligence and an artificial intelligence which can be found in papers gathered by S. Legg and M. Hatter [1,2]. We will connect the artificial intelligence with abilities to calculate and argue, perceive and realize the relations and analogies, to study (at examples), to store and look for information, to use a natural language, to classify and generalize, adapt to new situations in the course of the solution of complex problems [1].

Unlike the review [3] where we first of all were interested in possibilities of application of methods of an intellectual data analysis in case of support of information security of cloudy computing environments, in the real operation we will try to look at the considered data domain from the point of view of an information security expert.

There are many powerful arguments in favor of such choice, however we will be restricted by only two:

- a special role of such expert, including need to behave rationally and responsibly in quickly changing environment;
- a need "to arm" the expert with the effective computer tools of methods of an intellectual data analysis allowing to expand his professional opportunities.

J. Rak et al. (Eds.): MMM-ACNS 2017, LNCS 10446, pp. 28–33, 2017.
DOI: 10.1007/978-3-319-65127-9_3

However first of all, it is necessary to pay attention to three major tasks which effective solution defines success of the considered intellectual systems:

1. a choice of adequate means of knowledge representation, giving a chance to intellectual computer system to operate with knowledge necessary for the expert;
2. a choice of procedural tools of dependencies generation out of the data, allowing to use a computer system for extraction of the hidden dependencies out of the accumulated empirical data and to do it in the absolutely "transparent" way for an information surity expert;
3. an opportunity to carry the causal analysis, that is necessary to select the reasons of analyzable security events, the attacks, etc. That allows to organize reliable counteraction to the registered harmful activities.

The paper has the following structure. The Sect. 2 presents the main model of information security in information systems. In Sect. 3 our concept of data mining in information security support is defined. Conclusion is devoted to the discussion of the methodology and unsolved problems.

2   The General Model of Information Security in Information Systems

Any decision to provide information security (local or global) is described by the following commutative diagram [4]:

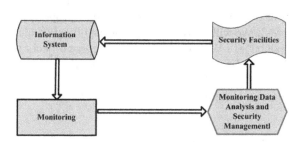

Fig. 1. Architecture of information security subsystem

Preliminary expert analysis and development of preventive information security measures do not make it possible to consider the entire amount of potential harmful effects on contemporary information systems. Currently, development and implementation of information security solutions are far behind possibilities of implementation of new information technologies. It is necessary to significantly accelerate analysis (even preventive) of the security state and it is necessary to invent measures aimed at usage of modern methods for information security. Analysis and management are the weakest part in the diagram (Fig. 1). It is not possible to automatically analyze the information security of large systems either in real-time or off-line. Therefore, the identification of empirical causal relationships and prediction of the effects in various situations of the functioning of information systems should be delegated to the machine amplifier of human intelligence.

3   Data Mining in Monitoring and Analysis

Due to limitation of speed of the modern computers a analysis of monitoring data is carried out in two directions. Let's call the first direction "speedy". This direction consists in that, knowing the causality and dependencies of monitoring data with threats of information security, danger is quickly identified with the help of signatures. Let's call the second direction "deep". This direction consists in search in monitoring data of origins and connections with threats to an information system.

The general idea of the deep analysis is the following. Originating dangers generate anomalies in data of monitoring. Therefore the first step of the analysis is detection of anomalies. This methodology is based on Tukey's ideas [5].

To results of anomalies search it is possible to apply JSM technology of data mining for detection of anomalies causalities, and for generation of hypotheses [6]. Confirmation or non-confirmation of hypotheses (abduction) on the extending data finishes the execution of the deep analysis.

We will provide the short description of JSM-data analysis [7]. We will designate through $U = \{a_1, ..., a_n\}$ – a set of characteristics (descriptions of the objects) which are found in data of monitoring. We will assume that there are positive examples of objects concerning occurrence of property p which we will index by the sign "+". We will mark examples of the objects which don't contain property p by the sign "−". We will mark contradictory objects by the sign "0". We will mark indefinite objects with the sign "τ". Thus, data analysis is carried out in four-digit logic.

Set of characteristics is represented as union of three sets $U = U^+ \cup U^- \cup U^c$, where

- U^c – characteristics of situations in which objects appear;
- U^+ – the characteristics of the positive examples which don't belong to the description of situations;
- U^- – the characteristics of the negative examples which don't belong to the description of situations.

As well as in the paper [8], an appearance of "0" has its own causality which we don't consider.

Let's cluster the characteristics $U_1^c, ..., U_r^c$ in the description of situations according to some measure of closeness. We consider sets of characteristics of one cluster as one situation.

Let's find the causalities of the positive examples. Let objects $O_{i_1}, \ldots, \varnothing_{i_s}$ be the positive examples which correspond to the situation U_1^c. Let's consider intersections

$$\bigcap_{j=1}^{s} O_{i_j} = \overline{u} \subseteq U.$$

If $\overline{u}$ is Galois closure [9], then it is possible to call $\overline{u}$ by the empirical causality of "+" in situation U_1^c.

The empirical causalities of "+" and of "−" for each situation are similarly built.

Let's check the causalities on other data in case of identical situations. The analysis will be finished if all data in identical situations confirm the causality of "+" and of "−". Appearance of "0" in extension data means an existence of errors in data analysis or existence of own causalities for appearance of "0". If the set of errors grows, then the analysis should be started anew. New data appears out of the set of data indexed by "τ"

It is possible to be restricted by "feeble" causalities and to throw out all data classified by "0".

We will consider Tukey [5] methodology for detection of anomalies. Let "normal" data be defined. These data undertake as a standard (regression). Then the considerable deviation from a standard data according to some measure of closeness is considered as anomaly. Here again it is necessary to define a concept of a situation, i.e. a set of characteristics of monitoring data, which are stably classified as "normal" data. In identical situations it is easier to reveal anomalies.

When searching of anomalies according to [5] it is better for further JSM-application to carry out data analysis with usage of bans of probability measures. Statistical techniques with zero probabilities of errors of false alarms are developed for the discrete models. These methods are based on a concept of the ban of a probability measure [10–12]. Conditions when in case of zero probability of false alarm the probability to miss violation is equal to 0 [12,13] are found.

We will integrate methodology of Tukey [5] and data mining by JSM-method. We will consider that "+" are anomalies, and "−" are objects with normal behavior in information system.

The concept of a situation is defined both in Tukey [5] methodology, and in JSM methodology. Naturally, they need to be integrated. Then all anomalies are divided into not crossed classes corresponding to identical situations. Further by JSM-method we look for the causalities of anomalies and "normal" behavior. We confirm them with abduction. As a result we will receive signatures of "+" and signatures of "−" for each of situations. These signatures should be used in the "speedy" analysis.

The experimental confirmations of the provided methodology aren't sufficient due to the lack of automation yet. However the set of confirmations by means of experiments isn't empty. Search of failure in network which used the RabbitMQ messenger on the basis of the OpenStack [14] cloud platform has been done. Owing to absence of the software the analysis of failures was carried out manually. The main feature of the experiment consists in that traditional logs didn't allow to establish the failure causalities, but the analysis which is carried out by means of the described above methods allowed to establish the failure reason.

The methodology of the JSM-analysis of the reasons of appearance of the selected properties taking into account situations is approved in sociological researches [8].

The main problem in applications of the described methods is computing complexity of solvable tasks. However some success in overcoming a problem of complexity is achieved. In some cases the JSM-method can be described by means of Galois compliances. The method of an accelerated check of closeness of sets is found in Galois closures [9].

4   Conclusion

For the usage of data mining it is necessary to find adequate means of information representation which should be analyzed in problems of information security support. The paper offers to build such representation as the objects created by "normal" data of an information system behavior, and as the objects created by monitoring of anomalies.

For detection of anomalies it is offered to use traditional methodology of Tukey. This methodology is based on comparing of "normal" data and significant deviations from them.

The information security expert, first of all, is interested in finding of causalities of anomalies. In this regard it is offered to consider appearance of anomalies as target property p, causalities of appearance of which we look for. Then the objects generated by anomalies are considered as the positive examples "+", and the objects generated by "normal" behavior are considered as the negative examples "−".

At the same time it is necessary to consider dynamism of the computer environment. This information in methodology of data mining is defined as a situation within which the analysis of causalities is carried out.

Development of application of data mining methodology to an information security support is connected to the creation of software for work of the information security expert.

The main problem in application of data mining for information security support is high complexity of the majority of algorithms. Therefore art of usage of complexity decreasing methods in data mining tasks defines an efficiency of information security support constructed on their basis.

Important issues of creation of measures of closeness which now become the important direction of scientific research aren't considered in the paper.

Acknowledgements. The research is supported by Russian Foundation for Basic Research (project 15-29-07981).

References

1. Legg, S., Hutter, M.: A collection of definitions of intelligence. Technical report, IDSIA-07-07, 15 June 2007
2. Legg, S., Hutter, M.: Universal intelligence: a definition of machine intelligence. J. Minds Mach. **17**(4), 391–444 (2007). arXiv:0712.3329v1 [cs.AI]
3. Grusho, A., Zabezhailo, M., Zatsarinnyi, A., Piskovskii, V., Borokhov, S.V.: On the potential applications of data mining for information security provision of cloud-based environments. J. Autom. Documentation Math. Linguist. **49**(6), 193–201 (2015). doi:10.3103/S0005105515060023
4. Grusho, A.A., Grusho, N.A., Timonina, E.E., Shorgin, S.Y.: Possibilities of secure architecture creation for dynamically changing information system. J. Syst. Means Inform. **25**(3), 78–93 (2015)
5. Tukey, J.W.: Exploratory Data Analysis. Addison-Wesley Pub. Co., Reading (1977)
6. Finn, V.K. (eds.) Automatic Hypothesis Generation in Intelligent Systems. KD "LIBROKOM", Moscow (2009)
7. Anshakov, O.M.: About one interpretation of the DSM-method of automatic generation of hypotheses. In: Finn, V.K. (eds.) Automatic Hypothesis Generation in Intelligent Systems, pp. 78–91. KD "LIBROKOM", Moscow (2009)
8. Finn, V.K., Mikheenkova, M.A.: About Situation-Dependent Extension of the DSM-method of Automatic Generation of Hypotheses. In: Finn, V.K. (eds.) Automatic Hypothesis Generation in Intelligent Systems, pp. 428–445. KD "LIBROKOM", Moscow (2009)
9. Grusho, A.A., Zabezhailo, M.I., Zatsarinny, A.A.: On the advanced procedure to reduce calculation of galois closures. J. Inform. Appl. **10**(4), 97–106 (2016). doi:10.14357/19922264160410
10. Grusho, A., Timonina, E.: Prohibitions in discrete probabilistic statistical problems. J. Discrete Math. Appl. **21**(3), 275–281 (2011). doi:10.4213/dm1140
11. Grusho, A., Timonina, E.: Consistent sequences of tests defined by bans. Optimization Theory, Decision Making, and Operation Research Applications. Springer Proceedings in Mathematics and Statistics, pp. 281–291. Springer, Heidelberg (2013). doi:10.1007/978-1-4614-5134-1_20
12. Grusho, A., Grusho, N., Timonina, E.: Power functions of statistical criteria defined by bans. In: Proceeding of 29th European Conference on Modelling and Simulation ECMS 2015, pp. 617–621. Digitaldruck Pirrot GmbH, Germany (2016)
13. Grusho, A., Grusho, N., Timonina, E.: Statistical classification in monitoring systems. In: Proceeding of 30th European Conference on Modelling and Simulation ECMS 2016, pp. 658–662. Digitaldruck Pirrot GmbH, Germany (2015)
14. Grusho, A.A., Zabezhailo, M.I., Zatsarinny, A.A., Nikolaeb, A.V., Piskovski, V.O., Timonina, E.E.: Erroneous states classifications in dictributed computing systems and sources of their occurences. J. Syst. Means Inform. **27**(2), 30–41 (2017). doi:10.14357/08696527170203

Critical Infrastructure Protection
and Visualization

Extending FAST-CPS for the Analysis of Data Flows in Cyber-Physical Systems

Laurens Lemaire[(✉)], Jan Vossaert, Bart De Decker, and Vincent Naessens

imec-DistriNet, Department of Computer Science, KU Leuven, Leuven, Belgium
{laurens.lemaire,jan.vossaert,bart.decker,
vincent.naessens}@cs.kuleuven.be

Abstract. Cyber-physical systems are increasingly automated and interconnected. Strategies like predictive maintenance are on the rise and as a result new streams of data will flow through these systems. This data is often confidential, which can be a problem in these low-security systems. In addition, more stakeholders are now involved and various cloud-based service providers are utilised. Companies often no longer know who gets to see their data.

This paper presents a methodology that aims to analyse these data flows. The methodology takes as input a set of data asset preferences and service policies, as well as the asset flow of the system. It then returns feedback in the form of an asset profile showing which stakeholders have access to what data assets, and conflicts between the preferences and the modeled situation. Several possible actors with different preferences are modeled for each stakeholder role in the system, the scenarios with the fewest conflicts are returned. The methodology is validated on a case study and has been added to the FAST-CPS framework.

Keywords: Cyber-physical systems · FAST-CPS · Data flows

1 Introduction

The term *cyber-physical system* (CPS) can be assigned to a broad range of applications, including industrial control systems, robotics, Supervisory Control and Data Acquisition (SCADA) systems, etc. Typically, a CPS is a network of interacting elements with physical input and output [9]. In the past decades, these systems have evolved from proprietary, isolated systems to complex interconnected systems that are remotely accessible. This has made them easier to use, but also easier to attack [6].

With the arrival of the Industrial Internet of Things (IIoT) and Industrie 4.0, new data streams flow through these cyber-physical systems, and more stakeholders are involved. For instance cloud platforms are increasingly used for data processing and storage. In the past, all the data usually remained in one network or multiple networks that belong to the same owner. Now various stakeholders are involved, and it is no longer clear who has access to what data.

© Springer International Publishing AG 2017
J. Rak et al. (Eds.): MMM-ACNS 2017, LNCS 10446, pp. 37–49, 2017.
DOI: 10.1007/978-3-319-65127-9_4

One technique that benefits from increased connectivity is *predictive maintenance (PdM)*. Here the machines will be monitored by various sensors that collect performance data, for example a vibration sensor. This data is sent to the equipment vendor who then runs predictive analysis algorithms on it to check whether maintenance is required or not. A PdM approach is beneficial for a company as it only schedules maintenance when needed, unlike *preventive maintenance* which schedules maintenance at regular intervals, even when the system may not need it. However, additional stakeholders are involved in the industrial process, and new streams of data are sent around. As a result, system owners no longer have a clear view of what data is being sent to which stakeholder.

It is important for the companies behind a CPS to adequately protect the data in the system. Leaked data from customers, suppliers, or other stakeholders in the system could result in reputation damage for the company. In addition, leaked algorithms, sensor data, performance data, etc. could benefit competitors and result in economic loss.

Contribution. The contributions of this work are as follows:

1. A methodology is proposed that evaluates data flows in CPS. The methodology returns which stakeholders have access to data assets in the system, and any conflicts this causes with actor preferences.
2. Different possible scenarios are compared with each other. The assessor can consider various possible actors for each stakeholder role, and the system will automatically evaluate all possibilities and return the models with the least conflicts.
3. The methodology has been added to the FAST-CPS framework. This allows for incorporating security feedback into the data analysis.
4. The methodology is realized using a knowledge-base system. In this paper, the methodology is validated on a 3D printing ecosystem.

Outline. The paper is structured as follows. Section 2 focuses on related work in this area. Section 3 gives an overview of the methodology for analysing data flows in CPS. Section 4 describes how this methodology is implemented. Section 5 introduces the case study and presents the possible feedback of the tool. Finally, Sect. 6 concludes the paper.

2   Related Work

A lot of related work about controlled data release exists, but mainly in the context of user privacy. Examples include the work from Samarati et al. about the relation between data release and anonymity [13].

Preference and policy languages have been proposed to give users control over the information that they allow to release. P3P [3] allowed service providers to express their privacy policies formally. Users could then analyse these policies and decide whether or not to use the service. APPEL [4], a P3P preference exchange language, was introduced to automate this process. Users could now formally model their preferences and these were compared with the policies to determine whether they were compatible. Several follow-up preference and policy languages have been proposed since then [1,12].

Our methodology will incorporate preferences and policies about data, but in a business-to-business setting involving cyber-physical systems. Here the related work is limited. Nowadays, most of these systems utilise cloud service providers. Data protection in cloud systems has been studied [16], but no methodologies exist that analyse data flows in a CPS. However, some tools exist that analyse their security. CSET [8] allows the user to provide a network diagram of its system, and gives security feedback about firewall placement, etc. ADVISE [11], CyberSage [15] and CySeMoL [14] are tools that return the probability of an attacker reaching an attack goal. A fifth tool to analyse security in CPS is FAST-CPS [10], this tool attempts to find security vulnerabilities in CPS by incorporating various vulnerability databases such as the one from ICS-CERT. Our methodology has been added to this framework in order to use the security feedback when reasoning about data flows.

Decroix [5] uses a methodology similar to ours to reason about privacy in electronic services. In their work, only the preferences of the user are modeled and only one scenario is evaluated. In the methodology described in this paper, the assessor will provide various possible actors for each stakeholder role in the system. All actors will have a set of preferences associated with them. The methodology will then evaluate all possible configurations of actors and return the instances that produce the least conflicts.

3   Methodology

Figure 1 shows a general overview of the methodology. The assessor provides the necessary input to a logic-based engine that draws conclusions based on this

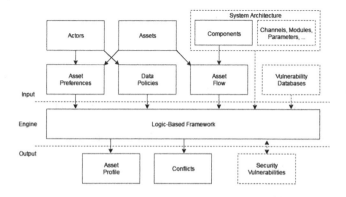

Fig. 1. The input and output of the methodology.

data. Dashed boxes indicate pieces of input that are optional, they are only required if the assessor wants to take security vulnerabilities into account. All components will be discussed in detail in this section.

The methodology evaluates data flows in CPS. Different possible scenarios are compared with each other. The assessor can consider various possible actors for each stakeholder role, and the system will automatically evaluate all possibilities and return the models with the least conflicts.

3.1 Input

The assessor first defines all the *Actors*, *Assets* and *Components* in the system. Next, the *Asset Preferences*, *Data Policies*, and the *Asset Flow* are compiled. Optionally, the assessor can model the entire system architecture and perform a *Security Analysis* of the CPS. The resulting *Security Vulnerabilities* of the system are then taken into account for the data flow analysis.

Concepts. First the important concepts are defined:

- A **Stakeholder** is a role in the cyber-physical system. Typical stakeholders include the *customer*, the *equipment vendor*, the *CPS company*, various *suppliers* and *cloud providers*. An optional stakeholder is the *Attacker* who attempts to exploit security vulnerabilities to compromise the system.
- An **Actor** is a specific instance of a stakeholder. Multiple customers or suppliers can be modelled, all of them are actors. The methodology presented in this paper will allow the assessor to select multiple possible actors for each stakeholder, the system will then evaluate all the different possibilities and return which actors are optimal for reducing conflicts.
- **Assets** are pieces of data that are important to actors with regards to confidentiality and privacy. These could be algorithms, data generated by sensors, customer information, etc. The methodology can also reason about *sets of assets*. Actors mark a set of assets as *identifiable* if the combination of the assets in the set reveals their identity.
- **Components** are the building blocks which the CPS consists of. These are hardware elements such as PLCs, switches, computers, etc. In order to model the data flow in the system, the assessor must also provide the relevant components and which stakeholder they belong to.

Asset Preferences. Each actor defines their asset preferences. Here we distinguish two types of preferences: the *operation preferences* and the *linkability preferences*. Operation preferences specify which stakeholders should be able to perform operations on data assets. An operation preference is represented as a first-order predicate *OperationPref(a,d,s,o)* containing:

- The actor whose preference it is.
- The data asset which the preference is about.
- The stakeholder that is allowed to perform operations on the asset.
- The operation that may be performed on the asset.

The operations currently supported by the system are *Process (P)* and *Store (S)*. The methodology utilises a whitelist approach where the actors specify the operations that are allowed in their preferences, rather than those that are not. This shortens the required input. As an example, a certain customer could indicate that only the CPS company can store his address details.

The other type of asset preferences are linkability preferences. These specify which stakeholders are allowed to link two or more assets. They are represented as a *LinkPref(a,d,d',s)* predicate containing the actor whose preference it is, an asset or set of assets, a second asset or set of assets, and a stakeholder that is allowed to link the two sets of assets. As an example, the CPS company is able to specify that only the equipment vendor can link machine IDs to machine problems. Other stakeholders in the system are allowed to see these data assets separately, but should not be able to link them.

As a subset of link preferences, the actor can also indicate which stakeholders are allowed to link a set of assets to the *identity* of the actor. In this case the engine will check which sets of assets are marked as *identifiable* for that actor, and ensure that none of the assets in the linkability preference can be linked to them.

Data Policies. The actors also specify their *data policies*. A data policy describes whether actors store received data, where it is stored, and how long. Policies are specified as a predicate *DataPol(a,d,l,i)*:

- The actor whose policy it is.
- The asset the policy is about.
- The location where the data is stored, this is a *component* in the system.
- The duration of storage, expressed in months.

Each actor also has a default policy. Assets for which there are no specific policies follow the default.

Actors that are cloud providers may also abide to certain *data directives and laws*, such as the US Patriot Act. This may entail that the data they have access to is also accessible by a third party, such as the US Government. The assessor models which actors fall under these data directives and laws.

Asset Flow. Finally, the *asset flow* is modelled. The assessor indicates which assets flow between components in the system, and where they are processed. This is done by indicating the sender component, receiver component, and the particular set of assets using a first-order logic predicate *AssetFlow(Component, AssetSet, Component)*. When assets are sent together, the receiver is able to *link* the assets in the set to each other. This is modeled with the predicate *Linked(AssetSet, Stakeholder)*. Another predicate *Processes(Component, AssetSet)* is used to indicate where the assets are processed.

It is possible to model several different flows for one CPS. In this case, the assessor will manually have to change the asset flow each time. The system will evaluate all actor possibilities for each flow. Results of the different flows can be compared at the end, and then the assessor can choose the optimal flow and actors for his design.

Security Vulnerabilities. Optionally, the assessor can provide the entire *system architecture* of the cyber-physical system using the FAST-CPS framework. The FAST-CPS framework allows the assessor to perform a security analysis on Cyber-Physical Systems [10]. The assessor models his system architecture in SysML, a modelling language derived from UML used for model-based systems engineering [7]. A security analysis of the system will then be performed by FAST-CPS [10]. Four types of security feedback are relevant to the data flow analysis and are fed back into the engine as input:

- A list of *component vulnerabilities.* Vulnerability databases such as the one from ICS-CERT are included in the FAST-CPS logic theory. When components such as PLCs and HMIs are modeled, the assessor provides the product type and the version. If the triple (*Component, Product, Version*) is found in one of the vulnerability databases, the component will be tagged with the relevant vulnerability. These vulnerabilities are further sorted into categories. For the data flow analysis methodology, the *DataLeakage, CompromisedAuth* and *PrivilegeEscalation* categories are relevant.
- *Security properties* of the communication channels in the system. The logic theory of FAST-CPS contains a set of commonly used protocols such as Modbus. These protocols have security properties associated with them regarding encryption and authentication. If a communication channel uses one of these protocols, the appropriate security properties are attached to the channel. If a protocol is used that is not yet supported by FAST-CPS, the user can add the security properties to the channel manually.
- Which attackers have *access* to components and channels in the system. Different attackers are modelled as part of the system architecture, these can be internal or external. The security analysis infers which attackers have physical or remote access to components and communication channels. The result is a predicate *Access(SystemPart, Stakeholder)* which will be used in the logic rules of the engine. Types *Component* and *Channel* are subtypes of *SystemPart*.
- An overview of which components and channels are used by the assets. The asset flow shows between which components the assets travel. If the full system architecture is modeled, the system can infer through which channels and components the assets pass. This is modelled with the predicate *Passes(SystemPart, AssetSet)*.

The methodology can then simulate the effects of the attacker compromising the component or channel vulnerabilities, provided the attacker has access to them.

3.2 Output

The assessor will provide several possible actors for each stakeholder role in the system. The logic-based framework will then evaluate all possible scenarios and return feedback for each of them. The first piece of output is an *asset profile.*

This profile consists of operations that stakeholders can perform on assets. This is represented as a first-order logic predicate: *AssetProfile(Stakeholder, Asset, Operation)*.

This profile is then compared with the asset preferences of the used actors to find *conflicts*. There are two types of conflicts, one corresponding to each type of preference. An *Operation Conflict* consists of four elements:

- The actor whose preference caused the conflict.
- The asset that the conflict is about.
- The stakeholder that the actor had a preference about.
- The operation that the stakeholder is able to perform on the asset.

Hence operation conflicts are represented by a *(Actor, Asset, Stakeholder, Operation)* four-tuple. For instance *OperationConflict(CustA, CustomerName, Sup, P)* indicates a conflict where the supplier is able to process the *Customer-Name* asset, and this clashes with the preferences of actor *CustA*. To populate *OperationConflict*, it suffices to compare *AssetProfile* with the operation preferences as follows:

$$AssetProfile(s, d, o) \land \neg OperationPref(a, d, s, o) \Rightarrow$$
$$OperationConflict(a, d, s, o)$$

The *Link Conflicts* are found in the same way by inspecting the *Linked* and *LinkPref* predicates and are represented by the *LinkConflict(Actor, AssetSet, AssetSet, Stakeholder)* predicate.

Various queries can now be performed. For instance, the assessor could request all models with the least number of conflicts by minimizing the cardinality of the union of conflict predicates:

$$Minimize \; |OperationConflict(a, d, s, o) \cup LinkConflict(a, d, d', s)|$$

3.3   Engine

The logic-based engine takes all of the input and analyses it to obtain the asset profile. This happens in three consecutive processing steps:

Asset Flow. First, the data asset flow is taken into account, creating a first overview of which stakeholders receive certain data assets, and where they are processed. To this end, the engine takes each asset flow triple *(component, asset, component)*, and checks which stakeholders own the components, to obtain the intermediate result *(stakeholder, asset, stakeholder)*. Similarly, assets that are processed at a certain component are now processed by the stakeholder who owns the component.

Data Policies. Next, the data policies are considered. This adds additional storage information to the asset profile. For instance, if the previous step resulted in a triple *(S, d, S')*, the engine will check which actors *A* and *A'* were selected to fill the role of stakeholders *S* and *S'*, and then the data policies of these actors will be investigated. If the actors store the asset *d*, the following triples are added to the asset profile: $(A, d, Store)$ and $(A', d, Store)$.

In addition, the engine will check which data directives and laws the actors fall under. Some actors will be required to keep all their data accessible for a third party. For instance if actor *A* falls under the Patriot act, the actor *USAGov* will also be able to store *d*.

Security Analysis. Finally, the feedback of a security analysis can be taken into account. When the asset flow is mapped on the system architecture, the engine knows through which intermediate components and communication channels the assets will pass. The security feedback shows which of these components and channels are vulnerable, and which attackers have access to them.

As an example, the security analysis may indicate that a certain communication channel uses a protocol that does not provide encryption. In this case, any attacker that has access to this communication channel can eavesdrop on the assets travelling through it:

$$Access(c, Attacker) \land \neg Encrypted(c) \land Passes(c, d) \Rightarrow$$
$$AssetProfile(Attacker, d, o)$$

Access(SystemPart, Stakeholder) and *Passes(SystemPart, AssetSet)* are first-order logic predicates that are output of the security analysis, indicating which stakeholders can access system parts, and what assets pass by them respectively. The *Encrypted(Channel)* predicate indicates that the data through a channel is encrypted as part of the protocol. When this is not the case, it is still possible that the data travelling through the channel has been encrypted by an application, this must be modelled in the asset flow by the assessor.

The security analysis will also return a list of component vulnerabilities. Only some of the vulnerability categories are relevant for the asset profile: *DataLeakage, CompromisedAuth* and *PrivilegeEscalation*. For these three categories, logic rules are written that detail their impact on the profile. For instance, if an asset travels via a component that has a *CompromisedAuth* vulnerability, the attackers that can access this component also have access to the asset, as they can bypass the authentication mechanism by compromising the vulnerability. This is represented with the following rule:

$$Access(c, Attacker) \land CompromisedAuth(c) \land Passes(d, c) \Rightarrow$$
$$AssetProfile(Attacker, d, o)$$

4   Realisation

This section describes how the methodology was implemented. IDP was chosen as logic programming tool, allowing for an easy integration with FAST-CPS. IDP is a declarative programming system that supports reasoning on expressions in a language that extends first-order logic. An IDP instance consists of a *structure*, a *theory*, and a *vocabulary*. The vocabulary defines types, predicates and functions that are used in the other two parts. The theory contains logic rules, while the structure contains the model of the system.

Mapping the concepts defined in the previous section to IDP types in the vocabulary is straightforward. As an example, types *Stakeholder, Actor, Asset* and *Operation* are defined in the vocabulary to model preferences. A predicate *OperationPref(Actor, Asset, Stakeholder, Operation)* is used to combine the four types and list the operation preferences of actors. Link preferences and data policies are added to the structure in similar fashion.

When the engine starts, the logic theory expands the model and populates an *AssetProfile(Stakeholder, Asset, Operation)* predicate. The rules used to fill this predicate can be translated into first-order logic definitions. A *definition* is a set of rules defining a concept, e.g. a logic predicate, in terms of other concepts. For example, this definition is used to find the set of operation conflicts:

$\forall a[Actor] \ d[Asset] \ s[Stakeholder] \ o[Operation]:$
$OperationConflict(a, d, s, o) \leftarrow AssetProfile(s, d, o) \land$
$\neg OperationPref(a, d, s, o).$

A term U is defined to be the union of conflict predicates. The *main()* procedure of the IDP instance then minimizes this term and returns all models with the least number of conflicts:

$result = minimize(Theory, Structure, U, Vocabulary)$
$printmodels(result)$

The predicate *ActorUsed(Stakeholder, Actor)* that combines actors with stakeholders is left empty in the structure. Hence, the evaluator will try all combinations of actors and stakeholders, check what the least number of conflicts is across all models, and then return all these models. Then the assessor can decide on the final design of his system. The necessary constraints have been put on the *ActorUsed* predicate to ensure that only sensible models are used, i.e. an actor *CustA* will not be used as the *Vend* stakeholder.

5   Validation

In the case study, the assessor is a company that owns a set of 3D printers which are used by their customers, mostly other companies. The owner of the printing company wants to design a system in which there are no conflicts between actors. To this end, several possible actors and system flows will be considered and their implications on the asset preferences evaluated. In total there are 384 different configurations of the case study.

5.1 Input

First the stakeholders and possible actors are defined. The printing company (Print) is the central stakeholder. The customer (Cust) has to send a model to the printing company. If necessary, the customer can contact a developer company (Supp) that creates this model for them. In order to use the available printers effectively, the printing company forwards this information to a scheduling service which is located in the cloud (SCloud).

The printing company also wants to employ predictive maintenance to assure the printers continue to function properly. For this purpose, they will contact the equipment vendor (Vend) and add a vibration sensor to their machines. Depending on the type of sensor used, this sensor data could either travel through the printing company networks before it reaches the equipment vendor, or it could travel straight to the equipment vendor over a telecommunications cloud (TelCo). The equipment vendor also opts to use a cloud service provider for its predictive maintenance analysis (PCloud).

Table 1. Different flows of the case study.

Flow	Description
1	The vibration sensor is connected to the printing network, no Supp.
2	The vibration sensor is connected to the printing network, Supp is used.
3	The vibration sensor uses LoRaWAN, no Supp.
4	The vibration sensor uses LoRaWAN, Supp is used

System Flows. Four different system flows are considered. Table 1 summarizes them. When the vibration sensor used is a LoRa sensor, the data travels straight to the equipment vendor through a Telecommunications provider (TelCo stakeholder). Alternatively, the data travels through the printing network. Further, flows 2 and 4 feature the *Supp* stakeholder, indicating the customer does not have a model yet.

Table 2. Actor operation preferences

Actor	Asset	Cust	Print	Vend	Supp	SCloud	PCloud	TelCo	Public
Cust A	*Model*	SP	SP			SP			
	CustomerName	SP	SP						
Cust B	*Model*	SP	SP		SP	SP			
	CustomerName	SP	SP			SP			
Vend A	*PdMAlgorithm*			SP			SP		
	SensorData			SP			SP	P	
Vend B	*PdMAlgorithm*			SP			SP		
	SensorData		SP	SP			SP	P	

Actors. 4 different customers are modelled with varying asset preferences, 2 different suppliers (only applicable in Flows 2 and 4), 2 different equipment vendors, and 2 different service providers for both the scheduling and predictive maintenance services, SAP HANA and AWS EC2 for the former, SAP HANA and Azure for the latter. Finally, the printing company also has two sets of asset preferences for flexibility if required.

An example representation of *operation preferences* for the case study is shown in Table 2. Two different customers and equipment vendors are shown. For each actor, all relevant assets are given a row in the table. The columns contain the different stakeholders in the system and the values show what operations these stakeholders are allowed to perform on the assets. S indicates assets can be stored, P indicates assets can be processed. Cust A is the most protective of its data, allowing only the printing company and their chosen cloud provider to see their model. Customer B trusts some of his data to the supplier also. Equipment vendors A and B disagree on whether the printing company should get to see the sensor data or not. *Linkability preferences* are modelled similarly.

In terms of data policies, all three cloud provider actors opt to store the received data indefinitely. SAP HANA falls under the EU DPD while Azure and AWSEC2 fall under the Patriot act.

5.2 Feedback

For each of the 384 cases, all conflicts were returned, as well as the actors whose preferences caused them.

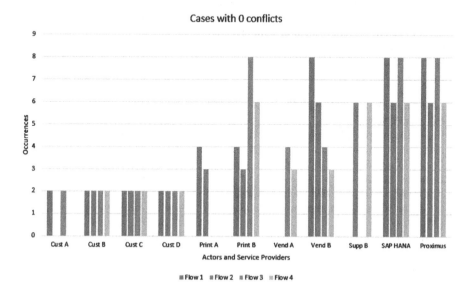

Fig. 2. Feedback about instances with zero conflicts.

The main aim is to find instances with zero conflicts and then select system flows and actors accordingly. The graph in Fig. 2 shows how often a particular actor is involved in instances with zero conflicts. Actors Supp A, AWS EC2 and Azure are not included in the graph as they always cause conflicts.

In case there are no models with zero conflicts, the methodology can still return useful feedback. For instance, assessors can model a case study with actor x or y and see which actor causes less conflicts. Another type of feedback could be which of 2 particular actors are causing more conflicts in certain flows.

6   Conclusions

This paper presents a methodology that allows an assessor to model a cyber-physical system and see which stakeholders have access to which pieces of data. The methodology evaluates multiple combinations of actors and returns the ones that create the least conflicts. The methodology is realised using a logic-based approach and validated on a 3D printing ecosystem. The methodology has been added to the FAST-CPS framework.

References

1. Becker, M.Y., Malkis, A., Bussard, L.: S4p: a generic language for specifying privacy preferences and policies. Microsoft Research (2010)
2. Bogaerts, B., De Cat, B., De Pooter, S., Denecker, M.: The IDP framework reference manual (2012)
3. Cranor, L.: Web privacy with P3P. O'Reilly Media, Inc., Sebastopol (2002)
4. Cranor, L., Langheinrich, M., Marchiori,M.: A P3P preference exchange language 1.0 (APPEL1. 0). W3C working draft (2002)
5. Decroix, K.: Inspecting privacy in electronic services (2015)
6. ENISA. Protecting industrial control systems: recommendations for EUROPE and member states (2011)
7. Friedenthal, S., Moore, A., Steiner, R.: A practical guide to SysML: the systems modeling language. Morgan Kaufmann (2014)
8. Homeland Security, H.C.C.: Cset: cyber security evaluation tool (2014)
9. Lee, E.A.: Cyber physical systems: design challenges. In: 2008 11th IEEE International Symposium on Object Oriented Real-Time Distributed Computing (ISORC), pp. 363–369. IEEE (2008)
10. Lemaire, L., Vossaert, J., Jansen, J., Naessens, V.: Extracting vulnerabilities in industrial control systems using a knowledge-based system. In: Proceedings of the 3rd International Symposium for ICS & SCADA Cyber Security Research, p. 1 (2015)
11. LeMay, E., Ford, M.D., Keefe, K., Sanders, W.H., Muehrcke, C.: Model-based security metrics using adversary view security evaluation (advise). In: 2011 Eighth International Conference on Quantitative Evaluation of Systems (QEST), pp. 191–200 IEEE (2011)
12. Li, N., Yu, T., Anton, A.: A semantics based approach to privacy languages. Comput. Syst. Sci. Eng. **21**(5), 339 (2006)

13. Samarati, P.: Protecting respondents identities in microdata release. IEEE Trans. Knowl. Data Eng. **13**(6), 1010–1027 (2001)
14. Sommestad, T., Ekstedt, M., Holm, H.: The cyber security modeling language: a tool for assessing the vulnerability of enterprise system architectures. IEEE Syst. J. **7**(3), 363–373 (2013)
15. Vu, A.H., Tippenhauer, N.O., Chen, B., Nicol, D.M., Kalbarczyk, Z.: CyberSAGE: a tool for automatic security assessment of cyber-physical systems. In: Norman, G., Sanders, W. (eds.) QEST 2014. LNCS, vol. 8657, pp. 384–387. Springer, Cham (2014). doi:10.1007/978-3-319-10696-0_29
16. Wang, C., Wang, Q., Ren, K., Lou, W.: Privacy-preserving public auditing for data storage security in cloud computing. In: INFOCOM, 2010 Proceedings IEEE, pp. 1–9. IEEE (2010)

Visualization-Driven Approach to Anomaly Detection in the Movement of Critical Infrastructure

Evgenia Novikova[1,2(✉)] and Ivan Murenin[1]

[1] Department of Computer Science and Engineering,
Saint Petersburg Electrotechnical University "LETI", Professora Popova Street 5,
Saint-Petersburg, Russia
imurenin@gmail.com, novikova.evgenia123@gmail.com
[2] Laboratory of Computer Security Problems, St. Petersburg Institute for Information
and Automation (SPIIRAS), 14th Line, 39, Saint-Petersburg, Russia

Abstract. Detection of anomalies in employees' movement represents an area of considerable interest for cyber-physical security applications. In the paper the visual analytics approach to detection of the spatiotemporal patterns and anomalies in organization stuff movement is proposed. The key elements of the approach are interactive self-organizing maps used to detect groups of employees with similar behavior and heat map applied to detect anomalies. They are supported by a set of the interactive interconnected visual models aimed to present spatial and temporal route patterns. We demonstrate our approach with an application to the VAST MiniChallenge-2 2016 data set, which describes movement of the employees within organization building.

Keywords: Cyber-physical security · Spatiotemporal movement patterns · Anomaly detection · Self organizing map · Heat map

1 Introduction

A wide range of applications may benefit from analysis of moving point data sets, also known as trajectories. Mining trajectories helps to establish object life patterns, reveal constraints existing in the underlying environment, for example, rules or security policies, restricting access to the specified zones, or infrastructure available to the individuals, i.e. places of interests, ATMs, etc. [1]. Another important application of the trajectory analysis is the generation of the features of the object life pattern to detect possible anomalies in observing data sets [2]. The roots of the detected anomalies may be different: they can be rather harmless like a driver encountering problems in the unknown place, or they can be signs of possible crime, for example an employee violating company security policies. Thus, the analysis of the trajectories can be used to provide air, road traffic and maritime safety by monitoring location, speed, trajectory and detecting unexpected travel impediments. Monitoring movements of the employees of critical infrastructure and hazardous industries supports monitoring compliance of the safety and access control policies and is useful in detection of inside threat [3].

© Springer International Publishing AG 2017
J. Rak et al. (Eds.): MMM-ACNS 2017, LNCS 10446, pp. 50–61, 2017.
DOI: 10.1007/978-3-319-65127-9_5

This paper presents an approach to detection of the spatiotemporal anomalies in organization stuff movement based on a combination of data mining and visualization techniques. A set of interactive visualization models supports understanding of the existing patterns in employees' movements and highlights possibly anomalous situations. We propose to form behavior patterns depending on a week day as daily routine of the company stuff may vary depending the week day. To understand what temporal patterns in employee's movements exist, we develop a special glyph that displays a set of days of week sharing the same pattern. Patterns are displayed using two visual models – the one is stacking based model with time bar reflecting the sequence of the monitored zones visited by employee, and the second one is a graph of connected controlled zones used to reflect spatial attributes of the pattern. The deviation in employees' movements is displayed using a heat map linked to detailed view on moves. Thus, an analyst has a possibility to understand the character of the detected anomaly.

Specifically, our main contribution is an approach to analysis of the movements of critical infrastructure stuff that handles multi-dimensional data (including employee groups and job classification) with the temporal features for the context of physical security. Its key elements are the interactive self-organizing maps used to detect groups of employees and days with similar behavior, enriched with specially designed glyph able to reflect periodicity in movement depending on a day of week and a heat map applied to detect anomalies and enforced by anomaly ranking mechanism.

To demonstrate the efficiency of the proposed approach we tested it on data set provided within VAST Challenge 2016 [4].

The rest of the paper is organized as follows. Section 2 discusses the related work on approaches to anomaly detection in time series and visualization models used to investigate object movement. In Sect. 3 we describe the proposed visual analytics approach to anomaly detection in employee movements. Section 4 presents case study used to evaluate approach, discusses results and defines directions of the future research. Conclusions sum up our contributions.

2 Related Work

In case when there is no possibility to obtain patterns of normal behavior by making observation the most widely used approach is based on the clustering of the trajectories. The obtained clusters are then used to describe normality model for anomaly detection. Clusters may be found by centroid based approaches, hierarchical models, or density-based approaches [5]. Automatic methods may discover interesting behavioral patterns and anomalies but in the most cases they need to be supported by the visualization techniques explaining the final result [6, 7]. A neural clustering method, also known the self-organizing map (SOM) combines multidimensional data clustering and projection techniques, and produces visualization of the clusters reflecting distance between them. Shreck et al. applied SOM to analyze trajectories and propose a visualization–driven framework for adjusting SOM output [8]. However, they focused mainly on the analysis of spatial attributes of trajectories. In [9] both spatial and temporal attributes are investigated; however, they are analyzed separately by selecting all temporal attributes for one geographical location or all spatial attributes for one time unit. Authors enriched SOM visualization by special images displayed within SOM cells. The goal of these images is to explain the result of clustering tool.

In general case existing models could be divided into three groups – static or interactive maps often enriched with glyphs encoding movement attributes, space-time cubes, and stacking based visualizations [6].

Maps are the most obvious way for presenting location aware data. Trajectories or cluster of trajectories are represented by lines. The movement attributes such as time, speed, type of the moving object are encoded by line color or specially designed glyphs. For example, in [10] the color of lines presenting routes of moving points is used to encode type of vehicles (car, bus, pedestrian, bicycle and others) and speed values. In cases when the exact trajectory is not important flow maps are used. Flow maps are visualization models focusing on determining destinations and sources of the routes. The quantities of the flows are usually mapped to two visual variables: the width and the color saturation of the flow lines, and the glyphs are used to characterize the type of the flow destination or source. Interesting modification of the flow maps used to analyze population migration is presented in [11]. The regions of interest serving as destination and source points of migration are located circumferentially and displayed as segments of the ring. The flows are displayed as splines connecting corresponding ring segments. However, all map-based visualization share one common disadvantage – they are not able to display spatial and temporal attributes of the movement simultaneously.

Space-time cube is a 3D-visualization technique designed to present spatial and temporal characteristics of the movement simultaneously. According to it, points of the trajectories are displayed in three dimension space, where vertical axis stands for time usually. In [12] authors presents an extension of the space-time cube called trajectory wall. In contrast to traditional space time cube the third display dimension is used to represent a set of trajectories. The vertical axis is divided into bins, each containing one trajectory. Trajectories are represented by bands split into segments, which are colored according to the values of attributes related to trajectory points. As the trajectories can be ordered in the third dimension according to their temporal order then this visualization model can be viewed as a space–time cube where the absolute time is transformed to the temporal order of the trajectories. Like all 3D visual models the space time cubes could be ineffective because of occlusions and cluttering of the trajectories.

Stacking based visualization of the routes is based on time graph, also known as time line. One axis represents time, and another – values of spatial attributes of the trajectory point. Each route is represented by a curve or polygonal line. To display a set of trajectories, stacked curves or bands synchronized within time scale are used. Bands can be divided into segments colored according to values of attributes. For example, in [13] color is used to display type of position (café, shop, office).

3   Visualization Driven Approach

When designing our approach to analysis of the employees' movement we tried to answer on the following questions the analyst would be interested in:

1. Are there any groups of employees having similar routes?
2. What is the common pattern in co-workers' movement belonging to one group? How does it change depending on day of week? How does it correlate with employee's position in the organization?
3. Are there any deviations in employee's movement?
4. What is the character of the anomalies, i.e. how often, when and where did they take place?

Answering these questions step by step, the analyst forms the overall understanding of the existing movement patterns in organization firstly, and then focuses on details describing possible anomalies. The visualization models and underlying data mining techniques used in the proposed approach support the described scheme of the analysis process.

Figure 1 shows the main view of the software prototype implementing our approach. The first SOM-based view, *Employees SOM View* (view A) shows groups of employees with alike movement trajectories, the second SOM-based view, *Days SOM View* (view B), highlights existing periodicity in movement arranging days of week in groups of similarities. The *Graph View* (view D) conveys information about spatial component of the movement only. View *C* has two tabs – Pattern View (Fig. 1) and Anomaly View, and contains stacking based visual model named *BandView*. The *BandView* model links spatial and temporal data on movement and is used to display detailed information on behavior patterns or periods with anomalous activity depending on what tab is active. The heat map view E displays deviations in behavior within groups of employees or groups of days with similar movement patterns. The *Property View* (view F) gives detailed information about an object represented by each selectable graphical element of the models, e.g. single move of the employee, controlled zone, group of the

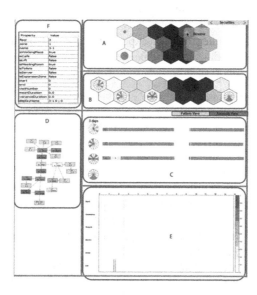

Fig. 1. The first version of the application GUI

employees, employee etc. in table view. All views are interactive and interconnected. Clicking on each graphical element of all data visualization models an analyst updates information displayed in the linked views. In the subsections below we discuss the data preprocessing step and describe proposed visualization and interaction techniques in detail.

3.1 Data

In general case logs from proximity card readers describing employees' movement have following format: <timestamp, employee ID, controlled zone ID>. There are could be some additional fields such as status (entrance permitted or denied), employee access level, etc. These data could be enforced by description of the control zone arrangement, employees' position within organization hierarchy, location of the employees' work place in the context of the controlled zones. In our approach we deal with logs containing information only who and when entered controlled zone, and show that these data are enough to form behavior patterns and discover signs of the anomalous activity.

The specific feature of the logs from proximity card readers registering employees' movement is that they appear irregular, and interval between logs for one employee may vary from tens of seconds to tens of hours. Furthermore, some employees can make a lot of moves within organization building due to their role profiles, while others rarely leave their work place. Thus, the lengths of time series describing their movement may vary significantly.

In our approach we transform each time series to a vector of the fixed length. We divide the whole time interval presented in logs into a sequence of the equal time slots, and calculate number of visits and duration of staying in each controlled zone for each time slot and each employee. The attribute of the vector generated in this way describes an activity of the particular user in the given controlled zone during given period of time. The attributes are ordered by time slots firstly and then by controlled zones. Currently the default duration of the time slot is 4 h, experiments showed that it is enough to detect even minor temporal deviations in movement equal to 5 min.

3.2 The SOM-Based Views

To detect groups of employees with similar behavior and outliers, we use SOMs known also as Kohonen maps [14]. It is a type of artificial neural network that is trained using unsupervised learning to map multidimensional input data into a low-dimensional (typically two-dimensional) space. The SOM is a topology-preserving data transformation technique meaning that the cluster centers associated with nodes located next to each other are more similar than clusters located far from each other.

One of the major problems with SOMs is obtaining data without missing values for each attribute. However, in our case data preprocessing step guarantees producing vectors with values for each dimension.

In our approach we use U-Matrix presentation of the SOM [15]. It shows data structure by displaying the average distances between weight vectors of neighboring units. The darker color of the node, the more it differs from the neighbors. The adjacent light nodes are quite similar to each other. Nodes containing clusters' centers are marked with circle glyph. Its size reflects the number of objects in the cluster.

The SOM is used twice in the proposed approach. The purpose of the Employees SOM view is to detect groups of co-workers with similar behavior. The attribute vector describes activity of the employee during all period of time, and deviations in the movement taking place once or rarely do not influence on the result of the clustering. This enables us to assume that this SOM shows differences in movement existing due to peculiarities of the employee's role in the organization. Each element of the SOM view is selectable; by clicking on it an analyst gets detailed information about cluster members, and updates the view of the second SOM, the Graph View, the Pattern View and the Heatmap View.

We assume that employees may have responsibilities implemented on some regular basis depending on the day of week; these duties may cause periodical changes in the employee's movement. The goal of the second SOM is to detect groups of days with similar behavior for the selected group of employees revealing thus periodicity in their movement. To construct the Days SOM, we use weight vectors of cluster centroids of the Employees SOM, transform it to a set of vectors representing days by splitting it into vectors of smaller length and cluster it using SOM. Then we determine what day of week contains in each group of days to discover dependencies of the movement from day of week. The result of clustering is displayed using U-Matrix, however, the SOM nodes are complemented with a special glyph that displays the distribution of the days in the cluster according to the day of week. In many organizations the employee's activity routine depends on type of the week in the year – odd or even. We designed a *WeekCircle* glyph able to display movement patterns having periods equal to one or two weeks. It may be divided into 7 or 14 sectors depending what periodicity model – 7 day or 14- day is selected. The model of the glyph for the 14-days period is shown in the Fig. 2. The right half of the WeekCircle represents odd week, and the left half of it represents even week. The Mondays are displayed by the top sectors and Saturdays – by the bottom sectors, thus odd week is in mirror reflection with even one. Figure 2 presents two glyphs reflecting what days of week the group contains. The left glyph shows that the cluster consists of Mondays, Wednesdays and Fridays of the odd week meaning that the employee or group of employees has particular duties implemented every second Monday, Wednesday and Friday. The right glyph indicates that the group contains weekends only. The Days SOM view allows also detecting days with anomalous behavior if these anomalies have long term character, i.e. their duration exceeds an hour. The day with such type of anomaly would constitute a separate cluster located in the close neighborhood to another cluster.

Fig. 2. The *WeekCircle* glyph showing the distribution of the days according to the day of the week

We implemented interaction techniques for the Days SOM view similar to the Employee SOM view. An analyst can set up the SOM size, get detailed information about each SOM cluster. By clicking on the node of the SOM the analyst updates the Property View, the Graph View, the Pattern View and Anomaly View.

3.3   The BandView Visualization Model

The goal of the BandView model is to link spatial and temporal attributes. It is a stacking based visualization technique. The horizontal axis corresponds to the time. The route of an employee is presented using segmented bar. Each segment represents time interval during which the employee was in the given controlled zone. The color of the segment is used to encode the zone itself. The color scheme is constructed in the following way. Each floor of the organization building is assigned a certain color. The palette for the zones located on one floor is created by changing brightness of the floor color. The greater the number (ID) of the controlled zone, the darker the color of the corresponding segment. The Fig. 3 shows routes of the co-workers of one department during one day. The zones of the first floor are displayed in brownish colors, zones of the second floor – in greenish colors, and zones of the third floor – in blue colors. Obviously, the majority of the employees spend their work time on the second floor, and only one person has an office on the third floor.

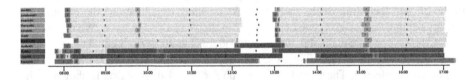

Fig. 3. The BandView representation of the employees' moves during one day.

The BandView model is used in the Pattern View and the Anomaly View. In the Pattern View it displays spatiotemporal patterns for the groups of employees and is used in conjunction with the WeekCircle model. The Y-axis of the BandView represents clusters of the days with similar routes. If no node in SOM-based views is selected the Pattern View displays raw data. In this case Y-axis represents stuff members ordered by the department. To analyze raw data, we implemented flexible filtering mechanism allowing constructing complex logical expressions using all available attributes of the move: employee ID, department, office, duration of staying in the zone, zone ID, floor, etc.

In the Anomaly view it shows movements of co-workers belonging to one cluster during one particular time interval (group mode) or routes of the employee during days belonging to one cluster (day mode). An analyst may switch between these two modes, however their availability is determined by the structure of the employees' cluster. If it consists of more than two persons then both modes are available to the researcher, otherwise the day mode is used. In the group mode Y-axis represents employees forming one cluster, and the scale of the timeline is limited to one day. In the second mode Y-axis displays a set of days belonging to one cluster ordered by time. However, in both modes BandView allows detecting where, when anomaly took place and how long it lasted; because it enables visual comparing of the routes.

3.4   The Graph View

The graph is used to display controlled zones visited by employees. The graph vertexes corresponds to controlled zones, adjacent zones are linked by edges. The graph of the controlled zones can be constructed on the basis of logs from proximity card readers or map of controlled zones.

The Graph View is controlled by two views – the Employees SOM View and the Days SOM View. These two views determine what data are to be displayed. When clicking on the element of the Employees SOM, the Graph View displays zones visited by a group of employees. The Days SOM View refines data to be displayed – the Graph View shows spatial pattern of the movement for this group during selected set of days.

The zones visited by the employee are mapped on this graph and highlighted by the color. They are colored in accordance with color scheme used in the BandView visualization model. The unvisited zones are displayed in grey.

3.5   HeatMap View

The goal of the heat map is to show the presence of possibly anomalous deviations in the stuff personnel movement. We consider that anomalies come out in irregular insignificant changes in the behavior of the subject, therefore we suggest investigating the deviations within group of employees or group of days having similar movement pattern. Like the Anomaly View the Heatmap View has two modes. In the first mode it displays deviations in routes of employees constituting one cluster. The heat map is constructed in the following way. The Y-axis corresponds to the employees in the cluster; and X-axis represents attributes of the vector generated from the log data as it is described above. In the second mode Y-axis displays days of one cluster, and X-axis displays attributes of the vectors describing person activity during given day. Each element of the heat map represents distance of an attribute value of the sample from the cluster centroid.

However, displaying the distances directly may produce rather noisy picture on the one hand when the distances are comparable, or hide some deviations on the other hand, if distance variance is high. To solve this problem we use anomaly ranking mechanism based on calculation of the z-score for each attribute deviation from cluster centroid. Z-score reflects how far the current value of the attribute from its mean value. Discretization approach used on the data preprocessing stage of the approach allows forming data samples for the time slots characterizing employee activity for the given period of time considering some time periodicity (day, week, month, etc.). This makes it possible to assess deviations in employee route, for example, on the time interval from 8 am till 12 pm in the morning for each work day.

The zones of the heat map with suspicious bursts of the activity can be selected and examined in detail in the Anomaly View.

4   Case Study and Discussion

To evaluate our approach we use a dataset provided by the VAST Challenge 2016: Mini-Challenge 2 [4]. It contains logs of the proximity card readers that cover individual building zones. When an employee with proximity card enters a new controlled zone, his/her card is detected and recorded. It should be noted that most, but not all, areas are available to staff members even if they forget their proximity cards. The dataset contains a two-week set of logs. An analyst is also provided with building layout for the offices, including the maps of the controlled zones, a list of employees, including their department and office assignments.

We assumed that the employees within one department may have similar movement patterns and decided to analyze logs grouped by the employee department. We discovered that the majority of the employees within one department moves alike, and there are small groups whose behavior is different due to the specific responsibilities and location of the work place. Figure 4 shows the result of clustering of the employees of the security department. It is clearly seen that there are 5 groups of co-workers having similar movement pattern. One of these groups is rather numerous, while others consist of one-two persons.

Fig. 4. Result of the SOM clustering of the employees belonging to one department

The members of the most numerous group have only two periodical patterns in their movement – one is for the work days and another - for the weekdays. Their work days usually start approximately at 7.50 am and finish at 5 pm. They leave the building approximately at 12 pm for an hour. We consider that they go outside for lunch. The members of this group spend the most of their work time in the 2–3 zone located on the second floor where their offices are located. Every 1, 5–2 h they leave zone and visit adjacent zone 2–7 for 5–10 min. The 2–7 zone contains offices and toilets. As they visit only one zone of the second floor this route hardly could be considered as a go-round, more likely they simply go out to refresh. At the weekends they do not come to work.

Analysis of the heat map displaying deviations in their routes allowed us to spot easily anomalies in the routes of two employees on the second day of the period investigated (Fig. 5). The BandView visualization of the movements of the selected group of employees for this day showed that the logs from proximity card readers are missing for one employee while another employee has doubled logs. Interestingly that the second doubled log has a timestamp several seconds later than the first one. These two facts – the absence of the logs for one employee and doubled logs for another – allowed us to assume that the first employee used the proximity card of the second employee to enter the controlled zone.

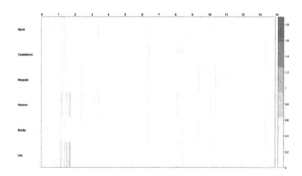

Fig. 5. Deviations in the routes of the most numerous group of the security employees

Two clusters closest to this group consist of one employee each. Their routes are rather similar to movements of the employees of the first cluster as their offices are located in the 2–3 zone, where they also spend most of their working time. However, one employee (the upmost left cluster) does not leave 2–3 zone in the first half of the day. The distinctions in the route of employee presented by the right cluster in the bottom row of the SOM are much greater – he leaves building for lunch one hour earlier at 11 am in order to be in the 1–7 zone during standard lunch time.

The rest two groups lay apart from the others in the SOM. The rightmost cluster consists of two employees whose offices are located in the first floor. They expose two periodical patterns depending on the day of week. One of them visits the 2–3 zone every Tuesday in the first half of the work day, while another visits the same zone every Thursday in the first half of the day. We spot interesting deviation in moves of the one employee of the given cluster. He visited 3–4 zone for 3 min located on the third floor only once during all two-week period. According to the zone plan lifts and stairs are located there. We could assume that the employee visited this zone accidently, for example by pressing wrong lift button. However, to be more precise we need more information about who else from the stuff was in this zone at that moment. The last cluster located in the upper right corner of the Employee SOM contains only one employee. From the BandView it is clear that his/her office is in the third floor. Analysis of the office assignments shows that the third floor is occupied by representatives of the administrative and executive department, thus allowing us to admit that this employee is a chief of the security department. His moves are rather diverse and strongly depend on the day of week. He starts his work day with visit of the local café located in the 1–2 zone and then goes upstairs in his office. Every Tuesday and Thursday he goes to the 2–3 zone and spends there approximately half an hour and then returns to his office. The BandView of the raw data for the moves of the security staff allows us to conclude that the department meeting takes place every Tuesday and Thursday. It is also possible to find out that the representative of the security stuff has to be on the first floor from 8 am to 5 pm. For this reason some security stuff has lunch break at different time intervals; and employees whose work places are located in the first floor visit meetings only once per week to ensure the presence of the security at the building entrance.

We were also able to determine anomalies when employee visits the zone in the unusual time, when they do not return to their working place, forget using proximity switch when leaving the building. In many cases analysis of the stuff interaction would improve understanding of the anomaly origin. The BandView model can be helpful in understanding possible interaction between stuff members. But it works only when the set of employees displayed is limited and not exceeding 10–15 persons, otherwise it is very difficult to spot meetings of the co-workers.

Therefore, one of the primary tasks of the future work is the implementation of the visual analytics techniques allowing investigation of the interactions both individual and group between the stuff members in dynamics. Another direction of the future work is concerned with analysis of the data obtained from the different type of sources. For example the logs of the operating system such as login/logout events, keyboard events provide evidences that employee is at his working place. Readings from the building sensors such as building heat-ventilation system may also explain the anomalous behavior of the employee. The correlation of these data needs elaboration of the new visual analytics techniques considering the character of the source logs.

5   Conclusions

In the paper we proposed the visual analytics approach to detection of spatiotemporal patterns and anomaly in employees' movement. The key elements of the approach are interactive SOMs used to detect groups of employees and days with similar movement patterns, and heat map used to detect anomalies. They are supported by graph based and stacking based visualization technique to present spatial and spatiotemporal patterns and anomalies. We presented core interaction techniques linking all visual displays and supporting analysis process.

To illustrate our approach, we used data set provided by the VAST Challenge 2016. In the paper we discuss result obtained, and define future directions of work devoted to the enhancement of the prototype, elaboration of visualization techniques and usability evaluation of the proposed visualization analytical system.

Acknowledgement. This research has been supported by grant of the RFBR # 16-07-00625.

References

1. Millonig, A., Maierbrugger, M.: Identifying unusual pedestrian movement behavior in public transport infrastructures. In: Proceedings of Movement Pattern Analysis Workshop (MPA2010), pp. 106–110. Zurich (2010)
2. Lerman, Y., Rofe, Y., Omer, I.: Using space syntax to model pedestrian movement in urban transportation planning. Geogr. Anal. **46**(4), 392–410 (2014)
3. Pan, X., Han, C., Dauber, K., Law, K.: A multi-agent based framework for the simulation of human and social behaviors during emergency evacuations. AI Soc. **22**, 113–132 (2007)
4. Vast Challenge Homepage. http://vacommunity.org/. Accessed 10 Mar 2017
5. Kisilevich, S., Mansmann, F., Nanni, M., Rinzivillo, S.: Spatio-temporal clustering: a survey. In: Data Mining and Knowledge Discovery Handbook, pp. 855–874 (2010)

6. Andrienko, N., Andrienko, G.: Visual analytics of movement: an overview of methods, tools and procedures. Inf. Vis. **12**(1), 3–24 (2013)
7. Novikova, E., Kotenko, I.: Analytical visualization techniques for security information and event management. In: Proceedings of 21st Euromicro International Conference on Parallel, Distributed, and Network-Based Processing, pp. 519–525 (2013)
8. Schreck, T., Bernard, J., Von Landesberger, T., Kohlhammer, J.: Visual cluster analysis of trajectory data with interactive Kohonen maps. Inf. Vis. **8**(1), 14–29 (2009)
9. Andrienko, G., Andrienko, N.: Exploration of massive movement data: a visual analytics approach. In: Proceedings of 11th AGILE International Conference on Geographic Information Science (2008)
10. Guo, H., et al.: Tripvista: triple perspective visual trajectory analytics and its application on microscopic traffic data at a road intersection. In: Proceedings of IEEE Pacific Visualization Symposium (PacificVis), pp. 163–170 (2011)
11. Sander, N., Abel, J., Bauer, R., Schmidt, J.: Visualising migration flow data with circular plots. In: European Population Conference (2014)
12. Andrienko, G., Andrienko, N., Schumann, H., Tominski, C.: Visualization of trajectory attributes in space–time cube and trajectory wall. In: Buchroithner, M., Prechtel, N., Burghardt, D. (eds.) Lecture Notes in Geoinformation and Cartography. Cartography from Pole to Pole, pp. 157–163. Springer, Heidelberg (2014)
13. Guo, C., et al.: Dodeca-rings map: interactively finding patterns and events in large geo-temporal data. In: IEEE Symposium on Visual Analytics Science and Technology, pp. 353–354 (2014)
14. Kohonen, T., Honkela, T.: Kohonen network. http://www.scholarpedia.org/article/Kohonen_network. Accessed 10 Mar 2017
15. Ultsch, A.: Self-organizing neural networks for visualization and classification. Information and Classification, pp. 307–313 (1993)

Detection and Mitigation of Time Delay Injection Attacks on Industrial Control Systems with PLCs

Emrah Korkmaz, Matthew Davis$^{(\boxtimes)}$, Andrey Dolgikh, and Victor Skormin

Binghamton University, Binghamton, NY 13902, USA
{ekorkma1,mdavis7,adolgikh,vskormin}@binghamton.edu

Abstract. National security agencies are increasingly concerned about cyber threats to Industrial Control Systems (ICS). For this reason, the detection and mitigation of cyber-attacks on ICS, as well as addressing the consequences of these attacks, are extensively researched. This paper describes the efforts of the cyber research team at Binghamton University that created an experimental cyber research testbed, designed as a power station equipped with low-watt electric machinery and industrial control and sensory systems, common in modern ICS. This paper presents a comprehensive study of time delay injection attacks on networked control systems, in which an attacker injects extra time delays into the feedback and forward channels of control systems. These attacks enable the adversary to interfere with the control system and create system instability, causing anomalous operational regimes and potentially forcing the system to crash. A technology based on an online recursive estimation of network time delays is proposed and validated by simulation studies and experiments on the testbed to mitigate any time delay injection attacks.

Keywords: Industrial control systems · Cyber-Physical systems · Testbed · Cyber-Security · Time delay injection attack · Time delay detection

1 Introduction

A recently published report by the Industrial Control Systems Cyber Emergency Response Team (ICS-CERT) indicates that many organizations have Internet-connected control systems and are not even aware that they are directly accessible from the Internet [1]. Recently, industrial communication technologies are being moved on top of the standard Ethernet/TCP/IP stack of protocols [2]. Using Ethernet protocols in ICS provides benefits such as expanding the functionality of control devices, allowing remote control, and utilizing virtual machines within the network. Technology products, such as remote Human Machine Interface (HMI) software on smartphones or tablets enable operators to manage ICS remotely. Although these advantages enable control systems engineers to build cost-effective and user-friendly ICS, this networked connectivity opens doors to a massive amount of cyber-attacks targeting the ICS [3]. To prove this point, we successfully deployed a time delay injection attack on our laboratory testbed. The impact of this time delay injection attack on an ICS was examined, and a method of using recursive delay

© Springer International Publishing AG 2017
J. Rak et al. (Eds.): MMM-ACNS 2017, LNCS 10446, pp. 62–74, 2017.
DOI: 10.1007/978-3-319-65127-9_6

estimation was implemented to accurately determine the injected time delay length within a short time period from the time of injection.

The rest of this paper is structured as follows: Sect. 2 presents the background of this research. Section 3 describes the designed testbed architecture and gives information about the Internet connection components. In Sect. 4, the effect of the time delay attack injection on ICS is discussed. Section 5 presents the recursive estimation based time delay detection technique and the obtained results. Finally, Sect. 6, contains the conclusions and further research on this topic.

2   Related Research

Over the past two decades, there was no lack of publications addressing time delays in ICS as well as demonstrating various control approaches [4–6]. Although most strategies were well justified by control theory and offered viable solutions, these solutions were not developed in the context of cyber-security. For instance, the authors in [7] present a discrete-time jump system approach in which a V-K iteration algorithm was utilized to design stabilizing controllers. However, the controller design was performed under the assumption that there were random and bounded delays between the sensor and the controller which is not always true for malicious delays. Another approach [8] addresses tuning the PID controller by PLC programming, based on models of unstable processes with a random time delay. This research is somewhat relevant to our study; however, the described stability conditions may not be sufficient for purposely designed time delay injection attacks. The authors in [9] propose gain scheduling for a PID controller to compensate for extra time delays in the system; however, control system stability cannot be assured for random delay values. Due to this lack of existing literature about the cyber-security implications of time delays in ICS, a cyber-security study of time delay attacks is performed for ICS in this paper.

There are several implementations and interpretations of network time delay attacks in literature. Larsen in [10] describes a time delay attack as a stale data attack. The attacker manipulates the timing of encrypted packets on the associated network, resulting in a difference between the physical and logical states of the process. Consequently, the control system may be driven to an arbitrary state. Krotofil et al. [11] suggest that for an effective stale data attack to drive the system to an unsafe condition, the adversaries must determine the optimal time duration of the attack. The researchers introduce this type of attack as a wormhole attack. With this attack method, an adversary establishes a link between the network nodes and can create delays over the network to drop packets maliciously [12, 13].

Time delay injection attacks on power systems are not uncommon. An adversary could exploit vulnerabilities along the communication links, which would cause the loss of critical information, and therefore unstable operation conditions can result [14]. The authors in [15] indicate that a time delay switch (TDS) attack can be performed to sabotage and degrade the performance of a smart grid. In another study, the authors propose a time delay detection mechanism to mitigate these attacks and introduce a modified controller in the case of a time delay injection [16]. This controller is only designed to control the power grid and the time delay injection is performed only in the feedback channels of the control system. However, in many cases the time delay can be injected into both the feedback and forward channels of the control network.

3   Industrial Control System Security Testbed

The ICS Security testbed built at Binghamton University features a digital control system that could typically be found in a power generation station at fossil fuel or nuclear power plants, electric grid, etc. The testbed is suitable for the deployment of typical cyber-attacks and the detailed monitoring of system operations, thus providing researchers with an unlimited amount of critical data [17]. The testbed components can be broken down into five categories:

3.1   Physical System

This equipment is used to investigate the effects of cyber-attacks on power generation hardware in two different power generation setups. The first unit is composed of a 0.25 HP 3-phase AC motor and a 0.33 HP permanent magnet DC motor which are connected via a coupling tie-in shaft. The PowerFlex 525 AC Drive controls the RPM of this motor-generator assembly. A series of single-phase loads are attached to the DC generator to safely dissipate the power, thereby protecting the system from overload conditions. The second power generating unit operates a 3-phase AC blower motor that drives a 12 V DC generator through airflow-based coupling. The airflow can be restricted externally thus simulating disturbance effects on air handling port. A separate PowerFlex 525 AC Drive is used to control the electrical power provided to the AC blower motor-generator module to manipulate the motor speed.

3.2   Measurement Devices

An Allen-Bradley 1794 Flex I/O module functions as a monitoring device for both power generation units. The power output of both the DC motor and the DC blower motor are connected to inputs of the Flex I/O, which then measures the voltage. Information about these voltages is transmitted to the ControlLogix controller which uses this information to display the values in the HMI as well as potentially alter the PowerFlex PID parameters to adjust the generated voltage.

3.3   Programmable Controllers

The testbed contains two different types of PLCs: an Allen-Bradley ControlLogix, which is an advanced controller, and an Allen-Bradley Micro850, which is a simpler multiple-IO controller. The ControlLogix 1756-L61 PLC is used as the central controller. Programming the ControlLogix device can be done using Rockwell Automation's RSLogix 5000 software. The power dissipation from the direct-coupled power generation unit is controlled by programming the Micro850 controller to alter the distribution of power to various single phase loads and a small DC motor. Rockwell Automation's Connected Components Workbench software is used to create the ladder logic diagrams for programming the Micro850.

3.4 Communication Infrastructures and Software

The components on the testbed communicate over the testbed network using the EtherNet/IP protocol and Common Industrial Protocol (CIP). To perform time delay injection attacks on the testbed, a traffic shaping VM is deployed on the testbed network. It is implemented via FreeBSD and DummyNet software [18]. This VM allows DummyNet-enabled bridges to be created using the existing PC hardware without disrupting any existing software installations of ICS components [19].

3.5 Scada-HMI

Human machine interface (HMI) systems permit operators to visualize and manipulate the testbed operations. On this testbed, the operator can observe and adjust the real-time output voltages of both power generation units. Proficy HMI/SCADA iFIX software is used to build, monitor, and control the entire HMI system.

4 Time Delay Injection Attack

The inherent time delay in ICS, perceived as a system stability issue, was addressed in various comprehensive studies [20–22]. However a time delay, when purposely designed and injected into the system by an adversary, is an effective method of attacking the network. For cyber-physical systems (CPS), packet delays on the control network might result in the deterioration of system performance and the loss of stability. Typical information technology (IT) computers and networks do no suffer from this timing criticality, therefore time delays on ICS networks deserve special attention.

The time delay can be created on both the forward and feedback channels of the control system (see Fig. 1). As described in the previous section, the PowerFlex drives and the measurement device are connected to the ICS network. While the PLC

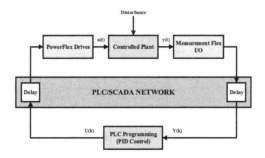

Fig. 1. Closed-loop diagram of testbed

communication with the PowerFlex drives is through the forward channel, the communication with the measurement devices is through the feedback channel.

4.1 Attack Model

Understanding the attack model and the threat scenario is important for preventing control system attacks. An attacker with network access can influence and disrupt the basic control functions, rather than only the longer-term controls commonly associated with a SCADA environment. Although simple time delay attacks do not require any expert knowledge, in many stale data attacks the attackers must directly manipulate the integrity of communications between field devices and controllers [11]. To execute a successful time delay injection attack, the adversary needs to conduct extensive reconnaissance work to identify the data flow of the control network which consists of sensors, controllers, and motor drives. To successfully exploit the network vulnerability, the attacker can use a network traffic shaping tool to create arbitrary delays within the targeted control network. As seen in Fig. 2, the attacker's computer is deployed on the testbed, which facilitates an experimental investigation of the ways and means of data traffic manipulation in the attacked control network. It is safe to assume that the attacker gains access to the control network and can inject time delays into the communication channels. Consequently, the immediate measurement of the desired process output $Y(t)$ and the output of the actuators $U(t)$ will be replaced by delayed ones,

$$Y^{DEL}(t) = Y(t - \tau) \text{ and } U^{DEL}(t) = U(t - \tau) \tag{1}$$

where τ is the desired delay magnitude, defined by the attacker.

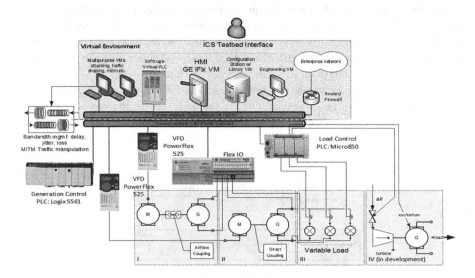

Fig. 2. Testbed architecture

The magnitude of the delay injected by the attacker must be chosen carefully because the added delay in the control system can be detected by the ICS and the sensor control code. If such a delay is detected by the devices on the network, the devices will automatically enter a fault condition which halts the system. However, the extra delay cannot be detected if it is injected gradually and each increment does not exceed the maximum change in delay value that would invoke the termination procedure in the system. We believe this is due to delay adaption code built into the network's enabled sensors that reacts to sudden significant delay increments but adapts to small ones.

4.2   Time Delay Attack

The testbed was configured to maintain a specified output voltage under varying load conditions to investigate the effectiveness of time delay attacks. This function was realized via a PID based controller in the feedback control loop. The blower motor's set point voltage value was chosen as 1.9 volts, which is small enough to protect attached devices from any potential overvoltage problems. The direct-coupled motor-generator module of the testbed operated at a frequency proportional to that of the blower motor. The direct-coupled motor-generator module can generate voltages up to 400 volts, and thus its voltage control is paramount because of the overvoltage values that might occur and potentially damage attached devices.

Detectable Delays

First, a time delay attack on the testbed with a 100 ms delay was deployed. It was detected almost immediately by the devices on the network, resulting in fault conditions on the PowerFlex drives and stopping the motor-generator modules. The experiments showed that the extra delay causes connection time outs and clears the data table of the drive so that the networked drives are no longer under the control of the PLCs. If the operators of the ICS encounter "communication interrupted" fault codes stemming from a time delay attack, they are to perform system debugging and effectively mitigate the problem. However, the "connection time outs" are a very common issue in a variety of interconnection protocols [23], and the time delay attack cannot be easily identified as the source of the fault. Although this attack method can be perceived as an ineffective way to stop a power generation unit, if it is conducted on a real power plant it may cause blackouts in a large portion of the electric power grid, depending on the specific configuration of each controller at each facility/unit and the type of the process.

Undetectable Delays

The EtherNet/IP based devices can also be subjected to a gradual time delay attack. This attack allows for much larger delays to be introduced without detection. Consider the graphs featured in Fig. 3. The upper graph depicts the output frequencies of the PowerFlex drives while the lower graph shows the measured output voltage of the air blower motor-generator module. In this experiment, during the first 100 s there was no network delay in either the feedback or forward channels. For the time delay attack to be successful, it must begin with subtle delay values that should be increased gradually over time. Thus every 10 s the delay value was increased by an additional 10 ms. In this case, the PowerFlex drives and PLC computers do not generate any fault conditions and give no indication of the time delay increase. The delay in the network prevents the PLC PID block from observing the actual process conditions and prevents the generation of timely control efforts [24]. The internal data table of the controller is supposed to update its input tags and output values based on the configured requested packet interval (RPI) parameter. However, the controller does not update the input and output data with the desired RPI. Instead, it updates all data at the maliciously altered time delay interval. It could be seen that the RPI value of 10 ms does not allow for the detection of small delay increments under 10 ms [25]. Consequently, the control task is still carried out by the PLC and PowerFlex drives, but the desired control performance is not achieved. This loss of desired control performance results in oscillations of the PID response due to the network delay, which effectively increases the dead time of the process and invalidates the tuning of the PID controller. When the controller is improperly tuned, it fails to dampen the oscillatory process in the control loop.

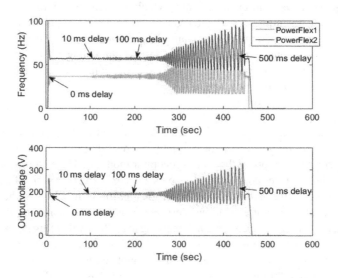

Fig. 3. Measured output voltage and frequency values of drives

At each cycle, the amplitude of the oscillation increases and eventually exceeds the operational safety limits. An overvoltage condition is forced by this time delay attack and causes the system to produce a very high output voltage (over 300 volts). As the delay increases, the stale data becomes a dominant factor in the control loop instability. It was noticed that as the time delay exceeds 150 ms, the system becomes unstable; with a delay of approximately 500 ms, the system crashed, burning out all the light bulbs that functioned as a resistive load for the direct-coupled generator.

It should be noted that having the testbed offers the "attackers" the luxury of having information crucial for the deployment of a successful attack. Although real attackers will not be able to determine attack parameters yielding the desired impact based on system configuration and PID response, the information required to design a time delay attack can be obtained from open sources, such as Wikipedia, data sheets, companies, and various side channels. If an attacker has access to the network, the task becomes trivial. The attack can also be mounted blindly by slowly ramping up the delay value.

5 Mitigation Technique

Literature presents many mitigation and control techniques for time delayed ICS [7–9]. While many of them offer a valid approach to dealing with time delays in ICS, they cannot be easily implemented with a real-world PLC. In this paper, we propose a novel, simplistic but very functional, time delay detection approach and validate it with a Simulink model and through actual implementation for a PLC.

5.1 Simulation Setup

A multiple model approach for the detection of various time delays in the control systems is proposed. After implementing and testing in the Simulink environment, it was implemented and tested on a PLC. Modeling the peculiarities of a real-world PLC and digital IO in such a way that the output of the Simulink model was consistent with the real PLC proved to be difficult. The modeling addressed issues such as the nonlinear behavior of the blower, unknown dead zones, motor ramp up, breaking curves, high system inertia, etc. The model development, validation, parameter estimation, and tracking was based on the techniques suggested in [22].

The detection methodology can be explained as follows. Assume that $R(t), Y(t), Y^{OBS}(t)$ and $Y^{MOD}(t)$ are correspondingly the input, output, observed output, and modeled output of a dynamic channel of an ICS. It is understood that $Y(t) = F[R(t)]$ is the input-output relationship describing the dynamic channel that reflects the relevant physical phenomena. Due to the delay in the information channel, τ, the observed output is $Y^{OBS}(t) = Y(t - \tau) \neq Y(t)$. For this reason, a mathematical model based on the system input $R(t)$ and observed output $Y^{OBS}(t)$, $Y^{MOD}(t) = \Phi[R(t)]$ would not properly represent the relationship $Y(t) = F[R(t)]$. Consequently, $Y^{MOD}(t)$ will differ from $Y(t)$. One can easily establish that the coefficient of determination of the model $Y^{MOD}(t) = \Phi[R(t)]$ is expected to be low [22]. Now consider mathematical models $Y^{MOD}\left(t, T_j\right) = \varphi\left[R\left(t - T_j\right)\right]$, built based on the system input $R(t - T_j)$ and the observed output $Y^{OBS}(t)$, where $T_j, j = 1, 2, 3, \ldots$ is one of the several alternative delays inserted in the channel of the input variable $R(t)$. It is understood that the most accurate model, resulting in the minimum discrepancy between $Y^{OBS}(t)$ and $\dot{Y}^{MOD}\left(t, T_j\right)$ or the largest value of the coefficient of determination, is the one where delays T_j and τ have close numerical values. The principle of operation of the delay estimation procedure is shown in Fig. 4.

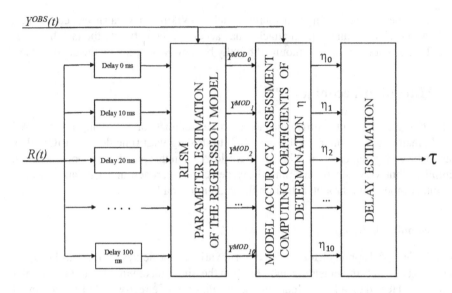

Fig. 4. RLSM model approach for different delay values

To implement this approach, first a mathematical model $Y^{MOD}(t, T_j) = \varphi[R(t - T_j)]$ was developed for the no-delay conditions in the form of a Z-domain transfer function

$$\frac{Y^{OBS}(z)}{R(z)} = \frac{b_2 z^{-1} + b_1 z^{-2} + b_0 z^{-3}}{1 + a_2 z^{-1} + a_1 z^{-2} + a_0 z - 3} \tag{2}$$

or in the discrete-time domain (where i = 1, 2, 3, … is the discrete-time index):

$$Y^{OBS}(i) = -a_2 Y^{OBS}(i-1) - a_1 Y^{OBS}(i-2) - a_0 Y^{OBS}(i-3) + b_2 R(i-1) + b_1 R(i-2) + b_0 R(i-3) \tag{3}$$

It has been established that the third order of the model is sufficient for the accurate description of the dynamic channel in question. Further increases in the order of the model practically do not increase the value of the coefficient of determination. It could be seen that the discrete-time version of the model is a regression equation, with input variables X, output variables Y, and parameters A, defined in Eq. (4). $\Delta = 10$ ms is the time step of the discrete-time control/monitoring procedure of the testbed. Parameters of this equation were estimated using the Least Squares Method.

$$X(t) = \begin{bmatrix} x_1(t) \\ x_2(t) \\ x_3(t) \\ x_4(t) \\ x_5(t) \\ x_{6[}(t) \end{bmatrix} = \begin{bmatrix} Y^{OBS}[(i-1)\Delta] \\ Y^{OBS}[(i-2)\Delta] \\ Y^{OBS}[(i-3)\Delta] \\ R[(i-1)\Delta] \\ R[(i-2)\Delta] \\ R[(i-3)\Delta] \end{bmatrix}, Y^{OBS}(t), \text{and } A = \begin{bmatrix} a_2 \\ a_1 \\ a_0 \\ b_2 \\ b_1 \\ b_0 \end{bmatrix} \tag{4}$$

Upon the completion of the parameter estimation task for the no-delay model, the procedure runs the RLSM for the parameter estimation of the ten models that include various delay magnitudes, and the parameters of the no-delay model are utilized as the starting parameter values. Now input variables X and output variables Y are shown in Eq. (5) where T_j is the delay value inserted in the j-th model, $j = 1, 2, 3, \dots, 10$.

$$X(t) = \begin{bmatrix} x_1(t) \\ x_2(t) \\ x_3(t) \\ x_4(t) \\ x_5(t) \\ x_{6[}(t) \end{bmatrix} = \begin{bmatrix} Y^{OBS}[(i-1)\Delta] \\ Y^{OBS}[(i-2)\Delta] \\ Y^{OBS}[(i-3)\Delta] \\ R[(i-1)\Delta - T_j] \\ R[(i-2)\Delta - T_j] \\ R[(i-3)\Delta - T_j] \end{bmatrix} \text{ and } Y^{OBS}(t) \tag{5}$$

The validity of the RLSM-supported models is periodically checked by computing the appropriate coefficients of determination, and the model with the highest value of the coefficient of determination or the lowest variance of the modeling error points at the most accurate estimate of the delay injected in the network. This RLSM model has been successfully implemented in the Simulink software and applied to the simulated ICS featuring the testbed, as seen in Fig. 5. Thus, the system operator could be alerted to the presence of a potentially unnoticeable network delay that is still capable of altering the system dynamics, and the operator can assess the delay magnitude so that timely precautions can be taken against the time delays on the control systems. Also, the knowledge of the time delay can be used to drive a gain scheduling procedure for the main PID controller. This way the stability of the control system and its performance can be maintained at an acceptable level even under attack [9].

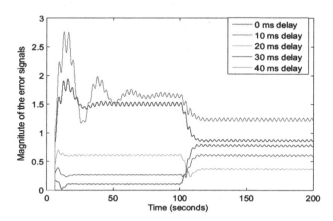

Fig. 5. Time delay detection

5.2 Experimental Implementation

Experimental implementation and testing is the optimal way to demonstrate the feasibility and efficiency of the described technology. Therefore, the delay detection/estimation approach, implemented in PLC code, was deployed on the testbed and utilized the "real" testbed data. First, a third order "no-delay" model was established thus providing starting parameter values to ten tunable regression models. A finite-memory RLSM procedure [22] was employed for parameter tuning of the individual models. As per Fig. 5, a provision was made for the assessment and display of the accuracy of the individual models. During the first 100 ms "no-delay" operation of the testbed only one model, describing the no-delay system showed a very low variance of the modeling error, associated with the measurement noise. After 100 s, a 20-ms delay was injected into both network channels of the control system. At this point, the variance of the modeling error began changing. Within about 10 s of the delay injection, the magnitude of the delay was accurately determined. Given that ICS are so time critical, accurately determining the time delay within a short time from injection is critical for the system's optimal operation. Since this ICS testbed operates as a fully functioning ICS, the results of this experiment are not limited to only this testbed as this technology can be successfully applied to any general ICS.

6   Conclusion and Future Work

In this paper, a time delay injection attack was deployed on both the forward and feedback channels of an ICS testbed. The results show that small delay values on control systems are not detected by system devices and their effects are minimal for the testbed. However, gradually increasing time delays may force the control system into an unstable state. The results of this research can be summarized as follows:

- A practical detection approach for time delay attacks on a PLC controlled, continuous process is formulated.
- A bank of models is built by monitoring a real controlled plant and capturing its dynamics using the recursive least squares method (RLSM).
- The approach operates by assessing the individual accuracy of the bank of models describing the real controlled plant with various delays in the loop.
- The approach was successfully implemented and tested in the Simulink environment and the testbed environment.

Future work for this research includes real-time implementation of the described technology in conjunction with a gain scheduling system for a PLS based controller.

Acknowledgement. This research was funded in parts by the Air Force Office of Scientific Research grant "Semantic Approach to Behavior Based IDS and its Applications" (Number FA9550-12-10077) and by the Office of Naval Research grant "Security Approach for Industrial Control Systems" (Number N00014-15-1-2759).

References

1. ICS-CERT   monitor.   https://ics-cert.us-cert.gov/sites/default/files/Monitors/ICS-CERTMonitorMay-Jun2015.pdf. Accessed 14 July 2016
2. Antonioli, D., Tippenhauer, N.O.: Minicps: a toolkit for security research on cps networks. In: Proceedings of the First ACM Workshop on Cyber-Physical Systems-Security and/or Privacy, pp. 91–100. ACM (2015)
3. Cruz, T., Barrigas, J., Proença, J., Graziano, A., Panzieri, S., Lev, L., Simões, P.: Improving network security monitoring for industrial control systems. In: 2015 IFIP/IEEE International Symposium on Integrated Network Management (IM), pp. 878–881. IEEE (2015)
4. Fan, W.-H., Cai, H., Chen, Q.-W., Hu, W.-L.: Stability of networked control systems with time-delay. Kongzhi Lilun yu Yingyong/Control Theory Appl. (China), 21(6), 880–884 (2004)
5. Michiels, W., Niculescu, S.-I.: Stability, control, and computation for time-delay systems: an eigenvalue-based approach, vol. 27. Siam (2014)
6. Wang, F.-Y., Liu, D.: Networked control systems. Springer, London (2008)
7. Xiao, L., Hassibi, A., How, J. P.: Control with random communication delays via a discrete-time jump system approach. In: Proceedings of the 2000 American Control Conference. vol. 3, pp. 2199–2204. IEEE (2000)
8. Lee, Y., Lee, J., Park, S.: PID controller tuning for integrating and unstable processes with time delay. Chem. Eng. Sci. 55(17), 3481–3493 (2000)
9. Gupta, R.A., Chow, M.-Y.: Performance assessment and compensation for secure networked control systems. In: 34th Annual Conference of IEEE Industrial Electronics. IECON 2008, pp. 2929–2934. IEEE (2008)
10. Larsen, J.: Controlling without modifying: the stale data problem. In: S4x16, Miami, US, January 2016
11. Krotofil, M., Cardenas, A., Larsen, J., Gollmann, D.: Vulnerabilities of cyber-physical systems to stale data: determining the optimal time to launch attacks. Int. J. Crit. Infrastruct. Prot. 7(4), 213–232 (2014)
12. Lee, P., Clark, A., Bushnell, L., Poovendran, R.: A passivity framework for modeling and mitigating wormhole attacks on networked control systems. IEEE Trans. Autom. Control 59(12), 3224–3237 (2014)
13. Hu, Y.-C., Perrig, A., Johnson, D.B.: Wormhole attacks in wireless networks. IEEE J. Sel. Areas Commun. 24(2), 370–380 (2006)
14. Sridhar, S., Hahn, A., Govindarasu, M.: Cyber–physical system security for the electric power grid. Proc. IEEE 100(1), 210–224 (2012)
15. Sargolzaei, A., Yen, K.K., Abdelghani, M.: Time-delay switch attack on load frequency control in smart grid. Adv. Commun. Technol. 5, 55–64 (2013)
16. Sargolzaei, A., Yen, K.K., Abdelghani, M.: Preventing time-delay switch attack on load frequency control in distributed power systems. IEEE Trans. Smart Grid 7(2), 1176–1185 (2016)
17. Korkmaz, E., Dolgikh, A., Davis, M., Skormin, V.: Industrial control systems security testbed. In: 11th Annual Symposium on Information Assurance (ASIA 2016), pp. 13–18, June 2016
18. Rizzo, L.: Dummynet: a simple approach to the evaluation of network protocols. ACM SIGCOMM Comput. Commun. Rev. 27(1), 31–41 (1997)
19. Carbone, M., Rizzo, L.: Dummynet revisited. ACM SIGCOMM Comput. Commun. Rev. 40(2), 12–20 (2010)

20. Hu, J., Wang, Z., Gao, H., Stergioulas, L.K.: Robust sliding mode control for discrete stochastic systems with mixed time delays, randomly occurring uncertainties, and randomly occurring nonlinearities. IEEE Trans. Ind. Electron. **59**(7), 3008–3015 (2012)
21. Yang, R., Liu, G.-P., Shi, P., Thomas, C., Basin, M.V.: Predictive output feedback control for networked control systems. IEEE Trans. Ind. Electron. **61**(1), 512–520 (2014)
22. Skormin, V.: Introduction to Process Control. Springer, Cham (2016)
23. Dolgikh, A., Birnbaum, Z., Skormin, V.: Customized behavioral normalcy profiles for critical infrastructure protection. In: 8th Annual Symposium on Information Assurance (ASIA 2013), Albany, NY, pp. 15–22, June 2013
24. Liu, G.-P., Xia, Y., Chen, J., Rees, D., Hu, W.: Networked predictive control of systems with random network delays in both forward and feedback channels. IEEE Trans. Ind. Electron. **54**(3), 1282–1297 (2007)
25. Dunning, G.: Controllogix Programmable Automation Controllers with Labs Second Edition. Delmar Cengage Learning (2014)

Choosing Models for Security Metrics Visualization

Maxim Kolomeec[1,3], Gustavo Gonzalez-Granadillo[2],
Elena Doynikova[1,3], Andrey Chechulin[1,3], Igor Kotenko[1,3(✉)],
and Hervé Debar[2]

[1] St. Petersburg Institute for Informatics and Automation of the Russian
Academy of Sciences (SPIIRAS), 39, 14 Liniya, St. Petersburg, Russia
{kolomeec,doynikova,chechulin,ivkote}@comsec.spb.ru
[2] Institut Mines-Télécom, Télécom SudParis, CNRS UMR 5157 SAMOVAR,
Evry, France
pci_gustavo@yahoo.com,
herve.debar@telecom-sudparis.eu
[3] St. Petersburg National Research University of Information Technologies,
Mechanics and Optics, 49, Kronverkskiy Prospekt, Saint-Petersburg, Russia

Abstract. This paper aims at finding optimal visualization models for representation and analysis of security related data, for example, security metrics, security incidents and cyber attack countermeasures. The classification of the most important security metrics and their characteristics that are important for their visualization are considered. The paper reviews existing and suggested research by the author's data representation and visualization models. In addition, the most suitable models for different metric groups are outlined and analyzed. A case study is presented as an illustration on the way the visualization models are integrated with different metrics for security awareness.

Keywords: Visualization model · Security metrics · Cost-sensitive metrics · Countermeasure selection · Security assessment

1 Introduction

Nowadays, cyber security situational awareness and countermeasure selection become more and more relevant as soon as cyber technology becomes an essential part of our life. The appropriate mitigation of a given attack depends on the optimal selection of security countermeasures. In order to select a countermeasure, it is important to identify its attributes and properties as well as the consequences of its application. A great number of researches propose cost-sensitive models [1, 2] including various security metrics to evaluate threats and select security countermeasures. However, due to the complexity and sophistication of current attacks, the detection and reaction process requires additional tools to help security analysts in the decision making process.

Approaches in this domain propose visualization models (e.g., graphical models [3, 4], and geometrical models [5, 6]) to estimate and analyze the impact of cyber events, making it possible to represent graphically scenarios of multiple attacks and to

© Springer International Publishing AG 2017
J. Rak et al. (Eds.): MMM-ACNS 2017, LNCS 10446, pp. 75–87, 2017.
DOI: 10.1007/978-3-319-65127-9_7

select optimal countermeasures accordingly. However, the main issue faced nowadays is to be able to select the appropriate model for the studied scenario.

In this paper, *we propose to analyze security metrics and visualization models with the aim of obtaining conclusions on the best match among them in order to help operators in the security monitoring and selection of security countermeasures against a given attack scenario.*

The rest of the paper is structured as follows: Sect. 2 introduces the different types of metrics used for the security assessment and countermeasure selection. Section 3 presents the geometrical and graphical models used for the visualization of security events. Section 4 discusses the complexity and usefulness of visualization models. Section 5 describes visualization tools that implement suggested models, and provides a case study to illustrate the applicability of our approach. Related works are presented in Sect. 6. Finally, conclusions are presented in Sect. 7.

2 Metrics for the Security Assessment

Currently there are a lot of metrics for the security assessment and countermeasure selection [1, 2, 7–12]. These metrics can be classified according to the object of assessment. There are metrics that characterize networks, cyber attacks, attackers, security incidents, and integral metrics that characterize common security level of the analyzed system and that are used for the countermeasure selection [4, 13]. These objects can be compound (like network and attack) or not (like security incidents, attackers and countermeasures). In addition, all these objects interact in the process of security assessment and countermeasure selection that lead to the connections between some groups of metrics (when the metrics of the next group are calculated using the metrics of the previous group) and to the appearance of new metrics.

Network incorporates interconnected hosts, network hardware and services, hosts include different software. Software and hardware, in its turn, include vulnerabilities and weak places. From the security assessment point of view, for instance, the next examples of metrics can be outlined: the metrics that characterize a network – Percentage of Hosts without Known Severe Vulnerabilities [12]; the metrics that characterize hosts and software/hardware – Criticality, Business Value; the metrics that characterize vulnerabilities – Exploitability, Impact [11].

We consider an attack as a sequence of attack actions that exploit network vulnerabilities. From the attack and attack action point of view the next metrics can be outlined: Severity, Complexity, Impact, and Probability. Metrics of this group are calculated using metrics of the previous network group. In addition, new knowledge on the possible attacks allows getting new metrics for the network objects, for example, Number of Attacks through the Host [4, 13].

We consider security incident as a product of events correlation process. The following metrics that characterize security incidents can be outlined: Severity, Confidence Level [4, 13]. New knowledge on the security incidents allows getting new metrics for the network and its objects, for example, Number of Incidents, Number of Compromised Hosts. It also allows refining metrics of the attacker group, for example, current position in the network and skills, and attack group, for example, Attack Probability [4, 13, 14].

The main metrics that characterize countermeasures are: Countermeasure Efficiency, Collateral Damage Potential, and Countermeasure Cost. Integral metrics that are used to define common security level include: Risk, Attack Surface [9, 10], and Expected Losses [15]. For the countermeasure selection, cost sensitive metrics are used. Cost sensitive metrics are widely proposed as a viable approach to find an optimal balance between intrusion damages and response costs, and to guarantee the choice of the most appropriate response without sacrificing the system functionalities.

The Net Present Value (NPV) allows discounting all expected costs and benefits from an investment to its present value, taking into account the time value of money. The Internal Rate of Return (IRR) considers the compounded annual rate of return the project is expected to generate. The ROI index compares the benefits versus the costs obtained for a given investment [1]. The Return On Security Investment (ROSI) is a relative metric that compares the differences between the damages originated by attacks (with and without countermeasures) against the cost of the countermeasure. The Return On Response Investment (RORI) provides a qualitative comparison of response candidates against an intrusion by considering response collateral damages response effects on intrusions [7].

3   Visualization Approaches

The current state of the art in visualization tools propose a wide range of models. It is suggested to select conditionally two kind of visualization models: *geometrical* models [5, 6] and *graphical* models [3, 4], to estimate the impact of cyber security events and to select countermeasures accordingly. The rest of the section details such models.

3.1   Geometrical Models

This section presents the different visualization models that use geometry as a tool to compute the impact of cyber attacks and security countermeasures within an information system.

We have proposed a **polygonal model** to calculate the impact of cyber events in a 2-dimensional system. The approach considers information about all entities composing an information system (e.g., users, IP addresses, communication protocols, physical and logical resources, etc.), as well as contextual information (e.g., temporal, spatial, historical conditions) to plot cyber attacks and countermeasures as polygons of n sides. A variety of geometrical instances (e.g., regular and irregular polygons such as: line segments, triangles, squares, pentagons, etc.) results from the analysis of the entities' information included in a system, attack and/or countermeasure [16].

Each side of the polygon is computed as the contribution of the entity in the execution of an event. The contribution for the user account dimension, for instance, can be evaluated as the number of users affected by a given attack over the total number of active users from the system. Following the CARVER methodology [17], which considers six criteria (i.e., criticality, accessibility, recuperability, vulnerability, effect, recognizability), we assign numerical values on a scale of 1 to 10 to each type of elements within the axis. As a result, we obtain a weighting factor (WF) that is associated to each type of elements. Examples of visualization of attacks and countermeasures in the polygonal system are shown in Fig. 1.

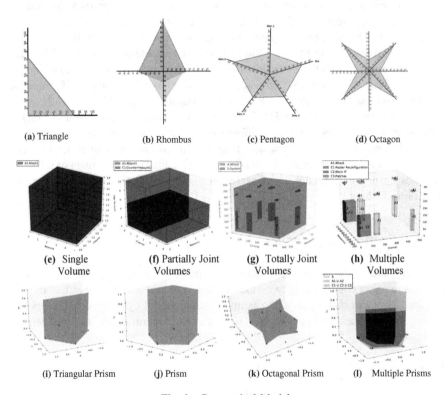

(a) Triangle   (b) Rhombus   (c) Pentagon   (d) Octagon

(e) Single   (f) Partially Joint   (g) Totally Joint   (h) Multiple
Volume   Volumes   Volumes   Volumes

(i) Triangular Prism (j) Prism   (k) Octagonal Prism   (l) Multiple Prisms

Fig. 1. Geometrical Models

Three-dimensional model allows to compute the volume of an information system, an attack and/or a countermeasure or a group of them. We identified three main dimensions that contribute directly to the execution of a given attack: User account (subject), Resource (object), and Channel (the way to execute actions, e.g., connect, read, write, etc.) [6]. The projection of the three axis in our coordinate system generates a parallelepiped in three dimensions. The volume of this parallelepiped is equal to the absolute value of the scalar triple product of all three vectors. The volume calculation requires the computation of the contribution of each axis represented in the coordinate system. This contribution is determined as the sum of each set of axis entities (e.g., user account type, port class, resource type) times its associated weighting factor. Examples of visualization of attacks and countermeasures in a 3D system are shown in Fig. 1.

A **prismatic model** is proposed to represent cyber security events (e.g., attacks, countermeasures) as prismatic instances of n-sides. The base of the prism integrates the information from the target's side (internal entities), whereas the height of the prism integrates the information from the attacker's side (external entities). The approach considers information about all entities composing an information system and the attacker's information (e.g., knowledge, motivation, skills, etc.), to plot cyber attacks and countermeasures in a geometrical system. The ultimate goal of our model is to help organizations make the most cost-effective decisions in minimizing the risk of the studied cyber events [18]. A variety of geometrical instances (e.g., regular and irregular prisms) results from the analysis of the internal and external information related to a given cyber security event. Examples of visualization of attacks and countermeasures in an N-Prismatic system are shown in Fig. 1.

3.2   Graphical Models

Graphical models are based on elements of Visual Grammar [19] such as abstract objects (dot, line, plane, demission, format), abstract structures (basic, formal, gradation, concentric radial, centrifugal and not-formal structures), specific objects (shape, size, color, tone, saturation, opacity), acts (repeat, mirror reflection, rotation, scaling, movement, offset) and relationships (attraction, symmetry, balance, cluster, diffusion, domination, variation, overlay). The combinations of these elements create different graphical models, that user can simply interpret.

Graphical models can be classified by different ways, but the simplest classification is separation on numerical models – graphics that can visualize data objects; and not numerical models – graphics that can visualize data objects and links between them.

The basic examples of numerical models are: charts [20] (Fig. 2a) – data visualized using specific objects as lines, areas, color and other; parallel coordinates [20] (Fig. 2b) – data are represented as polylines that crossing the metric scales; trilinear coordinates [20] (Fig. 2c) – models in which objects are situated in trilinear coordinates; wind roses [20] (Fig. 2d) – modes where data represented as polylines (like in a parallel coordinates) that crossing the metric scales, but scales located as radial structure; interval graphs [20] (Fig. 2e) – processes are represented as lines or arcs, where their overlay on specific axes represents the concurrent execution of processes.

The basic not numerical models are: graphs [20] (Fig. 2) – models where objects are represented as vertexes and links – as edges; matrices [20] (Fig. 2) – objects are represented as axes and links – as their crossing; treemaps [20] (Fig. 2) – hierarchical models where objects are visualized as areas and links as object placement (if objects are linked, they are located in each other); graphs with glyphs [20] (Fig. 2) – graph models in which vertexes are replaced by the stacked pie-charts for possibility of placement more metrics of objects; Voronoi diagrams [3] (Fig. 2) – models where objects are represented as polygons and links – as tiny lines between the polygons; Chord diagrams [21] (Fig. 2) – objects are represented as donate chart and links – as edges between chart`s pieces; geo-maps [20] (Fig. 2) – models in which other models overlapping on geographical maps.

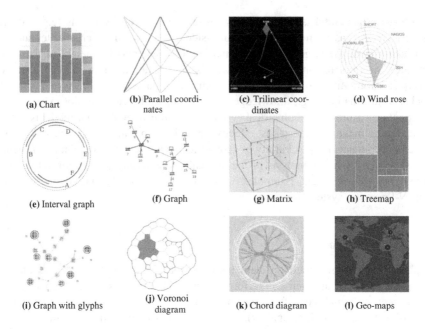

(a) Chart

(b) Parallel coordinates

(c) Trilinear coordinates

(d) Wind rose

(e) Interval graph

(f) Graph

(g) Matrix

(h) Treemap

(i) Graph with glyphs

(j) Voronoi diagram

(k) Chord diagram

(l) Geo-maps

Fig. 2. Graphical models

Above mentioned models have different advantages that depend on the use of metrics for model construction and of the context in which the model is used.

4 Complexity and Usefulness of Visualization Models

It is important to understand that there is no universal visualization model that can represent all stages of risk analysis process. That is why analytics usually use slices of data. Such slices have different properties, for example: dependencies of services have topology of links, events sequences are structured by time, network and its segments have hierarchy, and countermeasures have no links or dependencies (if they do not represent a connected set of different countermeasures).

At the same time, each model can describe only few sets of metrics: for example, 2D linear charts have 2 axes, line thickness, color and opacity; and some analytics trying to combine or create new visualization models that can contain more metrics especially for selected slice. Therefore it is not trivial to choose or create appropriate visualization models. To understand how to choose model for data slices we propose *the methodology that choose a visualization model or hierarchically create a model depending on the properties of slice*. This methodology includes 4 simple steps: (1) data slicing, (2) definition of set of models, (3) generation of a set of new models and (4) model choosing from the set.

Step 1 – data slicing. Depending on the risk analysis goal we need to select the data subset – slice. Typical case that can become a problem is when the data set consists of too many objects (example: host with 50 attributes) or data set is deeply nested (example: data represent networks that contain hosts with software vulnerabilities). If we try to visualize this set, we will obtain a complex image. That is why it is strongly recommended to minimize the set structure to few necessary attributes and nesting levels using data aggregation. Data aggregation is a complex standalone task, and it will be considered in future works.

Step 2 – definition of a set of models. At this step we associate data slice with visualization models. To do this, we have to select the attributes of the slice. The set of basic attributes that we can determine is a more detailed description of "numerical" and "not numerical" data classification:

- *Not linked* – the slice that can be described as an object or independent list of objects characterized by numerical data. For example: list of vulnerabilities, aggregated parameters of network, attacker parameters.
- *Not structured linked* – the slice that contains dependent data. The basic example is the network topology.
- *Planar linked* – the slice that contains dependent data that can be represented as a planar graph. The basic example is the network topology on the physical level.
- *Hierarchy linked* – the slice that contains dependent data that can be represented as a tree. An example – an attack tree.
- *Multiply linked* – the slice that contains dependent data with different types of links. For example, a network topology (not structured links) including an attack tree (hierarchy linked).

Examples of association with models from Sect. 3 are shown in Table 1.

Table 1. Association of data slice attributes with models

Data slice attributes		Model
Not linked		All geometrical models, charts, parallel coordinates, trilinear coordinates, wind roses, interval graphs
Linked	Not structured	Graphs, glyphs, matrices
	Planar structured	Graphs, glyphs, matrices, Voronoi diagrams,
	Hierarchy structured	Graphs, glyphs, matrices, treemaps
	Multiply structured	Graphs, glyphs, matrices, Chord diagrams

Step 3 – generation of a set of new models. It is absolutely possible that data in the selected slice are deeply nested. The simple example of this case is the slice that contains 3 nested sets: hosts with the network topology, software on the hosts that depend on each other, independent software vulnerabilities.

Each of these nested sets represents different level of abstraction. We can try to visualize all levels at the same time in one visualization model, but it is possible that results will be difficult to read. Another approach is to visualize each abstraction level on demand, for example, to expand a host by a click, but in this case we will not see the whole data at the same time. Another approach is to create a specific visualization model for the selected slice.

The basic way of the model creation is the hierarchical visualization, where every abstract level is a single visualization model. According to this, we have to separate the slice by abstraction levels.

For example, slice for definition of the impact propagation via service dependences can be separated on two abstract levels: (1) high level – services and their dependencies with weights; (2) low level – service characteristics (intrinsic criticality and vulnerability level). For every abstraction level we select the model according the association between properties and models (see Table 1). Results for a given example are shown in Table 2. Finally, the model of low level overlaps with the elements of the model of high level. Examples are graphs with glyphs (Fig. 2), in which glyphs overlap with graph nodes, and geo-maps, in which graphs overlap with geographical maps (Fig. 2).

Table 2. Abstraction levels of the slice

Abstraction level	Data description	Properties	Model
High	Services and their dependencies with weights	Not structured	Graphs, glyphs, matrices
Low	Services characteristics	Not linked	All geometrical models, charts, parallel coordinates, trilinear coordinates, wind roses, interval graphs

Step 4 - Model choosing from the set. At the last step we have the set of the models that we selected at step 2 and the models that we created at step 3. It is always better to choose models that can be easy readable and have no external dimensions. It is also common to find a situation when a final set contains only hard readable models. It means that the selected slice has many abstraction levels or too many data dimensions. The best solution is to reduce selected data slice and go to step 1.

5   Implementation and Verification of the Approach

Implementation. Data visualization models were developed as a web-application prototype that was implemented on JavaScript using Node.js on server side, and D3.js with THREE.js on client side. Software architecture is pretty similar to visualization pipeline [22] and it is shown in Fig. 3.

Fig. 3. Software architecture

Using the application we can load metrics and other data as CSV files. There is a possibility to load 2 types of CSV: (1) file with objects and (2) file with links. Numerical models need only file with objects, not numerical – both of them. After that we can simply connect graphical attributes of the models (size, color, dimensions, etc.) with attributes from CSV. As a result, we can visualize data using models in different ways and select the most easy-readable variant.

Case study. For case study we present a small corporative network with the following metrics and network attributes:

- *Host attributes* – number of software instances, number of services, number of ports, performance rate, type of device, number of users, date of update, number of incidents, medium severity of incidents, number of vulnerabilities, vulnerability, compromising status, number of attacks, probability of attack, criticality.
- *Links attributes* – type of connection (optical fiber, wi-fi, etc.), level of connection according to OSI model, traffic volume, noise immunity, channel capacity, status of participation in the attack, number of attacks, criticality.

Hosts and links of physical level were visualized by the web-application prototype to show the network topology. The result is shown in Fig. 4: network contains hosts of different types (see Table 3). For visualization approach verification we provide two examples. The first example is URL rewriting. The second example presents the visualization of the computer network risks and attack routes for situational awareness.

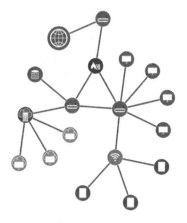

Fig. 4. Physical network topology (Color figure online)

Table 3. Network structure

external network	
user PC	router
wi-fi	mobile device
firewall	data base
virtualization server	virtual machine

Example 1. Example of geometrical visualization – URL Rewriting. The general process starts when the attack (e.g., A3) accesses the URL of an external web application and studies its behavior, and then the attacker rewrites the URL of the web application to bypass any implemented security check (login, cookies, session). As a result, the attacker bypasses security checks and accesses restricted information.

Examples of countermeasures associated to attack A3 are: Deny or redirect requests (C6); Disable URL-rewriting mode (C7); and Activate automatic expiring URLs (C8).

The graphical representation of each countermeasure vs. the detected attacks is depicted in Fig. 5, where the blue parallelepiped represents attack A3 and the green parallelepiped represents the countermeasures based on the affected users, resources and channels.

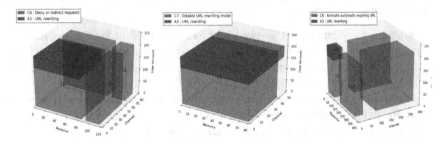

Fig. 5. Example of geometrical visualization of the attack and the countermeasure

Example 2.

Step 1. For situational awareness we select the next data slice from network attributes: host attributes – medium severity of incidents, compromising status, number of attacks, probability of attack, risk; links attributes – network level of connection, status of participation in attack, number of attacks, criticality.

Step 2. According to Table 1 the slice is classified as "multiply structured" because network level of connections can be represented as a fully connected graph and we need to visualize the attacker's route. According to Table 1 the possible models are: graphs, glyphs, matrices, chord diagrams. If we use graphs, the final model will be hard to read because some edges must represent network connections and some edges – attacker`s route. As a result users cannot effectively make out different types of edges. The rest of models cannot represent not -structured connections and attacker's route at the same time and we need to create a specific visualization model.

Step 3. For hierarchical visualization we need to divide slices on different levels of abstraction (see Table 4).

Our decision (Fig. 6) is to visualize high level as matrix, medium level as graph, and low level as glyphs. Hosts are shown as diagonal glyphs, links – as glyphs above the diagonal. Host's glyphs consist of 4 parts: criticality (top-left), probability (top-right), risk (bottom-left) and number of vulnerabilities (bottom-right). Link's glyph has 2 parts: criticality (top) and probability (bottom). The network that was provided in the case study is shown in Fig. 4 at the left side and the network with attacker route (internet –> router –> firewall –> router –> database) is shown at the right side. The numerical parameters were normalized to values between zero and one are represented with blue, yellow, orange and red colors.

Table 4. Abstraction levels of the slice

Abstraction level	Data description	Properties	Model
High	Hosts and links	Not structured	Graphs, glyphs, matrices
Medium	Attacker's route	Not structured	Graphs, glyphs, matrices
Low	Host and links attributes	Not linked	All geometrical models, charts, parallel coordinates, trilinear coordinates, wind roses, interval graphs

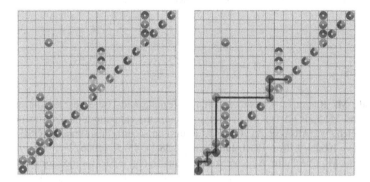

Fig. 6. Matrices with glyphs

6 Related Work

Current researches focus on simulation and visualization models as a tool to improve the evaluation and selection of security countermeasures. Dini and Tiloca [8], propose a simulation framework that evaluates the impact of cyber-physical attacks. However, countermeasures are not considered in the evaluation process.

Kundur et al. [23], propose a paradigm for cyber attack impact analysis that employs a graph-theoretic structure and a dynamical systems framework to model the complex interactions amongst the various system components. The approach concentrates on the attack impact but leaves aside the impact of mitigation actions in the evaluation. Duan and Cleand-Huang [24] consider heuristic methods and genetic algorithm approaches for the process of selecting a set of countermeasures. However, due to complexity of the search space, the heuristic approach is neither optimal, nor complete. Howard et al. [9] and Manadhata et al. [10] propose a model that measures quantitatively the level of exposure of a given system called the attack surface model. This latter is limited to the source code of the software to compare the risk level among similar options.

7 Conclusions

In this paper we presented a review and analysis of existing and suggested research on data representation and visualization models. We outline the most suitable models for different metric groups (including security and cost sensitive metrics) to match with geometrical and graphical visualization models. The methodology that was suggested in the paper can be used for selection and creation of new visualization models for different stages of risk analysis. We also proposed the case study and examples of metrics visualization. The future works will be focused on research of user cognition for efficiency analysis and optimal ways for metrics representation.

Acknowledgements. This research is being supported by the grant of RSF #15-11-30029 in SPIIRAS.

References

1. Schmidt, M.: Return on Investment (ROI): Meaning and Use. Encyclopedia of Business Terms and Methods (2011). http://www.solutionmatrix.com/return-on-investment.html
2. Sonnenreich, W., Albanese, J., Stout, B.: Return on security Investment (ROSI) a practical quantitative model. J. Res. Pract. Inf. Technol. **38**(1), 45–56 (2006)
3. Kolomeets, M., Chechulin, A., Kotenko, I.: Visualization model for monitoring of computer networks security based on the analogue of voronoi diagrams. In: International Cross-Domain Conference, and Workshop on Privacy Aware Machine Learning for Health Data Science (2016)
4. Doynikova, E., Kotenko, I.: Countermeasure selection based on the attack and service dependency graphs for security incident management. In: Lambrinoudakis, C., Gabillon, A. (eds.) CRiSIS 2015. LNCS, vol. 9572, pp. 107–124. Springer, Cham (2016). doi:10.1007/978-3-319-31811-0_7
5. Gonzalez Granadillo, G., Garcia-Alfaro, J., Debar, H.: Using a 3D geometrical model to improve accuracy in the evaluation and selection of countermeasures against complex cyber attacks. In: Security and Privacy in Communication Networks, pp. 26–29 (2015)
6. Gonzalez Granadillo, G., Alvarez, E., El-Barbori, M., Garcia-Alfaro, J., Debar, H.: Selecting optimal countermeasures for attacks against critical systems using the Attack Volume model and the RORI index. J. Comput. Electr. Eng. 13–34 (2015)
7. Kheir, N., Cuppens-Boulahia, N., Cuppens, F., Debar, H.: A service dependency model for cost-sensitive intrusion response. In: 15th European Symposium on Research in Computer Security (ESORICS), pp. 626–642 (2010)
8. Dini, G., Tiloca, M.: A simulation tool for evaluating attack impact in cyber physical systems. In: International Workshop Modelling and Simulation for Autonomous Systems, pp. 77–94 (2014)
9. Howard, M., Wing, J.: Measuring relative attack surfaces. In: Computer Security in the 21st Century, pp. 109–137 (2005)
10. Manadhata, P., Wing, J.: An attack surface metric. J. IEEE Trans. Softw. Eng. **37**(3), 371–386 (2011)

11. Mell, P., Scarforne, K., Romanosky, S.: A complete guide to the common vulnerability scoring system (CVSS) version 2.0. In: FIRST-Forum of Incident Response and Security Teams, p. 23 (2007)
12. The Center for Internet Security. The CIS Security Metrics, 175 p. (2009)
13. Kotenko, I.V., Doynikova, E.: Dynamical calculation of security metrics for countermeasure selection in computer networks. In: 24th Euromicro International Conference on Parallel, Distributed and network-based Processing (PDP 2016), pp. 558–565. IEEE Computer Society, Los Alamitos (2016)
14. Singhal, A., Ou, X.: Security risk analysis of enterprise networks using probabilistic attack graphs. NIST Interagency Report 7788, Gaithersburg: National Institute of Standards and Technology, 24 p. (2011)
15. Puangsri, P.: Quantified return on information security investment - a model for cost-benefit analysis. Master Thesis, Delft University of Technology (2009)
16. Gonzalez Granadillo, G., Garcia-Alfaro, J., Debar, H.: An n-sided polygonal model to calculate the impact of cyber security events. In: International Conference on Risks and Security of Internet and Systems (2016)
17. Special operations forces intelligence and electronic warfare operations, appendix D: Target analysis process, Federation of American Scientists (1991). http://www.fas.org/irp/doddir/army/fm34-36/appd.htm
18. Gonzalez Granadillo, G., Rubio-Hernan, J., Garcia-Alfaro, J., Debar, H.: Considering internal vulnerabilities and the attacker's knowledge to model the impact of cyber events as geometrical prisms. In: Conference on Trust, Security and Privacy in Computing and Communications (2016)
19. Leborg, C.: Visual Grammar, 1st edn, p. 96. Princeton Architectural Press, New York (2006)
20. Kolomeec, M.V., Chechulin, A.A., Kotenko, I.V.: Methodological primitives for phased construction of data visualization models. J. Internet Serv. Inf. Secur. (JISIS) 5(4), 60–84 (2015)
21. Holten, D.: Hierarchical edge bundles: visualization of adjacency relations in hierarchical data. IEEE Trans. Vis. Comput. Graph. 12(5) (2006)
22. Haber, R.B., McNabb, D.A.: Visualization idioms: a conceptual model for scientific visualization systems. In: Visualization in Scientific Computing, pp. 74–93. IEEE Computer Society Press (1990)
23. Kundur, D., Feng, X., Liu, S., Zourntos, T., Butler-Purry, K.L.: Towards a framework for cyber attack impact analysis of the electric smart grid. In: International Conference on Smart Grid Communications, pp. 244–249 (2010)
24. Duan, C., Cleland-Huang, J.: Automated safeguard selection strategies. In: CTI Research Symposium (2006)

Security and Resilience
of Network Systems

iCrawl: A Visual High Interaction Web Crawler

Deeraj Nagothu$^{(\boxtimes)}$ and Andrey Dolgikh

Binghamton University, Binghamton, NY, USA
{dnagoth1,adolgikh}@binghamton.edu

Abstract. This paper presents "iCrawl", a visual high interaction client honeypot system. Web-based cyber-attacks have increased exponentially along with the growth of cloud-based web application technologies. Web browsers provide users with an entry point to these web applications. The iCrawl system is designed to deliver a high interaction honey client that is virtually indistinguishable from a real human-driven client. The system operates by driving an actual web browser in a fashion closely resembling a genuine user's actions. Unlike most crawlers iCrawl attempts to operate over visual elements on the web page, not code elements. The honeypot system consists of pre-configured decoy virtual machines. Each virtual machine includes spider program, which upon execution automates the process of driving the web browser and crawling the targeted website. It performs browsing by observing the page and simulating human user input through mouse and keyboard activity. The data collected from the crawling is stored in a graph database in the form of nodes and relations. This data captures the context and the changes in system behavior due to interaction with the crawled website. The graph data can be queried and monitored online for structural patterns and anomalies.

The iCrawl system is enabling technology for studying sophisticated malicious websites that can avoid detection by the simpler crawlers typically utilized by well-known security companies.

Keywords: Automatic web crawling · High interaction honeypot · System data collection · Humanlike web interaction

1 Introduction

Web technology has become the primary mean of communication for many people around the world. Initially, web pages consisted of mostly plain text, pictures, and simple HTML code. As the technology matured, users were permitted to actively change the content on the Internet by posting or sharing their content. Today every user system has a web browser installed which acts as an entry point for many Internet resources. The purpose of the web browser is to get a webpage requested by the user from a remote server and display it to the user in a human readable format. Modern browsers are very sophisticated pieces of software. The advancements in web browser technology have led to an increase in the complexity of the web page processing on both the server side and client side. Modern webpages are designed with more complex components such as CSS, JavaScript, jQuery, etc. Server side technology stack is even more complicated.

© Springer International Publishing AG 2017
J. Rak et al. (Eds.): MMM-ACNS 2017, LNCS 10446, pp. 91–103, 2017.
DOI: 10.1007/978-3-319-65127-9_8

Thus, any web browser, like Google Chrome, Mozilla Firefox, Internet Explorer, or Safari, can contain many bugs. Potential malicious hackers can use these bugs to gain various forms of control over user's system or personal data. Thereon the attacker could also use the compromised victim's system to exploit other systems available in the local network further. Therefore, ensuring the safety of web-based applications on both the server side and client side has become of utmost importance.

Due to the inherent complexity of the web browsers there exists a significant number of different kinds of attacks exploiting various aspects of the web browser structure, network architecture in general and human psychology. Attack types like Drive-by-Download or cross-site scripting can be launched by a malicious attacker to gain access and control over the client system without the user's consent. Since many users are not aware of client-server interaction protocols, there is a high probability of being targeted by such attacks. To counteract the advances in web-based attacks and provide increased safety to unprotected clients, the malicious webpages must be identified and blacklisted.

Active honeypot technology is a popular approach to the identification of the malicious websites. Honeypots are decoy machines setup like a client system and act as bait for attackers. These honeypots are continuously monitored for the activity taking place and provide information regarding the attack techniques used by an attacker. To enable detection of highly selective malicious websites, a honeynet client which closely resembles the actual target victim machine is required. These systems are classified based on the type of interaction between the client and the server. The classification of such decoy systems, also known as honeypots is as follows:

- Low Interaction Honeypot System – The client system is designed based on an emulation of actual client software. This system increases the scope of search but decreases the accuracy of detection.
- High Interaction Honeypot System – In high interaction, the client system runs actual software as decoy system. This system increases the accuracy of detection but the scope of search decreases.

This paper presents iCrawl, a high interaction client-based honey-net system. This system is used to crawl suspicious webpages simulating typical human browsing behavior. Human behavior is modelled as a person using mouse and keyboard to interact with the webpage instead of directly reading web links from webpages. This allows capturing hidden weblinks which are activated upon mouse clicks. The iCrawl system is designed to gather information about the user system statistics and the webpage data. This information is stored in a graph database for later analysis of the system behavior if any suspicious activity was observed. The information collected by the iCrawl can also be used to study the attack types and attack vectors used by the attackers. This implementation of iCrawl system could also be used to collect information regarding any suspicious behavior on the web.

1.1 Browser Threat Landscape

Malicious web pages can contain software which upon execution can exploit certain vulnerabilities within browser software, protocol or server side software. Exploitable vulnerabilities previously unknown to the software manufacturers or security community are called zero day vulnerabilities. Detection of zero-day of vulnerabilities and the malware exploiting them is herder then detection of previously seen malware. As per the Internet Security Threat Report 2016 by Symantec, the number of zero-day vulnerabilities in web browsers and website plugins have increased by 125% in the year 2015 [1]. The report also states that 78% of scanned websites had vulnerabilities, of which 15% of websites were critical. This shows that the number of discoverable bugs in the world-wide web has drastically increased in a very short duration of time. In another report produced by Kaspersky Labs [2], around 121,262,075 malicious contents like scripts, exploits and executable files were detected and 34% of users were subjected to at least one web attack over the course of the year. Per Kaspersky, the overall statistics report in Fig. 1 for the year 2015 [2] states that most the exploits originated from web browsers.

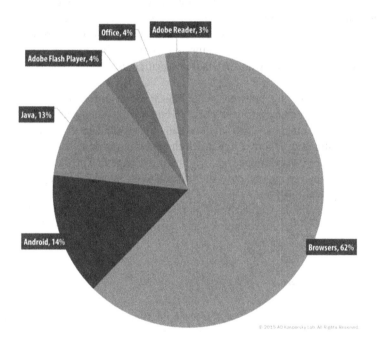

Fig. 1. Distribution of exploits used in cyberattacks in 2015

1.2 Consequences of Web Attacks

In 2015, D.R. Patil et al. presented a survey on malicious webpage detection techniques. He categorized major browser-based exploits which have been classified as the most common web based attacks against web browsers [3]. Web application vulnerabilities are classified based on the type of attack vector used and the technique used to exploit the browser system. The taxonomy of well-known browser attack vectors and attack types are Drive by download attack, SQL Injection Attack, Cross Site Scripting attack,

Clickjacking attack, JavaScript Obfuscation, Email based Phishing attacks and HTTP flood DDoS attack. The consequences of these web based attacks include data breach in companies resulting loss of customer's private information like credit card details. Attacks like Distributed Denial of service results in effecting the host computer to act like a zombie in control by a C&C server.

2   Crawling Approach

This research proposes to enable detection of the malicious web pages by implementing a high interaction client honeynet system referred to as "iCrawl" which closely resembles an actual user's system. This honeynet is designed to mimic the human behavior of browsing a web page and collects the corresponding browsing data. The system performs automated browsing activity by simulating actual mouse movement over the web page emulating moving the cursor across the page and generating clicks.

Virtual machines referred as crawlers, are used as a platform where the crawling scripts can be executed. The Crawler setup is deployed in an isolated network using private VLAN and secure firewall such that any malicious exploit could not escape the isolation.

Most of the competing crawler technologies use a different type of crawling approach. In those approaches, true behavior of human browsing is not properly implemented for improved efficiency. This method can be easily and very often automatically detected by the attacker. Whereas in iCrawl, the crawling is done based on "click and open" approach using a real mouse and keyboard interaction. The data collected from crawling is stored in a graph database and utilized to correlate the data gathered based on node-to-node relationships.

iCrawl uses chrome as web browser platform since around 47% of internet users prefer chrome [4], which makes the system less suspicious and provide more data regarding exploitation of chrome.

3   Graph Database

A graph database is used to store and process the data collected by the crawlers [4]. Graph database is a category of NoSQL database which implements an efficient mechanism to store and process graph data. The graph representation includes nodes and edges, here edges are referred as relationships. The major advantage of a graph database is its ability to traverse through a graph of greater depths [6, 7].

Figure 2 represents an example of a graph database. It shows a user's order history with various attributes. For example, a query for description of most recent order then it returns details based on all relationships named most recent. When a query is sent, it accesses the primary list of relationships then analyzes the list based on keywords in query and then iterate further accordingly.

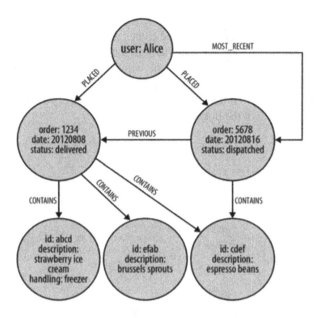

Fig. 2. Example of a user's order history in graph database [4]

In our research work we used the Neo4j graph database. Neo4j uses a declarative graph query language called Cypher [5]. The Cypher query language is used to create nodes and relations between nodes. Its simple structure allows users to ask the database to find data which is like a pattern. Cypher uses ASCII-Art presentation of the queries. For example, it uses parenthesis to represent nodes. The representation of its outlook is as follows,

$$(a)-[:Relation]-> (b)$$

Create, Delete, Set, and Remove commands are used to operate on the creation of nodes, relations, and updates the corresponding properties

4   iCrawl Setup

The iCrawl is dedicated to a single task of browsing a targeted webpage. This system consists of a virtualized environment with virtual machines acting as client machines. The iCrawl system is designed to have minimal detection of the bot and is also used to collect data regarding the browsing activity at the same time. The browser used in iCrawl is Google Chrome since most internet users prefer this browser.

The virtual machines are hosted on physical servers using VMware vSphere virtualization software. Each virtual machine is pre-configured with Windows operating system along with Google Chrome browser and spider program for crawling.

Figure 3 shows the setup for the iCrawl testbed. The crawlers are operating with a single coordinator node and multiple workers. The virtual machine "Crawler Control" is the coordinator crawler also used as a parent virtual machine. The parent virtual machine is used as the source to make linked clones sharing virtual disk and the runtime state with the parent virtual machine. The runtime state is captured with the snapshot of the parent VM and used to create linked clone with that state. The major advantage of making linked clones is the capability to share a transient state between the crawlers like SSL session or the browser cookies. Another major advantage is the low performance impact and the efficiency of the linked clones.

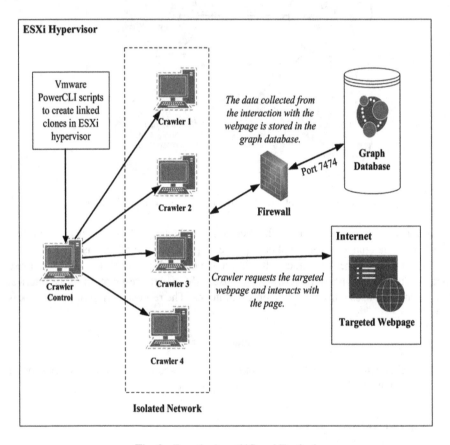

Fig. 3. Functioning of iCrawl Testbed

VMware VSphere PowerCLI is used to automate the process of creating linked clones. The PowerShell scripts allow communication with the ESXi hypervisor and allow alterations to the hardware of the virtual machine if required. The PowerCLI commands upon execution creates required number of linked clones based on the snapshot of the parent VM in a container pool. All the virtual machines in container pool are created in sync. Once the container of linked clones is created, the PowerShell scripts power on the container of virtual machines.

The Crawlers in the container are placed in a controlled isolated network. The isolation does not allow any suspicious activity to escape from its closed network, which ensures the safety of the external network. A firewall is setup to enable communication with the graph database. Crawlers are given a specific target and each crawler interacts with the webpage. During the crawling, the interaction data collected by the spider program is saved in the Neo4j graph database. Neo4j graph database is run on another virtual machine and it is configured in such a manner that the crawlers can access the Database using Neo4j system's IP address and port 7474(default).

4.1 Functioning of Spider Program

The Spider program drives an actual web browser (e.g. Chrome) in the host machine with the help of Selenium browser automation library [8]. Selenium provides access to page source of each webpage visited. Spider program uses Beautiful Soup as an HTML parser [9], which allows the crawler to parse through the page source data collected and extract the essential data. Other simulating packages are utilized to control the mouse and the keyboard actions. The spider program also collects the data regarding the browser based activity. It uses a Chrome development API to collect data regarding the browser processes like the inbuilt task manager of Chrome browser. Along with the process manager extension in the chrome browser, an additional tool is used to get information regarding system events.

Psutil is a system utilities module designed for Python [10]. This module gathers information regarding the running processes in the system. The spider program gathers the PID of the tab opened using the process manager and this PID is used to find details regarding the effects of the tab on the system. During the process of monitoring the system events, the spider program also monitors if there is any new system process created in the background when a new tab was accessed. As the virtual machine is configured in such a manner that there will not be any other processes running in the background apart from the browser session, any new process created in the background is detected. The details regarding the new process is collected using psutil and stored in the database along with other information gathered from the process manager extension.

The collected data is stored in Neo4j graph database in the form of nodes and the type of relationship between the nodes. Every time there is a new tab opened, a new transaction is created and all the data is stored in form of a node. After the information is stored in the database the transaction is committed and closed. The Python module used for interaction with the database is py2neo [11]. Py2neo is used to execute Cypher queries in the database and get the results. Cypher queries could be used to constantly monitor status regarding the data which is being stored and this feature allows the crawler to function standalone. Figure 4 represents the spider program flow consisting each task as a separate module.

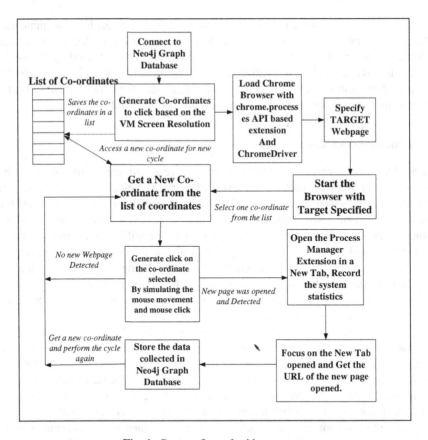

Fig. 4. Process flow of spider program

4.2 Distributed Crawling

Each crawler is setup to work automatically with no need for human supervision. The spider program is executed as soon as the VM is powered on. The current iCrawl setup has 4 crawler virtual machines running on each host named Crawler-1, Crawler-2, Crawler-3 and Crawler-4.

The naming is given when the PowerShell scripts are executed for generating linked clones of the parent virtual machine. The base crawling of the targeted webpage is done by Crawler-1 and it is called as stage-1 crawling. It collects all the information regarding the main target webpage including the links it has in the main webpage. Every new URL encountered by "Crawler-1" is pre-allocated with another crawler's name along with a flag set as "not crawled yet". After the crawling is completed, a completion flag is set with the Main tab node. Other crawlers like Crawler-2, -3, & -4 are used to perform stage-2 crawling. This 4 VMs setups can be replicated to increase the speed of the crawling.

Figure 5 represents the functioning of a script which is responsible for starting the spider program in the virtual machine at power on. This crawler setup enables the iCrawl technology to perform level 2 depth crawling i.e. collect data regarding the webpages which are connected to the main target website.

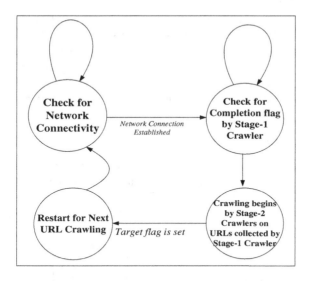

Fig. 5. Batch script functioning in state diagram

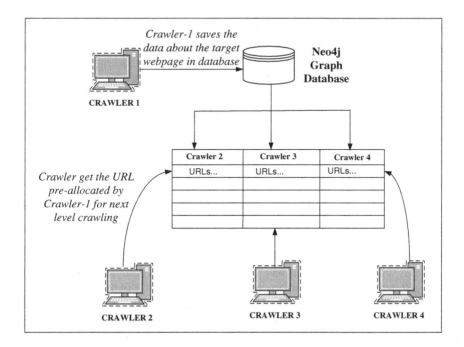

Fig. 6. Distributed crawling by Stage-1 and Stage-2 crawlers

Figure 6 represents the distributed crawling. Stage-1 crawler initially collects the URLs and the webpage data in the main website. During the crawling process, each new URL encountered by the stage-1 crawler is marked with the names of the stage-2 crawlers. This allows distribution of tasks among the stage-2 crawlers. Once the crawling is completed by the stage-1 crawler, stage-2 crawlers begin the data collection process. The spider program executes cypher query to get the list of URLs allotted for specific crawlers. Each stage-2 crawler selects one URL at a time from the list and upon completion it marks the URL as "target crawled." The data collected by stage-2 crawlers is stored in the graph database in relation with the data collected by stage-1 crawler.

4.3 Data Collected and Purpose

The iCrawl system collects various types of data regarding the system and stores the data in the graph database in each node in the form of node attributes. Data represented by a node consists of information related to web page opened in a browser tab. Data like Name of the Tab, Process ID used to get information regarding system events, CPU utilization, Network Consumption, JavaScript Memory, Page URL, executable for the process, command line representing the arguments and flags used to start the process, process time and system memory utilization.

These attributes collected by the spider program in each crawler virtual machine can be employed as sensors to continuously monitor the data collected. These sensors can be used to identify if there is any unusual consumption of memory by a process. It can also be used to detect significant traffic consumption indicating some exchange with the server in the background. Since the system processes are regularly monitored, any new process created in the system is captured. The details like the location of the executable and the command line could be used to detect what triggered the process and to study the effects of that process.

The collected structural data can be queried with Neo4j Cypher query. The cypher query

```
MATCH (n:Main_Tab)-[m]-(k)-[l]-(p)-[o]-(q)-[y]-(z) WHERE
n.Crawler = "Crawler-1" AND n.Main_URL = "www.amazon.com"
RETURN n,m,k,l,p,o,q,y,z
```

retrieves the data related to primary target page 'www.amazon.com'. The visualization of this data is featured in Fig. 7.

The graph in Fig. 7 consists of nodes which represent various kinds of information: the visited pages, new tabs and a new process trees initiated by the web page as well as additional system information pertaining to the visits.

Table 1 represents the summary of memory consumption between two websites amazon and slickdeals. The Mean and the standard deviation is computed based on the values collected from crawling up to depth of 2. The difference in the values indicates that even very simple measurements can be utilized as a signature for identification of different web back-ends and therefore can be used for identification of malicious pages within legitimate web-site. If there is any attack like drive by download or cross-site scripting attack, then there will be a change in the normal behavior of the data.

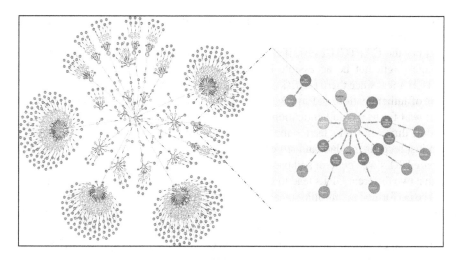

Fig. 7. Neo4j graph database visualization of amazon.

Table 1. Comparison of memory consumption between amazon and slickdeals

	Amazon	Slickdeals
Mean	72619.5 K	177093.7 K
Standard deviation	17782.7 K	51556.2 K

5   Limitations

Even though iCrawl implements human interaction behaviors there are certain cases where the system could be detected as bot. CAPTCHA test could be used to detect the iCrawl system. The spider program is not programmed with a module which could solve the CAPTCHA test. The spider program is designed to perform unorganized random mouse clicks on the webpage which could trigger suspicion. The random clicking activity could also be detected if the host tracks the mouse movement and generates a heat map based on clicks or mouse movements. Webpages which have complex design like popups and drop-down menu based interface could be difficult for spider program to crawl through resulting in missing few links in the page.

6   Future Work

iCrawl system could still be detected as a bot as discussed earlier. To overcome such detection in the future this system should be able to implement more accurate human-like behavior. Heat maps can be generated prior to crawling of the target through image processing and the coordinates which will be generated more concentrated on the areas where major content of the web is available.

To escape the popup blocks and make the crawler click through the dropdown menus, the crawler should be able to react to visual changes embedded in the page and perform the crawling accordingly. This can either be performed by studying the page source code or processing visual clues.

As per the CAPTCHA test, if the test is not passed then the actual content of the webpage might not be accessible but most of the malicious webpages do not use CAPTCHA test since there is a risk of losing the client. CAPTCHA's are generally used in case of authentication, and attacks like drive by download or Cross site scripting attack do not wait for user's authentication.

Some different URLs lead to the same destination webpage. The current implementation just records the data and stores it in the database. This system should be able to compare URLs web content and based on the similarity factor of the content it could be said that two different URLs lead to same destination webpage. This similarity checking could be performed in multiple stages to avoid in-depth analysis of every URL collected. In the first stage the level of similarity in the URL could be checked. If the similarity is high, such as around 90% or above, then the destination webpages could be concluded as similar pages. And if the similarity is around 60–80% then webpages could be further investigated by comparing the webpage content.

7   Similar Work

There were many implementation of crawler technology which includes both high interaction and low interaction clients. Few implementations involve similar approach to iCrawl. High interaction clients like Strider HoneyMonkey [12] which was used to detect exploits based on a system state change. Shadow honeypot which features anomaly based detection of malicious content [13] and Capture-HPC which is also used to find malicious servers in the internet. Low interaction clients like Thug client, HoneyC and YALIH are deployed to detect malicious content by interacting with malicious websites. There still exists a problem of detection as a bot. The low interaction clients trade fidelity for speed which results in higher probability of detection. These bots are usually designed to collect data from existing webpage HTML content, hence the web links which were obfuscated would be missed. Few bots emulate the browser by using browser headers [14] which makes honey-bot detection a bit harder. Nevertheless, improved low interaction bots are easily identified by many large web platforms like amazon or google as they have low fidelity and don't behave like human driven browser.

8   Conclusion

With the increase of web browser attacks, it is crucial to develop a system to study such attacks and develop preventative measures. This research paper presents "iCrawl," a high interaction client honeypot system. The iCrawl system is used to perform browsing activity analogous to the human interaction on targeted malicious websites without any need for human intervention. This feature allows iCrawl to circumvent defensive measures deployed by malicious server's operators and enables us to study targeted webpages without being categorized as bot. iCrawl drives an actual browser which makes it look more like a human user thus avoiding many bot detection techniques. iCrawl scales by performing browsing activity on various domains and collect data regarding the browsing activity in parallel virtual machines. The implementation of browser interaction is performed using a Python-based spider program. The decoy VMs referred as crawlers, are instantiated in an isolated virtualized environment. Multiple crawlers are deployed to increase the scale of browsing on a website using PowerShell scripts. The crawlers are configured with the spider program to drive web browser, collect data from the targeted web page and store it in Neo4j graph database. The Cypher query language used in Neo4j permits succinctly expressing complex queries through the graph data. The combination of high interaction human-like browsing and graph-based data collection and representation is the major advantage of the presented technology. The collected data includes information regarding the web page activity and its effects on the system. Neo4j stores the gathered data in the form of nodes and relations, establishing a network of interconnected nodes. The overall picture of this graph database could represent how each web page is connected to others. This data will be utilized to perform graph network analysis and enable us to study malicious website cliques.

References

1. Symantec: Internet Security Threat Report (2016). https://www.symantec.com/security-center/threat-report. Accessed 3 Nov 2016
2. Garnaeva, M., Wiel, J.V.D., Makrushin, D., Ivanov, A., Namestnikov, Y.: Kaspersky Security Bulletin, Overall Statistics for 2015. https://securelist.com/analysis/kaspersky-security-bulletin/73038/kaspersky-security-bulletin-2015-overall-statistics-for-2015/. Accessed 3 Nov 2016 (2015)
3. Patil, D.R., Patil, J.B.: Survey on malicious web pages detection techniques. Int. J. u- e- Serv. Sci. Technol. **8**(5), 195–206 (2015)
4. U.S federal Government: Digital Analytics program. https://analytics.usa.gov/. Accessed May 2017
5. Robinson, T., Webber, J., Eifrem, E.: Graph Databases. O'Reilly Media, Sebastopol (2013)
6. Neo4j: What is Graph Database? https://neo4j.com/developer/graph-database/. Accessed 13 Nov 2016
7. Vicknair, C., et al.: A Comaprison of Graph Database and a Relational Database (2009)
8. Selenium, Selenium WebDriver (2012). http://www.seleniumhq.org/projects/webdriver/. Accessed 18 Nov 2016
9. Richardson, L.: Beautiful Soup (2004). https://www.crummy.com/software/BeautifulSoup/. Accessed 18 Nov 2016
10. Rodola, G.: Psutils (2009). https://github.com/giampaolo/psutil. Accessed 19 Nov 2016
11. Small, N.: Py2neo v3 (2011). https://github.com/nigelsmall/py2neo. Accessed 19 Nov 2016
12. Wang, Y.M., et al: Automated web patrol with strider HoneyMonkeys: finding web sites that exploit browser vulnerabilities. In: 13th Annual Symposium on Network and Distributed System, San Diego, California, USA (2006)
13. Anagnostakis, K.G., et al.: Detecting targeted attacks using shadow honeypots. In: USENIX Security Symposium (2005)
14. Dell'Aera, A.: Thug, Github (2011). https://github.com/buffer/thug. Accessed 12 Nov 2016

Race Condition Faults in Multi-core Systems

Leonard Popyack[1,2(✉)] and Jay Biernat[2(✉)]

[1] Utica College, Utica, NY, USA
ljpopyac@utica.edu
[2] ANJOLEN Inc., New Hartford, NY, USA
biernatjay@gmail.com

Abstract. Finding race condition faults in multi-threaded programs now running on multi-core processors is akin to the proverbial needle in a haystack problem. This research narrows the search space by implementing a novel method of modulating the relative execution difference between potential conflicting threads in a deterministic way. Various methods including hardware and software simulation methods were explored. The results of finding lucrative execution speed differences was experimentally performed, and the results are discussed in this paper.

Keywords: Race conditions · Multi-core systems · Multi-threaded programming · Faulty computer programs

1 Introduction

Executing multi-threaded programs on multiple processors is normal today. Programs may contain hundreds of threads each executing as if it had exclusive use of the CPU, memory, and hardware resources. This is the model that is generally taught in classes. However, there is always interaction between threads and processes. Some of these interactions are intentional, and some are not. These unintentional interactions can have unwanted effects, including race conditions and data leakage between threads. A race condition occurs when a device or system makes an attempt to perform two or more operations at the same time but not in the proper sequence. These properties are some of the very hardest security problems we face today as illustrated by many of the vulnerabilities and exploits that are being exposed in malicious code [1]. This paper will show how a dynamic defense can be achieved by controlling threads, processes, and processor assignment to threads. Identifying areas of code which can be corrected before the mainstream use of the subject program can also reduce faults in the field.

Normal execution of a program is generally linear or has full-stop/full-go characteristics as found in multitasking operating systems. In general no attempts are used to graduate or control the execution speed once a context switch has occurred. Race conditions often occur due to poor programming practices or random conditions that were never anticipated. These race conditions in a multi-threaded program can be very hard to find [2], however, and source code analysis alone may miss specific conditions which occur in modern multi-core processors that share resources (such as L2 cache). It is also

© Springer International Publishing AG 2017
J. Rak et al. (Eds.): MMM-ACNS 2017, LNCS 10446, pp. 104–114, 2017.
DOI: 10.1007/978-3-319-65127-9_9

difficult to accomplish source code analysis for large programs. Attackers use fuzzing techniques and small timing changes (Nop instruction injection) to elucidate some race conditions.

2 Research Hypothesis

The idea presented here is to carefully control and deterministically modulate the code execution patterns to dynamically sense and explore properties of information security. Can specific conditions be identified in which race conditions are more likely to occur?

Figure 1 highlights the execution environment in which threaded code is run in a multi-core system. In general, the scheduler is often broken down even further to have a separate component for each processor, but we will assume only one scheduler is being used, just as a programmer would.

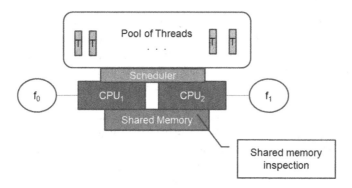

Fig. 1. Execution test environment for measuring race condition faults on multi-core systems.

The main approach taken was to create test condition code with known race faults which occur specifically in multi-core systems which utilize modern task and thread schedulers. This test code utilizes shared memory locations over multiple threads. Normal spin locking techniques are utilized which would protect the code from race conditions in a normal single processor configuration. When introduced to a multi-core system, faults can occur due to a couple factors. These factors include using a threading model not built for multi-core, poor programming practices, and random errors.

3 Testing

3.1 Hardware Approach

The first approach looked at was trying to craft a multi-core execution environment in which we had complete control over the modulation capability of the clock timing for each individual core. At first glance, this method seems very elegant and desirable to explore the timing control of each thread as it executes on individual cores.

Several architectures were examined to see if individual control of the clock frequency could be controlled. Imagination MIPS Creator CI20 was a great candidate in part because there was an announcement of an open MIPS design available to academia. However, after examination of the clocking control, this would be nearly impossible to separate the core clocking without disrupting other synchronous operations (mainly memory management). It also did not have Linux support at the time.

We next spent some time implementing an OpenRISC design of our own, but Linux only had support for single core and we would need to develop all the multi-core support ourselves. We had a very nice design based on an Altera Cyclone V FPGA. We also had a very flexible clock generator implemented based on using a Silicon Labs SI5338, Quad Clock Generator. In the end, this approach was turning into a large engineering effort and was abandoned for a software approach.

3.2 Software Approach

Instead of modulating the clock frequencies of the cpu cores via hardware, we simulated this functionality in our test software by introducing artificial delays into individual threads. This required carefully controlling threads and maintaining the cpu affinity of each thread to exactly one cpu core. The larger the delay inserted into a thread, the lower the simulated execution frequency is on that core. These delays can be modulated however we like.

Because this approach used no hardware modifications, we had to accept the fact that we had little to no control over the Level 2 cache replacement and other exceptions like System Management Mode exceptions. We re-instrumented our original test program to add control and test features. It now acts as a glorified hybrid simulator, running on the unmodified hardware we wish to test while still allowing us to modulate one running thread against another in a fairly predictable manner.

The end goal was to look for those magic conditions which precipitate race condition faults. We called these areas 'hot spots', and they could be used to highlight more vulnerable conditions where code could be expected to generate race condition faults.

In our test code, two threads are created and given access to two variables in shared memory. These threads were referred to as the *main looper thread* (also referred to as the *looper thread*) and the *conflict thread*. The main looper thread sets the two variables, value1 and value2, equal to a counter. The conflict thread checks the values of value1 and value2, and if their values are different, a fault has occurred.

4 Initial Results

Initially, the test code was run in a virtual machine (Windows 10 host with Ubuntu 14.04 guest) and on bare metal on a laptop also running Ubuntu 14.04. Our initial results indicate the presence of many hot-spot, which appear to be periodic.

Figures 2, 3, 4 show our initial results. In the shown graphs, the number of delays corresponds to the number of NOP instructions strategically inserted into a thread's executed code. Note that these initial tests were run by gathering fault rate data for every fifth inserted delay. This was done to control the runtime of these tests. As the delays are modulated, we see some interesting patterns in the observed fault rates.

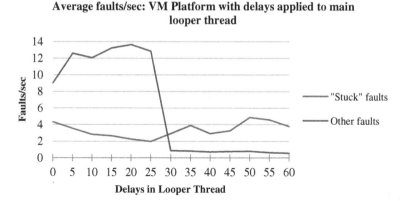

Fig. 2. Virtual Machine tested race condition faults. The above figure displays the "fault sticking" phenomenon. Also noticeable is the region of high fault rates that drops near zero once the delayed execution in the main looper thread reaches a critical amount.

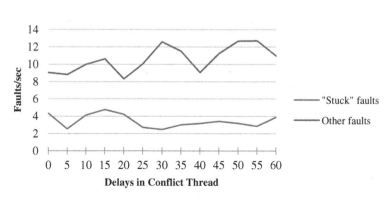

Fig. 3. Regardless of the appearance of these "stuck" fault rates, the behavior of the other fault rates are exhibiting some periodic tendencies.

Guest VM Results. Figures 2 and 3 show the average fault rates that occurred while running our test code in the Ubuntu VM. The race faults observed while modulating delays in the main looper thread are shown in Fig. 2. Examining the VM fault rates labeled as "other", we observe that when delays are applied to the main looper thread, there is a rather large region of race faults that occur during low numbers of delays. This region of high race faults then suddenly drops to near zero as the amount of delays increases. There appears to be a threshold for modulating the execution of the looper

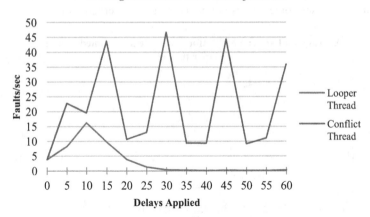

Fig. 4. Fault rates from testing our code on bare metal on a laptop. The periodicity of the fault rates from modulating the conflict thread is much more pronounced here than it was on the VM.

thread, past which the thread's execution speed is too slow to allow for a higher fault rate.

Figure 3 summarizes the fault rates observed when delays are applied to the conflict thread. Here, the fault rate does not drop to zero as the delay increases. Instead we observe what seems to be some periodic behavior with peaks in the fault rate approximately every 15 delays. These quasi-periodic peaks may be indicative of "hot spots" where the program is most vulnerable.

We observed another interesting phenomenon while running our test code in the VM (also shown in Figs. 2 and 3). About half of our collected data for any given delay would fall between 3 and 5 faults/s, regardless of the behavior of the "other" fault rates for that delay. We termed this phenomenon *fault sticking*. We theorize that this tendency for the program to fall into a certain fault rate is due to an unknown cache state when the program begins to run. Later versions of our test code flood the cache before starting to better control the level 2 cache.

Bare Metal Results. When moving the code over to bare metal (Fig. 4), we do not observe these "stuck" fault rates as we did within the VM. The strength of the peaks (hot spots) from delaying the conflict thread is much more pronounced, as is the periodic nature of the fault rates. The fault rates from modulating the execution in the looper thread peak in the lower delays before decreasing and approaching zero, similar to what was seen during the VM testing. Overall, the behavior of the fault rates is similar between the VM and bare metal platforms. However, we did not see the appearance of "stuck" faults when testing on bare metal as we did on the VM.

5   Cloud Server

To expand confidence in the results and to explore diverse execution environments, we turned to cloud servers. These are servers whose actual execution environment we had little control over and which were generally located at a provider's facility. We chose to perform tests on two of the most accessible cloud platforms, Google Cloud, and Amazon Elastic Compute Cloud (Amazon EC2).

The test code is designed for multi-core computing platforms. When running the code on bare metal and within a VM hosted on a physical laptop, we know that the threads' cpu affinities are tied to the actual, physical cpu cores that are part of a machine's hardware. While we can specify the number of cpus on a given cloud VM, these cpus are virtualizations of a processor thread (a vCPU) and not necessarily an actual hardware cpu core. We also have no control over how the hypervisor is scheduling the use of these cores or how the resources of our VM instance may be moved within the cloud infrastructure during the execution of the code.

Because runtime was less of an issue while running our test code on the cloud, we were able to collect data in instances where delays were applied in both the looper and conflict threads at the same time, not just in one thread or the other. These results show how modulating the execution speeds of both cores at once may affect the frequency of race faults.

Google Cloud Results. Figure 5 shows the average fault rates collected on Google Cloud. It should be noted that on the Google Cloud VM, the individual fault rates collected to compute the averages shown in the figure varied widely with any given combination of delays. Often, the standard deviation of the fault rates was just as large as the mean of the fault rates. For example, the average fault rate in our test code with 10 main looper thread delays and 10 conflict thread delays was 7.70 faults/s. The standard deviation of these fault rates was 6.50 faults/s. This makes the figure somewhat difficult to interpret.

However, very generally, it appears that increasing delays in the main looper thread will cause the fault rate to decrease (which was also observed on the VM and bare-metal platforms). Increasing delays in the conflict thread does not show any strong pattern, and does not show the periodic behavior observed previously in the VM and bare-metal data.

We believe that the varying computational power, and the ability of Google to move our VM around within their infrastructure, introduces variability in our tests that we cannot control. Figure 6 shows the available processing power we had available for a typical run, which may be the cause of the large variance between faults rates sampled at a single delay profile.

Average faults/sec: Google Cloud Platform

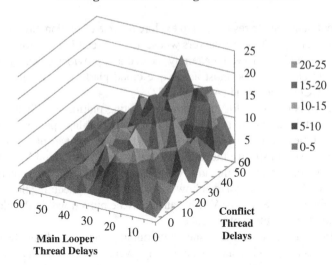

Fig. 5. Race condition faults generated on the Google Cloud platform. We see that high delays in the main looper thread suppress race faults, even when delays are used to modulated execution in the conflict thread.

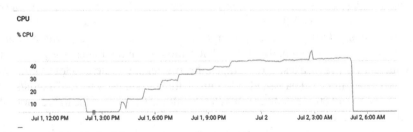

Fig. 6. Typical available processing power being used on our Google Cloud VM. This test ran for over 12 h between 4 PM and 5 AM the following day.

Amazon EC2 Results. The average fault rate data collected on Amazon EC2 is shown in Fig. 7. Unlike the data collected on Google Cloud, the individual fault rates collected for the same delay profile on Amazon EC2 have a much smaller variance, allowing us to make more confident generalizations about the data. Consistent with our other testing platforms, modulating the execution of the main looper thread with increasing delays causes the fault rates to quickly approach zero.

Average faults/sec: Amazon EC2 Platform

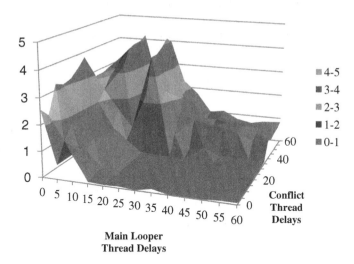

Fig. 7. Amazon EC2 computing platform shows predictable decrease in fault rates as the looper thread is modulated with increasing delays. (Note the reverse ordering of the looper thread delay axis for better viewing.)

However, we do not see any periodic behavior in the fault rates obtained by modulating the conflict thread execution. It is interesting that the farther we abstract away from execution on bare metal, the less periodic the fault rate data from delaying the conflict thread becomes. These results indicate the importance of studying the special security concerns of this platform, especially as more and more data is processed on the cloud.

Also of note are the fault rate hot spots that exist in areas where both the looper and conflict threads are being delayed. On the Google Cloud platform, we even see that the highest fault rates we observed were occurring in these conditions. This indicates that modulating the execution of both cores is important for finding the conditions of most (and least) vulnerability.

6   Single Board Computing Platforms

Finally, we wanted to look at how very small execution environments which use multi-core processors might behave. The test code was ported to a Raspberry Pi 3 single board computer, which contains a 1.2 GHz 64/32-bit quad-core ARM Cortex-A53 processor. After collecting fault rates at a quantization of 1 delay instead of 5 delays, some interesting results were collected from this small embedded system.

Figure 8 shows the fault rates observed from modulating a single thread at a time on the Raspberry Pi (also shown are the same results from our bare metal tests for comparison). Like on the bare metal platform, we see clear oscillations when delays are applied in the conflict thread. This again seems to suggest that the physical hardware (or abstraction from it) plays a large role in the formation of race conditions.

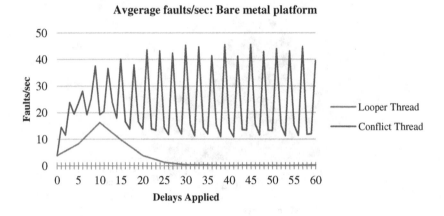

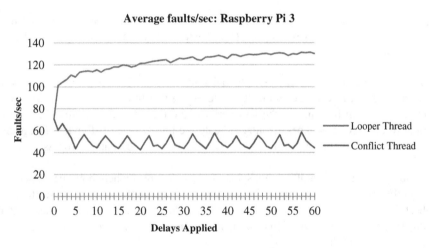

Fig. 8. (Top) Fault rates from the bare metal x86 based platform for comparison. (Bottom) Fault rates from Raspberry Pi 3. Fault rate oscillations due to conflict delay modulation are similar on both platforms. When modulating the looper thread delays, the Raspberry Pi's fault rate saturates instead of dropping to near zero.

Unlike on the bare metal laptop, fault rates in the Raspberry Pi will slowly rise to a saturation level when delays are applied to the main looper thread (as opposed to approaching zero). This is very strange, since even on the cloud platforms we tested, fault rates had a tendency to decrease as the looper thread delays were increased. The Raspberry Pi is the only platform we tested to exhibit this rise to a saturation level.

Also interesting is the extremely high fault rates we observed. The Raspberry Pi's ARM processor produced the highest number of race fault conditions with our test code out of all the platforms tested. Fault rates between 120–140 faults/s were consistently observed.

We suspect that the very high fault rate saturation with the ARM processor may be from a different cache replacement algorithm than that of other processors. Figure 9 shows how when we use our cache flooding technique to minimize the effects of the cache replacement artifacts, it still runs away into fault rate saturation. One thing is certain, embedded processors such as those used in smartphones, tablets, and other such devices are far more susceptible to race condition faults then that of any devices we have used so far. Table 1 summarizes the observed fault rates of the various multi-core execution environments tested. Fault rates are a minimum 290% higher on the embedded processor than that of desktop or server platforms.

Avgerage faults/sec: Rasperberry Pi 3 with cache flooding technique

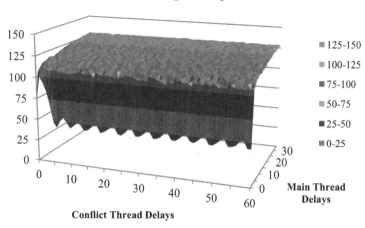

Fig. 9. Minimizing the effects of cache replacement has little effect on quickly reaching high fault saturation.

Table 1. Platform Measurements

Platform (all running Linux)	Highest fault rate observed (faults/sec)
Bare metal on laptop	48
VM hosted on Win10 laptop	22
VM on Google Cloud	23
VM on Amazon EC2	8
Raspberry Pi	137

7   Conclusions and Further Research

By controlling CPU affinity and carefully modulating or delaying potential race condition conflicting threads, so-called hot spots can be observed in which race conditions can be observed. This information can work in reverse as well. Areas which do not generate many race condition faults can be assigned as 'safer' zones to execute code on multi-core systems. However, all multi-core systems observed will fix the execution speed of each core to that of the system clock. If future multi-core systems could separate the core execution speeds, a unique method of race condition avoidance could be achieved. This is room for further research.

This material is based upon work supported by the US Air Force Research Laboratory (AFRL) office of Scientific Research (AFOSR) under Contract No. FA9550-15-C-0038. Any opinions, findings and conclusions or recommendations expressed in this material are those of the author(s) and do not necessarily reflect the views of AFOSR.

References

1. The Undocumented PC: A programmers Guide to I/O, CPU's, and Fixed Memory Areas, Chap. 15, 2nd edn. In: van Gilluwe, F. (ed.) CMOS Memory and Real-Time Clock
2. Cowan, C., Beattie, S., Wright, C., Kroah-Hartman, G.: RaceGuard: kernel protection from temporary file race vulnerabilities
3. Bishop, M., Digler, M.: Checking for race conditions in file accesses. Computing Systems 9(2), 131–152 (1996). http://olympus.cs.ucdavis.edu/bishop/scriv/index.html
4. Zalewski, M.: "Delivering Signals for Fun and Profit" understanding, exploiting and preventing signal-handling related vulnerabilities. http://lcamtuf.coredump.cx/signals.txt
5. A Practitioner's Guide to Software Test Design, Secure Programming with Static Analysis
6. McGraw, G., Viega, J.: Building secure software: how to avoid security problems the right way. http://www.informit.com/articles/article.aspx?p=23947
7. David Wheeler at IBM's Institute for Defense, Secure Programmer: Prevent Race Conditions. http://www.ibm.com/developerworks/library/l-sprace/index.html

Security Requirements for the Deployment of Services Across Tactical SOA

Vasileios Gkioulos[1]([⊠]) and Stephen D. Wolthusen[1,2]

[1] Norwegian Information Security Laboratory,
Norwegian University of Science and Technology, Gjøvik, Norway
{vasileios.gkioulos,stephen.wolthusen}@ntnu.no
[2] School of Mathematics and Information Security,
Royal Holloway, University of London, Egham, UK

Abstract. Service Oriented Architectures (SOA) have been identified as a suitable mediator towards the attainment of the requirements imposed by modern warfare. Earlier studies focused primarily on the strategic domain, or the adaptation of such systems to the requirements of the tactical domain. Yet, the underlying constraints are significantly different between the two, with direct impact both on security and quality of service. In this article we approach the security aspect of tactical SOA, focusing on the specifics of the services while operating under the constrains and requirements of modern battlefields. Selected elements of our analysis within the project TACTICS are presented, as they have been utilized for the extraction of operational and technical requirements towards the development of a suitable tactical service infrastructure.

1 Introduction

Military operations are dependable on maintaining interoperability across the strategic and tactical domains. The strategic domain is commonly stationary or deployable, with over-provisioned infrastructure that supports elements such as headquarters, air combat command, intelligence command, mission control centres and medical treatment facilities. Contrary to that, the tactical domain is based on mobile infrastructures of ad-hoc nature supporting the communication requirements of the deployed units within the context of a tactical operation and across a given AoO (Area of Operations). The military units that must be served by the tactical SOA are commonly expected to be at levels equal or lower to a brigade, while tactical operations are commonly executed at the level of a company, platoon or section. Such operations present significant variations in terms of the AoO environment, expected mobility patterns, deployed assets, available resources, required services, information exchange models and mission sub-objectives. Yet, a tactical service oriented architecture must enable service provisioning across these variations, allowing the support of mission specific objectives according to established security and quality of service requirements.

Tactical networks bear some similarities to commercial Mobile ad-hoc (MANET) and mesh networks. Yet, due to their military orientation, they differentiate over a multitude of characteristics including the utilised technologies,

© Springer International Publishing AG 2017
J. Rak et al. (Eds.): MMM-ACNS 2017, LNCS 10446, pp. 115–127, 2017.
DOI: 10.1007/978-3-319-65127-9_10

their set of requirements and the imposed constraints. The introduction of NEC (Network Enabled Capability) and NCW (Network Centric Warfare) paradigms within the domain of military networks, promoted the use of SOA for the attainment of these functionalities. However, the majority of existing SOA implementations have been developed focusing towards the enterprise domain, relying on infrastructures that can provide bandwidths of 100Mbits/sec or more on a permanent basis. Contrary to that, the common capacity of tactical networks is less that 1 Mbits/s, and they are deployed for short periods of time, while the common operational status is within the military VHF/UHF bands. Additionally to the use of an error-prone and constraint communication medium, mission (e.g. enforcement of radio silence) and terminal (e.g. computational capacity, buffer size, battery) related constraints can also impede communications. Thus, both message and service delivery cannot be guaranteed.

Accordingly, our earlier studies [1–9] within the EDA (European Defence Agency) project TACTICS focused on the investigation of suitable techniques, for the deployment of such mechanisms across contemporary C2 (Command and Control) and C4I (Command, Control, Communication, Computers and Intelligence) systems. TACTICS, aims to enable NCW and NEC, through the integration of information sources, effectors and services. Under this scope, the overarching objective is the definition, development and demonstration of a Tactical Service Infrastructure (TSI) architecture compatible with the realistic constraints and requirements of contemporary military operations. The developed TSI must allow existing tactical radio networks to participate in a core SOA infrastructure, while providing and consuming a set of required functional services. Additionally, the TSI must provide robust and efficient information transport within the tactical domain, but also to and from the strategic domain.

Maintaining a distinction between the information resources and the services (as the means to process information), is crucial for the attainment of security requirements in the environment of tactical SOA. Thus, in this article we focus on the services as the core element of TSI, presenting selected elements of our study, towards the extraction of corresponding operational and technical requirements for their development. The selected methodology allowed the identification of assets, threats and security requirements, according to tactical scenarios, developed based on contemporary and future operational perspectives from the participating member states (non-disclosed). This allowed the extraction of operational and technical requirements, for the development of the TSI architecture with increased security related impact. Under this scope, risks have been assessed according to three evaluation criteria. These refer to the strategic value of the involved information assets, the criticality of the underlay information management services and the attainment of corresponding protection goals. The remainder of this paper is structured as follows. Section 2 introduces related work. Sections 3 and 4 present the assets, and direct or transitive threats that emerged from the analysis of the aforementioned scenarios. Finally, Sects. 5 and 6 highlight the identified operational and technical requirements for the development of services within tactical SOA.

2   Related Work

A multitude of earlier studies was focused on the investigation of security aspects related to commercial MANETS [10–13]. Yet, as described earlier, contemporary tactical ad-hoc networks present distinct sets of constraints and requirements, due to their unique operational and architectural characteristics. Thus, they must be distinctly investigated focusing primarily on the attainment of requirements imposed by tactical operations. Bass et al. [14] suggested a qualitative risk analysis method for complex network centric military operations. The authors focus on operations where information superiority is critical, analysing basic information assurance concepts and suggesting a risk management methodology for defence in depth. Kidston et al. [15] provided a generic study in respect to threat mitigation in tactical networks. The authors assessed the significant differences between commercial and tactical networks, supporting that, despite the similarities, security analysis and solutions cannot be considered a priori transitive within the two. Furthermore, the authors proposed a cross-layer security framework for the attainment of the corresponding security requirements.

Jacobs [16] provided a thorough examination of the adversary types, along with the corresponding threats they pose, towards a war-fighter information network. The author categorised the adversaries to spies, traitors, intelligent agents, information warriors and hostile soldiers, analysing each category in terms of expertise, access, backing and risk tolerance. Additionally, an overview of cryptographic methods has been provided, towards the mitigation of system vulnerabilities. Burbank et al. [17] evaluated the use of MANETs towards the realisation of the requirements of network centric warfare. Although the main focus of this study is not related to security aspects, the authors provide a thorough presentation of the requirements of tactical networks and the capabilities of current technologies towards their realisation.

Wang et al. [18] evaluated some of the security challenges and goals of tactical MANETS, suggesting a hierarchical security architecture for communication security management across large scale tactical ad-hoc networks. Additionally, Kidston et al. [19] presented a cross-layer architecture for network performance optimization, according to their analysis over system specific quality of service requirements. As presented earlier the requirements of NEC and NCW, promoted the use of service oriented architectures, for enabling such capabilities across tactical networks [20–28]. Yet, the field has not been studied in depth from the scope of security, or the operational assumptions do not coincide with the realistic constraints of the modern battlefield. Setting the services as the core element of tactical networks, within the constrained nature of the operational environments and infrastructures, impose a unique set of security requirements which we seek to identify and analyse within this study.

3   Asset Identification and Categorization

As stated earlier, the goal of this study was to define operational and technical requirements with security related impact, for the deployment of services across tactical SOA. Identifying and categorising the available assets, including the developed services, allowed the mapping and analysis of functional, transitive and symmetric interactions across them. This initial step is crucial for the identification of transitive risk propagation across the assets, and the analysis of mitigating measures from the perspective of the developed services.

AS-01, Personnel: According to the preservation of life requirement, the personnel involved in an operation is the asset of utmost criticality. This applies both to the decision making commanding officers, and, within the context of tactical operations, primarily to the network users deployed across the AoO.

AS-02, Information: Tactical SOA rely on the utilisation of cross-layer information for the establishment of the environmental context by defining objects, activities, and relations. In this context information assets have been categorised as:

1. *AS-02.1, System specific:* Information that relate to the TSI architecture, such as:

   - Service interfaces
   - Service functionalities
   - Service input/output formats
   - Message/packet processing chain
   - Available cryptographic algorithms
   - Service choreography diagrams
   - Available overlay architectures
   - Available routing protocols
   - Security policy architecture
   - QoS policy architecture

2. *AS-02.2, Mission specific/Static:* Information that are established at the mission preparation stage and maintain absolute or high probability of remaining static through the mission execution stage, such as:

   - Deployed personnel (attributes)
   - Deployed functional services
   - Expected areas of operations
   - Deployed terminals (attributes)
   - Pre-shared cryptographic keys
   - Social/hierarchical relationships among the deployed personnel and terminals
   - Objectives/guidance information
   - Precedence/Aggregation levels

3. *AS-02.3, Mission specific/Dynamic:* Information generated by services, users and infrastructure during the mission execution stage, or are initialized during mission preparation, but are of dynamic nature, such as:

   - Blue/red force tracking
   - Messaging services inputs/outputs
   - Routing protocol data and statistics (available resources, link metrics)
   - Terminal/service trust levels
   - Terminal resource metrics
   - Information dissemination paths
   - Service registry data and statistics

AS-3, Software: Software within a tactical SOA refers to the operating system and the deployed TSI architecture. Military systems commonly utilize commercial operating systems, such as Linux, Microsoft Windows or OS-X. Yet, some special purpose domains are developed over operating systems specialised for military embedded systems. The TSI architecture refers to a set of core and functional services deployed across the tactical nodes in order to provide all the required mission and system-specific functionalities (e.g. unit positioning, medical evacuation alert, logging, session management, access control, information filtering/labelling).

AS-4, Hardware: Hardware resources refer to the deployed terminals. It must be noted that within tactical networks highly diverse platforms are deployed, referring to ground, air, naval, deployed unmanned and satellite communications. Despite the diversity of these platforms in terms of capabilities, constraints, requirements and mobility, interoperability must be guaranteed for the support of the required functionalities.

AS-5, Network: Network resources are a critical asset within the constrained environment of tactical networks, since they directly affect the aforementioned elements through the information dissemination, service choreography and resource allocation processes. In that sense network resources refer not only to the available bandwidth, but also to a variety of other elements that may effect service delivery, such as computational capacity, battery level, packet queue size, memory size and radio range.

Figure 1 presents the model of interactions across the identified assets, that has been developed and used during the next steps of our analysis. Software/Services (AS-03) are consumed by other services, and by the process of Personnel (AS-01) consuming or generating Information (AS-02). Furthermore, Service consumption can generate and consume Information, but also consumes Hardware (AS-04) and Network (AS-05) resources (which as a process also generates information).

An example of how the model has been used in the next steps of our analysis (in conjunction with the identified threats and requirements), can be extracted by the used scenarios as follows: The team leader of a section (AS-01) generates a medical evacuation alert message (AS-02), with the use of the MEDEVAC functional service (AS-03). In this scenario, the TSI must be developed according to technical specifications that allow the satisfaction of security requirements not only across the direct action path (e.g. encryption and integrity protection of the MEDEVAC request), but also on potential transitive paths, such as:

- Information leakage through the transitive consumption of other services (e.g. Distributed service registry, QoS Handler-Through the message prioritization process).
- Transitive Denial of Service attacks, if the consumption of the MEDEVAC functional service is dependable on the consumption of other (AS-03, AS-04, AS-05) assets.
- Information leakage through the consumption of AS-04 and AS-05 assets, for the prioritized routing of the MEDEVAC alert.

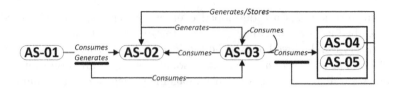

Fig. 1. Interactions across the identified assets.

4   Analysis of Transitive Threat Impact for Tactical SOA

As presented earlier, the threats imposed to commercial and tactical networks have been thoroughly analysed in existing bibliography. Yet, for the purpose of this study it was critical to identify transitive relationships, in order to define technical requirements that could minimize security related risks. The selected basis of our analysis was ENISA (European Union Agency for Network and Information Security) threat taxonomy [29]. Thus, filtering threats related to SOA across tactical environments, and identifying the affected assets in conjunction with the model presented in Sect. 3, allowed the mapping of transitive impact propagation. The identified interactions can be seen in Table 1, where Potential Threat Sources (PS), Direct Impact (DI), High Transitive Impact (HTI) and Low Transitive Impact (LTI) of threats, are presented.

An example of the scenarios used for this analysis, can be extracted in respect to the "Loss of stored information" threat. Internal sources of the threat are identified in AS-01 (misuse), AS-03(software failure), and AS-04 (equipment failure). The direct impact is located in the lost information itself, while high transitive impact is traced at the assets consuming information (AS-01 and AS-03). Yet, low transitive impact can be traced to AS-04 and AS-05, since recapturing (or requesting retransmission), and reprocessing the lost information, will require the consumption of hardware and network resources in an already constrained network.

5   Identified Operational Requirements

Setting the services as the core network element instead of the radio links, impose a unique set of requirements and vulnerabilities, that necessitate the incorporation of additional elements into the security paradigm of currently developed tactical architectures. In this section we aim to filter and analyse these elements that are specific to the service architecture and require the development of specialized controls or the suitable adaptation of the existing. Within the TSI, the deployed services obtain the role of network entities. In this sense the available core and functional services must be treated not only as network resources that can be invoked by the users, but also as agents that can consume resources on their own right, such as bandwidth and other services.

Table 1. Transitive threat impact analysis for tactical SOA

Threat	AS-01	AS-02	AS-03	AS-04	AS-05	External
Lack of resources						
Lack of network capacity	PS/LTI	HTI	PS/HTI	LTI	PS/DI	PS
Lack of processing power	PS/LTI	HTI	PS/DI	PS/LTI	LTI	PS
Lack of storage capacity	PS/HTI	DI	PS/HTI	PS/LTI	LTI	PS
Physical damage						
Destruction of equipment due to enemy activity	LTI	PS/HTI	LTI	DI	HTI	PS
Destruction of equipment due to accidents or misuse	PS/LTI	HTI	LTI	DI	HTI	
Loss of equipment possession	PS/LTI	HTI	LTI	DI	LTI	PS
Failures						
Equipment failures - performance degradation (due to exposure to environmental conditions, hazardous materials, and operational conditions)	LTI	HTI	HTI	PS/DI	LTI	PS
Software failures - performance degradation	HTI	LTI	PS/DI	LTI	LTI	PS
Loss of stored information	PS/HTI	DI	PS/HTI	PS/LTI	LTI	PS
Unintentional leakage of information in transit	HTI	DI	PS/LTI	LTI	PS/LTI	
Unauthorized/ Malicious actions						
Misuse of services	PS/HTI	HTI	PS/DI	LTI	LTI	
Misuse of hardware resources	PS/HTI	LTI	PS/HTI	DI	LTI	
Misuse of information	PS/HTI	DI	PS/HTI	LTI	LTI	
Misuse of network resources	PS/HTI	LTI	PS/HTI	LTI	DI	
Intentional disclosure of information	PS/HTI	DI	PS/HTI	LTI	LTI	
Incorporation of untrustworthy information	PS/DI	HTI	PS/DI	LTI	LTI	PS
Incorporation of malicious software (trojans, worms, viruses, bots, cracks, malware)	PS/LTI	DI	PS/DI	HTI	HTI	PS
Tampering with hardware resources	PS/HTI	LTI	PS/HTI	DI	LTI	PS
Tampering with software	PS/HTI	HTI	PS/DI	LTI	LTI	PS
Tampering with the network configuration	PS/HTI	LTI	PS/HTI	LTI	DI	PS
Social engineering	PS/DI	DI	HTI	LTI	LTI	PS
Active attacks (flooding, Wormhole, Black hole, Rushing, Byzantine, Replay, Snooping, Fabrication, Denial of Service, Sinkhole, Man in the middle)	LTI	HTI	HTI	LTI	DI	PS
Passive attacks (traffic analysis, eavesdropping, monitoring)	LTI	HTI	HTI	LTI	DI	PS

Consequently, in this section we attempt a mapping of the functional requirements that emerged from our study, for the mitigation of the aforementioned threats, to well established and generic security requirements. This approach has been selected because thorough technical details of existing (such as those deployed at the strategic domain) or currently developed (aiming at the tactical domain, such as TACTICS TSI) military SOA, have not or can not be fully disclosed. It must be noted that approaching this topic from the perspective of services, does not exclude but is complementary to generic and information centric security requirements, as described earlier [1], while transitive dependencies also apply.

1. *Availability*: It does not only refer to information, but also the means to process these (meaning the deployed services), which must be available at the time they are required directly or transitively. Availability of information is generally understood in the sense of timeliness, which does not necessarily imply any particular speed of processing, but rather depends on the specification of a deadline. If no such deadline exists, the information must be available on demand, which may be considered a stronger requirement. For code and services, the goal of availability formulates a metric identifying the ability to process information and provide functionalities. For realistic tactical systems, availability is closely related to reliability and is often expressed as a probabilistic metric. In reliability theory, availability expresses the degree to which a system is in a specified operable and committable state during a mission, when it is called for, at an unknown (modelled as random) time. This fraction is often described as a mission capable rate (0 to 1).

2. *Confidentiality*: A service must not disclose information to unauthorised entities (including other services) allowing the deduction of its state. This does not explicitly establish confidentiality between principals or services. Depending on the required granularity this may be achieved in the simplest case (however approximately) through access control mechanisms, but otherwise may require formulation over explicit information flows. We also note that information flows under non-deductibility are not limited to the deliberate exchange of information. As an example consider the use of radio frequencies which allows the observation of the fact that services communicate in a transitive manner, regardless of encryption or even traffic flow confidentiality. Similarly the use of a name service or service registry that is itself not kept confidential can allow the deduction of information regarding the internal state of the principal.

3. *Control*: Services must not relinquish possession of protected functionalities. This implies protection against tampering or the possibility of tampering within transitive or delegated service invocations. Such capabilities, including service substitution, are fundamentally required within tactical SOA. Yet, at each step of such invocation links, control must be maintained and reassured. Applying the notion of trust within this context, operations on information must only be performed if the service performing the operation can be believed to act in the interest of the service providing the data to be

processed. In a more generic but equally significant approach, a service must be capable of initiating processing in a trusted state.

4. **Integrity**: The TSI must not allow information flows that may have been subject to modification by services at different levels of integrity than the originating principal. This is realised typically at different levels for data and services. For data, detecting whether any modification has occurred, and possibly the originating service of such modification, is a necessary component. Particularly for services, integrity can be shown at the level of identity, but as data may also be subjected to transformations either at the syntactical or even at the semantic level. This requires a clear understanding of metrics other than non-modification. Additionally, integrity may be considered as axiomatic or be represented by trust in a service, modelled explicitly either dynamically or statically. We note that integrity may be called into question when modification is possible rather than on demonstrating that it has occurred in actual fact. Furthermore, modifications must also map omission or suppression of information, rather than only differences between a received or stored copy of information and the original.

5. **Authorisation**: All service functionalities on or affecting protected information (direct, transitive or delegated service invocations) must be subjected to authorisation. This is an indirect prerequisite for accountability and information-related protection. It must be noted that information flows and modifications may arise from local state change or previous and subsequent operations, requiring explicit consideration of such processing as part of the set of operations to be controlled.

6. **Authenticity**: Authenticity is a property that may again refer to information and services, and must not be confused with authentication, since it refers to obtaining proof or a relative metric to verify a claim either of origin or, more generally, of the provenance of a datum after processing. Authenticity can be proven ephemerally, but may also need to be verified after longer time periods have elapsed. In the former case, the proof or measure of authenticity exists for the duration of an interaction among services, whilst in the latter the proof or measurement must be stored or transported, and is itself the subject of protection. Where authenticity is to be shown over longer time periods, the notion of time or ordering must typically be included explicitly since violations of integrity of a datum or services operating on data may invalidate authenticity, or give rise to claims that data is not authentic.

7. **Authentication**: All information processing entities must be uniquely identified and authenticated. This is primarily required for accountability, but is also implicitly required in confidentiality and integrity protection mechanisms for information at the processing level.

8. **Traceability and Non-repudiation**: An unbroken chain must be retained documenting the provenance and transfer of information across all services, ensuring the inability of a principal to deny that a datum was generated, transferred or modified. The above can also be formulated positively in terms of requiring a service that provides proof of the integrity and origin of data, including the authenticity of this assertion with high assurance, where the

integrity and authenticity must be possible to maintain without the cooperation of the principal whose datum is the subject of the non-repudiation proof.
This is largely supported by integrity and authenticity assurance mechanisms,
but requires additional information to be retained for each service involved
in an information flow.

6   Identified Technical Requirements

The presented results of our theoretical analysis, allowed the identification of
technical requirements, towards the architectural development stage of TAC-
TICS. The identified requirements of high criticality for the mitigation of the
aforementioned threats include:

1. Service definition according to standard formats, (e.g. XSD, WADL, WSDL)
   ensuring interoperability with the existing subsystems deployed within the
   strategic domain, and coalition operations.
2. Any implemented service invocation processes must support existing protocols, (e.g. SOAP, WSIF) ensuring interoperability with the existing subsystems deployed within the strategic domain, and coalition operations.
3. End to end dynamic service discovery and delivery must be supported across
   multiple domains.
4. Edge proxy functionality must be supported, in order to allow suitable and
   secure translation of messages and services.
5. Support a variety of message exchange schemes (anycast, broadcast, multicast, unicast) for dissemination of policy critical updates and service man-
   agement/invocation.
6. A distributed and best-effort updated service registry/repository must be
   provided, in order to enhance service availability.
   - During service discovery, a consumer must be able to identify all the reach-
     able services/providers according to the defined security policy privileges.
7. Support of a dynamic and capable of preconfiguring publish/subscribe
   exchange pattern.
8. Support of store and forward functionality.
9. Support of bandwidth reservation functionality.
10. Service substitution and delegation must be conditionally supported, not
    only within the same or neighbouring nodes, but also within allied forces.
    - This also applies for the security services including policy mechanisms.
11. The service discovery mechanism functionalities are independent of other
    core services and, within the TSI, constrained only by the security policy.
    - Externally, the service providers available resources must also be taken
      into account.
12. Required services and policies can be added or updated on-line, during the
    mission execution stage, given that the needed resources become available.
    - This should also be feasible using an unmanned operational node (e.g.
      UAV-Unmanned Aerial Vehicle)

13. Suitable mechanisms must be established in order to allow message prioritization both for system and mission specific messages. (e.g. security policy updates, dynamic attribute dissemination (trust levels), mission alerts).
    - Similarly, prioritization in congested environments must be allowed for the exposure of high criticality services.
14. The TSI supports a variety of overlay/underlay routing protocols, in order to allow adjustments according to user mobility and disruptions, utilising and/or maintaining multiple routes.
15. Security management and service protection is established at multiple levels and variable granularity within the SOA stack
16. The TSI can include a variety of core services, which are deployed across the tactical nodes at the mission preparation stage, according to node capabilities and mission requirements.
    - The minimum set and most lightweight versions of core services deployed in a tactical node must allow service discovery, message exchange and security. This would allow the stand alone operation of the node within is-landed or heavily congested environments.
17. Service dedicated access control, integrity protection, confidentiality, provenance assurance and trust management mechanisms are established within the security policy, as discrete network entities, as presented earlier.
18. Service features are evaluated and adapted dynamically to network and node resources, as well as user requirements, according to service performance indicators and SQM (Service Quality Management).

7   Conclusions

The constraints of tactical networks impose significant limitations to the realization of suitable SOA based solutions. Overcoming these limitations, while maintaining the enforcement of security requirements for the protection of the deployed assets is a critical task. In this article we presented our analysis and results in respect to the secure deployment of services, as the means to process information and provide functionalities in tactical SOA. Analysing the interactions across the identified assets within pre-established scenarios, allowed the identification of potential transitive risk propagation paths. Focusing on the services as the main agent of such systems, operational and technical requirements have been established towards the development of a secure tactical service infrastructure. It must be noted again that approaching this topic from the perspective of services, must be enforced as complementary to generic and information centric security requirements, as described in our earlier studies.

Acknowledgments. The results described in this work were obtained as part of the European Defence Agency project TACTICS. The project is jointly undertaken by ITTI (PL), MCI (PL), Patria (FI), Thales Communications & Security (FR), FKIE (DE), Thales Deutschland (DE), Leonardo (IT), Thales Italia (IT), NTNU (NO), and their partners, supported by the respective national Ministries of Defence under EDA Contract No. B 0980.

References

1. Gkioulos, V., Wolthusen, S.D.: Securing tactical service oriented architectures. In: 2nd International Conference on Security of Smart cities, Industrial Control System and Communications (SSIC) (2016)
2. Gkioulos, V., Wolthusen, S.D.: Enabling dynamic security policy evaluation for service-oriented architectures in tactical networks. In: Norwegian Information Security Conference (NISK-2015) (2015)
3. Gkioulos, V., Wolthusen, S.D.: Constraint analysis for security policy partitioning over tactical service oriented architectures. In: Grzenda, M., Awad, A.I., Furtak, J., Legierski, J. (eds.) Advances in Network Systems. Architectures, Security, and Applications. AISC, vol. 461, pp. 149–166. Springer, Cham (2017). doi:10.1007/978-3-319-44354-6_9
4. Gkioulos, V., Wolthusen, S.D.: Reconciliation of ontologically defined security policies for tactical service oriented architectures. In: International Conference on Future Network Systems and Security-FNSS (2016)
5. Gkioulos, V., Wolthusen, S.D.: A security policy infrastructure for tactical service oriented architectures. In: 2nd Workshop on the Security of Industrial Control Systems and of Cyber-Physical Systems (CyberICPS 2016), in conjunction with ESORICS (2016)
6. Gkioulos, V., Wolthusen, S.D., Flizikowski, A., Stachowicz, A., Nogalski, D., Gleba, K., Sliwa, J.: Interoperability of security and quality of service policies over tactical SOA. In: IEEE Symposium on Computational Intelligence for Security and Defense Applications (IEEE CISDA 2016) - IEEE Symposium Series on Computational Intelligence (IEEE SSCI 2016) (2016)
7. Aloisio, A., Autili, M., D'Angelo, A., Viidanoja, A., Leguay, J., Ginzler, T., Lampe, T., Spagnolo, L., Wolthusen, S.D., Flizikowski, A., Sliwa, J.: TACTICS: tactical service oriented architecture. CoRR abs/1504.07578 (2015)
8. Lampe, T.A., Prasse, C., Diefenbach, A., Ginzler, T., Sliwa, J., McLaughlin, S.: TACTICS TSI architecture. In: International Conference on Military Communications and Information Systems ICMCIS (2016)
9. Lopes, R.R.F., Wolthusen, S.D.: Distributed security policies for service-oriented architectures over tactical networks. In: Military Communications Conference, MILCOM 2015, pp. 1548–1553. IEEE, October 2015
10. Priya, S.B., Theebendra, C.: A Study on Security Challenges in Mobile Adhoc Networks (2016)
11. Kauser, S.H., Kumar, P.A.: MANET: Services, Parameters, Applications, Attacks & Challenges (2016)
12. Patidar, D., Dubey, J.: A hybrid approach for dynamic intrusion detection, enhancement of performance and security in MANET. In: Proceedings of the Second International Conference on Information and Communication Technology for Competitive Strategies, ICTCS 2016, pp. 81:1–81:5. ACM, New York (2016)
13. Kannammal, A., Roy, S.S.: Survey on secure routing in mobile ad hoc networks. In: 2016 International Conference on Advances in Human Machine Interaction (HMI), pp. 1–7, March 2016
14. Bass, T., Robichaux, R.: Defense-in-depth revisited: qualitative risk analysis methodology for complex network-centric operations. In: Military Communications Conference, MILCOM 2001, Communications for Network-Centric Operations: Creating the Information Force, vol. 1, pp. 64–70. IEEE (2001)

15. Kidston, D., Li, L., Tang, H., Mason, P.: Mitigating security threats in tactical networks. Technical report, DTIC Document (2010)
16. Jacobs, S.: Tactical network security. In: Military Communications Conference Proceedings, MILCOM 1999, vol. 1, pp. 651–655. IEEE (1999)
17. Burbank, J.L., Chimento, P.F., Haberman, B.K., Kasch, W.T.: Key challenges of military tactical networking and the elusive promise of manet technology. Comm. Mag. **44**(11), 39–45 (2006)
18. Wang, H., Wang, Y., Han, J.: A security architecture for tactical mobile ad hoc networks. In: Second International Workshop on Knowledge Discovery and Data Mining, WKDD 2009, pp. 312–315, January 2009
19. Kidston, D., Li, L.: Management through cross-layer design in mobile tactical networks. In: 2010 IEEE Network Operations and Management Symposium - NOMS 2010, pp. 890–893, April 2010
20. Lund, K., Eggen, A., Hadzic, D., Hafsoe, T., Johnsen, F.T.: Using web services to realize service oriented architecture in military communication networks. IEEE Commun. Mag. **45**(10), 47–53 (2007)
21. Birman, K., Hillman, R., Pleisch, S.: Building Net-centric Military Applications over Service Oriented Architectures (2005)
22. Suri, N.: Dynamic service-oriented architectures for tactical edge networks. In: Proceedings of the 4th Workshop on Emerging Web Services Technology, WEWST 2009, pp. 3–10. ACM, New York (2009)
23. Russell, D., Xu, J.: Service oriented architectures in the delivery of capability. In: Proceedings of Systems Engineering for Future Capability (2007)
24. Croom, Jr., C.E.: Service-oriented architectures in net-centric operations. Technical report, DTIC Document (2006)
25. Johnsen, F.T., Flathagen, J., Hafsøe, T.: Pervasive service discovery across heterogeneous tactical networks. In: MILCOM 2009 - Military Communications Conference, pp. 1–8. IEEE, October 2009
26. Russell, D., Xu, J.: Service oriented architectures in the provision of military capability. In: UK e-Science All Hands Meeting, Citeseer (2007)
27. Russell, D., Looker, N., Liu, L., Xu, J.: Service-oriented integration of systems for military capability. In: 11th IEEE International Symposium on Object and Component-Oriented Real-Time Distributed Computing (ISORC), pp. 33–41. IEEE (2008)
28. Candolin, C.: A security framework for service oriented architectures. In: MILCOM 2007 - IEEE Military Communications Conference, pp. 1–6, October 2007
29. Marinos, L., ENISA: ENISA Threat Taxonomy A tool for structuring threat information Initial Version 1.0. Technical report, January 2016

Adaptive Security

Nodal Cooperation Equilibrium Analysis in Multi-hop Wireless Ad Hoc Networks with a Reputation System

Jerzy Konorski and Karol Rydzewski[(⊠)]

Faculty of Electronics, Telecommunications and Informatics,
Gdansk University of Technology, Gdansk, Poland
jekon@eti.pg.gda.pl, k.rydzewski@o2.pl

Abstract. Motivated by the concerns of cooperation security, this work examines selected principles of state-of-the-art reputation systems for multi-hop ad hoc networks and their impact upon optimal strategies for rational nodes. An analytic framework is proposed and used for identification of effective cooperation-enforcement schemes. It is pointed out that optimum rather than high reputation can be expected to be sought by rational nodes.

Keywords: Ad hoc network · Cooperative security · Utility · Cost · Reputation system · Cooperation · Strategy

1 Introduction

Wireless ad hoc networks are gaining popularity as a growing number of areas of human activity require omnipresent and self-configuring connectivity. One of the greatest advantages of this network concept – the lack of central infrastructure and governing authority – is its greatest challenge as well. Until its inception, standards ruling networks' operation were obeyed ensuring their optimal performance. In the ad hoc paradigm, this fundamental law is disputed, as the autonomy of network nodes enables them to neglect collective welfare and selfishly optimize their individual utility [1]. Motivations behind these decisions may be of different origin, to boost node's performance, lengthen operational life, etc. Some of these effects may be introduced intentionally by node's software programmers, others may emerge out of non-hostile optimization techniques employed. The scarcity of resources, namely of battery power and bandwidth, aggravate the problem.

Selfishness ensures a better performance of a node compared to nodes following the primarily altruistic network standards. The impact on the network is minimal until there are few selfish nodes. However, other nodes in the network may quickly learn to acquire the same strategy. As the number of selfish nodes grows, the network performance drastically deteriorates and eventually the network disintegrates, calling into question its very mission. This is clearly a security (more precisely, cooperation security) issue, since it directly impacts the inter-nodal communication capability.

Such considerations are not unusual in the realm of game theory [2]. They are used to explain a well-known phenomenon in multi-hop networks, where players following

© Springer International Publishing AG 2017
J. Rak et al. (Eds.): MMM-ACNS 2017, LNCS 10446, pp. 131–142, 2017.
DOI: 10.1007/978-3-319-65127-9_11

their best interest choose strategies resulting in non-optimal solutions for everyone, including themselves. In such games, the only solution improving the game results seems to consist in shaping the game in such a way that the non-cooperative (selfish) strategies become non-optimal for the players, and in promoting cooperative ones.

The idea of discouraging network nodes from becoming selfish underlies the idea of *reputation systems*. Such a system, fed with experience reports from nodes that have had interactions with other nodes, disseminates information that helps deciding whether a certain node can be trusted to deliver a service on a certain service level. Other nodes, having this information can make decisions whether or not to cooperate with such a node, without any prior experience with it. This leads to the economic concept of *indirect reciprocity* [3], where nodes are rewarded or punished for their prior cooperative or noncooperative behavior towards nodes different from the ones they are currently interacting with. Such a system, to be useful and to actually encourage nodes to cooperate, has to be carefully designed to reshape the payoff matrix of the arising game so that globally non-optimal behavior becomes non-optimal to individual nodes as well.

In this paper we examine some state-of-the art principles of reputation systems with a special interest on how they influence individual nodal strategies and how these strategies influence network operations, in particular if they actually discourage undesirable behaviors. This paper is structured as follows: in Sect. 2 we briefly present the state of the art in reputation systems and previous work; in Sect. 3 used metrics are discussed; Sect. 4 discusses reputation systems' typical design assumptions and their impact on nodal strategies; Sect. 5 examines possible nodal responses to modifications of utility functions; finally, Sect. 6 summarizes our findings and concludes the paper.

2 Related Work

In recent years, reputation systems have become a popular research avenue addressing the problem of selfish nodes and cooperation enforcement. The basic concept entails a method of monitoring nodes' behavior, a behavior-rating algorithm, reputation calculation and an algorithm of leveraging the calculated reputation in network operations. The key part of a reputation system is the cooperation detection and evaluation. The *watchdog* mechanism [5–10] is widely used in numerous wireless network environments. Its principle of work is based on omnidirectional characteristics of antennas typically employed by wireless network nodes. Assuming this, a node's neighbors that are situated within the radio range can overhear all its communication. This mechanism is, however, innately unable to address non-uniform radio range, transmission impairments, and unpredictable collisions. Other solutions focusing on identifying a single misbehaving network node are based on a subnetwork of cooperating nodes observing the environment in their proximity and sending reports to other nodes. Such approach is exemplified by the Two-ACK scheme [5], based on additional short range ACKs sent by the intermediate nodes on a given path, and on the flow conservation presumption [6]. According to it, cooperative intermediate nodes keep a count of transit traffic and share it with other nodes; thus they are able to identify nodes responsible for "leaking" packets. A different concept, deriving agent reputation from composed service of multiple agents [7], is used in [8] for detection of selfish nodes in military wireless sensor networks of a hierarchical directed tree topology. The detection and avoidance of malicious nodes is orchestrated by a sink node. The operation of this system is divided into rounds, in each of which the sink node changes the network topology. The sink node gathers statistics on network behavior. Based on the delivery ratio for packets sent by a given source node, as well as the network topology and its changes, the sink is able to deduce malicious and suspicious nodes in the network. A similar concept [9], based on end-to-end ACKs is used to deduce behavior of intermediate nodes from multiple reports on different paths in a MANET network; certainty levels of the results can be computed.

Based on the results obtained from various detection mechanisms, usually in the form of delivery or forwarding ratios, nodes' reputation is calculated. Many reputation systems serve just to discern cooperative or misbehaving nodes measuring their behavior against a predefined desirable pattern [4] and returning a binary value describing a node's positive or negative rating. Sometimes this binary metric is extended to define intermediate states or to indicate nodes of uncertain reputation. Alternatively, a more fine–grained view of a node is created [9], typically with real-valued reputation levels between 0 and 1, where 0 represents a completely uncooperative node and 1 a fully cooperative one. Usually reputation reflects nodes' behavior in a certain period of time and may be constantly recalculated. In some systems, when a node is labeled as uncooperative, it is regarded as such forever, whereas other systems offer possibilities to regain positive, cooperative rating, either by resetting it after a predefined period of time or offering a "redemption" opportunity.

The use of the calculated reputation can be twofold. On the service requesting side it is often used as an extension to routing algorithms assisting in path selection. A well-known solution, called *pathrater* [4], attempts to select a path without misbehaving nodes. If such a path is unknown to exist at the moment, a path rediscovery phase is triggered. However, some authors, e.g., [10], stress that routing around misbehaving nodes in fact rewards them, as they incur lower costs of participating in the network; accordingly, they propose to route part of the traffic via lower-reputation nodes. This gives a node a possibility to regain ("redeem") high reputation and diversifies traffic among multiple nodes, while discouraging whitewashing (i.e., changing identity to restore unblemished reputation). On the service provision side, specifically when the service consists in forwarding transit packets, punishment may be administered by only forwarding packets originated at a cooperative source node, or doing so with a probability depending on the source node's reputation level [10]. Some systems use only the service requesting side, which may actually promote misbehaving nodes, giving a selfish strategy so called *evolutionary stability*. Recently, this concept, well-known in game theory and in biology [3], has been linked to reputation systems to provide a more in-depth explanation of indirect reciprocity. In [3], a vast number of possible behaviors (or strategies) coupled with reputation systems are critically examined in order to identify evolutionarily stable (strategy, reputation system) pairs that perform well against nonstandard alien behavior. Best performing pairs are found to adhere to similar principles: by giving help to a good agent, the donor also earns a good reputation, whereas refusal of help to a good agent brings a bad reputation; refusing to help ill-reputed agents does not undermine a good reputation. The authors note that ensuring evolutionary stability against a group of alien agents entails regarding helping a good agent as good, and helping a bad agent as bad. Thus indirect reciprocity, i.e., cooperative behavior toward third parties, is promoted.

In [11], a game-theoretic study of nodes' behavior dynamics is presented and an attempt is made to search an equilibrium. The authors propose a reputation system where nodes locally observe the behavior of paths they are using based on their delivery and deduce therefrom the behavior of every node. The authors associate the gain of a node with sends a successfully delivered source packet or receives a desti-nation packet; the loss is associated with forwarding a transit packet on behalf of some other source node. The parameters under nodes' control are: the forwarding ratio of transit traffic on a given incoming link, the amount of outgoing traffic and a threshold value of packets dropped by other nodes on a given outgoing link. Based on those arbitrarily set values and a utility function, a node is able to adjust its behavior towards other nodes, which in extreme cases may even result in completely shutting a given network link. The influence of the network size and traffic volume is demonstrated – the more source traffic a node has, the better forwarding service it provides.

3   Network Resources and Utility Functions

We restrict the focus of a reputation system to packet forwarding along paths set up as sequences of nodes to traverse. However, our reasoning can be carried over to other types of network service. The service can be measured and quantified into a set of key performance indicators (KPIs), enabling evaluation and comparison of the imple-mented solutions. In the history of computer networks, a significant number of KPIs have been developed. A network node requests a specific amount of service to be provided by the network that it may regard as an abstract external entity. Due to different network phenomena, limited communication capacity, protocol constraints or node's policy, the node's requests can be serviced either in full or to some extent, or completely rejected. Each unit of service costs the requesting node and the servicing entity some defined cost, which we model as constant across all the nodes. Cost-based analysis of nodes' and network's operations is a well-established direction of research in computer networks. To discover and evaluate nodal motivations behind selfishness one needs to know what drives their behavior and how their costs (also referred to as *utilities*) are created. This knowledge allows one to build effective network solutions shaping nodal utility in a way that is desired from the network perspective.

To examine nodes' strategies in a simplified model we propose a concept of a game between a node X and the network N, pictured in Fig. 1. The two parties in this game are issuing towards each other service requests and are interested in achieving optimal performance. Hence, both employ techniques enabling them to evaluate another party behavior and to respond to it adequately. The network N employs a reputation system and utilizes the concept of indirect reciprocity, and is modeled by node X as a single, albeit complex entity. On the technical level, indirect reciprocity is ensured by an agreed upon (centralized or distributed) algorithm of reputation calculation, dissemination the reputation values among network nodes, and a specific algorithm of nodal response to the assigned reputation. There are many methods employed to resolve these issues, some of them were summarized in the related work section. Node X employs the concept of

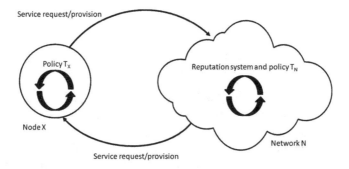

Fig. 1. Model of a game between node X and the network N.

rationality and ability to define its own cost-effective strategies. In the presented game model, following variables and parameters are taken into consideration:

- S_{XN} – amount of service (in service units) requested by node X from the network N.
- S_{NX} – amount of service requested by the network N from node X; in our model, for the sake of meaningful evaluation of node X's behavior, $S_{NX} > 0$ is assumed.
- $T_X \in [0, 1]$ – policy of node X stating what proportion of S_{NX} is to be provided,
- U_X – utility node X draws out of being connected to the network,
- b – available bandwidth (in service units),
- e – observation error reflecting the inability of the network N to correctly assess the behavior of node X because of the flaws in the network operation and/or radio environment,
- $R_X \in [0, 1]$ – reputation of node X related to the value of T_X evaluated by N in a way defined by chosen reputation system, i.e., R_X is a function of T_X, S_{NX} and e,
- $T_N \in [0, 1]$ – policy of the network N towards node X, i.e., the proportion of X's requested service S_{XN} that is provided; it is a function of R_X, and
- G – service value; a constant representing how valuable for node X is the service it requested from the network N, i.e., how much node X is determined to pay for S_{XN} if it is serviced by the network N.

The above variables and parameters result from the network design decisions, (in particular concerning the reputation system the indirect reciprocity mechanism), the radio environment, and the network's and node X's requirements for service. The policy T_X is the only variable that can be set according to node X's strategy. Because T_X is directly unobservable, the network can only rely on R_X calculated by the reputation system based on the past observations of node X's behavior. Ideally, if the system uses a fine–grained reputation metric. If $e = 0$ and the observations sample is large enough, R_X should reflect T_X precisely for the network N. We will use the assumption $R_X = T_X$ henceforth.

To evaluate node X's utility we propose a utility function (1), representing node X's gain from being connected to the network. The goal of node X is to select a strategy that maximizes its utility function with respect to the chosen service, i.e., forwarding source traffic, while taking some environmental limitations into account (2). Hence, the optimization problem for node X can be stated as follows:

$$U_X = f(G, S_{XN}, T_N) \tag{1}$$

$$T_X^* = \arg\max_{T_X \in [0,1]} U_X \left| S_{NX}(1 + T_X) + \frac{S_{XN}}{T_N} \le b \right. \tag{2}$$

U_X, is a function of node X's behavior, with respect to the amount of service it provides to the network N, as assessed by the network's reputation mechanism producing the value R_X, and the amount of service the node X receives from the network N. Node X, being in control only of its service policy, in response to the obtained U_X, assesses its optimal T_X to maximize its utility, taking into account the network's limited bandwidth for service provision (2). The bandwidth is consumed by issuing own requests taking into account requests that need to be reissued (i.e., S_{XN}/T_N), and processing network's requests (i.e., $S_{NX}(1 + T_X)$), where the $(1 + T_X)$ term comes from the nature of wireless network operation: S_{NX}, even if not processed by node X, consumes its bandwidth, since received requests occupy the radio medium and nothing can be broadcast at that time). Note that this model assumes that the rejected service requests should be reissued by node X until they are successfully processed by the network. In reality some threshold on number of reissues should be implemented to avoid a negative U_X. However, the aim of this work is to show the effects of node X's rational behavior, and introducing such thresholds could blur the overall picture.

The above game in which node X optimizes its utility against the employed reputation system, and the network attempts to accomplish its mission of providing network-wide connectivity and well-being continues in search of an equilibrium. The general problem (1) takes on various forms depending on the specific network services and operations, in particular the choice of the workings of the reputation system and the algorithm setting T_N in response to R_X. Examples of these specific formulations will be examined in Sect. 4.

4 Reputation Systems' Design Impact on Utility Function

There exist various methods of monitoring nodes' behavior as detailed in Sect. 2; most of them are not free from flaws that prevent them from determining nodes' behavior precisely. The complexity of wireless network operation as well as the diversity of possible factors influencing it make it impossible to eliminate those flaws completely. One way of dealing with this is to accept the measurements' imperfections and account for them when modeling the network's and reputation system's operation. This is the approach we follow here by including the e variable reflecting these flaws. Reputation, as an algorithm transforming observed node's behavior into numerical values of reputation, also has an impact upon the network's ability to distinguish and address various nodal behaviors.

The most important part of the reputation system, from the operational cost viewpoint, is the indirect reciprocity mechanism mentioned earlier, i.e., a set of algorithms constituting part of the network operation that reflect node X's reputation. Indirect reciprocity may transform a reputation system from a pure signaling tool into an enforcement mechanism fostering nodes' cooperative behavior. In what follows we examine common design concepts and their influence on node X's utility function.

4.1   Plain Multi-hop Ad Hoc Network

A plain multi-hop ad hoc network does not account for nodes' rationality and assumes that all the nodes follow some predefined standard behavior. In such a network, there is no reputation system and the network provides service in response to node X's service requests under a best effort policy regardless of its (not even monitored) behavior. This is equivalent of $R_X \equiv 1$, and the utility function (1) and node X's policy (2) are expressed as in (3) and (4), respectively:

$$U_X = (G - 1) \cdot S_{XN} - T_X \cdot S_{NX} \tag{3}$$

$$T_X^* = \arg\max_{T_X \in [0,1]} U_X \bigg|_{S_{NX}(1 + T_X) + S_{XN} \leq b} \tag{4}$$

X's utility (3) is the difference between the gain from having own service requests successfully serviced $((G - 1) \cdot S_X)$ and the cost associated with servicing the network's requests $(T_X \cdot S_{NX})$. We subtract 1 from G to reflect the cost associated with issuing the amount S_{XN} of requests, which lowers node X's gain.

4.2   Tit-for-Tat Reciprocity Mechanism

A tit-for-tat-type reciprocity mechanism enables the network N to respond in kind to node X's behavior, i.e., N provides requested service to X in the same proportion that X provides requested service to N: $T_N = T_X$. Formulas (1) and (2) transform into (5) and (6), respectively:

$$U_X = G \cdot S_{XN} - S_{XN}/T_N - T_X \cdot S_{NX} \tag{5}$$

$$T_X^* = \arg\max_{T_X \in [0,1]} U_X \bigg|_{S_{NX}(1 + T_X) + S_{XN} + \dfrac{S_{XN}}{T_N} \leq b} \tag{6}$$

Formula (5) contains a term representing node X's service requests rejected by the network that need to be reissued (S_{XN}/T_N), which was already discussed in (2). This replaces subtracting 1 from G in (3).

4.3   Reputation Metric

Reputation metrics in general need not impact the mechanisms of monitoring node X's behavior. As stated earlier, some common reputation metric types are fine-grained and binary. The former takes node X's observed behavior to be numerically equal to its reputation, optionally with some additional scaling to reflect all possible behaviors. The latter incorporates an algorithm of transforming all possible behaviors into a discrete, two-valued metric. Typically, this algorithm imposes a threshold t_S upon the ratio of S_{XN} and S_{NX}, the crossing of which changes R_X. The type of reputation metric does not directly influence formulas (1) and (2), as it only influences the shape of the function $R_X(T_X, S_{NX}, e)$.

4.4 S_{NX} Reflecting Node X's Reputation

Besides enabling tit-for-tat service provision, reputation is often meant to assist network nodes in selecting appropriate (trustworthy enough) nodes to interact with and request service from. The basic approach dictates that only highest-reputed nodes be considered. Other approaches are more refined and make use of lower–reputed nodes as well, allowing non-optimal performance.

In the latter case, irrespective of the actual policy T_N, it is often assumed that the network N is able to split its service requests to be alternatively serviced by nodes other than node X, hence node X gets only a part of the original amount of requested service S_{NX}. To achieve this, the network N requires an algorithm to transform R_X into a parameter determining the part of the original S_{NX} directed to the node X. For simplicity, we will assume this parameter is equal to R_X (a general derivation of an optimal transformation of R_X into this parameter is beyond the scope of this paper). Formulas (1) and (2) change into (7) and (8), respectively:

$$U_X = (G - 1) \cdot S_{XN} - R_X T_X S_{NX} \tag{7}$$

$$T_X^* = \arg\max_{T_X \in [0,1]} U_X \left| S_{NX}(1 + T_X)R_X + S_{XN} \leq b \right. \tag{8}$$

Equations (7) and (8) introduce R_X as a parameter influencing the amount of service requested by the network N from node X. The other terms are as in (3) and (4).

5 Rational Nodes' Strategies and Their Effects

In this section we examine the concepts presented in Sect. 4, either by themselves or in selected combinations employed in the state-of-the-art reputation systems. We will focus on the impact of a given solution on node X's utility and available strategies. We will anticipate how the behavior of node X impacts the network operation and check if a given solution encourages nodes to become cooperative. One of our goals in this analysis will be how the utility U_X and optimal T_X for node X change depending on the ratio M of the requested amounts of service:

$$M = \frac{S_{NX}}{S_{XN}} \tag{9}$$

5.1   Plain Multi-hop Ad Hoc Network

In a network without a reputation system, the utility function U_X given by (1) has two components – one representing service requests originating from node X, and another one representing the cost of providing service in response to the network N's requests. The policy T_X, the only part of the model controllable by node X and acting upon S_{NX}, is bounded only by the above cost and has no bearing upon S_{XN}. The dominant strategy of the node X in this situation is trivially $T_X = 0$, irrespective of any parameters defining the game, meaning a completely uncooperative node. Therefore, if every network node were to be rational in terms of costs and gains, and follow this strategy, the network would disintegrate.

5.2 S_{NX} Reflecting X's Reputation

Solutions using this concept have only one possibility of influencing forwarding decisions, which is by shaping the amount of service S_{NX} the network N requests from node X in step with R_X, and in this way shaping node X's utility. The incentives indicated in Sect. 5.1 become even stronger in Eq. (7), since S_{NX} typically increases as R_X increases. However, R_X is mainly influenced by T_X, therefore by staying uncooperative and so keeping a low reputation, node X can lessen the amount S_{NX}. Thus its optimal policy is $T_X = 0$. Apart from a high utility, the optimal strategy also ensures a greater amount of available bandwidth, as transit traffic avoids the node X. A frequently used variant of this solution introduces a threshold t_P on R_X below which no service is requested from node X; at the same time, no reciprocity mechanism is used. The optimal T_X changes and is now anywhere in $[0, t_P)$. However, from the network N's perspective, it produces the same effect as in the variant without the threshold implemented, since no service is provided by node X.

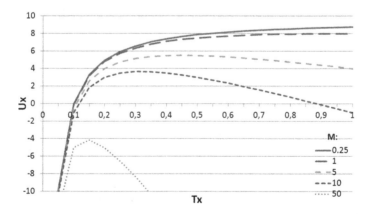

Fig. 2. Node X's utility vs. T_X; several U_X plots are shown for various M and $G = 10$.

5.3   Tit-for-Tat Reciprocity Mechanism with Fine-Grained Reputation Metric

In this subsection we analyze Eqs. (5) and (6) extended with R_X taken from (7) and (8) along with fine-grained reputation metric detailed in Sect. 4.3. The node X's optimal policy becomes more complex when playing against a network using a tit-for-tat fine-grained strategy, and becomes then more dependent on M. If $M < 1$, the optimal policy for X is $T_X = 1$. However, as M grows, the optimal T_X decreases though at much slower rate (Fig. 2), i.e., is roughly proportional to the logarithm of M. The utility at $T_X = 0$ is always infinite negative, i.e., no service is provided to X by the network N. In all cases charted on Fig. 2 constant G equals 10. However, as it can be observed on the dotted line chart, representing the case were $M = 50$, value G is insufficient to elevate U_X above 0. A rational node, in this case, should restrain from providing any service to the network, i.e. $T_X = 0$ as well as it should stop issuing its own request to the network.

5.4   Tit-for-Tat and Binary Reputation Metric

This subsection analyzes in detail Eqs. (5) and (6) along with binary reputation metric described in Sect. 4.3. Node X's strategy implements a threshold t_S on T_X which marks a border between $R_X = 0$ and $R_X = 1$. Below this threshold no amount of requested service S_{XN} is granted by the network, thus node X's utility is infinite negative the node has no perception of being connected. On the other hand, nodes with $T_X \geq t_S$ get their S_{XN} granted in full. Node X's optimal strategy in this game variant is $T_X = t_S$, because it still can refuse to service some part of S_{NX} and at the same time enjoy a full service of its requests and a full perception of being connected.

From the network N's perspective, in the error-free environment ($e = 0$), the optimal value of t_S would be 1, as it would force X to be fully cooperative and there would be no discrepancy between the proportion of service provided by N and X. However, in reality the wireless network environment is not perfect, i.e. $e > 0$, and proceeding this way would exclude some cooperative nodes from the network. The specific number of excluded nodes depends on the actual value of e. Given its stochastic nature, optimal selection of t_S is hard.

5.5   Tit-for-Tat and Fine-Grained Strategy with a Threshold

The last strategy examined in this paper is a modification of the tit-for-tat strategy analyzed in Sect. 5.3, with a threshold t_S on R_X above which the network N starts to send its service requests to node X. The optimal T_X in this case should be just below t_S in a general case. However, if $M \leq 0.5$ then the policy T_X in $[t_S, 1]$ turns out to give a slightly better performance due to the lower cost of servicing S_{XN}.

This strategy poses the same problem of accurate definition of the threshold value as in the binary metric case. However, the discrepancy between the amount of service received and provided by the network N is eliminated, as is the problem of partially cooperative nodes. The most serious issue with this strategy is the optimal T_X that makes node X useless to the network, and creates a strong incentive for all nodes to follow it to minimize their costs if the amount of service requested from them is significant.

6 Summary

We have introduced a framework for analysis of cost incentives driving nodal behavior under a reputation system, enabling comparison of different solutions and evaluation of new concepts. We have sketched some of the most common strategies of reputation systems for wireless ad hoc networks and enabled an analytical confirmation of some heuristic findings, such as the necessity of incentive-driven reputation systems in ad hoc networks, the need of indirect reciprocity towards rational nodes and the insufficiency of merely signaling uncooperative behaviors. We have showed the possibility of creating a reputation system able to shape nodes' utility functions in a way that will enforce a non-trivial service provision, by making it a strategy of highest utility for a rational node. Another contribution is made by pointing out the risk of excessive exploitation of high-reputation nodes in a way that lowers the amount of service provided to the rest of the network. Thus a need for creation of a fair load vs. reputation balancing mechanism in ad hoc networks has been shown. In the near future, the qualitative findings of this paper will be verified through extensive simulations of realistic wireless network environments and a more detailed analysis.

Acknowledgment. Preliminary ideas of the paper were developed during the Future Internet Engineering project supported by the European Regional Development Fund under Grant POIG.01.01.02-00-045/90-00.

References

1. Li Z., Shen, H.: Analysis of the cooperation strategies in mobile ad hoc networks. In: Proceedings of MASS 2008, Atlanta, GA (2008)
2. Fudenberg, D., Tirole, J.: Game Theory. MIT Press, Cambridge (1991)
3. Ohtsuki, H., Iwasa, Y.: How should we define goodness? — reputation dynamics in indirect reciprocity. J. Theor. Biol. **231**(1), 107–120 (2004)
4. Buchegger, S., Le Boudec, J.: Performance Analysis of the CONFIDANT Protocol (Cooperation of Nodes: Fairness In Dynamic Ad-hoc Networks). École Polytechnique Fédérale de Lausannen, Lausanne (2002)
5. Liu, K., Deng, J., Varshney, P., Balakrishnan, K.: An acknowledgment-based approach for the detection of routing misbehavior in MANETs. IEEE Trans. Mobile Comput. **6**(5), 536–550 (2007)
6. Graffi, K., Mogre, P., Hollick, M., Steinmetz, R.: Detection of colluding misbehaving nodes in mobile ad hoc and wireless mesh networks. In: Proceedings of IEEE GLOBECOM, Washington DC (2007)
7. Yu, H., Shen, Z., Miao, C., Leung, C., Niyato, D.: A survey of trust and reputation management systems in wireless communications. Proc. IEEE **98**(10), 1755–1772 (2010)

8. Sivanantham, S., Kirankumar, K., Akshaya, V.: Detection and avoidance of intrusion, packet drop and modification in WSN. Int. J. Adv. Res. Comput. Commun. Eng. 2(11) (2013)
9. Konorski, J., Rydzewski, K.: A centralized reputation system for MANETs based on observed path performance. In: Proceedings of 8th IFIP WMNC, Munich (2015)
10. Konorski, J., Orlikowski, R.: A reputation system for MANETs and WSNs using traffic shedding. In: Proceedings of International Conference on Applied Sciences in Biomedical and Communication Technologies, Rome (2010)
11. Karakostas, G., Kharaud, R., Viglas, A.: Dynamics of a localized reputation-based network protocol. In: 2013 International Conference on Parallel and Distributed Computing, Applications and Technologies (2013)

Network Anomaly Detection
Based on an Ensemble
of Adaptive Binary Classifiers

Alexander Branitskiy[1,2] and Igor Kotenko[1,2(✉)]

[1] St. Petersburg Institute for Informatics
and Automation of the Russian Academy of Sciences,
39, 14 Liniya, St. Petersburg, Russia
{branitskiy,ivkote}@comsec.spb.ru
[2] St. Petersburg National Research University of Information Technologies,
Mechanics and Optics, 49, Kronverkskiy prospekt, Saint-Petersburg, Russia

Abstract. The paper proposes a technique for constructing the ensemble of adaptive binary classifiers on the example of solving the problem of detection of anomalous connections in the network traffic. The detectors are used in the role of the atomic units of object classification, the principle of functioning of each ones is recognition of only one class of objects among all the others. Formation of the decisive classification rule is based on the standard procedures and includes majority voting, stacking and combining using the arbiter based on the dynamic competence regions. The novel features of the proposed technique, which contains the presented approaches, are possibility to establish an arbitrary nesting of the classifiers and lazy involvement of classifiers due to the descending cascade learning of the binary classifier ensemble. The results of experiments using the open data set for calculating the performance indicators of detection and classification of network anomalies are provided.

Keywords: Network anomalies · Network connections · Network attack detection · TCP/IP protocols · Binary classifier ensemble

1 Introduction

With the continuous development of modern technology there is a large increase in network traffic transmitted using the TCP/IP family of protocols [1]. To ensure the security and increase fault tolerance of terminal and switching devices it is required to use a special software — network-based attack detection and prevention systems. Their main function is monitoring and analyzing the captured packets in terms of their anomalous content at different levels of the network protocol stack. Since the data in the Internet are transmitted separately on the basis of separate, but related to each other blocks (IP-fragments), the analysis at the level of individual packets is not sufficient to identify the majority of network anomalies, which are aimed to seizure or disablement of the computing host. Among these anomalies it can be mentioned viral activity, overloading the network equipment, denial of service (DoS) attacks, port and host scanning. Typically to detect such types of attacks a much larger number of packets are

© Springer International Publishing AG 2017
J. Rak et al. (Eds.): MMM-ACNS 2017, LNCS 10446, pp. 143–157, 2017.
DOI: 10.1007/978-3-319-65127-9_12

needed, which are combined into the minimum network flow — connection, features of which play the role of input arguments to customize adaptive models. In the paper as such models we apply multilayer neural network, neuro-fuzzy network based on Takagi-Sugeno inference and support vector machine (SVM). Also for improving the quality characteristics of individual models we propose to use several classifier ensembles, namely majority voting, stacking, and Fix and Hodges method.

This research continues the development of a number of papers devoted to the analysis of security and response to attacks in computer networks as well as to detection of targeted attacks in distributed large-scale critical systems [2] and is based on the authors' previous papers [3, 4].

The scientific contribution of this paper is to present a technique which is designed for performing the combination of heterogeneous classifiers with the application to the field of detection of anomalous network connections. It should be noted that this approach can be used outside this field to solve more general problems of pattern recognition.

The novelty of the proposed approach is that unlike existing analogues it is more flexible and within it we can create various ensembles of classifiers without strict binding to a specific method of combining classifiers. In addition, instead of using one classifier for recognizing all specified types of attacks, this approach is aimed at applying the binary classifiers for constructing the multi-class model that enables greater scalability and reduces the training time of such model.

The second section contains a formulation of the problem in the performed research and a brief survey of related papers which are relevant to detection of network attacks using the combined approaches and adaptive classifiers. In the third section we present a technique of a hierarchical construction of a binary classifier ensemble to detect anomalous network connections. The fourth section includes experimental evaluation of the proposed technique with the use of open dataset of network raw dump. The fifth section considers main conclusions and future work.

2 Formulation of the Problem and Related Work

The problem of detecting the anomalous network connections through combining the classifiers can be formulated as follows.

The base classifiers are given $F^{(1)}, \ldots, F^{(s)} : \mathbb{R}^n \to 2^{\{0,\ldots,m\}}$, which were trained on the set of labeled feature vectors of network connections $\chi = \{(X_i, c_i)\}_{i=1}^{M}$ $(c_i \in \{0, \ldots, m\})$.

Within the ensemble of base classifiers the aggregating function $G : \{0, \ldots, m\}^s \times \mathbb{R}^n \to 2^{\{0,\ldots,m\}}$ is defined in such a way, that it takes the output values of classifiers $F^{(1)}, \ldots, F^{(s)}$ as input arguments. Each of the presented classifiers $F^{(1)}, \ldots, F^{(s)}, G$ as output values generates a the set $\{c_i'\}_{i=0}^{m'} \subset \{0, \ldots, m\}$ $(0 \leq m' \leq m)$, whose elements indicate the possible class labels in terms of this classifier. Besides, the function G can be a complex multilayer procedure, which makes it difficult to develop a common approach to construct the classifier ensemble. It is required to customize the function G such that the empirical risk functional of its composition with base classifiers

$\psi_\chi\big(G \circ \big[F^{(1)}, \ldots, F^{(s)}, \mathrm{id}\big]\big) = \frac{1}{M} \cdot \#\big\{X_i | G\big(F^{(1)}(X_i), \ldots, F^{(s)}(X_i), X_i\big) \neq \{c_i\}\big\}_{i=1}^{M}$ did not exceed the arithmetic mean of the empirical risk functional of individual classifiers $F^{(1)}, \ldots, F^{(s)}$: $\psi_\chi\big(G \circ \big[F^{(1)}, \ldots, F^{(s)}, \mathrm{id}\big]\big) \leq \frac{1}{s} \cdot \sum_{j=1}^{s} \psi_\chi\big(F^{(j)}\big)$.

The total average used in the right part can be replaced by $\min_{j \in \{1, \ldots, s\}} \psi_\chi\big(F^{(j)}\big)$.

Figure 1 shows one of the possible schemes of combining the binary classifiers using functions $F^{(1)}, \ldots, F^{(s)}, G$.

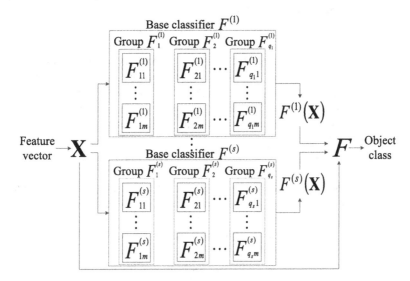

Fig. 1. A proposed approach for combining the binary classifiers

Detection of anomalous network connections using adaptive classifiers is actively researched field. For solving this problem in [5] it is proposed to use K radial basis neural networks. Each of these networks is trained on different disjoint subsets $D_1, \ldots, D_K$ of the original training dataset D. Such subsets are generated using the method of fuzzy clustering, according to which each element belongs to the region D_i with a certain membership degree of u_i^X. Each subset D_i $(i = 1, \ldots, K)$ is composed of those elements that have the greatest membership degree with respect to this subset among all other subsets. As the authors emphasize, due to such preliminary decomposition the generalization ability of base classifiers is improved and time of their training is reduced since for their configuring only those objects are employed which are most densely grouped around the formed center of the training subset.

To combine the output results $Y_1, \ldots, Y_K$ of these classifiers, taking the vector X as an input argument, the multilayer neural network is used. Its input vector is represented as a set of elements obtained by applying a threshold function to each component of the vector $u_i^X \cdot Y_i$ $(i = 1, \ldots, K)$. A similar approach has been used previously in [6], where feed-forward neural networks served as base classifiers and input for an aggregating module was composed of the direct values of vectors $u_1^X \cdot Y_1, \ldots, u_K^X \cdot Y_K$.

In [7] the analysis of the records of network connections is performed by neuro-fuzzy models and SVM. The authors determine four main stages in the proposed approach. On the first stage the generation of training data is performed by means of K-means clustering method. The second stage is training of neuro-fuzzy classifiers. On the third stage the input vector is formed for SVM. The final stage is attack detection using the latter classifier.

In [8] an individual neural network with one hidden layer is constructed for detecting each of three types of DDoS attacks which are conducted with the use of protocols TCP, UDP and ICMP. The last layer of each of these neural networks consists of single node, the output value of which is interpreted as the presence or absence of DDoS attacks of the appropriate type. The proposed approach is implemented as a module in the Snort and tested on real traffic network environments.

In [9] to detect DoS attacks it is proposed to use an approach, which combines the method of normalized entropy for calculating the feature vectors and SVM for their analysis. In order to detect anomalies six parameters are extracted from network traffic, numerically expressed as the occurrence intensity of different values of selected fields within the packets during the 60 s window. In this approach, the network parameters are calculated using the method of normalized entropy, and they are used as the input for training and testing data based on SVM.

In [10] to detect DoS attacks and scanning of hosts the authors consider an approach based on consecutive application of a vector compression procedure and two fuzzy transformations. First, principal component analysis is applied to the input eight-dimensional feature vector of network connections, which allows to reduce its dimension to five components with preserving the relative total variance at the level of more than 90%. The next step is the training or testing of the neuro-fuzzy network, the output value of which is processed by the method of fuzzy clustering.

Our approach is based on these papers, but we suggest to apply the binary classifiers for constructing the multi-class model for recognizing different types of attacks. The approaches of combining the binary classifiers are considered in the next section.

3   Technique of a Hierarchical Construction of a Binary Classifier Ensemble to Detect Anomalous Network Connections

The general representation of the suggested technique for detecting the anomalous network connections is illustrated in Fig. 2 and consists of the following stages: (1) Construction of a classifier tree; (2) Generation of network connection parameters; (3) Preprocessing of network connection parameters; (4) Hierarchical bypassing of a classifier tree in width; (5) Detection and classification of network anomalies.

The first stage of the technique may be characterized as preparatory, it consists in the selection of the structure of individual binary classifiers (detectors), including dimension and quantity of layers, learning parameters and algorithms, types of activation functions, membership functions and kernels. For each detector the set of training rules can be made. By specifying a different combinations of such rule sets we can form

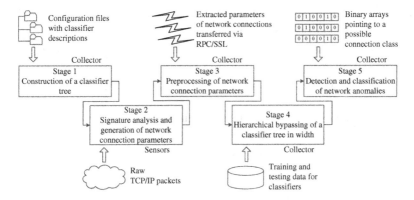

Fig. 2. Main stages of the technique for detecting the anomalous network connections

a group of detectors each of which is constructed on the basis of one of the adaptive models: neural network [11, 12], neuro-fuzzy network [13, 14] and SVM [15, 16]. The detectors within such group is combined through approaches one-against-all, one-against-one [17] or their affiliated variations. In the first approach each detector $F_{jk}^{(i)} : \mathbb{R}^n \to \{0,1\}$ $(k = 1, \ldots, m)$ is trained on data $\{(X_l, [c_l = k])\}_{l=1}^M$, and functioning the group of detectors is described using the exclusionary principle:

$$
F_j^{(i)}(X) = \begin{cases} \{0\}, & \text{if } \forall k \in [1,m] F_{jk}^{(i)}(X) = 0 \\ \left\{ k \big| F_{jk}^{(i)}(X) = 1 \right\}_{k=1}^m, & \text{otherwise} \end{cases}.
$$

In the second approach each of $\binom{m+1}{2} = \frac{(m+1) \cdot m}{2}$ detectors is trained on the set of objects which belong to only two classes k_0 and k_1, — $\{(X_l, 0)|c_l = k_0\}_{l=1}^M \cup \{(X_l, 1)|c_l = k_1\}_{l=1}^M$, where $0 \leq k_0 < k_1 \leq m$, and functioning the group of detectors can be set using the max-wins voting:

$$
F_j^{(i)}(X) = \left\{ \arg \max_{c \in \{0,\ldots,m\}} \sum_{k=c+1}^m \left[F_{jck}^{(i)}(X) = 0 \right] + \sum_{k=0}^{c-1} \left[F_{jkc}^{(i)}(X) = 1 \right] \right\}.
$$

As one of the affiliated variations of previous approaches for combining the detectors we can mention the classification binary tree. We have already investigated it from the experimental point of view in our earlier paper [3]. Formally this structure is recursively defined as follows:

$$
CBT_S = \begin{cases} \left\langle F_{jL_SR_S}^{(i)}, CBT_{L_S}, CBT_{R_S} \right\rangle, & \text{if } \#S \geq 2 \\ S, & \text{if } \#S = 1 \end{cases}.
$$

Here $S = \{0, \ldots, m\}$ — the original set of class labels, $L_S \subset S$ — a randomly generated or user predefined subset of S ($\#L_S < \#S$), $R_S = S \backslash L_S$, CBT_{L_S} — a left classification binary subtree, CBT_{R_S} — a right classification binary subtree, $F^{(i)}_{jL_SR_S}$ — a node detector trained on elements $\{(X_l, 0) | c_l \in L_S\}^M_{l=1} \bigcup \{(X_l, 1) | c_l \in R_S\}^M_{l=1}$, i.e. the detector output is configured to be equal 0 if the input object X_l has label $c_l \in L_S$, and 1 if the input object X_l has label $c_l \in R_S$. Therefore functioning the group of detectors nested in each other is given via the recursive function ϕ:

$$F^{(i)}_j(X) = \phi(S, X),$$

$$\phi(S, X) = \begin{cases} S, & \text{if } \#S = 1 \\ \phi(L_S, X), & \text{if } \#S \geq 2 \wedge F^{(i)}_{jL_SR_S}(X) = 0 \\ \phi(R_S, X), & \text{if } \#S \geq 2 \wedge F^{(i)}_{jL_SR_S}(X) = 1 \end{cases}.$$

Using the function ϕ we can perform an unambiguous search of the class label of the input object. This is due to since a disjoint partition of the set of class labels takes place at each step during the descent down the classification tree, then only one possible class label remains after reaching the terminal detector. Therefore conflict cases of classification through the classification tree are not possible within the group $F^{(i)}_j$, although they may occur for other two approaches considered above.

Another approach is a directed acyclic graph that combines $\binom{m+1}{2} = \frac{(m+1)\cdot m}{2}$ detectors into a linked dynamic structure which can be given by the following formula:

$$DAG_S = \begin{cases} \left\langle F^{(i)}_{jSk_0k_1}, DAG_{S \backslash \{k_0\}}, DAG_{S \backslash \{k_1\}} \right\rangle, & \text{if } \#S \geq 2, \text{ where } k_0 \in S, k_1 \in S \\ S, & \text{if } \#S = 1 \end{cases}.$$

As in the approach one-against-one each node detector $F^{(i)}_{jSk_0k_1}$ is trained on the basis of elements $\{(X_l, 0) | c_l = k_0\}^M_{l=1} \cup \{(X_l, 1) | c_l = k_1\}^M_{l=1}$ ($k_0 < k_1$). Bypassing of the graph is performed using a recursive function Ξ which specifies an element-by-element detachment of the set S:

$$F^{(i)}_j(X) = \Xi(S, X),$$

$$\Xi(S, X) = \begin{cases} S, & \text{if } \#S = 1 \\ \Xi(S \backslash \{k_1\}, X), & \text{if } \#S \geq 2 \wedge F^{(i)}_{jSk_0k_1}(X) = 0 \\ \Xi(S \backslash \{k_0\}, X), & \text{if } \#S \geq 2 \wedge F^{(i)}_{jSk_0k_1}(X) = 1 \end{cases}.$$

If the detector $F^{(i)}_{jSk_0k_1}$ votes for the k_0-th class of the object X, i.e. $F^{(i)}_{jSk_0k_1}(X) = 0$, then the label k_1 is removed from the set as obviously false, otherwise the label k_0 is excluded. The process is repeated until the set S degenerates into the one-element set.

Table 1 shows the characteristics of the considered schemes for combining detectors in a multiclass model which is intended to associate an input object to one or more of $(m+1)$ class labels.

Table 1. Characteristics of the schemes for combining detectors

Scheme for combining detectors	Number of detectors to be trained	The minimum number of detectors involved in the classification of objects	The minimum number of detectors involved in the classification of objects
One-against-all	m	m	m
One-against-one	$\frac{(m+1)\cdot m}{2}$	$\frac{(m+1)\cdot m}{2}$	$\frac{(m+1)\cdot m}{2}$
Classification binary tree	m	1	m
Directed acyclic graph	$\frac{(m+1)\cdot m}{2}$	m	m

Only one, namely the classification binary tree, has a variable number of detectors, which can be used in the process of classifying the objects. The minimum value is reached when the detector $F_{jL_SR_S}^{(i)}$ is activated which is located in the tree root and trained to recognize only one object among all the rest and $F_{jL_SR_S}^{(i)}(X) = 0$ $\left(F_{jL_SR_S}^{(i)}(X) = 1\right)$, i.e. when $\#L_S = 1 (\#R_S = 1)$. The maximum value is achieved when the tree is represented by a sequential list and the most remote detector is activated in it. In the case of a balanced tree this indicator can be equal to $\lfloor \log_2(m+1) \rfloor$ or $\lceil \log_2(m+1) \rceil$.

In Fig. 1 we have presented an example when each classifier $F^{(i)}$ $(i = 1, \ldots, s)$ contains q_i groups $F_j^{(i)}$ $(j = 1, \ldots, q_i)$, each of which combines m detectors $F_{jk}^{(i)}$ $(k = 1, \ldots, m)$ using the approach one-against-all.

Each group of detectors $F_j^{(i)}$ is trained on different arbitrary bootstrap samples which include duplicate and reordered elements from the original training set χ. Combining the groups $F_j^{(i)}$ into the classifier $F^{(i)}$ is implemented on the basis of majority voting:

$$
F^{(i)}(X) = \left\{ c \left| \underbrace{\sum_{j=1}^{q_i} \left[c \in F_j^{(i)}(X) \right]}_{\xi_i(c)} > \frac{1}{2} \cdot q_i \wedge \xi_i(c) = \max_{c' \in \{0,\ldots,m\}} \xi_i(c') \right. \right\}_{c=0}^{m} .
$$

For constructing the ensemble rule G [18, 19] which combines the output results of classifiers $F^{(i)}$ we have implemented following methods: (1) majority voting representing a weighted average of the sum of individual classifier outputs; (2) stacking, complemented by the introduction of an additional attribute — a cluster number retrieved by K-means; (3) Fix and Hodges method, representing a combining the classifiers using the arbiter based on the dynamic competence regions and a nearest neighbor method. All of these methods are described in more detail in [3].

To complete the task of parsing we have implemented the interpreter, supporting the operations of conditional branching, vector concatenation, vector summation, component product and division. In progress of the interpreter the correctness of the handled configuration files is checked as well as the object fields are initialized within the constructed classifier tree which is a structure with terminal nodes in the form of detectors and nonterminal nodes in the form of classifiers or aggregating functions.

The considered technique implies a distributed architecture of systems realizing it. In such systems the collection of initial data is performed by secondary nodes — sensors, and processing of aggregated data streams is performed on a centralized server — collector. Since the developed system consists of several independent components such approach of system construction allows to achieve increased fault tolerance and greater flexibility in data processing.

The second stage of the technique is performed on the sensor side and consists in applying the developed algorithm to reassemble the raw packets into network connections, extracting their parameters and performing the signature analysis by means of several developed parallel modifications of the substring search algorithms. For this purpose we have examined the performance of Aho–Corasick [20–22] and Boyer–Moore [21–23] algorithms on the Snort selected signature records and implemented their improved analogues using the technologies OpenMP and CUDA.

The event-driven analyzer of network traffic was implemented by which 106 network parameters were extracted. Among them it should be called connection duration, used network service, intensity of sending the special packets by the host, the number of active connections between a certain pair of IP-addresses, flag of changing the TCP-window scale after actual establishing of the session, current state of TCP-connection, various flags of scanning packets presence on the levels TCP, UDP, ICMP и IP, etc. The classification of these parameters is presented in Fig. 3.

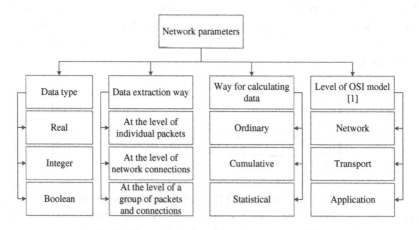

Fig. 3. The classification of network parameters

For measuring the value of intensity of sending/receiving the packets we have used the adapted sliding window method. The method essence is to split a given time interval $\Delta_0^{(L)} = [0, L]$ with length L, during which a continuous observation of a number of parameters is carried out, into several smaller intervals $\Delta_0^{(L')}, \Delta_\delta^{(L')}, \ldots, \Delta_{\delta \cdot (K-1)}^{(L')}$ with identical length $0 < L' \leq L$. The beginning of each such interval has an offset $0 < \delta \leq L'$ relatively beginning of the previous interval. As $\bigcup_{i=0}^{K-1} \Delta_{\delta \cdot i}^{(L')} \subseteq \Delta_0^{(L)}$ and $\bigcup_{i=0}^{K} \Delta_{\delta \cdot i}^{(L')} \supset \Delta_0^{(L)}$, then $K = 1 + \lfloor \frac{L-L'}{\delta} \rfloor$. During time intervals $\Delta_0^{(L')}, \ldots, \Delta_{\delta \cdot (K-1)}^{(L')}$ the snapshots of parameter values $\omega_0, \ldots, \omega_{K-1}$ are made and their average value (intensity) ϖ within the time window with length L' is calculated by the following formula: $\varpi = \frac{1}{K} \cdot \sum_{i=0}^{K-1} \omega_i$. In this paper we have used an interval which value of the parameter L is equal to five seconds. The length of the smoothing interval L' was chosen to be equal to one second. The offset δ is set to a half-second. That such approach allows to eliminate sparse and occasional network bursts and decrease the false positive rate.

The third stage begins with listening to the packets incoming from the sensors, containing the calculated connection parameters and transmitted using the protocol RPC/SSL. We have chosen such protocol pair to ensure the communication between collector and sensors, because it ensures both fast and safe sending data. RPC is a well-proven and successfully passed the test of time technology that allows to organize easily the compact transfer of binary data streams. SSL, in turn, is widely used for creating an encrypted channel between the data transmitters.

Before the detectors will be immediately trained, preprocessing of parameters is carried out for reducing the effect of their substantial variability. Many methods, including neural networks and *principal component analysis* (PCA), are sensitive to such fluctuations and require that all the features of handled vectors had the same scale. Therefore, the first step of preprocessing of each component x_{ij} of the vector $X_i \in \{X_i\}_{i=1}^M$ includes its normalization using the function $f(x_{ij}) = \frac{x_{ij} - x_j^{(min)}}{x_j^{(max)} - x_j^{(min)}}$ (when $x_j^{(max)} = x_j^{(min)}$ it can be assumed $f(x_{ij}) = 0$), where $x_j^{(min)} = \min_{i=1,\ldots,M} x_{ij}$ and $x_j^{(max)} = \max_{i=1,\ldots,M} x_{ij}$. The second step is reducing the number of insignificant features, which is achieved by PCA [24, 25]. Such method is described as a sequence of the following steps: (1) To calculate the mathematical expectation of the random vector, which is represented by the set of training elements $\left\{ X_i = \{x_{ij}\}_{j=1}^n \right\}_{i=1}^M$: $\bar{X} = (\bar{x}_1, \ldots, \bar{x}_n)^T = E[\{X_i\}_{i=1}^M] = \frac{1}{M} \cdot \sum_{i=1}^M X_i = \left(\frac{1}{M} \cdot \sum_{i=1}^M x_{i1}, \ldots, \frac{1}{M} \cdot \sum_{i=1}^M x_{in} \right)^T$; (2) To generate elements of an unbiased theoretical covariance matrix $\Sigma = (\sigma_{ij})_{\substack{i=1,\ldots,n \\ j=1,\ldots,n}}$:

$\sigma_{ij} = \frac{1}{M-1} \cdot \sum_{K=1}^M (x_{ki} - \bar{x}_i) \cdot (x_{kj} - \bar{x}_j)$; (3) To calculate eigen values $\{\lambda_i\}_{i=1}^n$ and eigen vectors $\{v_i\}_{i=1}^n$ of the matrix Σ as roots of equations: $\det(\Sigma - \lambda \cdot I) = 0$ and $(\Sigma - \lambda \cdot I) \cdot v = 0$; (4) To sort eigen values $\{\lambda_i\}_{i=1}^n$ in decreasing order and corresponding eigen vectors $\{v_i\}_{i=1}^n$: $\lambda_1 \geq \ldots \geq \lambda_n \geq 0$; (5) To select the required number of $\hat{n} \leq n$ of principal components: $\hat{n} = \min\{z | g(z) \geq \varepsilon\}_{z=1}^n$, where $g(z) = \frac{\sum_{i=1}^z \lambda_i}{\sum_{i=1}^n \lambda_i}$ — an informativeness measure, $0 \le \varepsilon \le 1$ is an expertly selectable value; (6) To center the input feature vector X': $X'_c = X' - \bar{X}$; (7) To project the centered feature vector X'_c into the new coordinate system, described by the orthonormalized vectors $\{v_i\}_{i=1}^{\hat{n}}$: $Y' = \left(y'_1, \ldots, y'_{\hat{n}}\right)^T = (v_1, \ldots, v_{\hat{n}})^T \cdot X'_c$, where $y'_i = v_i^T \cdot X'_c$ is called i-th principal component of the vector X'. The experimental results showed that the re-normalization after compression using the PCA is not necessary.

The fourth stage of the technique is the most cumbersome in terms of computational resources and consists of the following recursively repeating sequences of operations: calculation of dependencies of the current classifier, generation of input signals for the current classifier, training of the current classifier. A special tree-like structure for storing the classifiers was developed which allows to perform an effective top-down descent by all the chains of dependencies, from the top-level classifier to terminal nodes, represented as detectors. Training of each classifier generates a request for training of the underlying classifiers, indicated in the list of its dependencies, and generation of their output data for creating the input data of the overlying classifier. The consequence of thus used cascade training is the possibility of lazy loading of the classifiers: only those classifiers are involved in training and recognition, which are found directly or indirectly in the list of dependencies of the classifier, which is responsible for generation of the general solution in the ensemble of classification rules. This property is especially beneficial in the analysis of dynamic rules for training the classifiers, i.e. such rules, the successful or unsuccessful activation of which leads to a call of another rule. In particular, this is typical for the classification tree when rules are nested in each other. Thus, this makes it possible to avoid cases of useless calls of a detector, which output value is known not to affect the final result of the ensemble.

The fifth stage of the technique includes two modes: (1) the mode of evaluating the effectiveness and (2) the mode of functioning. In the first mode the indicators are calculated which are presented in the next section, in the second mode the system diagnostics is performed without a priori knowledge of the actual class of an identified network connection.

4 Experiments

For the experiments we have used the data set DARPA 1998, represented as pcap-files with raw packet images and csv-files with connection labels. For our research we have selected two classes of DoS attacks, four classes of attacks associated with scanning of ports and hosts and one class represented by normal connections. A detailed description of generated sets of training and testing data are given in Table 2.

The following indicators of detection and classification have been chosen in respect of which an evaluation of classifiers was carried out: (1) The rate of detection correctness: $TPR = TP/(TP + FN)$, where indicator TP is the number of correctly detected anomalous connections, FN is the number of errors of the second type; (2) The rate of false positives: $FPR = FP/(FP + TN)$, where FP is the number of errors of the first type, TN — the number of correctly detected normal connections; (3) The rate of classification correctness: $CCR = CC_{COR}/(TP + FN + FP + TN)$,

Table 2. Training and testing data sets

Training data set	
Total amount	7000
Absolute and relative amount of unique records	5962 (85.17%)
Test data set	
Total amount	101113
Absolute and relative amount of unique records	53733 (53.14%)
Absolute and relative amount of unique records, which are not seen while training	47771 (47.25%)

where CC_{COR} is the total number of elements, which class was correctly identified, on a joined data set, consisting of normal and anomalous connections; (4) The rate of conflict cases of correct classification: $CCR' = CC_{CONFL}/(TP + FN + FP + TN)$, where CC_{CONFL} is the total number of elements, for which the output value of the ensemble contains several classes, on a joined data set, consisting of normal and anomalous connections including a correct class; (5) The rate of generalization capability upon detection: $GAR = TP_{UNQ\backslash TR}/(TP_{UNQ\backslash TR} + FN_{UNQ\backslash TR})$, where indicators $TP_{UNQ\backslash TR}$, $FN_{UNQ\backslash TR}$ represent respectively the number of correctly detected anomalous connections and the number of errors of the second type, which are calculated on unique data of the test set, strictly excluding any data of the training set; (6) The rate of overfitting upon detection: $OVR = TPR_{UNQ\_TR} - GAR$, where the indicator TPR_{UNQ_TR} corresponds to the rate of detection correctness on the unique data of the training set. Using the PCA we have reduced the dimension of the feature space from 106 to 33 components.

Performance indicators obtained are given in Table 3. Cells in the first three columns contain values of respective performance indicators calculated for each of three ensembles. The last column corresponds to the average of the outputs of individual base classifiers represented as neural networks with a hyperbolic tangent activation function, neuro-fuzzy networks with bell-shaped membership functions and SVM with radial basis kernels.

Table 3. The values of performance indicators

Indicators	Majority voting	Stacking	Fix and Hodges method	Average of base classifiers
TPR	99.78%	99.82%	99.78%	99.3%
FPR	0.46%	2.89%	3.01%	1.32%
CCR	98.46%	97.76%	96.7%	97.9%
CCR'	0%	0%	0.01%	0.09%
GAR	99.72%	99.74%	99.72%	99.58%
OVR	0.2%	0.2%	0.2%	−0.76%

Using the proposed technique we have improved *TPR* by 0.48% in the case of majority voting and reduced the false positive rate by 0.86% as compared with the average of individual base classifiers. It can also be seen that for majority voting the indicator *CCR* was increased by 0.56%, the indicator *GAR* was increased by 0.16%, and the probability of occurrence of cases of conflict classification of objects has decreased to zero. Such small gain is caused by presence of the already high performance indicators of individual classifiers, which are presented as a group of detectors which are trained to recognize only one class of attacks. In the case of other approaches for combining the classifiers the rate of false positives has been greatly risen, while maintaining the detection correctness rate comparable with the approach of majority voting.

Since one of our main purposes is to decrease the empirical risk functional, i.e. to increase *CCR*, we have carried out several additional experiments for more detailed and accurate evaluating an unbiased assessment of such indicator. For this purpose we have used 3-fold cross-validation. The essence of such procedure is as follows. The data set Q which contains 53733 non duplicated instances of network connections was splitted into 3 disjoint subsets Q_1, Q_2, Q_3, each of which have approximately the same value of cardinality ($\#Q_1 \approx \#Q_2 \approx \#Q_3$). And in each set Q_k there are elements of all seven classes of connections in such a way that the subsample corresponding to each specific class has approximately the same size within each set Q_k ($k = 1, 2, 3$). The training process of base classifiers was performed thrice by means of the sets $\{Q_i \cup Q_j\}_{i<j \wedge i=1,2,3 \wedge j=2,3}$. Depending on these sets we have selected the testing set Q_k which differs from them ($k \neq i \wedge k \neq j \wedge k = 1, 2, 3$), performed the testing process of three base classifiers and three ensembles using the set Q_k and calculated the performance indicator $CCR_{bk}^{(BC)}$ for each b-th base classifier ($b = 1, 2, 3$) and $CCR_{ek}^{(EN)}$ for each e-th ensemble ($e = 1, 2, 3$) which aggregates the base classifiers.

The final values of the indicators $CCR_b^{(BC)}$ and $CCR_e^{(EN)}$ for the b-th base classifier and for the e-th ensemble were obtained by averaging the corresponding values computed previously: $CCR_b^{(BC)} = \frac{1}{3} \cdot \sum_{K=1}^{3} CCR_{bk}^{(BC)}$ and $CCR_e^{(EN)} = \frac{1}{3} \cdot \sum_{K=1}^{3} CCR_{ek}^{(EN)}$. Similarly we have calculated $TPR_b^{(BC)} - FPR_b^{(BC)}$ and $TPR_e^{(EN)} - FPR_e^{(EN)}$ for each b-th base classifier and e-th ensemble. The values obtained for each of these indicators are schematically displayed in Fig. 4. As before in these experiments we have used the approach one-against-all at the lowest level for combining the detectors into the base classifier (group).

Using the Fix and Hodges method the indicator of a classification correctness $CCR_3^{(EN)} = 98.26\%$ has been increased by 3.23% compared with the maximal value of such indicator $\max_{b=1,2,3} CCR_b^{(BC)} = 95.03\%$, obtained among base classifiers, namely using the neuro-fuzzy classifier. Applying the majority voting and Fix and Hodges method enabled to augment insignificantly (by 0.13%) the difference of indicators $TPR - FPR$, representing a compromise between the value of detection correctness of anomalous network connections and false positives.

A dependence of an averaged informativeness measure on the number of principal components selected is shown as a graph in Fig. 5.

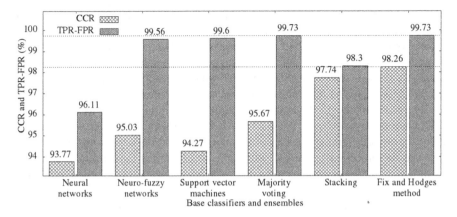

Fig. 4. The values of performance indicators obtained using the 3-fold cross-validation

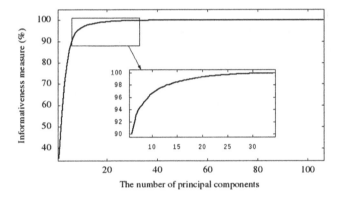

Fig. 5. A dependence of the informativeness measure on the number of principal components

It can be seen from this figure, after about the first 30 principal components a significant expansion of an informativeness measure has not been observed and the curve graph is almost completely degenerated into a constant function.

5 Conclusion

The paper presented a technique of a hierarchical construction of a binary classifier ensemble in the framework of solving the problem of detection of anomalous network connections. The novel features of the proposed technique are possibility to set an arbitrary nesting of classifiers in each other and lazy loading of classifiers due to the top-down cascade training of the classifier ensemble. There are five stages in the considered technique. At the first stage the individual classification of classifiers and the setting of rules for their training are performed. Examples of several schemes, which are based on the usage of such rules and allow to combine detectors in a multiclass model, were presented. Each of these schemes is supported at the level of the interpreter of the developed software tool which is designed to classify anomalous network connections. The second stage consists in carrying out a signature analysis of the content of individual and defragmented packets, assembling the network connections and extracting the network parameters which are applicable for analysis using adaptive classifiers. The third stage is characterized by preprocessing of such parameters by means of the methods of normalization and principal components. At the fourth stage the bypassing of the classifier tree is performed together with the alternation of processes training, testing of the classifiers and the dependency search. It is noted that the processes performed within this stage are the most resource intensive. The fifth stage consists in calculating the selected indicators of detection and classification of anomalous network connections.

The results of the experiments showed an augmentation of the classification correctness rate using the proposed technique compared with the individual base classifiers. In this paper we have carried out the comparative performance of the ensembles and base classifiers using the fixed approach for combining the detectors as one-against-all. Further it is planned to perform also a comparison of ensembles, but with an emphasis towards a low-level combining the detectors theoretically considered in this paper in the form of approaches one-against-all, one-against-one, classification binary tree and directed acyclic graph.

Acknowledgements. This research is being supported by the grant of RSF #15-11-30029 in SPIIRAS.

References

1. Comer, D.E.: Computer Networks and Internets, 6th edn, p. 672. Upper Saddle River, Pearson (2014)
2. Kotenko, I.V., Saenko, I.B.: Creating new generation cybersecurity monitoring and management systems. Herald Russ. Acad. Sci. **84**(6), 993–1001 (2014)
3. Branitskiy, A., Kotenko, I.: Hybridization of computational intelligence methods for attack detection in computer networks. J. Comput. Sci. Elsevier (2016). http://www.sciencedirect.com/science/journal/aip/18777503. Accessed 1 Aug 2016
4. Branitskiy, A., Kotenko, I.: Network attack detection based on combination of neural, immune and neuro-fuzzy classifiers. In: 18th IEEE International Conference on Computational Science and Engineering (IEEE CSE2015), pp. 152–159. Porto, Portugal (2015)
5. Amini, M., Rezaeenour, J., Hadavandi, E.: Effective intrusion detection with a neural network ensemble using fuzzy clustering and stacking combination method. J. Comput. Secur. **1**(4), 293–305 (2015)
6. Wang, G., Hao, J., Ma, J., Huang, L.: A new approach to intrusion detection using artificial neural networks and fuzzy clustering. Expert Syst. Appl. **37**(9), 6225–6232 (2010)
7. Chandrasekhar, A.M., Raghuveer, K.: Intrusion detection technique by using k-means, fuzzy neural network and SVM classifiers. In: International Conference on Computer Communication and Informatics (ICCCI), pp. 1–7 (2013)
8. Saied, A., Overill, R.E., Radzik, T.: Detection of known and unknown DDOS attacks using artificial neural networks. Neurocomputing **172**, 385–393 (2016)

9. Agarwal, B., Mittal, N.: Hybrid approach for detection of anomaly network traffic using data mining techniques. Procedia Technol. **6**, 996–1003 (2012)
10. He, H.-T., Luo, X.-N., Liu, B.-L.: Detecting anomalous network traffic with combined fuzzy-based approaches. In: Huang, D.-S., Zhang, X.-P., Huang, G.-B. (eds.) ICIC 2005. LNCS, vol. 3645, pp. 433–442. Springer, Heidelberg (2005). doi:10.1007/11538356_45
11. Haykin, S.: Neural Networks and Learning Machines, 3rd edn, p. 906. Pearson Prentice Hall, New York (2009)
12. Fausett, L.: Fundamentals of Neural Networks: Architectures, Algorithms and Applications, 1st edn, p. 461. Pearson Prentice Hall, New York (1994)
13. Takagi, T., Sugeno, M.: Fuzzy identification of systems and its applications to modeling and control. IEEE Trans. Syst. Man Cybern. **SMC-15**(1), 116–132 (1985)
14. Jang, J.-S.R.: ANFIS: adaptive-network-based fuzzy inference system. IEEE Trans. Syst. Man Cybern. **23**(3), 665–685 (1993)
15. Vapnik, V.N.: The Nature of Statistical Learning Theory, p. 188. Springer, New York (1995)
16. Duda, R.O., Hart, P.E., Stork, D.G.: Pattern Classification, 2nd edn, p. 680. Wiley, New York (2000)
17. Hsu, C.W., Lin, C.J.: A comparison of methods for multiclass support vector machines. IEEE Trans. Neural Netw. **13**(2), 415–425 (2002)
18. Zhou, Z.H.: Ensemble Methods: Foundations and Algorithms, p. 218. CRC Press, Boca Raton (2012)
19. Kuncheva, L.I.: Combining Pattern Classifiers: Methods and Algorithms, 2nd edn, p. 384. Wiley, New York (2014)
20. Aho, A.V., Corasick, M.J.: Efficient string matching: an aid to bibliographic search. Commun. ACM **18**(6), 333–340 (1975)
21. Aho, A.V.: Algorithms for finding patterns in strings. In: Handbook of Theoretical Computer Science, pp. 255–300. Elsevier Science Publishers (1990)
22. Stephen, G.A.: String Searching Algorithms, p. 256. World Scientific, Singapore (2000)
23. Boyer, R.S., Moore, J.S.: A fast string searching algorithm. Commun. ACM **20**(10), 762–772 (1977)
24. Pearson, K.: On lines and planes of closest fit to systems of points in space. London Edinburgh Dublin Philos. Magaz. J. Sci. **2**(11), 559–572 (1901)
25. Jolliffe, I.T.: Principal Component Analysis, 2nd edn, p. 488. Springer, New York (2002)

Cardholder's Reputation System for Contextual Risk Management in Payment Transactions

Albert Sitek[✉] and Zbigniew Kotulski

Institute of Telecommunications of WUT,
Nowowiejska 15/19, 00-665 Warsaw, Poland
asitek@tele.pw.edu.pl, zkotulsk@tele.pw.edu.pl

Abstract. Electronic card payments gained huge popularity mainly because of their simplicity, convenience and processing time. Unfortunately transaction processing rules are constant for every transaction, for example each transaction above some hard limit (50 PLN in Poland) must be authorized with PIN verification. One can notice that such an approach is simple, but is not optimal: that is why Contextual Risk Management systems for payment transactions started to be created. This paper presents a new Cardholder's Reputation System that can be used in Contextual Risk Management Systems. It is flexible thanks to a few parameters and allows to cover all possible transaction processes.

Keywords: Reputation systems · EMV · CVM · Payment systems

1 Introduction

Electronic card payments are getting more and more popular across the world. Only in Poland, there were more than 1 billion transactions performed in Q2.2016 [1]. Electronic payment transactions are performed in compliance with EMV specifications, see [2], the standard that has been firstly proposed by Europay, MasterCard and Visa in 1993. Currently it is promoted by EMVCo which associates all major Payment Card Schemes: Visa, Mastercard, JCB, American Express, Discover and UnionPay. Initially, payment card's data could be read by inserting card to the terminal: in a contact way, according to ISO 7810 specification [3]. Nowadays, Contactless Payment Cards (compliant with ISO 14443 [4]) are gaining huge popularity, especially in some countries like UK, Poland and Turkey. Transaction made with contactless card is 53% faster than a traditional magnetic stripe credit card transaction and 63% faster than using cash [2]. According to the newest report, more than 77% issued cards in Poland have contactless functionality [1]. Recently, thanks to services like Android Pay [5], or Samsung Pay [6], there is emerging trend observed on the market to emulate Contactless Payment Card with the smartphone [7]. Such a functionality is possible thanks to the Host Card Emulation technique (HCE) [8] and smartphones equipped with the Near Field Communication (NFC) interface [9]. Thankfully, contactless card emulated with the smartphone is treated and read as a physical

© Springer International Publishing AG 2017
J. Rak et al. (Eds.): MMM-ACNS 2017, LNCS 10446, pp. 158–170, 2017.
DOI: 10.1007/978-3-319-65127-9_13

one, so no changes are required in the payment infrastructure to support those cards correctly.

Payment transaction, compliant with the EMV specification [10], can be processed in many ways, for example can be authorized on-line (by sending an authorization request to the bank), or locally authorized off-line (by the card). Also cardholder can be verified in a different way, e.g. using PIN On-line (verified by the issuer), PIN Off-line (verified by the card, only for contact EMV), Signature, or NoCVM (no cardholder verification at all). The decision which authorization method and cardholder verification method should be used is being made based on terminal's configuration and data retrieved from the card (encoded on the card by the issuer during its personalization phase). Those parameters are for example:

(a) CVM Limit (Cardholder Verification Method Limit), only for contactless transactions, the amount above which the cardholder must be verified: currently 50 PLN in Poland.
(b) Floor Limit, the amount above which the transaction must be authorized on-line.

Those parameters are constant for every transaction: it means that each cardholder is treated in the same way, no matter what's his history and whole transaction context. Such an approach is simple, but it causes that a lot of transactions are processed "time and user experience-ineffectively". One can imagine that transaction flow could be adjusted to the given cardholder and to particular transaction, based on various factors. It may give a lot of benefits, e.g. shorter transaction processing time, greater cardholder's loyalty, better user experience etc. This issue has been raised for the first time in [11]. In this paper, Sitek proposed a new Cardholder Verification Method: One-time PIN, and decision if this method should be used is made by the issuer, based on transaction context (transaction's time, place, cardholder's history etc.). Unfortunately, the author did not propose any algorithm that could be used to decide whether cardholder verification should be performed or not. Another approach has been proposed in [12]. Authors presented dedicated solution for huge merchants (such as Tesco, Auchan etc.), where historical data are kept on merchant's server. Their architecture assumed that payment terminal, during the transaction, sends contextual information (transaction's amount, location, tokenized card's number etc.) to merchant's server and receives the decision whether it should be authorized on-line or off-line. They also proposed a simple example of algorithm that calculates floor limit for current transaction based on cardholder's reputation, transactions' periodicity factor and transactions' amount stability factor. Unfortunately, their reputation system has a few flaws, for example it is unable to detect the situation where cardholder cancels the PIN Off-line, enters it with success on second attempt, or a transaction with PIN On-line that has been declined because of lack of funds (but PIN has been verified).

In this paper a new cardholder's reputation system has been proposed. It distinguishes all possible transaction processes that are significant for cardholder's reputation, including contact and contactless EMV cards. Moreover, it is open to any customization, because of many parameters. Such a system has been designed to generate single reputation value that could be taken into account (together with other contextual factors, e.g. exact time, location etc.) in dedicated decision system (like [12]) that could produce final verdict, how current payment transaction should be processed.

The rest of the paper is organized as follows: Sect. 2 briefly presents current knowledge regarding reputation systems, Sect. 3 describes presented reputation system based on possible transaction processes, Sect. 4 outlines the way how the proposed system has been verified, Sect. 5 contains tests' results, Sect. 6 summarizes the paper and maps out future work.

2   Reputation Systems

According to Cambridge Dictionary [13], reputation can be defined as follows: *Reputation: the opinion that people in general have about someone or something, or how much respect or admiration someone or something receives, based on past behavior or character.* The concept of reputation can be easily mistaken with trustworthiness. In order to explain the difference between trust and reputation, an example from [14] can be quoted: "I trust you because of your good reputation" or "I trust you despite your bad reputation". Those sentences show, that reputation is only one of the factors that can have an impact on the trust. There can be a situation when relying party has some private knowledge about the trustee (for example some direct experiences), and these factors may overwrite any reputation during decision making. On the other hand, in case of lack of additional information, reputation can have crucial meaning during decision making process. Generally speaking, reputation systems assess the reputation of the user by aggregating the ratings that he received from other users [15]. Based on how reputation values are calculated, reputation systems are divided into a few groups:

- *Arithmetic-based*, where reputation values are calculated as simply sum of positive and negative ratings (e.g. eBay) or an average of all ratings (e.g. Amazon). Advanced models in this category compute a weighted average of all the ratings, where the rating weight can be determined by factors such as distance between rating, age of the rating and current score etc. [16]. The reputation system presented in this paper belongs to this group;
- *Probabilistic approach-based*, where reputation values are calculated by the statistical updating of probability density functions (PDF), see [17];
- *Fuzzy logic-based*: in this group of systems, trust and reputation can be represented as linguistically fuzzy concepts, where the membership functions describe to what degree an agent can be described as trustworthy or not trustworthy, see e.g. [18].

Taking into account how reputation is maintained in whole system, there are two groups of reputation systems: centralized and decentralized. The centralized systems have a central authority being responsible for the collection and storage of user's ratings, and for the calculation of reputation values and their dissemination [19]. Such systems are widely used in e-commerce [20], experts sites [21], etc. The decentralized systems have neither a fixed network topology nor a central authority that can be used to control the entities within the system. Instead of that, each entity is responsible for controlling its data and resources. In these systems, the storage of ratings and calculation of reputation are distributed among the entities within the system [15]. Such systems are used in decentralized environment like Peer-to-Peer Networks [22,23], Mobile Ad-hoc Networks [24,25], Wireless Sensor Networks [26], Multi-agent Systems (MAS) [27,28], etc. One can read a few wide surveys of currently developed trust and reputation system, see for example [14,19,29,30].

3   Cardholder's Reputation System

As mentioned in Sect. 1, presented reputation system covers all possible transactions' flows. In order to illustrate and identify them, the transaction's flow diagram has been created. Figure 1 presents all possible transaction's scenarios that can happen during the transaction. It takes into account both contact and contactless transactions. The diagram shows that each transaction flow can be simplified to a set of answers to the questions written in lozenges. For example, the contactless transaction that has been successfully authorized on-line with on-line PIN verification can be translated into YES|NO|NO|NO|YES|YES|YES|YES|NO. When we change "YES" to "1", and "NO" to "0", this transaction flow can be translated into 100011110. This shows, that each transaction flow can be presented as unambiguous binary string. The same transaction flow can also be presented in more human-readable form as CTLS_PIN_ONL_VRFD_ONL_APPR. Both notations will be used in the rest of this paper.

Each transaction flow has constant rating assigned to it. The set of ratings for all possible transaction flows are parameters of the reputation system. The cardholder's reputation for a forthcoming transaction n can be calculated as weighted average of last N transactions limited to the range $<R_{MIN}, R_{MAX}>$, see Eq. (1). N, R_{MIN} and R_{MAX} are parameters of the reputation system.

$$R_n = \begin{cases} R_{MIN} & \text{if } \overline{R}_{n-i} < R_{MIN} \\ \overline{R}_{n-i} & \text{if } \overline{R}_{n-i} \in \langle R_{MIN}, R_{MAX} \rangle \\ R_{MAX} & \text{if } \overline{R}_{n-i} > R_{MAX} \end{cases}, \text{ where } i \in \langle 1, N \rangle. \quad (1)$$

The proposed reputation system assumes that there must be at least N historical transaction stored in the system's database to calculate proper reputation value; otherwise cardholder's reputation is set to 0. Equation (2) shows the proposed formula how to calculate weights for the weighted average computation.

$$w_{Rni} = \frac{1}{2} e^{-\frac{t_n - t_i}{\tau_{RT} * AvgT}} * \text{erfc}(\frac{(n - i - 1) * 2}{x_d} + x_m), \quad (2)$$

where n is the index of current transaction, i is the index of i-th transaction, t_n is time of current transaction, t_i is time of i-th transaction, $AvgT$ is the average distance between transactions, τ_{RT} is the reputation system parameter (the decay factor), erfc is the Complementary Error Function, x_d is the reputation system parameter (a dispersion parameter of the erfc function), x_m is the reputation system parameter (a concentration parameter of the erfc function [32]).

Equation (2) has been proposed based on a set of experimental simulations. Usage of exponential function assures that historical reputation values will be

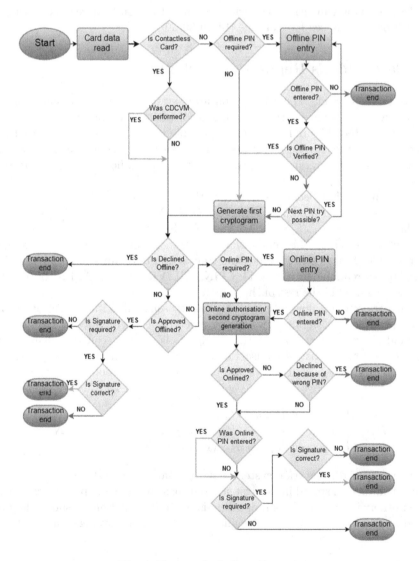

Fig. 1. Transaction's flow diagram

decaying accordingly to distance in time between current and historical transaction. On the other hand, the Complementary Error Function is responsible for decaying accordingly to how many transactions has been made between current and historical transaction.

4 Verification of the Model

In order to verify the reputation system, a lot of simulations need to be performed. The important thing is to select proper simulation software. According to [31], there are currently three options to develop and simulate models: spreadsheets, programming languages and dedicated software. Each of them have pros and cons, but in our opinion, the most suitable option is to simulate proposed model in spreadsheet. Simulating in spreadsheet is fast to develop and has all necessary features [33]. Therefore Microsoft Excel^{TM} 2013 has been used in our tests. In order to share common formulas across a few workbooks, dedicated Add-in has been developed.

As mentioned in previous sections, proposed reputation system has a lot of parameters. On the grounds of numerous simulation iterations, following values has been chosen for further simulations: $N = 5$, $R_{MIN} = -5$, $R_{MAX} = 10$, $\tau_{RT} = 6$, $x_d = 3$, $x_m = -1$. Table 1 presents chosen transaction flow's ratings for simulations, calculated by experts' knowledge, for transactions made according to Fig. 1. A reader must note that not all possible transaction flows has been listed. For example there is no Off-line Authorization for Contact transaction listed, because in real life this authorization method has been disabled in terminals' configuration. Moreover, some transaction flows are very rare, for example CTLS_ONL_APPR_SIG_VRFD (signatures for contactless cards, are uncommon). There are some interesting patterns that can be seen in Table 1:

(a) For PIN on-line: there is no difference whether transaction has been finally accepted or not. The key thing is if it has been declined because of wrong PIN code entered. For example CT_PIN_ONL_VRFD_ONL_APPR = CT_PIN_ONL_VRFD_ONL_DCLD = 7, but CT_PIN_ONL_FAILED = −10,

(b) PIN off-line: can be entered several times, in case of previous attempts appeared incorrect. Presented values assume that if cardholder made a mistake once, and finally transaction was accepted, then his reputation will increase (CT_2ND_PIN_OFFL_VRFD_ONLINE_APPR = 3). But if he made a mistake twice, his reputation will be decreased (CT_3RD_PIN_OFFL_VRFD_ONLINE_APPR = −2),

(c) After transactions, which flows have rating = 0: cardholder reputation for forthcoming transaction will slightly decrease because of decaying features of reputation weights.

Table 1. Chosen transaction flow's ratings

Description	Binary trace	Rating
CT_1ST_PIN_OFFL_VRFD_ONL_APPR	0111000100	7
CT_2ND_PIN_OFFL_VRFD_ONLINE_APPR	011011100100	3
CT_3RD_PIN_OFFL_VRFD_ONLINE_APPR	011011011100100	−2
CT_1ST_PIN_OFFL_CNCD	010	−15
CT_2ND_PIN_OFFL_CNCD	011010	−17
CT_PIN_ONL_VRFD_ONL_APPR	000011110	7
CT_PIN_ONL_VRFD_ONL_DCLD	0000110000	7
CT_PIN_ONL_FAILED	00001101	−10
CT_PIN_ONL_CNCD	000010	−15
CT_ONL_APPR_SIG_VRFD	000001011	5
CT_ONL_APPR_SIG_FAILED	000001010	−10
CT_ONL_DCLD	00000000000	0
CT_ONL_APPR	000001000	0
CTLS_PIN_ONL_VRFD_ONL_APPR	100011110	7
CTLS_PIN_ONL_VRFD_ONL_DCLD	100011100	7
CTLS_PIN_ONL_FAILED	10001101	−10
CTLS_PIN_ONL_CNCD	100010	−15
CTLS_ONL_APPR	10000100	0
CTLS_ONL_DCLD	10000000	0
CTLS_OFFL_APPR	10010	0
CTLS_OFFL_DCLD	101	0

5   Tests' Results

There has been several transaction scenarios proposed to show reputation system's behavior in certain situations. Because of the limitations of this paper, only the most interesting scenarios has been presented. Each test has been described in details in following subsections.

Table 2. Transactions' history before test

Time	Description	Binary trace	Rating
01.03.2016	CT_PIN_ONL_VRFD_ONL_APPR	000011110	7
08.03.2016	CT_PIN_ONL_VRFD_ONL_APPR	000011110	7
15.03.2016	CT_PIN_ONL_VRFD_ONL_APPR	000011110	7
22.03.2016	CT_PIN_ONL_VRFD_ONL_APPR	000011110	7
29.03.2016	CT_PIN_ONL_VRFD_ONL_APPR	000011110	7

There is an assumption that before first transaction in given test case, there was constant transactions' history (described in Table 2), so that computation of cardholder's aggregated reputation using Eq. (1) is possible.

Test 1 shows how cardholder's reputation will be rebuilt after unsuccessful on-line PIN verification. Table 3 presents chosen transactions' history to illustrate such a situation.

Table 3. Transactions' history for Test 1

Time	Description	Binary trace	Rating
05.04.2016	CT_PIN_ONL_FAILED	00001101	−10
12.04.2016	CT_PIN_ONL_VRFD_ONL_APPR	000011110	7
19.04.2016	CT_PIN_ONL_VRFD_ONL_APPR	000011110	7
26.04.2016	CT_PIN_ONL_VRFD_ONL_APPR	000011110	7
03.05.2016	CT_PIN_ONL_VRFD_ONL_APPR	000011110	7
10.05.2016	CT_PIN_ONL_VRFD_ONL_APPR	000011110	7

Figure 2 shows results of Test 1. First successful transaction after transaction with incorrect on-line PIN causes reputation to increase to the medium level, around 2.7. Only second successful transaction raises the cardholder reputation to satisfactory level, around 8.5. After third transaction, calculated reputation (R Real) is above R_{MAX} parameter, so it is cut away to the R_{MAX} value.

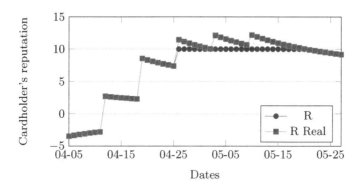

Fig. 2. Aggregated reputation from Test 1

Test 2 shows how cardholder's reputation will be rebuilt after two unsuccessful on-line PIN verifications. Table 4 presents chosen transaction history to illustrate such a situation.

Table 4. Transactions' history before tests

Time	Description	Binary trace	Rating
05.04.2016	CT_PIN_ONL_FAILED	00001101	−10
12.04.2016	CT_PIN_ONL_FAILED	00001101	−10
19.04.2016	CT_PIN_ONL_VRFD_ONL_APPR	000011110	7
26.04.2016	CT_PIN_ONL_VRFD_ONL_APPR	000011110	7
03.05.2016	CT_PIN_ONL_VRFD_ONL_APPR	000011110	7
10.05.2016	CT_PIN_ONL_VRFD_ONL_APPR	000011110	7

As shown in Fig. 3, after two incorrect PIN verifications, calculated reputation drops down dramatically. It reaches level below R_{MIN}, so that R stays at the level of $R_{MIN} = -5$. After first successful transaction, calculated reputation still remains below 0. Only second successful transaction causes reputation to increase, while next successful transaction causes calculated transaction to be cut away to R_{MAX} value. Comparing results of Test 1 and Test 2, one can see that after two successful transactions, cardholder's reputation is set to the similar level, while after first successful transaction reputation in Test 2 is much more lower than in Test 1. This is because of proper values of parameters responsible for decaying old ratings.

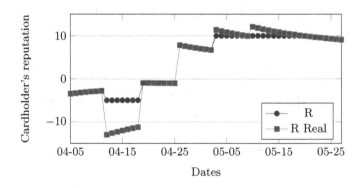

Fig. 3. Aggregated reputation from Test 2

Test 3 shows how good cardholder's reputation will decay because of set of transactions without cardholder verification. Table 5 presents chosen transactions' history to illustrate this scenario.

As shown in Fig. 4, excellent cardholder's reputation will decay completely after three transactions without any verification. Such a transaction may happen because the transaction amount was below CVM Limit, or some Contextual Risk

Management system (like [11,12]) decided to authorize the transaction without verification. Such a behavior is a result of decaying parameters and prevents Contextual Risk Management system from being abused.

Table 5. Transactions' history for Test 3

Time	Description	Binary trace	Rating
05.04.2016	CT_PIN_ONL_VRFD_ONL_APPR	000011110	7
12.04.2016	CTLS_ONL_APPR	10000100	0
19.04.2016	CTLS_ONL_APPR	10000100	0
26.04.2016	CTLS_ONL_APPR	10000100	0
03.05.2016	CTLS_ONL_APPR	10000100	0
10.05.2016	CTLS_ONL_APPR	10000100	0

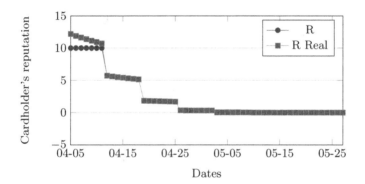

Fig. 4. Aggregated reputation from Test 3

Test 4 presents how presented reputation system will react on transaction canceled on second attempt of entering off-line PIN. Canceling off-line PIN on second attempt means that first attempt has failed and cardholder interrupted the transaction. It may indicate that this was an attempt to perform fraudulent transaction. Table 6 presents chosen transaction history to illustrate such a scenario.

As mentioned before, canceling PIN indicates suspicious behavior so that it is reflected in Fig. 5 correctly. Very good cardholder's reputation will drop down drastically after such a behavior. In this picture one can also see that cardholder's reputation slightly decreased after third transaction because of lack of verification, and it is constantly, slightly decreasing after some period of time without any transaction.

Table 6. Transactions' history for Test 4

Time	Description	Binary trace	Rating
05.04.2016	CTLS_PIN_ONL_VRFD_ONL_APPR	100011110	7
12.04.2016	CT_2ND_PIN_OFFL_CNCD	011010	−17
19.04.2016	CTLS_PIN_ONL_VRFD_ONL_APPR	100011110	7
26.04.2016	CTLS_PIN_ONL_VRFD_ONL_APPR	100011110	7
03.05.2016	CTLS_ONL_APPR	10000100	0
10.05.2016	CTLS_PIN_ONL_VRFD_ONL_APPR	100011110	7

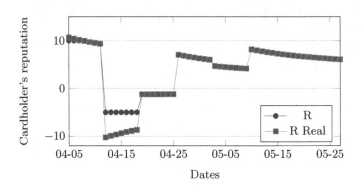

Fig. 5. Aggregated reputation from Test 4

6   Summary and Future Work

In this paper a new Cardholder's Reputation System has been proposed. It covers all possible transaction processes, what has been shown in Fig. 1. It also allows the end user to make some adjustments thanks to plenty of parameters. It is designed to be used in Contextual Risk Management systems like, for example, [12]. Such a system allows to control transaction processing based on various factors, mainly on cardholder's reputation, but also on other, like contextual information: transaction time, transaction amount, actual queue length, etc. The presented system has been validated with success by several simulations performed in the dedicated test environment based on Microsoft Excel^{TM}2013. Additional tests on real transactions' data (taken from one of the retail chain in Poland) are scheduled and will be finished in a few months. One can imagine the Contextual Risk Management System, that decides whether the Cardholder should enter the PIN number, or not. It makes its decision based on cardholder's reputation (calculated using the presented formulas), and some other factors like the Amount Stability Factor (a number indicating how current amount differs from previous ones), the Transaction Periodicity Factor (telling if the Cardholder is a loyal customer and she makes transactions frequently), etc. To prove its commercial applicability, such a system should be tested with production transaction data. In our opinion it is worth to focus future research in that topic.

References

1. Department of Payment System, National Bank of Poland: Information about payment cards 2nd quarter 2016 (2016). (in Polish)
2. EMVCo: EMV Specifications. http://www.emvco.com/specifications.aspx
3. ISO 7810 Specification. http://www.iso.org/iso/catalogue_detail?csnumber=31432
4. ISO 14443 Specification. http://www.iso.org/iso/home/store/catalogue_ics/catalogue_detail_ics.htm?csnumber=70170
5. Android Pay homepage. https://www.android.com/intl/pl_pl/pay/
6. Samsung Pay homepage. http://www.samsung.com/us/samsung-pay/
7. http://www.bankier.pl/wiadomosc/Eksperci-Platnosci-HCE-to-rynkowy-przelom-3323308.html
8. Host Card Emulation. https://en.wikipedia.org/wiki/Host_card_emulation
9. Near Field Communication. http://nfc-forum.org/what-is-nfc/
10. EMV Transaction Steps. https://www.level2kernel.com/flow-chart.html
11. Sitek, A.: One-time code cardholder verification method in electronic funds transfer transactions. Annales UMCS ser. Informatica, AI **14**(2), 46–59 (2014)
12. Sitek, A., Kotulski, Z.: Contextual management of off-line authorisation in contact EMV transactions. Telecommun. Rev. Telecommun. News 88(84), 8-9, 953–959 (2015). (in Polish)
13. Cambridge Dictionary, definition of "Reputation". http://dictionary.cambridge.org/dictionary/english/reputation
14. Jøsang, A., Ismail, R., Boyd, C.: A survey of trust and reputation systems for on-line service provision. Decis. Support Syst. **43**(2), 618–644 (2007)
15. Vavilis, S., Petrovic, M., Zannoe, N.: A reference model for reputation systems. Decis. Support Syst. **61**, 147–154 (2014)
16. Jøsang, A.: Trust and Reputation Systems. Foundations of Security Analysis and Design IV, FOSAD (2007)
17. Ciszkowski, T., Mazurczyk, W., Kotulski, Z., Hoßfeld, T., Fiedler, M., Collange, D.: Towards quality of experience-based reputation models for future web service provisioning. Telecommun. Syst. **51**(4), 283–295 (2012)
18. Damiani, E., Capitani, D., di Vimercati, S., Paraboschi, S., Pesenti, M., Samarati, P., Zara, S.: Fuzzy logic techniques for reputation management in anonymous peer-to-peer systems. In: Proceedings of the Third International Conference in Fuzzy Logic and Technology, Zittau, Germany (2003)
19. Koutrouli, E., Tsalgatidou, A.: Reputation systems evolution survey. ACM Comput. Surv. **48**, 3 (2015). Article 35
20. Resnick, P., Zeckhauser, R.: Trust among strangers in internet transactions: empirical analysis of ebay's reputation system. In: The Economics of the Internet and E-Commerce, vol. 11 of Advances in Applied Microeconomics. Elsevier Science (2002)
21. Costagliola, G., Fuccella, V., Pascuccio, F.A.: Towards a trust, reputation and recommendation meta model. J. Vis. Lang. Comput. **25**, 850–857 (2014)
22. Gupta, M., Judge, P., Ammar, M.: A reputation system for peer-to-peer networks. In: NOSSDAV 2003, 1–3 June 2003, USA (2003)
23. Buchegger, S., Le Boudec, J.-Y.: A robust reputation system for P2P and mobile ad-hoc networks. In: Workshop on Economics of Peer-to-Peer Systems (2004)
24. Sen, J.: A distributed trust and reputation framework for mobile ad hoc networks. In: Third International Conference (CNSA 2010), Chennai, India, 23–25 July 2010 (2010)

25. Srinivasan, A., Teitelbaum, J., Liang, H.: Reputation and trust-based systems for ad-hoc and sensor networks. In: Boukerche, A. (ed.) On Trust Establishment in Mobile Ad-Hoc Networks. Wiley, New York (2007)
26. Roman, R., Fernandez-Gago, M.C., Lopez, J.: Trust and reputation systems for wireless sensor networks. In: Security and Privacy in Mobile and Wireless Networking, pp. 105–128 (2009)
27. Sabater, J., Sierra, C.: Reputation and social network analysis in multi-agent systems. In: First International Joint Conference on Autonomous Agents and Multiagent Systems, pp. 475–482 (2002)
28. Pujol, J.M., Sanguesa, R., Delgado, J.: Extracting reputation in multi agent systems by means of social network topology. In: The First International Joint Conference on Autonomous Agents & Multiagent Systems (AAMAS 2002), 15–19 July (2002)
29. Yan, Z., Zhang, P., Vasilakos, A.V.: A survey on trust management for Internet of Things. J. Netw. Comput. Appl. **42**, 120–134 (2014)
30. Noorian, Z., Ulieru, M.: The state of the art in trust and reputation systems: a framework for comparison. J. Theor. Appl. Electron. Commer. Res. **5**(2), 97–117 (2010). doi:10.4067/S0718-18762010000200007. Talca ago
31. Robinson, S.: Simulation: The Practice of Model Development and Use. Palgrave Macmillan, London (2014)
32. Kotulski, Z., Szczepinski, W.: Error Analysis with Application in Engineering. Springer, Dordrecht (2010)
33. Seila, A.F.: Spreadsheet simulation. In: Winter Simulation Conference, California, USA (2006)

Towards Self-aware Approach for Mobile Devices Security

Nanda Kumar Thanigaivelan$^{(\boxtimes)}$, Ethiopia Nigussie, Seppo Virtanen,
and Jouni Isoaho

Department of Future Technologies, University of Turku, Turku, Finland
{nakuth,ethnig,seppo.virtanen}@utu.fi

Abstract. We present conceptual design of self-aware security for mobile devices. The design is envisioned to bring self-awareness into the mobile devices security for optimal protection by regulating application activities. The proposed design contains three subsystems: *meta-level* enables self-awareness, *extended meta-level* extends protections to the base-level components through security mechanisms and *base-level* comprises of resources that are essential for applications execution. The presented design enables cooperation among security mechanisms (such as access control and anti-virus) as well as with self-aware agent. The cooperation is intended for better understanding of application activities that leads to recognizing threat patterns in advance. When a threat is predicted/detected, the self-aware agent communicates with the security mechanisms so that they can take the necessary actions. The design of the security mechanisms are elaborated using access control system and anti-virus as example cases.

1 Introduction

Mobile devices are becoming a predominant tool for accessing online information and services. The number of users accessing internet through mobile devices is estimated to reach 6.1 billion by 2022 and it will become the primary interface to access internet for more than 50% of users by 2018 [1,2]. Though mobile market is occupied by numerous manufactures, mobile platform is majorly dominated by two operating systems: Android by Google and Apple's iOS [3]. Both platforms allow developers to build applications and publish in market place by providing APIs [4,5]. The fact that mobile devices handle sensitive information and its resources can be accessed easily makes ensuring security and privacy a priority. In future, mobile devices will play a crucial role in the Internet of Things (IoT) by performing operations such as sensing and actuation, and also acting as an intermediate gateway for IoT devices. These activities will enhance the roles and usage of mobile devices but also increases its vulnerability to threats due to its involvement in various activities.

The emergence of new threats along with the lack of security awareness among the users makes mobile devices a lucrative target for attacks. Existing security

© Springer International Publishing AG 2017
J. Rak et al. (Eds.): MMM-ACNS 2017, LNCS 10446, pp. 171–182, 2017.
DOI: 10.1007/978-3-319-65127-9_14

features in iOS and Android provide privacy controls to protect sensitive information [6, 7]. There are a number of ways to overcome the restrictions. For instance, in Android platform, permission verification APIs that are used to verify the state of the required permissions may be exploited by application developers to force users to grant all permissions in order to nullify the advantage of runtime permission revocation control, which is available in Android 6.0 and higher versions. Numerous anti-virus are available to protect mobile devices from exploitation by malicious applications [25–28]. Most anti-virus are signature based and proprietary, failing to protect from new malicious applications behavior and also limiting the users choice. The security mechanism in Android like permission model act as access control system in order to prevent unauthorized access to resources. Several researches have been carried out in improving access control [8–11]. Policies of most access controls are coarse-grained and failed to regulate device level activities. In addition, the use of self-adaptation based on learning neither available nor capitalized in existing access control mechanisms. Hence, there is a need for self-adaptive fine-grained context-based access control for better control over application and device activities. In addition, embedding logic to accomplish the tasks of anti-virus to ensure the permanent existence of anti-virus mechanism into the platform for reliable detection of malicious activities.

In this work, we present a conceptual design that enables building of security mechanisms that can be configured and optimized by a self-aware agent. The main working principle of the design is to configure, control and direct the activities of various security mechanisms that are used to safeguard the mobile devices from applications exhibiting malicious behaviors. Furthermore, security mechanisms help the self-aware agent in the learning process by gathering the required information and communicating with it. This approach improves security of the device by optimizing the controls and detection ability of the anti-virus at runtime with minimal human intervention.

The paper is structured as follows. In Sect. 2, motivation and objectives of the self-aware security are discussed. The details of designing self-awareness and security mechanisms are presented in Sect. 3. The related works on modeling the self-aware agent are discussed in Sect. 4. Finally, future direction for realizing self-aware security in mobile devices and summary are presented in Sects. 5 and 6, respectively.

2   Motivation and Objectives

Mobile platforms like Android, expose device activities and resources through APIs. Several researches have been carried out to address permission overclaiming, abusing granted permission and security issues [8–12]. The platform developers have also strengthened the operating system by introducing encryption, SE Linux and runtime permission revocation [6, 7]. However, it is still possible for applications to gather information about the users and devices through various ways. For example, sensors and event broadcasts are not protected in Android, which can be exploited to get user activities and location information [22–24].

A number of solutions have been proposed to thwart the threats in mobile platforms, particularly in Android but most of them concentrated either on access control or prevention of identified threats [8–12]. These solutions failed to recognize the assimilation of mobile devices into internet-of-things (IoT) and the resulting change in the mobile usage landscape. The ongoing efforts in bridging IPv6 and BLE will facilitate easy integration of mobile devices in the IoT ecosystem [13–15]. One potential example of this integration is the capitalization of sensors available in mobile for information gathering through crowd sensing [16–19]. In addition, intercommunication between mobile devices is highly likely in future IoT applications. Once this opportunity is available, applications that try to harness the crowd sensing may exploit the mobile resources. In these scenarios, it is difficult to know the security or privacy threats in advance.

One of the limitations of the existing security measures is that the lack of cooperation between various security solutions though they are operate in the same device. For example, access control system performs its enforcement operations based on the given configuration without sharing or cooperating with the anti-virus applications. In access control, context are necessary to increase the policy granularity. However, the policy granularity and diversification are limited since the existing context based access control systems rely only on location, Wi-Fi, battery and time.

The objective of this work is to specify the concept of a self-aware security design that addresses the limitations of existing security measures and future challenges due to the change in mobile usage landscape. A self-aware system is capable of implementing appropriate measures at run-time in order to achieve and maintain the required performance [20, 21] by observing its environment and operations. The proposed security design is intended to achieve the following:

- To learn application behaviors through self-aware agent and communicate it with the security mechanisms which in turn take the necessary measures.
- To design security measures that are guided by the self-aware agent to achieve fine-grained control with minimal human involvement, leading to improved security.
- To devise cooperation strategy among security measures for improved understanding and detection of new threat types/malicious application activities.

3   Self-aware Security Design

Conventionally, security mechanisms are positioned to intercept the request calls from any applications (see Fig. 1). Based on the given configuration, it will decide further course of action. The configuration has to be performed manually by an administrator or a user depending on the complexity of the security mechanism and the interface provided for configuration. The security mechanisms do not possess any components or subsystems that can perform learning and optimization operations of other subsystems.

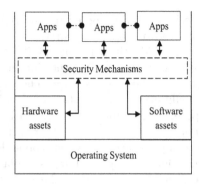

Fig. 1. Traditional mobile platform with security mechanisms

3.1 Self-awareness

Any system that has the capability to learn and adapt itself through continuous monitoring of its own operations and environment is termed as self-aware system. Design and implementation of a self-aware system is not an easy task but they offer numerous benefits upon proper employment. Some of the advantages are improved performance over time, efficient use of resources, reduced complexity, low required maintenance effort/time, detection/prevention of unexpected events, and better functioning of the entire system.

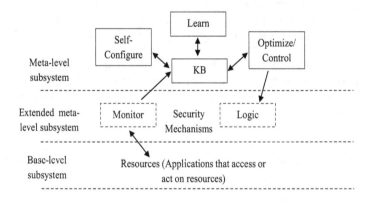

Fig. 2. Proposed self-aware reference architecture for mobile security

A system that shows any self-awareness property is comprised of two subsystems: meta-level that offers protection and base-level that requires protection [29]. A meta-level subsystem is responsible for the realization of self-aware property while base-level subsystem handles the domain functionality and it is protected/managed by the meta-level subsystem. The self-aware architecture of the proposed security design for mobile devices is given in Fig. 2. The main purpose of the given architecture is to secure the available resources in the mobile devices from being abused or exploited. The proposed design is slightly different from the architecture given in [29]. In our case, the monitor functions are categorized as an extended meta-level subsystem along with the security mechanisms since it aides the self-aware realization of meta-level subsystem by gathering information for learning and optimization process. In the proposed design, the security mechanisms are responsible for listening every resource request calls from applications and this is the main reason for the separation of monitor functionality from meta-level subsystem (self-aware agent). Furthermore, meta-level subsystem is not responsible for protecting the security mechanisms. Even the resources are not protected by the self-aware agent directly instead the security mechanisms are responsible for protection of resources under the guidance of the self-aware agent. This is the reason for the introduction of extended meta-level subsystem in the proposed architecture as can be seen in Fig. 2. Since resources do not have the ability to perform operations on their own, applications that use or act on the resources are included in base-level subsystem.

The modified mobile platform with the proposed self-awareness and controllable security mechanism is given in Fig. 3. The introduced components of the modified mobile platform are self-configure, learn and evaluate, controller, and knowledge base.

Self-configure: the purpose of self-configuration component is to update the settings of self-aware agent by considering the previous and current circumstances in order to fulfill the required objectives. It is also responsible for (re)defining the execution period for controller as well as learn and evaluate components.

Learn and evaluate: information gathered by the security mechanisms are analyzed to establish the common system behavior patterns. Upon detection of deviation in behavior pattern after successive execution, the appropriate changes will be deduced and submitted to knowledge base.

Controller: examines the provided recommendations and direct the operations of security mechanisms by changing their settings (for example, access control policies, encryption algorithms and enable/disable the entire security system). It is also responsible for restoring settings to previous states if the applied changes fails or causes abnormal behavior in the security mechanisms.

Knowledge base: act as a central repository for the storage of monitored information (in the form of logs), learning outcomes and execution settings of its components.

Security mechanisms, such as access control system and open anti-virus platform, acts as an extended components of the self-aware agent. The task of gathering information for learning will be handled by the security mechanisms since they have the ability to intercept every request. This will considerably reduce the workload of the self-aware agent and thus, allows it to invest more resources on learning tasks.

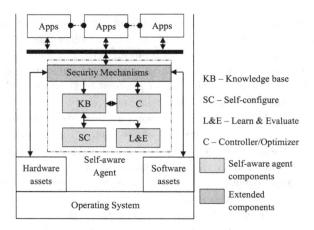

Fig. 3. Mobile platform with self-aware agent and security mechanisms

3.2 Security Mechanisms

In the current version of mobile platforms, each of the security mechanisms are designed as a self-contained system that operates independently and have complete control over its operations. For example, except policy configuration, access control system is completely self-contained. It does not have ability to cooperate with other security mechanisms. In the proposed self-aware security, cooperation among security mechanisms are introduced in order to achieve a holistic protection strategy that strengthen the overall security of the device. In addition, the security mechanisms cooperate with the self-aware agent as they are guided by the self-aware agent for enforcing the security measure. To have these cooperation, all critical operational requirements of the security mechanisms have to be separated from the core logic. In the proposed design, security mechanism contains only the core logic and its own execution parameters or requirements are controlled by the self-aware. The critical operations differ in different security mechanisms and hence, a special care has to be given when designing the security mechanisms and its interaction with the self-aware agent. The design of security mechanisms are elaborated using the following two example cases.

Access Control System. The access control system in self-aware security cooperates with the self-aware agent in order to perform dynamic policy administration by taking advantage of learning outcomes. Except the core logic, i.e., restriction enforcement, the rest of access control critical parameters has to be separated. The access control system must be classified into two subsystems so that it can handle device level and application level activities separately. The core logic must be extended to record all the activities intercepted during execution. For policy creation, both environment and feature based context have to be employed. In addition, new provisions to control the memory requirement

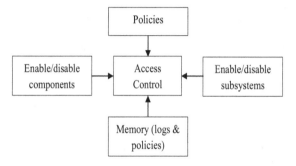

Fig. 4. Security mechanism: access control system security mechanism: access control system

(for logs and policy storage) and controlling of subsystems have to be established. The customized access control mechanism is shown in Fig. 4.

Open Anti-virus/Malware. Several vendors are providing proprietary anti-virus application to mobile devices [25–28]. The signatures will be updated periodically to detect malicious applications. Since they operate as a stand alone system application, it is not possible for any system to oversee the activities and/or cooperate with anti-virus applications. This limits their capacity of identifying new malicious activities. By cooperating with other security mechanisms and the self-aware agent, their detection capacity can be enhanced significantly. Thus, we are proposing a new open anti-virus security mechanism that will be managed by vendors as well as the self-aware agent collectively. The block diagram of the proposed open anti-virus is shown in Fig. 5. It will be designed as a part of the operating system and open to any vendors. The users can choose any vendor according to their preference and change the vendors at later stages. Compared to proprietary anti-virus application, the open anti-virus has to operate with two signature repositories. First repository will be used by vendors to

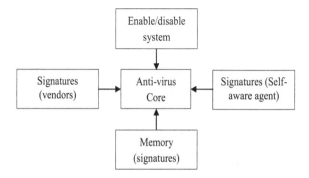

Fig. 5. Security mechanism: open antivirus

update the malicious applications' signatures and the other one by the self-aware agent to maintain its own learned malicious patterns. It will also have a provision to turn on/off the execution of core logic when it is ordered by the self-aware agent.

Overall Conceptual Design. The cooperation between the self-aware agent and security mechanisms is necessary to improve the security of mobile devices. In Fig. 6, the execution flow of application installation event between self-aware agent, access control and open anti-virus is illustrated. It shows the sequence of actions in the mobile platform during application installation event and gathering of information through observation of activities by security mechanisms. In the diagram, malicious verification of the application is initiated by install service but it can also be initiated by the access control system.

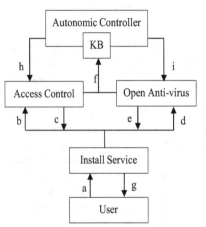

a.   Install action by user
b.   Policy verification
   i.   Is install allowed?
   ii. Is application origin allowed?
c.   Verification status
d.   Malicious application verification
   i.   Is malicious by vendor?
   ii. Is malicious by autonomic controller?
e.   Verification status
f.   Monitored information storage
g.   User notification (success or fail with reason for denial)
h.   Update policy repository and adapt execution settings
i.   Update malicious repository and adapt execution settings

Fig. 6. Conceptual design of self-adaptive security

4   Related Work

A number of researches have been carried out on self-aware computing for realization of autonomous systems. There are also models provided to design self-aware property based systems [30,31]. MAPE-K [30] is one of the earliest and most adopted architecture for modeling autonomic systems. It has five components: Monitor (M), Analyser (A), Planner (P), Executor (E) and Knowledge (K). The knowledge component is shared by MAPE components. SEEC is another framework for self-aware computing that employs Observes (O), Decide (D) and Act (A) components for modeling self-awareness [31]. The O and A components are similar to M and E components of MAPE-K and the tasks of A and P components are collectively carried out by D component in SEEC framework. In [32], a Self-Adaptive Authorization Framework (SAAF) is used to manage access control automatically for computers. It is specifically meant for systems having multi-user and access restrictions based on authority (e.g., administrator, researcher and supervisor). The same framework can be usable in multi-user mobile platforms like Android but it will apply restrictions at user level on applications accessibility. It may not work at resource feature level (e.g., deny network association if security is WEP) in mobile environment and also lacks context based restrictions. In case of mobile security, the self-awareness is primarily used in malware detection techniques [33–36].

The proposed security design of this work has components similar to MAPE-K and SEEC frameworks but it differs in operations. In our work, the tasks are shared between the self-aware agent and security mechanisms. The task of monitoring and enforcing security measures are performed by the security mechanisms while the self-aware agent handles learning and optimization tasks. Since security mechanisms possess greater ability to regulate the mobile device activities, they can perform monitor functions better than any other components. The security measure enforcement is similar to Executor (E) in MAPE-K. The separation of tasks allows to distribute the workload among the components of the security design and enables the cooperation of security mechanisms that results in achieving better security. The interaction between the single self-aware agent and multiple security mechanisms helps to construct holistic view of application behavior patterns distinctively. The security mechanisms are uniquely designed as such that their operations can be controlled easily through the deployment of self-aware agent.

5   Future Directions

Currently, we envisioned self-configuration as part of the self-aware agent. It is responsible for configuration of the learning and optimization/control processes. These processes cannot run continuously due to: (1) sufficient number of logs are required for optimal learning; (2) initiating learning process will result in resource wastage if there is no considerable number of logs recorded between successive learning sessions; and (3) the configuration process should not use resources when the device is busy. Determining sufficient number of logs that are required for optimal learning is necessary for achieving appropriate level of accuracy in pattern detection. The availability of logs depends on the successive time period for learning process execution. Care should be taken in determining successive time period for learning process execution and the period should be adaptable at runtime depending on several factors including environment, available resources and device usage history. If the interval is long, optimal learning can be achieved due to huge number of logs but device may fail to detect/prevent unexpected new events that are occurred during the waiting period. If it is short, it leads to unnecessary resource consumption and inefficient learning. Hence, an algorithm that is able to dynamically adapt the learning interval and the required number of logs will be developed.

Learning algorithm plays a decisive role in the detection of malicious activities and threats. The algorithm has to have high detection accuracy with very low false positives. Given that the operating environment is mobile platform, the algorithm should be light-weight that requires acceptable level of resources with low energy consumption. Thus, accuracy and resource requirement have to be taken into account when selecting and customizing the learning algorithm.

To create a secure ecosystem and to harness the self-aware agent benefits running in multiple devices, establishing communication among agents is a necessity. The self-aware agent has to be designed to operate as distributed intelligent system in order to recognize, cooperate, assist and share knowledge among its peers. In addition, they have to possess competitive traits to handle malicious agents. Therefore, self-aware agent needs to be designed to operate in hybrid mode by combining cooperative and competitive traits.

Finally, the security of knowledge base is critical as it always resides within the mobile devices. There are possibilities that the knowledge can be targeted by the adversaries with an intention of obtaining/spoofing learned behavior patterns or for preventing the execution of tasks by the self-aware agent. It is compulsory to design a dedicated subsystem to handle the any request targeted to knowledge base for authenticity verification before allowing to perform any manipulation.

6 Summary

In this paper, we presented the design of self-aware security for mobile devices at concept level. The presented design has three interactive subsystems that are tasked to provide maximal protection by taking advantage of self-awareness. For seamless cooperation among security mechanisms as well as with self-aware agent, new design approach for the security mechanism has been proposed, as existing designs results in non-cooperative self-contained security mechanisms. The cooperation enables the self-aware agent to have a holistic view of mobile device activities, leading to better prediction of threats and enforcement of appropriate measures by security mechanisms. The design of access control and anti-virus security mechanisms are presented as case studies.

Acknowledgement. The authors gratefully acknowledge Tekes (the Finnish Funding Agency for Innovation), DIMECC Oy, and the Cyber Trust research program for their support.

References

1. Ericsson. Ericsson Mobility Report, November 2016. https://www.ericsson.com/assets/local/mobility-report/documents/2016/ericsson-mobility-report-november-2016.pdf. Accessed 22 Feb 2017
2. Gartner. Gartner says by 2018, more than 50 percent of users will use a tablet or smartphone first for all online activities (2014). http://www.gartner.com/newsroom/id/2939217. Accessed 22 Feb 2017

3. International Data Corporation. IDC: Smartphone OS Market Share, Q3 (2016). http://www.idc.com/promo/smartphone-market-share/os. Accessed 22 Feb 2017
4. Apple Developer. API Reference Apple Developer Documentation. https:// developer.apple.com/reference. Accessed 22 Feb 2017
5. Android Developer. Package Index Android Developers. https://developer.android. com/reference/packages.html. Accessed 22 Feb 2017
6. Apple. iOS6 Software Update (2012). https://support.apple.com/kb/DL1578? locale=en_US. Accessed 22 Feb 2017
7. Android. Security Enhancements in Android 6.0. (2016). http://source.android. com/security/enhancements/enhancements60.html. Accessed 22 Feb 2017
8. Bugiel, S., Davi, L., Dmitrienko, A., Fischer, T., Sadeghi, A.-R.: Xmandroid: a new android evolution to mitigate privilege escalation attacks. Technische Universität Darmstadt, Technical report TR-2011-04 (2011)
9. Enck, W., Gilbert, P., Han, S., Tendulkar, V., Chun, B.-G., Cox, L.P., Jung, J., McDaniel, P., Sheth, A.N.: Taintdroid: an information-flow tracking system for realtime privacy monitoring on smartphones. ACM Trans. Comput. Syst. (TOCS) **32**(2), 5 (2014)
10. Heuser, S., Nadkarni, A., Enck, W., Sadeghi, A.-R.: ASM: a programmable interface for extending android security. In: Proceedings of 23rd USENIX Security Symposium (2014)
11. Wang, X., Sun, K., Wang, Y., Jing, J.: Deepdroid: dynamically enforcing enterprise policy on android devices. In: Proceedings of 22nd Annual Network and Distributed System Security Symposium (NDSS 2015). The Internet Society (2015)
12. Conti, M., Crispo, B., Fernandes, E., Zhauniarovich, Y.: Crêpe: a system for enforcing fine-grained context-related policies on android. IEEE Trans. Inf. Forensics Secur. **7**(5), 1426–1438 (2012)
13. Nieminen, J., Savolainen, T., Isomaki, M., Patil, B., Shelby, Z., Gomez, C.: RFC 7668 - IPv6 over BLUETOOTH® low energy. https://tools.ietf.org/html/rfc7668. Accessed 23 Feb 2017
14. Wang, H., Xi, M., Liu, J., Chen, C.: Transmitting IPv6 packets over Bluetooth low energy based on BlueZ. In: 2013 15th International Conference on Advanced Communications Technology (ICACT), PyeongChang, pp. 72–77 (2013)
15. Andersen, M.P., Fierro, G., Culler, D.E.: System design for a synergistic, low power Mote/BLE embedded platform. In: 2016 15th ACM/IEEE International Conference on Information Processing in Sensor Networks (IPSN), Vienna, pp. 1–12 (2016)
16. Skorin-Kapov, L., Pripužić, K., Marjanović, M., Antonić, A., Žarko, I.P.: Energy efficient and quality-driven continuous sensor management for mobile IoT applications. In: 10th IEEE International Conference on Collaborative Computing: Networking, Applications and Worksharing, Miami, FL, pp. 397–406 (2014)
17. Angelopoulos, C.M., Evangelatos, O., Nikoletseas, S., Raptis, T.P., Rolim, J.D.P., Veroutis, K.: A user-enabled testbed architecture with mobile crowdsensing support for smart, green buildings. In: 2015 IEEE International Conference on Communications (ICC), London, pp. 573–578 (2015)
18. Zhao, D., Ma, H., Liu, L.: Frugal online incentive mechanisms for mobile crowd sensing. IEEE Trans. Veh. Technol. **PP**(99), 1 (2016)
19. Shu, L., Chen, Y., Huo, Z., Bergmann, N., Wang, L.: When mobile crowd sensing meets traditional industry. IEEE Access **PP**(99), 1 (2017)
20. Guang, L., Nigussie, E., Rantala, P., Isoaho, J., Tenhunen, H.: Hierarchical agent monitoring design approach towards self-aware parallel systems-on-chip. ACM Trans. Embedded Comput. Syst. (TECS) **9**(3), 1–26 (2010)

21. Isoaho, J., Virtanen, S., Tenhunen, H.: Current challenges in embedded communication systems. In: Innovations in Embedded and Real-Time Systems Engineering for Communication. IGI Global (2012)
22. Zhou, X., Demetriou, S., He, D., Naveed, M., Pan, X., Wang, X., Gunter, C.A., Nahrstedt, K.: Identity, location, disease and more: inferring your secrets from android public resources. In: 2013 ACM SIGSAC Conference on Computer & Communications Security, pp. 1017–1028. ACM (2013)
23. Narain, S., Vo-Huu, T.D., Block, K., Noubir, G.: Inferring user routes and locations using zero-permission mobile sensors. In: 2016 IEEE Symposium on Security and Privacy (SP), pp. 397–413. IEEE (2016)
24. Zhou, Y., Jiang, X.: Dissecting android malware: characterization and evolution. In: 2012 IEEE Symposium on Security and Privacy (SP), pp. 95–109. IEEE (2012)
25. Avira Holding GmbH. Avira Mobile Security (version 2.1). https://itunes.apple.com/us/app/avira-mobile-security/id692893556. Accessed 28 Feb 2017
26. NortonMobile. Norton Security & Antivirus (version 3.17.0.3205). https://play.google.com/store/apps/details?id=com.symantec.mobilesecurity. Accessed 28 Feb 2017
27. Trend Micro Incorporated. Trend Micro Mobile Security (version 5.2.1089). https://itunes.apple.com/us/app/trend-micro-mobile-security/id630442428. Accessed 28 Feb 2017
28. Avast Software. Mobile Security & Antivirus. https://play.google.com/store/apps/details?id=com.avast.android.mobilesecurity. Accessed 28 Feb 2017
29. Weyns, D., Malek, S., Andersson, J.: FORMS: unifying reference model for formal specification of distributed self-adaptive systems. ACM Trans. Auton. Adaptive Syst. **7**(1), 61 (2012)
30. Kephart, J.O., Chess, D.M.: The vision of autonomic computing. Computer **36**(1), 41–50 (2003)
31. Hoffmann, H., Maggio, M., Santambrogio, M.D., Leva, A., Agarwal, A.: SEEC: a framework for self-aware computing (2010)
32. Bailey, C., Montrieux, L., de Lemos, R., Yu, Y., Wermelinger, M.: Run-time generation, transformation, and verification of access control models for self-protection. In: Proceedings of the 9th International Symposium on Software Engineering for Adaptive and Self-Managing Systems (SEAMS 2014), pp. 135–144. ACM (2014)
33. Guo, D.F., Sui, A.F., Shi, Y.J., Hu, J.J., Lin, G.Z., Guo, T.: Behavior classification based self-learning mobile malware detection. J. Comput. **9**(4), 851–858 (2014)
34. Shabtai, A., Tenenboim-Chekina, L., Mimran, D., Rokach, L., Shapira, B., Elovici, Y.: Mobile malware detection through analysis of deviations in application network behaviour. Comput. Secur. **43**, 1–18 (2014)
35. Li, F., Clarke, N., Papadaki, M., Dowland, P.: Behaviour profiling on mobile devices. In: International Conference on Emerging Security Technologies, Canterbury, pp. 77–82 (2010)
36. Tong, F., Yan, Z.: A hybrid approach of mobile malware detection in Android. J. Parallel Distrib. Comput. **103**, 220–31 (2016)

Anti-malware Techniques:
Detection, Analysis, Prevention

Resident Security System for Government/Industry Owned Computers

Matthew Davis[(⊠)], Emrah Korkmaz, Andrey Dolgikh, and Victor Skormin

Binghamton University, Binghamton, NY 13902, USA
{mdavis7,ekorkma1,adolgikh,vskormin}@binghamton.edu

Abstract. The use of government and industry computers is restricted regarding their access, software applications, operations, and auxiliary hardware. Nevertheless, such computers are often subjected to cyber-attacks and unauthorized usage, whether malicious or benign. The technology outlined herein provides a resident security system that upon deployment detects, registers, and reports instances of computer misuse, thus providing early detection of malware and functioning as a deterrent for computer criminals/misusers. This technology is based on behavioral profiling of computer operation. Developed under the USAF funding, it has been implemented and tested.

Keywords: Computer security · Attack detection · Behavioral modeling · System calls · Functionalities

1 General

As cyber warfare rages, offensive strategy centers around malicious insiders and the use of advanced malware. In the past, malware attacks were perpetrated by hackers and petty cyber criminals for self-gratification and blackmailing. Although these attacks sometimes led to massive computer epidemics, plenty of information for attack mitigation could be attained during the early stages of the computer epidemics. For example, conventional antivirus software provides a sufficient means for detection and prevention of attack of this type. However, malware developers of today are backed by foreign governments and criminal enterprises with practically unlimited funding. This modern malware exhibits various advanced features (encryption, poly- and metamorphism, mimicry, multi-partied operation, etc.), and is intended for espionage and even sabotage of physical systems. A new development in cyber warfare is a single attack against high-value targets (industrial and government facilities). Such malware is highly specialized for the target environment and is expected to "peacefully" coexist with the host until some malicious actions are initiated. It does not create these previously mentioned epidemics and thus does not provide data for attack mitigation: the first instance of the attack could also be the last instance.

Malicious insiders utilize the full power of human intellect that is unmatched by computers, excellent technical backgrounds, and being insiders, an understanding of "what to look for" and "how to access it" in the system. Per CERT, "a malicious insider threat to an organization is a current or former employee, contractor, or other business

© Springer International Publishing AG 2017
J. Rak et al. (Eds.): MMM-ACNS 2017, LNCS 10446, pp. 185–194, 2017.
DOI: 10.1007/978-3-319-65127-9_15

partner who has or had authorized access to an organization's network, system, or data and intentionally exceeded or misused that access in a manner that negatively affected the confidentiality, integrity, or availability of the organization's information or information systems." From this definition, it is evident that the phenomenon of the insider is multifaceted and cannot be described precisely.

What makes a cyber-attack an attack is the malicious intent of the perpetrator. Malware implements the malicious intent of its developer, which could be deduced from the operations performed by the attacked computer. However, in many instances cyber-attacks are perpetrated through the unauthorized use of benign, fully legitimate software that, for example, enables the attacker to steal proprietary/classified data or simply to utilize the computer for unauthorized operations. The malicious intent of the human attacker could become obvious from his/her actions. In both cases malice is present in the behavior of the computer and in most cases, could be detected by the analysis of system calls or computer log data. Theoretically, under proper monitoring malicious behavior leaves digital trails that could be observed and processed for the detection of malicious intent before the damage occurs. While monitoring systems could be intentionally disabled, this very action already could be indicative of malicious intent. The assured timely detection of a successfully perpetrated attack or even a malicious intent is also a desired outcome since the inevitability of detection is a good deterrence for the attacker.

This paper presents an approach that, when implemented within networked computers, automatically detects unauthorized computer activities that could be attributed to malware attack or computer misuse by a human operator. Combined with a highly perceptive visualization, it provides the means for the formalization and analysis of computer behavior and facilitates the application of both anomaly and misuse detection. This approach additionally results in a reduced computer vulnerability to malware, complicates the task of an insider attack, and significantly enhances the chances of timely attack detection. Intended for enhanced intrusion detection systems (IDS), it has been experimentally validated [1–3].

2   Behavioral Modeling

The authors perceive behavior as a semantic pyramid (see Fig. 1). The lowest level of the pyramid represents elementary actions (events) that could be registered by a monitoring system. There is a limited number of distinctive elementary actions, which can be conceptualized as letters of an alphabet. Although the flow of elementary actions provides complete information on the process in question, it has a very low discriminating power for the recognition of normal/benign and malicious activities. The highest level of the pyramid represents the functionalities, i.e. a combination of actions that regardless of their specific realization could be associated with a specific, recognized goal. Functionalities could be conceptualized as sentences, undoubtedly malicious or benign in the particular context. One can see that the highest level of the semantic pyramid cannot be subjected to monitoring and the functionalities are to be deduced from the flow of elementary events. The intermediate levels of the semantic behavioral pyramid are chosen to facilitate efficient behavioral modeling, i.e. the development of formal expressions relating functionalities to elementary events. One can say that to assure efficiency, simplicity, and versatility, the sentences on the highest semantic level are to be composed of words, i.e. objects formed at the intermediate levels.

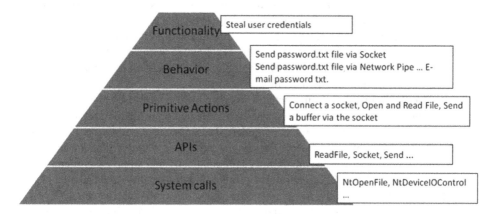

Fig. 1. Semantic pyramid of computer behavior.

In their current research, the authors suggested connecting system calls that are readily available in many operating systems in an object access mega-graph, providing detailed information on the computer behavior. Upon subjection to special compression procedures, a mega-graph falls into several well-separated components that represent functionalities and could be recognized by a human expert as such (see Fig. 2). Note that the shape of the individual components is defined by the visualization software and is irrelevant. However, the individual nodes are annotated and given the sufficient scale, each graph component could be easily understood by an expert. At the same time, individual components of the mega-graph that have already been discovered could be represented by Colored Petri Nets (CPN) suitable for off-line automatic analysis and on-line recognition in the flow of system calls.

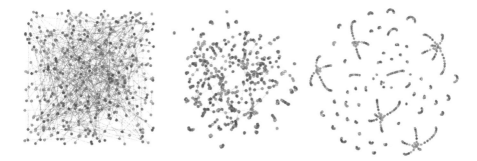

Fig. 2. Gradual emergence of functionalities by graph processing.

3   Establishing Normalcy

The essence of the off-line semantic analysis of the behavioral data is in the detection of the exhaustive set of unique functionalities describing normal operation (behavior) of the system in question. Each of these functionalities is constructed and represented using CPN. All system calls corresponding to the system functionality are connected in the order that they are observed, thus preserving the sequence of functionality operations. Additionally, each element of the functionality is contained within a connected component subgraph. These features, represented by CPN, form the system's normalcy profile, providing the basis for anomaly detection.

One can realize that in a similar fashion a system misuse profile, containing a set of known malicious functionalities, could also be established, thus facilitating the misuse detection. When a normalcy profile is compiled, the computer in question performs its regular, authorized applications while the system call flow is monitored and processed in real time. The functionalities are extracted automatically and when encountered for the first time are included in the normalcy profile: no functionality could be included more than once. Consequently, the number of included functionalities eventually levels off and stays unchanged for some arbitrarily chosen time, thus indicating that the stable normalcy profile exists and the extraction process is complete.

This could be an on-going process: any functionality unmatched to the normalcy profile could be "manually" added to the normalcy upon inspection. For example, the newly discovered functionalities associated with applying software updates and patches can be added to the normalcy profile. Figure 3 depicts a normalcy extraction process. It is worth mentioning that the task of functionality extraction (discovery) greatly benefits

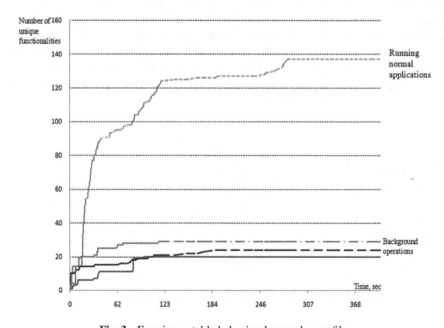

Fig. 3. Forming a stable behavioral normalcy profile.

from the existence of particular system calls clearly indicating the functionality completion. A misuse profile contains functionalities exposed by known software, generally malicious, or malicious in its contexts. It could be established by the execution of this software in a controlled environment. Functionalities of the normalcy profile and the misuse profile are represented by CPN, thus facilitating real-time functionality extraction from the flow of system calls.

4   Anomaly/Misuse Detection

Real-time application of the described technology implies that individual functionalities are being extracted from the flow of system calls and matched to the system normalcy profile and the system misuse profile using the specially developed graph matching tool. Functionalities matching the misuse profile undoubtedly represent malicious behavior patterns indicative of attacks. The unrecognized (anomalous) functionalities are treated as suspicious and are to be scrutinized. In addition, the system may detect and report an anomaly as an abnormal execution frequency of a legitimate functionality. The described approach is implemented in software and accompanied by extensive visualization [4, 5].

5   Detection of Misuse of an Office Computer

For verification and testing, the described system was deployed in a typical office computer environment that has only two legitimate applications: the Linux-based word processor Libre Office Writer and spreadsheet software Libre Office Calc. A customized normalcy profile for this computer was established by performing various tasks and modes of operation of these two software tools. The detected normalcy profile contained over three hundred functionalities that upon discovery, were automatically translated into Petri nets.

The real-time testing stage included "normal" usage of the computer, deployment of malware, utilization of illegitimate software, and performing prohibited operations. During this stage, an additional computer was employed to perform real-time application of the described security procedure and provide the appropriate visualization. Each figure below represents displays on the screen of the computer user (top) and the screen of his/her supervisor (bottom).

As seen in Fig. 4, the user runs the Libre Office Writer word processor and Libre Office Calc spreadsheet applications. The supervisor's screen demonstrates how the observed system calls (represented by different colors) are interconnected into graphs and individual functionalities are constructed. Note that the display does not show any completed functionalities: any completed functionality consistent with the normalcy profile is immediately removed from the display because it does not carry any important detection information.

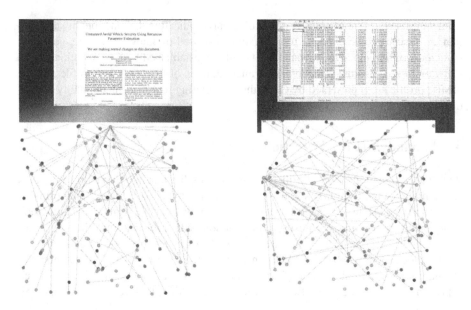

Fig. 4. Running approved applications: functionalities are being detected and removed from the picture upon matching the normalcy profile. (Color figure online)

The top left of Fig. 5 clearly indicates that the computer user is engaged in playing Solitaire. Although this application is clearly benign and will not be detected by an off-the-shelf antivirus software, in our context it is an illegitimate application. While

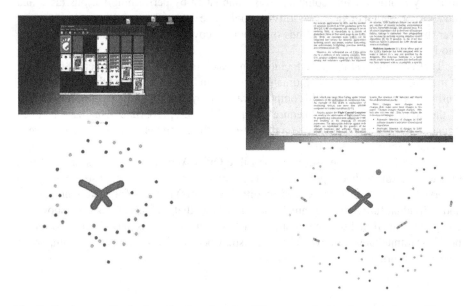

Fig. 5. Benign unauthorized application: functionalities unmatched to the normalcy profile are detected, marked in red, and preserved for future analysis. (Color figure online)

executed, Solitaire exposes several specific functionalities, unmatched by the existing normalcy profile, and the appropriate graphs are shown on the supervisor's display marked in red (lower left). The right section of Fig. 5 indicates that although the user resumed legitimate activity with the word processor, the indication of the perpetrated misuse is recorded on the supervisor's display for further actions.

The top left of Fig. 6 is a typical display accompanying the insertion of a USB drive into the user's computer which in many instances is prohibited. This action results in a sequence of interrelated system calls that are assembled into anomalous functionalities, displayed on the supervisor's computer in red (the evidence of previously detected Solitaire is still shown). The top right of Fig. 6 indicates that the user is copying data to the inserted USB drive. This is surely a prohibited action that is at the core of many notorious cases of information attacks. It could be seen that the supervisor's display shows the entire history of misuse-type attacks, perpetrated without any malicious software.

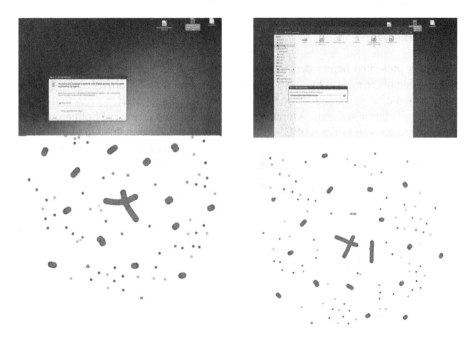

Fig. 6. Unauthorized insertion of a USB drive and copying files, indicating potential malicious insider activity is detected, registered, and reported.

The above experiments validate the proposed approach. These experiments were expanded to further test the ability of the software to detect system operations not captured in the established normalcy profile. The results are shown in Table 1, where all "illegitimate" operations implemented on the computer were detected and captured by the security software. These tested operations cover an assortment of potential computer misuses from playing games to adjusting system settings. Thus, the detection of a variety of operations is indicative of the versatility of the software.

Table 1. Security software detection of computer misuse

Illegitimate operations compared to normalcy profile	Detected by security software
System Settings	Yes
Firefox Web Browser	Yes
Thunderbird Email Service	Yes
LibreOffice Impress	Yes
LibreOffice Math	Yes
LibreOffice Draw	Yes
Plugging in USB Drive	Yes
Plugging in USB Webcam	Yes
Sudoku	Yes
Solitaire	Yes
Mines	Yes
Mahjongg	Yes

Results presented herein demonstrate the ability to detect computer misuse. The identification of the misuse so far is a different story. One should realize that the specific configuration of a "graph in red" on the supervisor's display is merely a function of the graph representation software. Moreover, there are several versions of Solitaire games and software, as well as types of USB drives. Additional research leading to the establishment of generic patterns or pattern libraries enabling misuse identification is required. Nevertheless, our software can provide annotation to the individual nodes of "graphs in red" thus enabling a professional to interpret the nature of computer operations performed by the sequence of "red nodes." In some ways, this task is similar to reading a code written in Assembler.

It is important to realize that in some cases inconsistency in object access graphs accompanying the connection of external hardware to a computer could be caused by some hidden malicious functions of the hardware. Therefore, the described technology has the potential for malicious hardware detection as well.

6 Detection of Malware Attacks

Attacked computers exhibit specific behavioral patterns that could be successfully detected by extracting specific functionalities from the flow of system calls. As indicated earlier, known attacks could be represented by a special library and detected as an instance of misuse. Unknown attacks could be detected as anomalies, represented by an annotated graph, and then later identified by an expert.

Figure 7 (left) depicts a display of system call sequences where completed functionalities (graph components) matched to the normalcy profile are removed, but the completed anomalous functionalities are shown in red. The right part of Fig. 7 previews the detected anomalous functionalities with necessary annotations enabling identification of the attack.

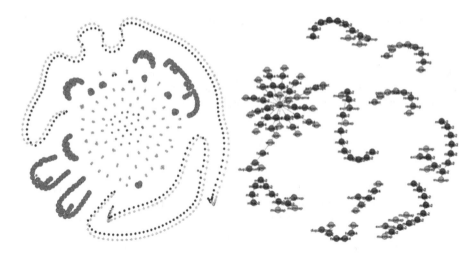

Fig. 7. Display and preview of anomalous functionalities for detection and identification.

7   Related Works

Behavior-based modeling approaches to computer security have been taken by other researchers as well. Denning makes use of computer subject activity profiles to monitor subject behavior with respect to objects such as files, programs, terminals, etc. This behavior is representative of the subject's signature normal activity with such objects [6]. Hofmeyer, Forrest, and Somayaji track system calls and collect normal behavior both synthetically and in a live user environment. This method utilizes recorded lengths of system call sequences to monitor computer operations, and identifies any operations that provide an unrecognized sequence of system calls [7]. Authors Balajinath and Raghavan describe a method of using genetic algorithms to learn user behavior on a system. User behavior is then compared in real-time to non-intrusive behavior to detect any potential intrusions [8]. Ye uses a Markov chain model to represent the temporal profile of normal behavior on computers and networks. This model learns from historical normal behavior, which is analyzed to infer the probability that current behavior is considered benign and non-intrusive [9].

8   Conclusion

Behavioral IDS utilizing anomaly based and misuse based detection is developed and presented. It employs an original graph reduction approach and utilizes Colored Petri Nets for the discovery and consequent real-time extraction of functionalities indicative of authorized and unauthorized, normal and anomalous computer behavior. The dependability of the described approach, when implemented in a resident security system, requires additional efforts, resulting in a protected domain within a computer where this security system will reside. The developed technology offers a potentially constructive approach for the processing of computer logs and the analysis of the behavior of network administrators.

Acknowledgement. The authors are grateful to the Air Force Office of Scientific Research and the Project Manager Dr. Robert Herklotz for the support of the authors' work in the computer security area. The authors are also grateful to Dr. A. Volynkin of CERT for the fruitful discussion of the research results.

References

1. Dolgikh, A., Birnbaum, Z., Liu, B., Chen, Y., Skormin, V.: Cloud security auditing based on behavioral modeling. In: Gamble, R., Ray, I. (eds.) International Journal of Business Process Integration and Management, vol. 7, issue 2. pp. 137–152. Inderscience, Genève, Switzerland (2014)
2. Birnbaum, Z., Dolgikh, A., Skormin, V.: Intrusion detection using n-grams of object access graph components. In: ICDS 2014, The Eighth International Conference on Digital Society, pp. 209–215. IARIA, Barcelona, Spain (2014)
3. Dolgikh, A., Nykodym, T., Skormin, V., Birnbaum, Z.: Using behavioral modeling and customized normalcy profiles as protection against targeted cyber-attacks. In: Kotenko, I., Skormin, V. (eds.) MMM-ACNS 2012. LNCS, vol. 7531, pp. 191–202. Springer, Heidelberg (2012). doi:10.1007/978-3-642-33704-8_17
4. Tokhtabayev, A.G., Skormin, V.A., Dolgikh, A.M.: Expressive, efficient and obfuscation resilient behavior based IDS. In: Gritzalis, D., Preneel, B., Theoharidou, M. (eds.) ESORICS 2010. LNCS, vol. 6345, pp. 698–715. Springer, Heidelberg (2010). doi: 10.1007/978-3-642-15497-3_42
5. Graph based intrusion detection. http://goo.gl/1N24qc. Accessed 17 July 2014
6. Denning D.: An intrusion-detection model. IEEE Trans. Softw. Eng. **SE-13**(2) (1987). IEEE, Lincoln, Nebraska
7. Hofmeyr, S.A., Forrest, S., Somayaji, A.: Intrusion detection using sequences of system calls. J. Comput. Secur. **6**(3), 151–180 (1998)
8. Balajinath, B., Raghavan, S.V.: Intrusion detection through learning behavior model. Comput. Commun. **24**(12), 1202–1212 (2001)
9. Ye, N.: A markov chain model of temporal behavior for anomaly detection. In: Proceedings of the 2000 IEEE Systems, Man, and Cybernetics Information Assurance and Security Workshop, vol. 166, pp. 171–174. West Point, NY, June 2000

tLab: A System Enabling Malware Clustering Based on Suspicious Activity Trees

Anton Kopeikin[1], Arnur Tokhtabayev[2(✉)], Nurlan Tashatov[1],
and Dina Satybaldina[1]

[1] L.N. Gumilyov Eurasian National University, Astana, Kazakhstan
[2] T&T Security LLP, Astana, Kazakhstan
arnur@tntsecure.kz

Abstract. We present a new approach for malware clustering in the domain of their behavior. To this end, we use a system called tLab that offers analysis and detection of modern complex malware including user-oriented and targeted attacks. Due to technologies used, tLab identifies and describes malware behavior at various levels of semantics, which makes it very instrumental in cluster analysis.

Technically, the system employs secure containers enabling user-dependent execution environment in malicious activity analysis. To provide effective malware detection, tLab has a technology for deep dynamic inspection of system-wide behavior, which allows for structural analysis and construction of so-called activity trees defined in the domain of system functionalities. Modified Hierarchical Colored Petri Nets are used for run-time recognition of system functionalities including obfuscated and distributed ones.

In this paper, we perform cluster analysis at the level of activity trees, which provide highly semantic representation of malicious behavior. Our clustering approach is evaluated with corpus of real malware families. Results demonstrated that the used activity tree domain enables excellent behavior clustering and provides better and more consistent results compared to antiviruses vendors.

Keywords: Behavioral malware clustering · Threat identification · Program behavior analysis · Malware detection · Functionality recognition

1 Introduction

Over last several years, malware production sees exponential growth [1]. Doubling in numbers every two years, malware already reached more than 600 million samples. Such exponential pace is apparently achieved by massive usage of malware generators and various complex packers, which essentially produce zero-day malware on-demand, e.g. when a victim visits a virus delivery site or when sending malicious documents. This ensures that each malware sample is unique and AV signature created for it will not match any other sample, which makes signature approach obsolete. To avoid more complex intrusion detection systems based on static analysis, adversaries employ code obfuscation including polymorphism and metamorphism techniques, which application was somewhat predicted thirty years ago in the first study of computer virus phenomena [2], i.e. so-called evolved copy of virus.

© Springer International Publishing AG 2017
J. Rak et al. (Eds.): MMM-ACNS 2017, LNCS 10446, pp. 195–210, 2017.
DOI: 10.1007/978-3-319-65127-9_16

Under such terms, the dynamic behavioral analysis seems to be the only credible approach to detect modern malware. However, recently, behavioral malware detection approaches encountered significant challenges due to difficulties in distinguishing specially crafted malware from goodware (legitimate software). To this end, modern advanced malware attempt to keep legitimate profile in their activity via using good-ware tools in the attack workflow. For instance, attack may use PowerShell scripts residing entirely in the windows registry, which almost removes non-trusted behavioral footprint [3]. Therefore, the entire attack could be outsourced to legitimate, even whitelisted software. Moreover, an adversary can perform so-called distributed attack that implies partitioning malicious functionality among several files, making each file individually benign, yet in combination they achieve malicious goal., e.g. private data exfiltration [4]. Since modern AV systems hardly correlate activity of several pro-cesses, such an attack may progress undetected.

Given such complexity in quality and massiveness in quantity of modern attacks, it makes sense to perform deep behavioral analysis on dedicated servers that provide all necessary computation power to apply comprehensive and heavy models to identify maliciousness in a sample activity. Such approach could be implemented as a next-generation sandbox that would enable high-level view of sample behavior for an expert who can bring in a verdict. Obviously, given the high volume of malware appearance, such a system needs to automatically group new samples, so that the expert would have to inspect only one representative sample to come up with the verdict for the entire group. Such malware grouping could be achieved by cluster analysis.

Currently, many AV vendors perform some sort of malware classification and clustering at the behavior level. However, as a recent trend many AV engines classify malware in a generic way, resulting in families' names being not informative regarding malware activity. Such classification leads to behavioral inconsistencies with respect to group members. This may happen due to complex malware, which behavior is not consistent in each execution. For instance, distributed attack may use different proxy processes and random artifact names (e.g. dropped files, processes etc.)

In this paper, we propose to address the challenge of clustering malware with respect to real semantic of the samples activity. Our goal was to properly cluster even complex and randomized malware such as distributed attack and ones with obfuscated behavior. To this end, we formulated and used a highly semantic behavioral model that is so-called activity trees. Such activity trees are determined at the level of simple and complex system functionalities having different threat level from benign to suspicious and malicious. We performed clustering analysis in the activity tree domain. In this research, we used the tLab system that allows for deep behavioral analysis and run-time recognition of complex functionalities [5]. The system uses Modified Hierarchal Colored Petri Nets (CPN) for dynamic analysis of the programs functionality.

This paper offers the following contributions: (i) we formulated and introduced of a semantic malware behavior model, i.e. activity tree; (ii) we proposed clustering in the domain of activity trees, which required representing the trees in the metric space; (iii) we evaluated real malware behavioral relationship and provided results validation (it required developing tree sorting method to compare them).

To demonstrate our approach, we performed clustering analysis on 2374 malware samples constituting more than 40 families. Finally, we overview behavioral similarity of malware samples based on clustering results.

2 Approach

2.1 tLab System Description

tLab system provides the identification of malware by the deep analysis of the its behavior, which is monitored in the isolated environment inside virtual containers [5]. The system uses a technology enabling behavior analysis at the level of activity trees specified in the functionality domain. The functionalities are recognized by modified Petri nets [6] revealing hidden complex activity at the level of the system calls.

As indicated in Fig. 1, tLab system contains an execution environment, which is a wrapper around the VirtualBox hypervisor, managing the isolated containers (virtual machines, VM). Inside each container there is a proprietary behavior detector, which performs deep, run-time analysis of the behavior of the examined samples to recognize malicious functionalities. Also, the detector traces the stream of the malicious activity spread and the correlation between executable objects. Moreover, inside the VM there is the simulator of the user activity, which emulates clicks on GUI elements belonging to untrusted objects. Finally, the detector forms behavioral reports (profiles).

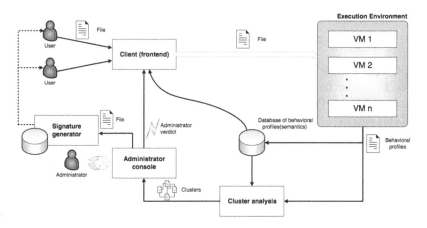

Fig. 1. Architecture of tLab system

Behavioral reports are saved in the base, which is used by the report analysis module. The module identifies the threat level for the executable object. The threat indicators are calculated on the base of the detected functionalities and activity trees. Here we distinguish various indicators including: persistence, OS intrusion, spyware activity, evasion, exploitation, proxy activity, network activity, atypical activity.

The given indicators depending on the malware behavior context can represent different threat levels from suspicious to malicious. A special algorithm is used to calculate the threat level, which considers many semantic factors, including the types of the detected functionalities, activity trees, behavior context of the executable object, execution environment settings, and the aspects of the object interaction with the user activity simulator. tLab collects different analytical data, from behavior models to threat indicators. Practically, such data can be used in data mining algorithms for further analysis of not only individual malware samples, but also their classes and families. In this paper, we focus on cluster analysis in the proposed domain of activity trees.

2.2   Functionality Recognition

From OS perspective, processes invoke API functions to perform system object operations that complete some semantically distinct *system actions*, such as writing data to a file or sending data to a specified IP address. We define individual functionality as a combination of such *system actions* that achieve a certain high-level objective.

The functionality is recognized in two stages: system calls and object manipulation (API traits). A manipulation may be performed through several alternative APIs operating on the same Kernel objects. API may invoke several additional minor system calls that are not critical for the manipulation implementation. Hence, only the essential, semantically critical part of an API should be recognized.

In our CPN models are employed for the recognition of malicious functionalities. A CPN could formally be defined as a tuple:

$$CPN = (C, P, T, A, N, F, G, E, I), \tag{1}$$

where: C – color set, P – set of places, T – set of transitions, A – set of arcs, N – node function, F – color function, G – guard function, E – arc expression function, I – initialization function [7].

CPN must reflect objects and manipulations. Hence, CPN places must represent the following states: created objects, which are ready to be manipulated; manipulations on the objects; pseudo states routing the control flow and functionalities.

As defined in (1), CPN has a *set of places* (P) that consists of four disjoint dedicated subsets – Object places, Manipulation places, Functional places and Pseudo places: $P = P_{obj} \cup P_{manip} \cup P_{fun} \cup P_{pseudo}$, such that, each Object place is associated with a unique OS object; every Manipulation place represents an individual operation with an object; any Functional place corresponds to a unique functionality and a Pseudo place. Functional place tokens represent successful recognition of the given functionality.

Places of CP-nets represent executed object operations; therefore, a transition must be attributed to execution of one of the equivalent system calls implementing the respective manipulations. The set of transitions consists of three sets: $T = T_{man} \cup T_{fun} \cup T_{pseudo}$, where T_{man} - represent system calls or a user level manipulation. T_{fun} - transitions, which constitute functionality trigger, T_{pseudo} - pseudo transitions that reflect conditional branches. Transition guard expressions check manipulation handles and parameters to ensure that transitions are enabled only by manipulations with correct attributes specified by functionality. It provides flexibility to distinguish similar yet semantically different functionalities.

2.3   Activity Trees

Revealing individual functionalities does not guarantee proper identification of the malicious activity. Because goodware frequently behaves like certain components in malware, e.g. installers, file encryptors and downloaders, making detection verdict based only on distinct functionalities may lead to false positives.

We must elevate the analysis semantics level, which in our view would be best represented by activity trees defined in the functionality domain. An activity tree is a directed acyclic graph representing the flow of functionalities invoked by related processes, i.e. chain of system events. Technically, this tree reflects inter-process and intra-process interaction between system objects. Here, the nodes correspond to various system objects (processes, files, registry keys, and network endpoints, etc), while edges symbolize interaction/operations. The root of the tree is always the malware sample being analyzed, nevertheless in some cases the processes interaction becomes the forest of trees due to the activity of OS components, initiated by the malware actions.

In Fig. 2, tLab shows the activity tree build for real malware sample. The tree starts with launching malware process. Then, the malware process starts process "pluguin. exe", which image was extracted in advance, and set it for autorun. Moreover, the sample injects into windows explorer that in its turn launches "pluguin.exe" again. Process plaguing.exe eventually performs some network activity. The advantage of visualizing malware as an activity tree lies in the ability to reflect proxy levels of the functionality. For instance, Fig. 2 indicates that network activity performed not by malware sample itself, but by its second-generation process child, which represents pure proxy activity frequently used in smart and targeted malware attacks.

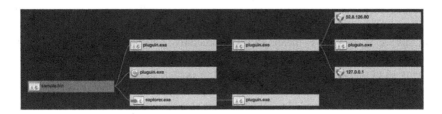

Fig. 2. Example of an activity tree

To sum up, our approach enables malware analysis and detection in the domain of activity trees. The choice of the domain is determined by the fact that the activity tree represents the most exact and informative image of a behavioral model of the malware. As far as the tree reflects the interaction of various malicious and suspicious functionalities, this allows for comparing and correlating even complex malware, such as distributed attacks. Besides, the behavioral model of malware, based on the activity tree, has the immunity to some methods of behavioral polymorphism, e.g. malware artefact names randomization (files, notes in the registry, etc.)

2.4   Behavioral Clustering

Application of classical clustering algorithms to malware behavior requires defining a metric feature space. The most straightforward way to represent behavior in a metric space would be fixed length functionality histogram. However, we need to reflect the structure of the activity, which cannot be provided by functionality histograms. Activity trees would best represent the feature space for malware behavior clustering. Though, the use of trees in their immediate form is not suitable for direct processing by cluster algorithms. We suggest using a numerical representation of the behavior tree, which, with some assumptions, still reflects the structure. To this end, we model an activity tree as a feature vector, which represents a tuple of frequency or presence of functionality binned by levels of the given activity tree.

$$ATV = (g(1, F_1), \ldots, g(1, F_n), g(2, F_1), \ldots, g(2, F_n), \ldots, g(m, F_1), \ldots, g(m, F_n)),$$

$$(2)$$

where for the activity tree having n functionality types and m levels: $g(i, F_j)$ is the frequency of j-th functionality (F_j) at the i-th level of the tree.

For instance, for the tree presented in Fig. 2, the tuple of the presence of only such functionalities as process creation and code injection would be: [1, 0, 1, 1, 1, 0, 1, 0], where the first pair corresponds to the level 1, the second pair to the level 2 etc. and odd element indicates process creation and even indicates code injection.

For certain functionality types, we consider only the presence of the functionality. To this end, samples of the same family can invoke the same functionality different number of times, for example, the number of extracted files with different names or number of Internet connections (C&C enumeration to find the available one). Therefore, due to such cases the related viruses can appear in different clusters. At the same time, the presence of functionalities at a tree level seems to be a stable attribute.

In this paper, we used K-means and Agglomerative Clustering algorithms. K-means is one of the simplest unsupervised learning algorithms, which follows a simple and easy way to classify a given data set through a certain number of clusters (assume k clusters) fixed a priori. The success of this algorithms depends on correctly defined number of clusters. We tried classical K-means to estimate the degree of simplicity of malware behavior similarity.

Agglomerative Clustering algorithm represents on a popular method for hierarchical cluster analysis. The algorithm starts with each of n samples as a separate cluster and iteratively merge the two nearest clusters to produce a single hierarchical clustering. We used agglomerative nesting algorithm with wards linkage method. Wards linkage method is preferred over other linkage methods because it achieved cophenetic correlation for our data. In our research, this clustering algorithm was aimed to reveal more complex behavioral relationship between malware samples. In our evaluation experiments, we used two distance metrics Cosine for functionality presence feature space and Euclidian for functionality frequency space respectively.

2.5   Results Validation

The selected feature space represents activity tree quite adequately, but not precisely. To estimate clustering performance with respect to malware behavior defined in actual activity trees, we developed method for class identification based on cluster data. Members of each class would have very similar or equivalent trees. The idea is to label classes based on some sort of distance between activity trees. To achieve this, we need to compare members with centroids. However, unlike K-means, Agglomerative Clustering algorithm (AC) does not compute centroids. In case of AC, the centroid of a cluster is considered a member that is the closest to all other members of the cluster. Then we can build the ground truth classes for the clustered samples. To this end we assign each member to the class that corresponds to the cluster which centroid is the nearest to the member with respect to activity trees. The number of ground-truth classes would be equal to the number clusters. Then we can perform external clustering evaluation.

To compare two activity trees, we use marked tree edit distance. This distance is defined as a minimal number of operations with marked nodes that needs to be executed to transform one tree to another, which can be computed by Zhang-Shasha algorithm [8]. In our experiments, we used an accelerated version of the classical Zhang-Shasha algorithm [9].

Due to the nature of our data, we had to perform tree normalization before computing tree edit distance. This happens since our activity trees are semantically insensitive to branch positions. At the same time, the tree edit distance algorithm in its classical form does not consider subtree isomorphism. Therefore, the algorithm may miscalculate the number of minimal operations.

The tree edit distance algorithm transforms one to tree to another using the following operations on nodes: insertion (i.e. insert node between parent and child vertices); removal (i.e. children node of the removed one get connected to its parent) and renaming. The used edit tree algorithm allows for assigning a weighting factor for each operation type. In our case the weighting factor was set to one.

Figure 3 demonstrates the result of calculation of the distance between two marked trees (the marker is a color). Various samples of the same malware family can perform actions in different order, and the given algorithm of the distance calculation considers the order of branches. Therefore, the calculation on the trees with large numbers of actions shows a long distance due to the large number of operations of renaming, although the same actions are performed. Hence, to make an additional minimization of the distance between activity trees their normalization was performed.

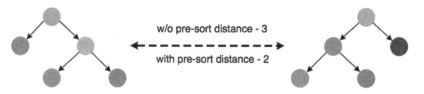

Fig. 3. Tree edit distance

Normalization lies in the sorting of the branches and leaves. Firstly, the sorting of braches is performed by the sum of child nodes and their frequency at each level. Then indiscernible nodes are sorted by their markings. If after this step there are still indiscernible nodes left, then the additional sorting is performed based on the internal structure of the children nodes, which takes into account the number of functionalities at each next level.

Below we present basic steps of used tree normalization algorithm:

1. Obtain the vectors representing the number of common type nodes at the different levels of the sorted branches;
2. Sort branches according to the total sum of children nodes and a vector in descending order;
3. If there are branches with indiscernible positions (identical outcomes of the previous step): sort branches inside this group according to the marker in the alphabetical order;
4. If there are branches with indiscernible position: sort branches inside this group according to the in-depth structure

Figure 4 demonstrate activity trees before and after the normalization respectively. As indicated in the graphs the algorithm performed the following transformation: the branch with the biggest number of nodes appeared at the top, and the nodes with identical in-depth structure (leaf nodes) became sorted in alphabetical order.

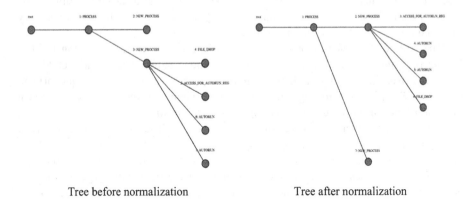

Tree before normalization   Tree after normalization

Fig. 4. Activity tree normalization examples

3   Experimental Evaluation

Currently, tLab system can detect more than 50 suspicious/malicious functionalities of different threat level. For this research, we pre-selected the following functionalities which threat level ranges from normal to malicious:

- New process creation
- Image set for autorun (via direct registry manipulation or proxy operations)

- New service installation (including obfuscated approach)
- Code injection to a legitimate process (via thread or DLL)
- Executable extraction (dropper)
- Connection to a remote host
- Renaming/moving of the dropped image
- Creation of a new task in task scheduler (task for image execution)

This selection is justified due to fact that any malware most frequently invokes these functionalities, because they play a part in almost any complex attack scenario.

3.1 Malware Set

In our experiments, we tested clustering performance with respect to malware families of 22 anti-virus engines. To this end, the sample set encompasses at least 25 families (Panda AV) and at most 462 families (McAfee). In our view, the most indicative and informative family labels are provided by DrWeb, which distinguished 41 distinct families in our sample. Having more than 3000 malware samples originally, we selected only those that constitute families having at least 30 members according to DrWeb. The resulting pre-selected representative malware set totaled 2374 samples.

To evaluate the degree of consistency between classification approaches of various AV engines we calculated their family size distribution presented in Fig. 5. It could be seen that with respect to the reference AV, i.e. Dr.Web, our sample set has certain distribution showing at least 30 samples per family. Figure 5 indicates that the family size distribution of VIPRE and Panda AVs are closest to the reference AV (Dr. Web). However, other AV engines do not match the reference distribution, meaning that AV engines differ quite significantly in malware classification.

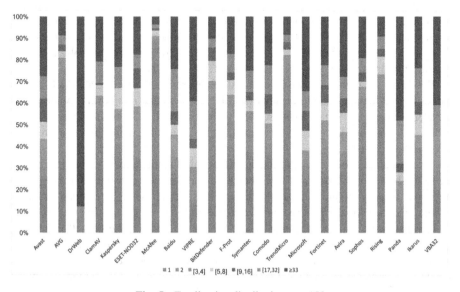

Fig. 5. Family size distribution per AV

Due to using purely generic naming conventions, some AV engines do not provide indicative classes. For instance, in our samples set McAfee has many too generic and non-informative signatures such Artemis!476B09D3AF3F, BackDoor-FCDE!-16FCA46305CA, PUP-FHQ!-E39887BBD499 etc. ThrendMicro defines malware in the same non-informative fashion, for instance TROJ_GEN.F0C2C00DE15 signature which seems to be auto-generated. Obviously, the aliases of such AV engines cannot be used as ground truth in our research. This justifies our chaise of the reference AV.

3.2   Behavioral Clustering

In the experiment, we pre-selected functionalities, which threat level ranges from normal to malicious (listed in Sect. 2.2). This selection is justified due to fact that any malware most frequently invokes these functionalities, because they play a part in almost any complex attack scenario.

We used scikit-learn package to perform Hierarchical Agglomerative Clustering (HAC) on sample set in our feature space that is presented by vector of the functionality frequency for each level of the activity tree.

Figure 6 shows bitmap of the clustered samples. The map indicates presence of the features, i.e. functionality at the different tree levels. The Y-axis indicates individual samples grouped by the obtained clusters. We show only clusters with at least five members. The X-axis depicts features sorted by the number the samples possessing the given feature. The feature labels denote a functionality name and the activity tree level at which the functionality was detected (L1 - the first level, L2 - second level etc).

As depicted in Fig. 6, functionality NEW_PROCESS_L1, i.e. new process start, is always observed at the first level of the activity tree, since malware sample launch is also considered as a new process. Looking at the second level of activity, one can see that malware frequently use other "proxy" processes to accomplish certain activity. Hence, the first two most frequently used functionalities at the second level are image drop/extraction (FILE_DROP L2) and new process launching (NEW_PROCESS L2). This indicates image drop and execute activity. Moreover, it could be observed that malware itself frequently sets for autorun (AUTORUN L2).

New service launch is always attributed to separate activity tree, at which it constitutes root. It happens due to peculiarities of the system call monitoring. As observed at system call level, to create a new service, a process, via LPC channel, sends a request to Services Control Manager (services.exe), which in its turn writes necessary records to Windows registry.

For each cluster, Fig. 6 clearly indicates the main functionalities represented by top ten sorted behavioral features. These depicted functionalities constitute the essence of the major activity of the cluster members. For some clusters, the bitmap provides enough evidence for samples risk level estimation.

For instance, by inspecting clusters 3, 12, 30, 33 and 35 one can attribute their samples to installers of unwanted or malicious software. Such installers usually extract executable images, launch new processes and set images for autorun. However, samples of cluster 35 demonstrate more aggressive persistence activity that is dropping an image

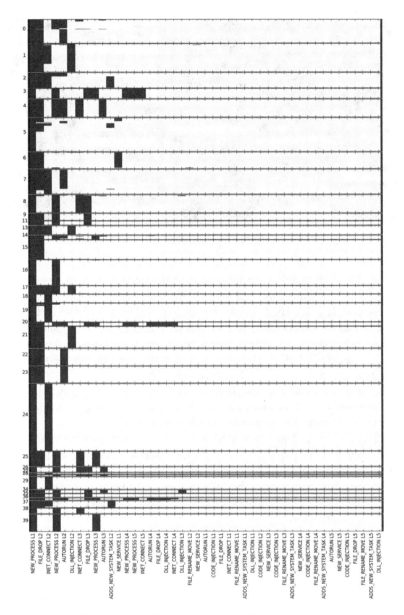

Fig. 6. Sorted feature bit map for clustered samples

and installing it as a service. Samples of clusters 24 and 26 establish internet connection and extract image, which may indicate either file dropper or downloader activity.

Samples of cluster 12 demonstrate complex activity that, at several levels of the tree, involves multiple functionalities including autorun set, new processes creation, image extraction and internet connection. Figure 7 shows the activity tree of a representative sample of the cluster 12. As can be seen at the plot, the sample performs a lot

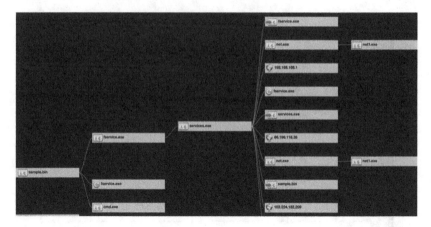

Fig. 7. Activity tree of representative sample of cluster 12

of proxy activity, especially at the forth level of the tree, such as additional autorun setting, multiple host connection and running previously dropped image.

Clusters as 0, 1, 2, 15, 16, 21 cannot be directly attributed to certain malware type. It is possible that the functionality of their samples depends on some unreached conditions, e.g. operation system settings, user account, execution time etc. Another reason may be that samples of this clusters simply did not execute any of the standard functionalities due to different attack pattern they commit.

In this paper, we evaluated our clustering approach only with respect to standard and most frequently used malicious functionalities. More extensive evaluation with all possible malicious indicators is planned in the future work.

To estimate to what degree our behavioral clusters are consistent with AV label classes we employed two popular external cluster evaluation metrics such as purity and completeness. For the given class ground truth (AV alias labels), the completeness metric measures how consistently the following property holds: members of a given class belong to the same cluster. Purity reflects the extent to which clusters contain only members of the same class.

Figure 8 depicts purity and completeness for aliases of five AV engines showing the best results. X-axis represents the number of clusters passed to HAC algorithm. Figure 8 also reflects cluster size distribution depicted in colored regions. As the plot indicates, when the number of cluster matches the number of reference AV families, i.e. 41 cluster, more than 60% of the clusters have more than 20 members (white colored region) and less than 17% clusters contain up to 5 members. This means that most samples were properly clustered with correct input data, which is confirmed by the completeness and purity values being 80% and 70% respectively. For 50 classes, F-Prot also shows good purity and completeness at the level of 80%. Apparently, these AV companies bring much attention to complex behavior patterns in classification process.

In general, for all AV engines, purity metric is increasing with the number of clusters and saturates at sixty. This means that for the given malware set, these AV

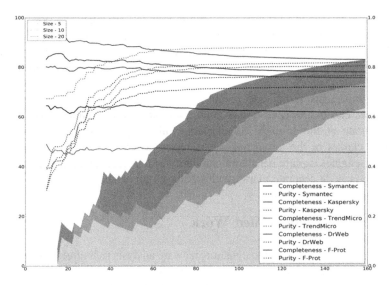

Fig. 8. Cluster purity and completeness with respect to AVs

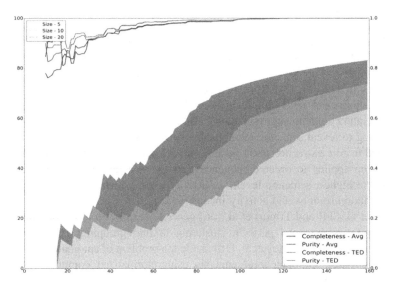

Fig. 9. Cluster purity and completeness with respect to tree edit distance classes

engines distinguish approximately the same number of malware classes, which correspond to up to 60 families.

To validate results of the clustering analysis based on the activity tree feature vectors (2), we produced class labels based on tree edit distance according to the methodology described in the previous section. To this end, we applied two algorithms in computing class labels. The first algorithm assigned class labels according to the closest centroid. The second algorithm, computes distance between a member to be classified and each cluster. Such a distance is calculated as average tree edit distance from the member to all cluster's members. Then we assign class label according to the shortest average distance.

Figure 9 presents purity and completeness of the clusters with respect to the obtained tree classes. As can be seen in the plot, the metrics computed by both algorithms saturate at the level of 80 clusters, which represents the tree number of behavioral classes of the tested malware samples. Therefore, even if in some cases several AV engines capture behavioral similarity of malware samples, in general most AVs fail to provide accurate malware clustering in the behavioral domain.

4 Background and Related Work

There are many works devoted to dynamic malware analysis techniques. Egele et al. [7] provide a detailed survey of various existing dynamic malware analysis systems. Jacob et al. [16] present a taxonomy of behavioral detection methods according to the reasoning techniques deployed in them. While dynamic malware analysis allows for extracting samples behavior, the system used in our research allows for identification of complex functionalities and provides a high-level semantic view the malware behavior in the space of activity trees.

Malware clustering in the behavioral domain was addressed in various publications [9, 10, 17, 23, 24]. Most of the proposed approaches employ vanilla clustering algorithms and selected appropriate feature space and distance metric.

Authors in [11, 17, 24] work with behavioral profiles generated by processing execution reports and generating feature sets. These works focus on scalable clustering by incorporating suitable approximations. BitShred [17] performs feature hashing and co-clustering to reveal semantic relationships between families. Their method requires preselected feature extraction and operates on vector data. Also, due to co-clustering it could not be applied to ordered sequence data for semantic analysis. Our approach works at the highest semantic level, i.e. activity trees, which is insensitive to certain behavior randomizations and activity inconsistencies.

Rieck et al. [24] and Trinius et al. [26] generate feature vectors based on n-grams from behavior reports and perform clustering to find groupings (class discovery). Wagener et al. [28] and Bailey et al. [10] tackle the problem of automated classification of malware based on behavioral analysis using normalized compression distance (NCD) metrics. Ye. et al. [29] proposed an ensemble method to generate consensus of multiple clustering using static features of unpacked malware.

Unlike n-gram based methods, our approach does not heavily depend on the sequence of functions execution. Instead, we correlate functionalities based on their semantic interdependency. This ensures that our clustering is robust to certain deviations in malware behavior such as interposition of the semantically distinct system actions, e.g. API invocations or primitive functionalities.

5   Conclusion

We introduced new malware clustering approach based on activity trees specified at the level of functionalities. Activity trees could be viewed as a high-level model suitable for accurate semantic analysis of the malware behavior interrelationship.

To this end we used the technology for deep dynamic inspection of system-wide behavior, which allows for structural analysis and construction of the activity trees defined in the domain of system functionalities. Modified Hierarchical CPNs are used for run-time recognition of functionalities including obfuscated and distributed ones.

The presented approach was evaluated on more than two thousand malware samples, which were clustered based on their activity trees. To this end, we represented trees in the specific metric space that captures the structure of the tree. The results showed better clustering performance compared to several AV vendors. Moreover, the results suggest such clustering is sustainable even with malware that may have randomized and interchanging behavior.

Acknowledgment. The tLab system was fully funded and developed by T&T Security LLP. The malware behavioral clustering research effort is funded by T&T Security LLP and is partially supported by scientific projects of L.N. Gumilyov Eurasian National University, Kazakhstan managed by the authors of this paper.

References

1. Malware Statistics Report by AV-Test Institute. https://www.av-test.org/en/statistics/malware/
2. Cohen, F.: Computer Viruses Theory and Experiments, Computers and Security, v. 6 (1987)
3. The Increased Use of PowerShell in Attacks. Whitepaper by Semantic Corporation (2016). https://www.symantec.com/content/dam/symantec/docs/security-center/white-papers/
4. Tokhtabayev, A.G., Skormin, V.A., Dolgikh, A.M.: Expressive, efficient and obfuscation resilient behavior based IDS. In: Gritzalis, D., Preneel, B., Theoharidou, M. (eds.) ESORICS 2010. LNCS, vol. 6345, pp. 698–715. Springer, Heidelberg (2010). doi:10.1007/978-3-642-15497-3_42
5. tLab (Version 1.5) [computer software], T&T Security LLP, Astana, Kazakhstan (2017)
6. Tokhtabayev, A., Skormin, V., Dolgikh, A.: Detection of worm propagation engines in the system call domain using colored petri nets. In: Proceedings of the IEEE IPCCC '07, USA, December 2008
7. Jensen, K.: Coloured Petri nets (2nd ed.): basic concepts, analysis methods and practical use, vol. 1, Springer, Berlin (1996)
8. Zhang, K., Shasha, D.: Simple fast algorithms for the editing distance between trees and related problems. SIAM J. Comput. **18**(6), 1245–1262 (1989)
9. Pawlik, M., Augsten, N.: RTED: a robust algorithm for the tree edit distance. Proc. VLDB Endow. **5**(4), 334–345 (2011)
10. Bailey, M., Oberheide, J., Andersen, J., Morley Mao, Z., Jahanian, F., Nazario, J.: Automated Classification and Analysis of Internet Malware (2007)
11. Bayer, U., Comparetti, P.M., Hlauschek, C., Kruegel, C., Kirda, E.: Scalable, behavior-based malware clustering. In: NDSS (2009)

12. Egele, M., Scholte, T., Kirda, E., Kruegel, C.: A survey on automated dynamic malware-analysis techniques and tools. ACM Comput. Surv. **44**(2), 6:1–6:42 (2008)
13. Falliere, N., Murchu, L.O., Chien, E.: W32.stuxnet dossier (2011). www.symantec.com White paper 2011
14. Gusfield, D.: Algorithms on Strings, Trees, and Sequences - Computer Science and Computational Biology. Cambridge University Press (1997)
15. Reversal and Analysis of Zeus and SpyEye Banking Trojans. Technical report, IOActive (2012)
16. Jacob, G., Debar, H., Filiol, E.: Behavioral detection of malware: from a survey towards an established taxonomy. J. Comput. Virol. **4**, 251–266 (2008)
17. Jang, J., Brumley, D., Venkataraman, S.: Bitshred: feature hashing malware for scalable triage and semantic analysis. In: Proceedings of the 18th ACM Conference on Computer and Communications Security, pp. 309–320. ACM (2011)
18. The flame: Questions and answers, May 2012. www.securelist.com
19. New malware classification system. www.securelist.com. Accessed June 2012
20. Rules for naming detected objects. www.securelist.com. Accessed 2012
21. Kirillov, I., Beck, D., Chase, P., Martin, R.: Malware attribute enumeration and characterization, MITRE (2011)
22. Langfelder, P., Zhang, B., Horvath, S.: Defining clusters from a hierarchical cluster tree: the dynamic tree cut package for r. Bioinformatics **24**(5), 719–720 (2008)
23. Li, P., Liu, L., Gao, D., Reiter, M.K.: On challenges in evaluating malware clustering. In: Jha, S., Sommer, R., Kreibich, C. (eds.) RAID 2010. LNCS, vol. 6307, pp. 238–255. Springer, Heidelberg (2010). doi:10.1007/978-3-642-15512-3_13
24. Rieck, K., Trinius, P., Willems, C., Holz, T.: Automatic analysis of malware behavior using machine learning. J. Comput. Secur. **19**(4), 639–668 (2011)
25. RSA. The Current State of Cybercrime and What to Expect in 2012. Technical report, RSA (2012)
26. Trinius, P., Holz, T., Gobel, J., Freiling, F.C.: Visual analysis of malware behavior using tree maps and thread graphs. In: 2009 6th International Workshop on Visualization for Cyber Security, pp. 33–38 (2009)
27. Ukkonen, E.: Constructing suffix trees on-line in linear time. In: IFIP Congress, pp. 484–492 (1992)
28. Wagener, G., State, R., Dulaunoy, A.: Malware behaviour analysis. J. Comput. Virology **4** (4), 279–287 (2007)
29. Ye, Y., Li, T., Chen, Y., Jiang, Y.: Automatic malware categorization using cluster ensemble. In: Proceedings of the 16th ACM SIGKDD International Conference on Knowledge Discovery and data mining, KDD 2010, pp. 95–104. ACM, New York (2010)

Malware Analysis and Detection via Activity Trees in User-Dependent Environment

Arnur Tokhtabayev[1(✉)], Anton Kopeikin[2], Nurlan Tashatov[2], and Dina Satybaldina[2]

[1] T&T Security LLP, Astana, Kazakhstan
arnur@tntsecure.kz
[2] L.N. Gumilyov Eurasian National University, Astana, Kazakhstan

Abstract. We present a new system that offers detection and analysis of modern complex malware including user-oriented and targeted attacks. These attacks stem from users' misbehavior, e.g. misinterpreting or ignoring security alerts, which lead to proliferation of malicious objects inside trusted perimeter of cyber-security systems (e.g. exclusion list of AVs). The attack mechanisms include strategic web compromise, spear phishing, insider threat and social network malware. Moreover, targeted attacks often deliver zero-day malware that is made difficult to be detected, e.g. due to distributed malicious payload.

The system provides a secure container enabling user-dependent environment in malicious activity analysis, which is achieved by user interaction simulation in real time. The user interaction simulator recognizes GUI components and clicks through them according to click patterns of a typical user, e.g. office employee. To provide effective malware detection, our team developed a new technology for deep dynamic inspection of system-wide behavior, which is based on structural analysis of so-called activity trees defined in the domain of system functionalities. We use Modified Hierarchical Colored Petri Nets for run-time recognition of system functionalities including obfuscated and distributed ones. We our system with corpus of real malware families. Results show high efficiency of our system in detecting and blocking malware while having low system overhead.

Keywords: Threat identification · Zero-day malware · Attacks on a user · Distributed malware · Targeted attacks

1 Introduction

In thirty years after the first study of a computer virus phenomena [1], more than half a billion viruses in the world were reported and 390 000 malware samples appear every day [2]. In addition to increasing volume of virus production, malware developers continuously have been searching for yet new ways to attack hosts and evade existing popular cyber-defense systems, e.g. anti-viruses (AV) and intrusion detection systems (IDS). To intrude, an attacker must solve at least two challenges: develop a malware that is not detected by AVs and deliver the malware to a victim host. Attackers advanced in both challenges.

To avoid detection, adversaries develop complex *zero-day malware* that is not yet known for current versions of AV. This ensures that each malware sample is unique and

© Springer International Publishing AG 2017
J. Rak et al. (Eds.): MMM-ACNS 2017, LNCS 10446, pp. 211–222, 2017.
DOI: 10.1007/978-3-319-65127-9_17

AV signature created for it will not match any other sample, which makes signature approach obsolete. Apparently, the credible approach to detect such malware is dynamic behavioral analysis. However, recently, behavioral malware detection approaches encountered significant challenges making it difficult to distinguish specially crafted malware from goodware (legitimate software).

First, behavior of legitimate software become more and more aggressive and deviant in the sense of performing side activity that is not related to their main functionality. For instance, many programs not related to networking, such as text editors, document viewers and file managers may perform online update that implies connecting to remote server and downloading an executable. This functionality is exactly what a downloader malware would perform. Another example would be legitimate ad installers that install several tools, set them to autorun and change web browser settings such as home page, extensions etc. Such an activity is usually performed by malware at the stage of persistence. Moreover, certain low-profile cryptors (ransomware) behave very similarly to several legitimate third-party archiving utilities. In other words, nowadays goodware perform functionalities that traditionally ware attributed to malware, hence it becomes increasingly difficult to distinguish goodware from malware at the behavior level.

Second, modern advanced malware attempt to keep legitimate profile in their activity via using goodware tools in the attack workflow. For instance, attack may use Powershell scripts residing entirely in the windows registry, which almost removes non-trusted behavioral footprint. Therefore, the entire attack could be outsourced to legitimate, even whitelisted software. Moreover, an adversary can perform so-called distributed attack that implies partitioning malicious functionality among several files, making each file individually benign, yet in combination they achieve malicious goal., e.g. private data exfiltration [3]. Since modern AV systems hardly correlate activity of several processes, such an attack will progress undetected.

One of the recent malware distribution method widely adopted by adversaries are *user-oriented attacks*, which are directed to user errors. These attacks include spear phishing, strategic web compromise, contaminated SEO, social network malware and insider threat. In fact, such attacks are often preceded by social engineering phases. As a result, the user is persuaded to ignore/overwrite alerts and recommendations of IDS. Then the user performs dangerous operations with vulnerable applications such as opening suspicious/malicious web links, executing suspicious files or opening documents with mistrustful script. In combination with zero-day exploits this leads to proliferation of malicious objects.

Due to high efficiency of these offensive approaches, they are also frequently used in professional targeted attacks against organizations or groups of people such as Advanced Persistence Threat (APT).

Unfortunately, current IDSs do not offer credible defensive solutions for these problems. It is clear, that one needs innovate solutions that must provide security even for an ignorant user.

In this paper, we present a novel intrusion prevention system based in a secure container that protects a host from abovementioned attacks. When necessity comes, secure container seamlessly analyzes malicious activity of vulnerable applications being under attack in a specific virtual environment that enables high fidelity in malicious activity analysis. Such high execution environment fidelity is achieved by user interaction simulation in real time. The user interaction simulator recognizes GUI components and clicks through them according to click pattern of a typical user, e.g. office worker.

Our system allows for run-time detection of malicious functionalities and deep analysis of the so-called activity trees to identify even specially crafted "well-behaving" malware. To this end, we applied Modified Hierarchal Colored Petri Nets (CPN) for dynamic analysis of the programs functionality.

The contributions of the paper are as follows: description of an emerging threat named user-oriented attacks, a novel malicious behavior analysis and detection technology based on activity trees defined in the functionality domain, introduction and evaluation of the developed container system that protects from zero-day and user-oriented attacks.

To demonstrate our approach, we implemented a prototype of the secure container system. The system has been tested for detection of several malicious functionalities and various malicious payloads.

2   System Description

The secure container system provides seamless malware identification at the level of program activity. The system enables object execution isolation and effective malicious activity analysis.

Isolation allows for running checked malware and seamlessly imitates all user interaction with vulnerable applications in segregated, disposable containers, which are backed by virtual machines. It ensures that such applications will not harm the OS being checked under attacking scenarios.

Malicious activity analysis allows for mitigating attacks by continuously monitoring processes behavior at run-time inside each container. We employ a technology of behavior analysis at the level of activity trees defined in functionality domain. Functionalities are recognized via modified CPN [4], which detects hidden and complex malicious functionality at the system call level.

2.1   Functionality Recognition

From OS perspective, processes invoke API functions or system calls to perform system object operations (manipulations) that complete some semantically distinct *system actions*, such as writing data to a file or sending data to a specified IP address. We define individual functionality as a combination of such *system actions* that achieve a certain high-level objective.

The functionality is recognized in two stages: system calls and object manipulation (API traits). A manipulation may be performed through several alternative APIs operating on the same Kernel objects. API may invoke several additional minor system calls that are not critical for the manipulation implementation. Hence, only the essential, semantically critical part of an API should be recognized.

In our system, CPN models are employed for the recognition of malicious functionalities.

A CPN is defined as a tuple:

$$CPN = (C, P, T, A, N, F, G, E, I), \tag{1}$$

where: C – color set, P – set of places, T – set of transitions, A – set of arcs, N – node function, G – color function, G – guard function, E – arc expression function, I – initialization function [5].

To recognize functionalities CPN must reflect objects and manipulations. Hence, CPN places must represent the following states: created objects, which are ready to be manipulated; manipulations on the objects; pseudo states routing the control flow and functionalities.

According to formalism 1, our CPN model has a *set of places* (P) that consists of four disjoint dedicated subsets – Object places, Manipulation places, Functional places and Pseudo places: $P = P_{obj} \cup P_{manip} \cup P_{fun} \cup P_{pseudo}$, such that, each Object place is associated with a unique OS object; every Manipulation place represents an individual operation with an object; any Functional place corresponds to a unique functionality and a Pseudo place. Functional place tokens represent successful recognition of the given functionality.

Places of CP-nets represent executed object operations; therefore, a transition must be attributed to execution of one of the equivalent system calls implementing the respective manipulations. The set of transitions consists of three sets: $T = T_{man} \cup T_{fun} \cup T_{pseudo}$, where T_{man} - represent system calls or a user level manipulation. T_{fun} - transitions, which constitute functionality trigger, T_{pseudo} - pseudo transitions that reflect conditional branches. Transition guard expressions check manipulation handles and parameters to ensure that transitions are enabled only by manipulations with correct attributes specified by functionality.

To provide flexibility to distinguish similar yet semantically different functionalities and overcome behavioral obfuscation, several modifications were introduced to CPN model. These modifications extend CPN recognition semantics and provide the following new properties.

Multidimensional token color function. This modification allows for storing multitude of system call attributes in the token to achieve efficiency in recognizing complex subsystem API (e.g. kernel32.CreateProcess). In fact, this feature minimizes overall CPN size.

Token genealogy. This modification enables tracing transitions firing sequence to identify system calls that initially triggered the certain functionality. This is applicable for resolving a functionality that can be implemented by alternative system calls. For instance, image auto-execute could achieved via setting registry or event task scheduler.

Token polymorphism. It implies dynamic token structure is mutable and is reshaped by certain events. Usually CPN tokens are defined by place type and their structure is fixed during Petri network simulation, only value can change, e.g. color. In our modification, token structure can change to adjust to variations of the functionality being recognized. Practically, one polymorphic token can be used in identifying several realizations of the same complex functionality. Moreover, such a token can reflect multitude of repetitive events without extending CPN structure (places/transitions). Finally, this feature, in principle, allows for building CPN that could self-adjust to recognize previously unknown realizations of the malicious functionalities.

2.2 Activity Trees

Revealing individual functionalities does not guarantee proper identification of the malicious activity. Because goodware frequently behaves like certain components in malware, e.g. installers, cryptors and downloaders, making detection verdict based only on distinct functionalities may end up in false positives.

Therefore, we must elevate the analysis semantics level that in our view would be best represented by activity trees defined in the functionality domain. An activity tree is a directed acyclic graph representing the flow of functionalities invoked by related processes, i.e. chain of system events. Technically, this tree reflects inter-process and intra-process interaction between system objects. In such a tree, the nodes correspond to various system objects (processes, files, registry keys, and network endpoints, etc.), while edges symbolize interaction/operations. In our case the root of the tree is always the malware sample being analyzed, nevertheless in some cases the processes interaction becomes the forest of trees due to the activity of OS components, initiated by the malware actions.

Figure 1 depicts a screenshot made in our system that shows the activity tree build for real malware sample. As indicated in the plot the tree starts from launching malware process. Then malware process starts process "pluguin.exe", which image was extracted in advance, and sets it for autorun. Moreover, the sample injects into windows explorer that in its turn launches "pluguin.exe" again. Process plaguing.exe eventually performs some network activity. The advantage of visualizing malware as an activity tree lies in the ability to reflect proxy levels of the functionality. For instance, Fig. 1 indicates that network activity performed not by malware sample itself, but by its second-generation process child, which represents pure proxy activity frequently used in smart and targeted malware attacks.

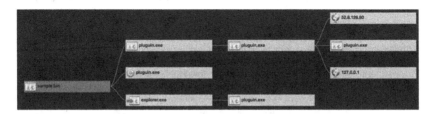

Fig. 1. Example of an activity tree

To sum up, our approach enables malware analysis and detection in the domain of activity trees. The choice of the domain is determined by the fact that the activity tree represents the most exact and informative image of a behavioral model of the malware. As far as the tree reflects the interaction of various malicious and suspicious functionalities, this allows for comparing and correlating even complex malware, such as distributed attacks. Besides, the behavioral model of malware, based on the activity tree, has the immunity to some methods of behavioral polymorphism, e.g. malware artefact names randomization (files, notes in the registry, etc.)

2.3 Behavioral Indicators

Currently, our system can detect more than 50 suspicious/malicious functionalities of different threat level. Depending on the activity context (activity tree), these indicators can be attributed to eight categories, so-called indicators described in Table 1. Each of the indicator reflect maliciousness/suspiciousness in a certain behavioral domain. Some

Table 1. Behavioral indicators

Category	Functional activity and goals
Persistence	This activity related to malware persistence, which enables malware to survive in the OS (e.g. after reboot, malware process termination or image deletion). The simple approach is to drop image and install it as a service or set itself for autorun. Some recent malware may employ more sophisticated self-persistence methods such as recurring system proxy tasks camouflaged via goodware (e.g. PowerShell scripts or system app piggybacking). The main challenge here is to distinguish malware persistence activity from legitimate installer of a goodware. For instance, both malware and goodware may drop image and set to autorun, however malware usually does not display dialog installer window offering a user to select setup configuration
OS invasion	Malware permanently changes state of the host software via modifying OS settings, overwriting system data or native executable objects. Such activity can weaken/disable OS security or destroy system/user data (e.g. via low level disk manipulation). Malware can also infect system executables programs to escalate privilege and hide its activity. User data encryption by ransomware also falls into this indicator category
Spy activity	User data theft, host/OS identification, system data acquiring to identify a user, hooking low level events and recording user interaction
Evasion	Hide malware presence (e.g. via switching behavior based on fingerprinted host or merging with goodware by performing all activity exclusively through system tools)
Exploit	Malware exploits legitimate applications causing deviated behavior of the hosting (vulnerable) application. To this and, malicious activity is conducted in the context of the hijacked legitimate processes. This may happen due to application exploitation or malicious script execution, e.g. macros executed by MS Word or JavaScript execution by Adobe Reader
Proxy activity	Malware infects a legitimate process by injecting a thread or DLL module, and then the infected process executes various suspicious functionalities. To this end, malware performs so-called proxy attack via a legitimate process (usually in attempt to escalate privilege or hide itself)
Network activity	This behavior could be observed in such malware as downloader, bot agents and backdoor. In most cases, purely network activity cannot be considered malicious by itself. However, in some cases network behavior could attributed as at least suspicious due to the context of the activity, for instance frequent DNS requests with the same domain name (indicative of covert communication channel via DNS protocol)
Atypical activity	This activity is not proven to be malicious, instead depending on the volume it at most could be considered suspicious. To this category we attribute verbose activity, such as highly repetitive create process functionality, too many internet connections or many file rename operations. Moreover, we also attribute process execution delay to this category

domains may be less suspicious, such as network and persistence, others may be attributed to proven maliciousness such as proxy and exploit. For some domains, sample activity threat level could heavily depend on context of the activity.

3   System Evaluation

We experimented with a corpus of 2374 malware samples which were firstly encountered during several recent years. The malware set accounts to dozens of families depending on chosen AV engine (41 in case of Dr.Web, and 25 in case of Panda). In our view, the most indicative and informative family labels are provided by Dr.Web, which we selected as a reference AV. This selection is justified due to fact that any malware.

In the experiment, we pre-selected the following most frequently invoked functionalities, that play a part in almost any complex attack scenario:

- New process creation
- Image set for autorun (via direct registry manipulation or proxy operations)
- New service installation (including obfuscated approach)
- Code injection to a legitimate process (via thread or DLL)
- Executable extraction (dropper)
- Connection to a remote host
- Renaming/moving of the dropped image
- Creation of a new task in task scheduler (task for image execution)

3.1   Detection Results

The results of our experiments are shown in Fig. 2 that represents a bit map of the samples. The map indicates presence of functionalities at the different activity tree levels, which we regarded as behavioral features. The Y-axis indicates individual samples grouped by the families of reference AV (Dr.Web). The X-axis depicts features sorted by the number the samples possessing the given functionality at the given activity tree level. The feature labels denote a functionality name and the activity tree level at which the functionality was detected (L1 - the first level, L2 - second level etc.).

As indicated in Fig. 2, our system detected suspicious and malicious indicators in samples of almost all malware families. Functionality NEW_PROCESS_L1, i.e. new process start, is always observed at the first level of the activity tree, since malware sample start is also considered as a new process. Looking at the second level of activity, where functionalities performed by malware itself, one can see that malware frequently use other "proxy" processes to accomplish certain activity. To this end, the first two most frequently used functionalities at the second level are executable extraction/drop (FILE_DROP L2) and new process launching (NEW_PROCESS L2). This indicates image drop and execute activity. Moreover, it could be observed that malware itself frequently sets for autorun (AUTORUN L2) and establishes connection to a remote host (INET_CONNECT L2).

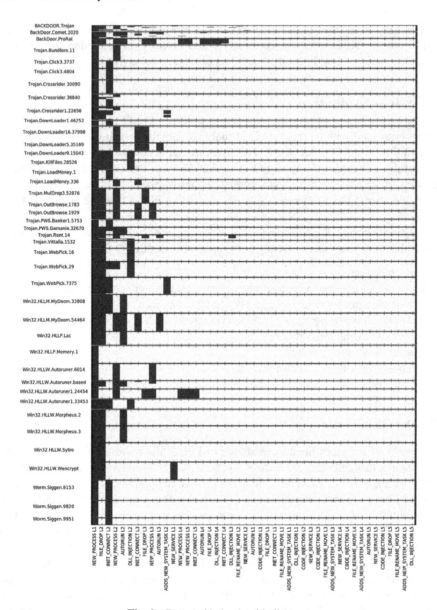

Fig. 2. Detected behavioral indicators

New service launch is always attributed to separate activity tree, at which it constitutes root. It happens due to peculiarities of the system call monitoring. As observed at system call level, to create a new service, a process, via LPC channel, sends a request to Services Control Manager (services.exe), which in its turn writes necessary records to Windows registry.

For some families, detected functionality precisely match their naming characteristics. For instance, in our system all 187 samples of "Trojan.Downloader" families exposed such functionality as "connection to a remote host" (INET_CONNECT). In addition, our system detected "executable extraction" functionality (FILE_DROP) in almost all "Trojan.Downloader" samples (160 files). The combination of these two functionalities indeed corresponds to image downloading activity. As Fig. 2 indicates all 27 samples of Trojan.DownLoader1 family did not expose "executable extraction" functionality in our system, what means that the samples connected to Internet, but did not drop any executable. This may happen due to two several reasons such as the sample recognized the execution environment of our system and evaded; sample was not able to successfully download an image from the vending server or sample stalled beyond the analysis time in our system. Note the mitigating malware evasion and stalling techniques is out of the scope of this paper and is not addressed in the used research version of our malware analysis system, however we plan to resolve these issues in the production version of the system.

While almost all malware families reveal several observed functionalities, samples of "Win32.HLLP.Memery.1" family did bot expose any functionality from the selected set of eight most frequent and standard functionality used in this evaluation test. To gain deeper insights into family behavior, we run samples of this family against all functionalities (more than 50) in our system.

Figure 3 shows screenshot of the behavioral report for a representative sample of the "Memery.1" family. As demonstrated in the report, our system detected several indicators of OS invasion category. For instance, malware performed "legitimate file modification" functionality with target file being windows system executable, which in this context signifies maliciousness. To this end, it seems that malware simply did not execute any of the standard functionalities due to different attack pattern, which is contamination of the host executables. In this paper, we evaluated our system only with respect to standard and most frequently used malicious functionalities.

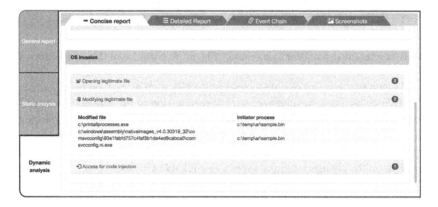

Fig. 3. Behavioral report

Indeed, our methodology allows for specifying and detecting any functionality. We believe that behavior-based detection of some complex malicious payloads, such as spyware activity or hidden ransomware behavior, may be most successful achieved by utilizing a strategically chosen group of several primitive behavioral indicators. On the other hand, secure container isolates all legitimate processes so that positives will not affect usability.

Finally, we evaluated performance of our user interaction simulator (UIS) with hundreds of modern malware and unwanted software (such as riskware, key generators). The experiments indicated that 94% of tested malware exposed GUI with which our system interacted. Figure 4 demonstrates a screenshot made by our system inside virtual container (Windows XP) just before UIS automatically clicked a button belonging to the GUI of the analyzed sample. Our system interacts only with GUI of sample process or non-trusted processes, which apparently derived from analyzed sample. To achieve user-like interaction, our system smartly selects a button to click based on the priority queue of the button names. To this end, UIS first clicks buttons representing options ("advanced", "options", "settings", etc.), then clicks buttons representing process continuation (e.g. "next", "continue", "proceed", etc.) and lastly clicks process termination buttons (e.g. "cancel", "deny", "decline", etc.). In the options windows, UIS activates all possible checkboxes. This scheme is perfect for completely preceding through various installers. The experiments indicated that most of the installers successfully completed installation process.

   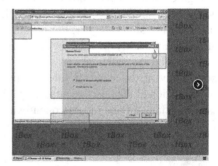

Fig. 4. User interaction simulator (auto-click)   **Fig. 5.** Recognition of the changed regions

It is known that it is impossible to read properties such as caption from some types of GUI. Hence, we implemented geometrical recognition of the screen difference. The result of such recognition is shown in the Fig. 5, where after clicking the button in Fig. 4, UIS highlighted in green the changed regions compared to the previous state. In our approach, if UIS did not detect or was not able to read GUI elements of a window, it may click on the changed regions expecting clickable elements there.

3.2 Runtime Overhead

The secure container prototype was executed in MS Windows 7 running on an Intel Core i7-3517U (2,4 GHz) processor with 4 Gb of ram. We recorded overhead for three activities: web browsing (google chrome), video watching in the browser and PDF reading in Acrobat Reader. Figure 6 shows system CPU overhead imposed by these activities performed when protected by secure container (solid line) and natively, without secure container (dashed line).

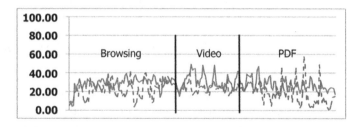

Fig. 6. System overheads with/without secure container

One can see that practically the secure container overhead is not much different from the native one. On average, secure container imposes about 7% CPU overhead versus native execution. As per memory, the system incurs only 3% overhead.

Such a low CPU overhead could be credited to our highly efficient behavioral monitoring module. In fact, that we hook only a small subset of the system calls that are part of a given modified CPN. Since the system call monitor is implemented in the Kernel mode, hooking a small subset of the system calls minimizes the number of computations needed to process by functionality detector.

4   Background and Related Work

Our system could be attributed to behavior-based IDS. The IDS such as [6–12] recognize only malicious activity in the context of a single process. Papers [6, 7] propose tracing sequences of system calls to reveal misuse in OS objects manipulations. In contrast, our approach recognizes of complex functionalities involving interrelated sessions of object operations of multiple processes.

Works [8, 9] target dynamic behavior analysis. One paper advocates for detection of a "gene of self-replication" from object operations and activity blocks. Others utilize so-called behavior graphs [9, 10]. Our modified CPN model represents an executed system call chain as one token residing in the corresponding place. Such token semantics allows for processing multiple system call chain instances to recognize an inter-process activity as well. In our case, usage of activity trees in the program behavior analysis provides additional discriminative power for our malware identification mechanism.

Adversaries may reduce "malicious footprint" to make the activity less suspicious in terms of behavioral statistics. They use mimicry attacks to match normality profile of IDS. Since we recognize activity on the highest semantic level which is activity trees in functional domain, it is hardly possible to conduct a mimicry attack such that it would go unnoticed while executing certain functionality represented in our modified CPN.

5   Conclusion

We introduced new malware analysis and detection system that enables identification of targeted and user-oriented attacks. To provide robust malware detection our system analyzes sample behavior using activity trees defined in the functionality domain. The system employs Modified Hierarchal Colored Petri Nets for run-time recognition of malicious and suspicious functionalities.

The system provides high fidelity in malicious activity analysis, which is achieved by user interaction simulation in real time. The user interaction simulator recognizes GUI components and clicks through them according to click pattern of a typical user, e.g. office worker. Due such features secure container system is instrumental in enabling security in such modes (scenarios) when typical AV products cannot guarantee security.

We evaluated the secure container prototype with corpus of real malware families. During evaluation, activity tree based analysis enabled deep structural insight view into malware behavior, which in general would assist in identifying even specially crafted "well-behaving" malware. Evaluation results showed high efficiency of secure container in detecting and blocking various malware while having low system overhead. Ultimately, secure container enabled us to securely and efficiently operate on insecure/malicious resources.

References

1. Cohen, F.: Computer viruses theory and experiments, Computers and Security, v. 6 (1987)
2. Malware Statistics Report by AV-Test Institute. https://www.av-test.org/en/statistics/malware/
3. Tokhtabayev, A.G., Skormin, V.A., Dolgikh, A.M.: Expressive, efficient and obfuscation resilient behavior based IDS. In: Gritzalis, D., Preneel, B., Theoharidou, M. (eds.) ESORICS 2010. LNCS, vol. 6345, pp. 698–715. Springer, Heidelberg (2010). doi:10.1007/978-3-642-15497-3_42
4. Tokhtabayev, A., Skormin, V., Dolgikh, A.: Detection of worm propagation engines in the system call domain using colored petri nets. In: Proceedings of the IEEE IPCCC '07, USA, December 2008
5. Jensen, K.: Coloured Petri nets (2nd ed.): basic concepts, analysis methods and practical use, vol. 1. Springer, Berlin (1996)
6. Bernaschi, M., Grabrielli, E., Mancini, L.: Operating system enhancements to prevent the misuse of system calls. In: Proceedings of the ACM CCS 2000, pp. 174–183 (2000)
7. Kang, D., Fuller, D., Honavar, V.: Learning classifiers for misuse and anomaly detection using a bag of system calls representation. In: Proceedings of the 6th IEEE Systems Man and Cybernetics Information Assurance Workshop (IAW), pp. 118–125 (2005)
8. Skormin, V., Volynkin, A., et al.: Run-Time detection of malicious self-replication in binary executables. J. Comput. Secur. 15(2), pp. 273–301 (2007)
9. Bayer, U., et al.: Dynamic analysis of malicious code. J. Comput. Virol. 2(1), 67–77 (2006)
10. Christodorescu, M., Jha, S., Kruegel, C.: Mining specifications of malicious behavior. In: Proceedings of the ESEC-FSE'07, NY, USA (2007)
11. Kouznetsov, V.: US Patent 6973577 B1: System and Method for Dynamically Detecting Computer Viruses Through Associative Behavioral Analysis of Runtime State, 6 December 2005
12. Martignoni, L., et al.: A layered architecture for detecting malicious behaviors. In: Proceedings of the RAID 2008 (2008)

A Concept of Clustering-Based Method for Botnet Detection

Hubert Ostap[(✉)] and Ryszard Antkiewicz

Institute of Computer and Information System, Faculty of Cybernetics,
Military University of Technology, Kaliskiego Street 2, 00-908 Warsaw, Poland
{hubert.ostap,ryszard.antkiewicz}@wat.edu.pl

Abstract. The aim of this paper is to present concept of the botnet detection method based on the network flow clustering. There are a lot of botnets implementations and there are a lot of methods of their detection. Usually those methods are only effective for specific groups of botnets for example, which are using IRC, HTML or P2P protocol for internal communication. Method presented below, called BotTROP is a concept how to detect different kind of botnets based on their synchronous activity.

Keywords: Security · Botnet detection · Clustering

1 Introduction

In the last several years, one can observe that the Internet threats are more frequent, better organized and the most important profit-oriented. Such situation is caused by constant moving more and more areas of business to the Internet, which also attracts criminals. There are a lot of types of cyber-attacks such as ransomware, spyware, DOS (Denial of Service). They are really dangerous not only for common users but also for advanced telecommunication systems. One of the most dangerous Internet threat are botnets. They consist of compromised computers called bots, which are controlled from C&C (Command & Control) without the permission and the knowledge of rightful owner [8]. C&C is one of the most important part of each botnet because it is used to manage whole network [6, 23]. Depending on the botnet architecture, it can consist of one C&C (centralized architecture) or group of them (decentralized architecture). Infected computers have also possibility to became C&C but this is much more common practice in decentralized architecture which is based for example on P2P protocol [26, 30].

There are a lot of botnet detection methods [1, 11]. This paper presents new concept of the botnet detection method based on the network flow clustering and allows to analyze any kind of communication protocol used by botnet. The rest of the paper is organized as follows. In Sect. 2 we provide an overview of botnets detection methods. In Sect. 3, we describe the idea of the new method – BotTROP. Section 4 presents the results of testing the effectiveness of the developed method. The fifth section contains a summary of this study.

© Springer International Publishing AG 2017
J. Rak et al. (Eds.): MMM-ACNS 2017, LNCS 10446, pp. 223–234, 2017.
DOI: 10.1007/978-3-319-65127-9_18

2   Overview of Botnet Detection Methods

Because of the huge number of botnets and their different implementations impressive number of defenses method was developed to fight with them. There are a lot of classification proposal of botnet detection methods in the literature [8, 9, 11, 22, 26, 27]. Especially interesting classification are proposed in [11, 26]. Garcia et al. [11] presents only taxonomy of network-based botnet detection methods, which was based on clearly defined classification criteria. However, in article [26] classification includes whole spectrum of botnet detection methods. Taking into consideration both articles, it seems to be possible to propose classification that will connect both propositions, using criteria of classification described in Fig. 1.

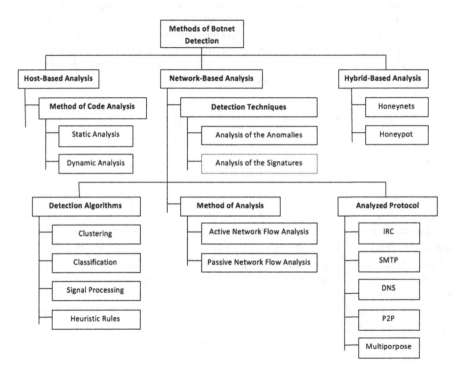

Fig. 1. Classification of the botnet detection methods

Methods based on the selected PC analysis (Host-Based Analysis) can be used during any time of botnet lifecycle. These methods require physical access to an infected machine to ensure possibility of localizing bot-software in the form of malicious process, service or driver. After securing malicious software, analysts can conduct reverse engineering to possess information about C&C address, its functionality and key indicators, which helps in the future to detect this botnet in more automatic way. When using methods from this group, the key action is to localize the infected host in the entire analyzed network. In modern network is almost impossible to analyze all of the hosts due to its number. This is the reason why reverse engineering is conducted after using a method from one of the other groups [16]. Host-Based group contain methods of code analysis: static and dynamic [25]. The first one retrieves all information about malicious file without running it, the second one involves running the file.

Methods based on the network analysis are most frequently used to fight against botnets because they don't need physical access to every host, moreover they are most frequently developed in nowadays [26]. Majority of these methods allow detecting infected machines based only on the network flow generated by them. Suspicious machine can be then analyzed using methods from the host-based group. Algorithms from this group can be also used during any time of botnet lifecycle. They allow detecting those botnets, which have not yet been used for any attack and they are still in the creation phase.

Network-Based Analysis consists of four smaller subgroups of the methods divided due to different factors. The first one involves methods that are directed on the characteristic of the network traffic especially anomalies and signatures. An example of the method based on detecting network anomalies is the method presented by Barthakur and Dahal [2]. It tries to detect anomalies in P2P protocol with Support Vector Machine (SVM) for network classification. The basic premise of this method is the fact that malicious P2P traffic has significant differences in comparison with legitimate traffic. The authors assume that using appropriate indicators of P2P traffic it is possible with high accuracy to distinguish legitimate P2P traffic and malicious used by a botnet. This sophisticated method can be used only against botnets using P2P for communication.

Algorithm presented by Sayoidand and Chanthakoummane [24] is a good representative of a method based on the signature analysis. They have developed improvements to the well-known Intrusion Detection System (IDS) – Snort. It is a network application that has implemented botnet detection method based on signature analysis. Without knowing anything about botnet it is impossible to create its signature.

The next subgroup of detection methods, from network analysis group, is the subgroup, which divide methods due to their mode of action: active and passive. The first one points to methods which modifies network traffic to retrieve information about potentially infected machines which are part of a botnet. The purpose of these methods is to localize infected computers by sending a modified traffic to the suspicious hosts. In the next step, received flow is compared with typical one. This kind of approach allows detecting implementation mistake and localizing not only infected machine but also C&C servers [17].

Today, it seems that more effective methods are based on a passive analysis of the network traffic. They allow detecting bots of even unknown botnets by analyzing only traffic without its modification. Those methods also don't require an access to the computers in the analyzed network. Method presented by Goebel and Holz [12] is a good representative of this subgroup. It tries to find malicious IRC servers, unusual ports for IRC communication and suspicious nick, which can be used by bots for communication with C&C. Unfortunately, this algorithm, is not widely used because of its restriction. It can be used only with unencrypted flow and it is effective against botnets that are using IRC protocol for communication. This method also need to analyze not only IP address but also transferred data to receive information about transferred parameters and values of IRC protocol such as nicks, command and others.

Botnet detection method based on data-mining (clustering, classification, etc.) use also passive network analysis [26]. Good representative of this group is BotMiner proposed by G. Gu, R. Perdisci, J. Zhang and W. Lee. Their method use clustering of botnet's communication and activity traffic. BotMiner perform cross-plane correlation using implemented clustering algorithms to detect bots [14].

The representative of classification methods is BotGAD [4, 5]. This algorithm is trying to detect synchronized action of bots called group activity. It is focused only on Domain Name System (DNS) flow analysis. Bots uses DNS protocol to resolve address of malicious domain name. Such activity is analyzed by group of sensors installed in few parts of networks.

Using BotGAD one can detect synchronous action of all device connected to the analyzed network. Unlike legitimate traffic, Botmaster usually sends his commands to all of the bots. Those, which receive it, trying to send him result of this command as fast as possible. Consequently results are transmitted in very close time. Apart from slight delays, all active bots will send result in synchronous manner, this is the reason why similarity factor between each session will be high. For example Elastic Zombie [20] and Blackshaded [18] botnets sends control packet to C&C confirming activity at specified time, respectively 30 s. and 45 s. Synchronous activity can be also detected during various action carried out by the botnet.

BotGAD is very good method but has few disadvantages. First of all it analyzes only DNS protocol. However, the main disadvantage is the fact that BotGAD needs to divide whole activity on time-windows with fixed length. They represent predefined and equal parts of the whole monitoring time. Those windows are used to group all source IP's of the analyzed destination IP. Chosen length of the time-window has significant impact on the effectiveness of the group activity detection. There is also method called BotSniffer, which works in very similar manner [13].

In the next section we will present method, which could identify group activity of bots without time windows and could analyze network flow based on any protocol. This method is the representative of Clustering methods.

Last subgroup of criteria divides methods of botnet detection according to the protocols that are used for internal communication between bots and C&C. Binkley and Singh [3] proposed method based on IRC communication. Their algorithm combines IRC tokenization with IRC message statistic to detect bots. Manasrah and Hasan [19] proposed DNS-based mechanism that is similar to BotGAD, but is much more limited because they use a MAC address as a identifier rather than IP, which makes this method unusable outside local network.

Authors of the article [28] proposed algorithm that identifying and tracking bots sending SMAP. The main disadvantage is necessity of providing an predefined IP set associated with SPAM bots.

Appropriate example of the botnet detection mechanism based on P2P protocol is an algorithm presented by Holz et al. [29]. They adopt method called Sybil attack [7] to access the Storm botnet and measure its features and use them to mitigate its spreading.

The last subgroup from methods based on analyzed protocol are multipurpose algorithms such as presented in [31]. Authors of this approach proposed system that is able to detected C&C by aggregating traffic with the same payload and destination IP in communication traffic. Suspicious computers are detected thanks to shared common characteristics.

Methods in Hybrid-Analysis group are based on Honeynets and Honeypots projects and allow detecting a large number of botnets. They are combination of Host-Based and Network-Based methods. When suspicious activity is detected in the network traffic or on the virtual machine, then the malicious PC is analyzed using static or dynamic analysis from Host-based method. For instance, solutions presented in [15, 21] describe approaches how to use honeynet-based methods for botnets detections.

In nowadays, thanks to high efficacy method based on Data-Mining with conduction of passive network analysis are most developed and researched, resulting in the largest number of publications [26]. This is the main reason why authors decides to improve one of the described method called BotGAD.

3   BotTROP – Clustering-Based Method for Botnet Detection

3.1   The Idea of the BotTROP

BotTROP identifies bots in some organization (network). We assume, that bots communicate with C&C servers outside the organization in similar moments. This feature of botnet is named synchronous activity [5]. BotTROP at first, records all public IP addresses (outside organization) (destination IP), which where destination of connections generated by nodes (source IP's). Next, for fixed destination IP, BotTROP use clustering method for grouping all source IP connected with analyzed destination IP regarding to specified protocols. In the next step similarity of identified groups of source IP's is analyzed. High value of similarity factor means that analyzed groups contain very similar source IP's and they are connecting with Destination IP in synchronous way. This fact indicates that identified group of source IP's (internal nodes of organization) could be bots of some botnet, and destination IP is the C&C server of that botnet.

Steps described above are done for all recorded public IP addresses and all analyzed protocols. Presented method is effective against all of the protocol used during network connectivity of any type. Details of BotTROP method are presented in the next section.

3.2   The Algorithm

In order to describe the clustering method of network traffic we define the following denotations:

$DIP = \{IP_i^D : i = 1, .., I_D\}$ - the set of analyzed destination IP addresses, I_D – number of analyzed IP addresses;

$PR = \{Pr_j : j = 1, .., I_{PR}\}$ – the set of protocols analyzed by the BotTROP, elements of the set PR can take values from the set $\{HTTP, IRC, DNS, TCP, TLSv1, ...\}$;

$SIP(IP_i^D, Pr_j) = \{IP_k^S(IP_i^D, Pr_j) : k = 1, .., I(IP_i^D, Pr_j)\}, i = 1, .., I_D; j = 1, .., I_{PR};$ - the set IP addresses, which connected with destination address IP_i^D using protocol Pr_j;

$T\left(IP_i^D, Pr_j, IP_k^S\right) = \left(t_r(i,j,k)\right)_{r=1,..I_T(i,j,k)}$, where $t_r(i,j,k)$ is the moment, when computer with address IP_k^S was connected with the destination address IP_i^D using protocol Pr_j in r-th session;

Further, we assume, that we have log of the network system, which contains: $DIP, PR, SIP\left(IP_i^D, Pr_j\right) and T\left(IP_i^D, Pr_j, IP_k^S\right)$

$$for\ i = 1,..,I_D; j = 1,..,I_{PR}; k = 1,..,I\left(IP_i^D, Pr_j\right); r = 1,..I_T(i,j,k).$$

$IP_{max}^S(i,j)$ – the source IP with highest connection rate to analyzed destination IP_i^D using protocol Pr_j.

Clustering of network traffic is carried out according to the following algorithm:

```
FOR  i = 1,..,I_D  DO
FOR    j = 1,..,I_PR  DO
//Determination of number of clusters for  destination  IP_i^D using protocol Pr_j//
e(i,j): =      max        I_T(i,j,k); IP_max^S(i,j): = arg    max       I_T(i,j,k);
          k=1,..,I(IP_i^D,Pr_j)                              k=1,..,I(IP_i^D,Pr_j)
END FOR;
FOR  r = 1,..I_T(i,j,e(i,j))  DO
Create set (cluster):  C(i,j,IP_max^S,r);
C(i,j,IP_max^S,r) := ∅;
END FOR ;
//Clustering of connections generated by source IP and directed to IP_i^D using protocol
Pr_j //
FOR  k = 1,..,I(IP_i^D,Pr_j)  DO
FOR  r = 1,..I_T(i,j,k)  DO
            C(i,j,IP_max^S,m) := IP_k^S(IP_i^D,Pr_j), where m:
|t_r(i,j,k) − t_m(i,j,IP_max^S)| = min_{n=1,..I_T(i,j,e(i,j))}|t_r(i,j,k) − t_n(i,j,IP_max^S)|;
END FOR ;
END FOR ;
//Calculation of average cosine similarity factor for the clusters of connections//
FOR  r = 1,..I_T(i,j,e(i,j)) − 1    DO
S_Cos(i,j,r) := 2·|C(i,j,IP_max^S,r)∩C(i,j,IP_max^S,r+1)| / (√|C(i,j,IP_max^S,r)|·√|C(i,j,IP_max^S,r+1)|);
S̄_Cos(i,j) := S̄_Cos(i,j) + S_Cos(i,j,r);
   END FOR ;
    S̄_Cos(i,j) := (1/e(i,j)) S̄_Cos(i,j);
END FOR ;
END FOR ;
```

Presented algorithm is used for every Destination IP in analyzed network flow. Implemented mechanism allows viewing result in every step of detection. Moreover it also has a lot of useful filters (protocols, Source IP, Destination IP) that help to reduce the data set resulting in a faster calculation.

At first it is trying to determine initial number of clusters and then assigning other Source IP's to the created clusters. Number of clusters that are created during calculation corresponds to number of connection from that source IP which connect to analyzed Destination IP the largest numbers of times. In the next step time of every connection of others IP are compared with time reference for each cluster. After comparison, analyzed connection is joined to that cluster where the distance is the smallest. In the next step cosine similarity is calculated for all subsequent clusters. There are a lot of similarity factors that can be used, but to the sake of comparison with BotGAD result cosine similarity factor was used. Average cosine similarity is the representation of similarity factor. Values of average cosine similarity close to 1 means that subsequent clusters contain very similar Source IP's. It means that source IP's from this clusters communicate with analyzed Destination IP in similar moments. It represents synchronous communication activity of source IP's and could show, that they are bots. The legitimate Source IP's communicates with Destination IP's at random moments and this caused low values of average cosine similarity. Schema shown below represents graphical representation of clustering method for destination IP_Ω (Fig. 2).

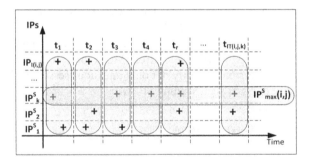

Fig. 2. Graphical interpretation of clustering method.

BotTROP is a method, that like BotGAD, could detect even unknown botnets based on groups activity identification in a network flow. But it do not use "time windows" and allows to analyze all protocols used by botnets. Preparing calculation for all of the Destination IP's can detect even decentralized botnets based on P2P protocol where role of clients and servers are time varying. It is possible because clustering method is used for every Destination IP. BotTROP analyzes whole network traffic and is able to detect not only "self-activity" but also "working activity" such as SPAM and DOS attacks.

4 Case Study

4.1 Description of Dataset

Testing data set comes from Malware Capture Facility Project [10] which is an effort from the Czech Technical University ATG Group establish for capturing and analyzing real malware traffic. The mains goals of the project are:

- Executing malware in honey-net for long periods of time,
- Analyzing captured network traffic,
- Labelling main parts of network traffic including attacks, background, normal and botnets phases.

There are a lot of data sets available on their server but for now only one was analyzed with BotTROP – CTU-Malware-Capture-Botnet-50 (ID 9).

This probe contains network traffic generated from 10 hosts, which were infected with Neris-botnet. When network capturing was started, the virtual-hosts were infecting one by one with the malware. The main activity of botnets is to send SPAM and to communicate with C&C using IRC protocol. The size of captured network flow is about 94 Gb (5 h and 18 min.) with 115, 415, 321 packets. Thanks to the Malware Capture Facility Project it is known that 6.5% is botnet Flow, 0.18% is C&C Flows, 1.57% is labeled as Normal Flow and Background Flow is 91.7%.

This data set was very helpful in verification of BotTROP effectiveness. Results from BotTROP were compared with information from MCFP project about CTU-Malware-Capture-Botnet. It was possible to verify not only malicious servers and infected hosts but also functionality of Neris such sending SPAM.

4.2 Results and Their Interpretation

For the better understanding result presented below show only small and selected part from all outcome. Results consist of many weird IP's with conjunction of high similarity factor that should be analyzed in wider context. In the tables below there are few interesting IP's and protocols with high similarity factor, which may indicate malicious activity. It was decided to show not only potential C&C but also legal severs like yahoo.com. It shows how BotTROP detects malicious activity like SPAM sending. All malicious PC send it using different mail servers but in synchronous way. Thanks to that presented algorithm was able to find which PCs where infected and what kind of servers were used. Results are grouped by protocols. In some cases connection number is not

Table 1. Comparison of BotGAD and BotTROP.

Domain name of destination IP address	Connections No.	BotGAD	BotTROP
mail.live.com	14	0,283	0,854
mail.com	42	0,00	0,556
yandex.ru	28	0,142	0,547
yahoo.com	18	0, 250	0,500

to big because data set was rather small but it was still possible to detect simultaneous activities (Table 1).

Because of the BotGAD limitation, it is possible to compare it with BotTROP only against DNS based botnets. Sample network traffic used during tests contains SPAM activity performed by the Neris botnet. Before sending malicious emails, each bot need to resolve domain mail server address to its IP address used to SPAM sending. This is the only area where BotGAD can detect synchronous activity. Table below contains comparison of the BotTROP and BotGAD with 25 s. time-windows. Mails servers used for SPAM sending are publicly accessible and used also by legitimate users.

All of the mail servers presented in the table above are used by botnet Neris to send SPAM [10]. This kind of activity is an example of synchronous activity, so this is the reason why the cosines similarity should be close to "1". Highest measure is never reach because those servers are also used by legitimate users, which doesn't act in synchronous way.

Father results contains only similarity factor calculated with BotTROP, because it is impossible to detected synchronous activity in network flow other that DNS with BotGAD. To provide privacy, all IP addresses are replaced with temporary name. Original IP addresses can be shared after email contact (Table 2).

Table 2. Similarity factor for HTTP protocol.

Domain name of destination IP address	Connections No.	Similarity factor
Unknown-1	21	1,00
Server-lu-1	97	1,00
Reverse-com-1	1292	0,79
Yahoo-server-1	162	0,64

The first two addressees were unable to resolve using public DNS, the third points to "server.lu" and the last one is one of the yahoo mail servers. It was probably used for spam sending (Table 3).

Table 3. Similarity factor for IRC protocol.

Domain name of destination IP address	Connections No.	Similarity factor
Unknown-2	12	0,66
Unknown-3	10	0,63
Unknown-4	9	0,50
Unknown-5	9	0,50

All IP' presented above was used as IRC servers, there were made only few connection from different computers in analyzed network but that communication was made in synchronous way. It is known that Neris botnet use IRC protocol to communicate with C&C. With very high probability those IP pointed in the table above belong to C&C's (Table 4).

Table 4. Similarity factor for SSL protocol.

Domain name of destination IP address	Connections No.	Similarity factor
peek4me-1	379	0,98

During testing SSL protocol with BotTROP it is possible to detect malicious servers that use encryption. It is also possible to localize legal mail servers that use SSL for authentication reason that were used to send SPAM. Results of the BotTROP detection show that there is only one suspicious server (peek4me_1). Because of high number of connection and high similarity factor it is possible that it plays an important role in botnet architecture (Table 5).

Table 5. Similarity factor for TCP protocol.

Domain name of destination IP address	Connections No.	Similarity factor
Unknown-9	52371	1,00
Hotmail-com-2	1016	0,75
tp-pl-1	24	0,70
Yahoo-com	1064	0,9

This protocol is the most general one, connection number are the biggest that is way similarity factor is also the most suspicious.

All the presented results show suspicious activates which were pointed to the IP's in tables. Not all of them are identified as malicious, some of them are legitimate mail servers but used in very unusual, synchronous manner. This kind of communication can be Bontet "working-activity". Unidentified IP's are potential C&C from where Bots receive commands.

5   Summary

BotTROP is a method for detection of any kind botnet. It utilizes the phenomenon that all current botnets generate network traffic in synchronous way, especially during "working-activity" such as DOS attack or SPAM. Synchronous actions are also performed during "self-activity" for management. Some implementation of malicious software have hardcoded period of time after which "ping" packet is send to C&C and thanks to clustering method it is possible to group such network flow and calculate similarity factor. Bots that are not sending "ping" at least must send request to the Botmaster commands. It is also possible to detect such communication because after receiving command from Botmaster, they are trying to send answer as soon as possible. Due to this, they are also generating synchronous network flow.

Presented method is time consuming especially when it is working on large data sets. Due to this fact further work on the project is aimed at improving the speed of the calculation for large data sets. In the nearest future presented method will be used against source IPs. This approach could reveal infected machines even in very small botnets. It is possible because botnets especially Hybrid and P2P-based generate a lot of repeated sequentially network traffic during finding active C&C when a lot of IPs addresses from bot's list are checked. Infected machines also generate a lot of traffic during SPAM campaign [7].

References

1. Anagnostopoulos, M., Kambourakis, G., Gritzalis, S.: New facets of mobile botnet: architecture and evaluation. Int. J. Inf. Secur. **15**(5), 455–473 (2013)
2. Barthakur, P., Dahal, M., Ghose, M.: A framework for P2P Botnet detection using SVM. In: International Conference on Cyber-Enabled Distributed Computing and Knowledge Discover (2012)
3. Binkley, J.R., Singh, S.: An algorithm for anomaly-based botnet detection. In: Proceedings USENIX Steps to Reducing Unwanted Traffic on the Internet Workshop (SRUTI 2006), pp. 43–48 (2006)
4. Choi, H., Lee, H.: BotGAD: detecting botnets by capturing group activities in network traffic. In: Proceedings of the 4th International ICST Conference on Communication System Software and Middleware, (Comsware 2009) (2009)
5. Choi, H., Lee, H.: Identifying botnets by capturing group activities in DNS traffic (2012)
6. Cooke, E., Jahanian, F., McPherson, D.: The zombie roundup: understanding, detecting, and disrupting botnet. In: Proceedings of SRUTI: Steps to Reducing Unwanted Traffic on the Internet, July 2005
7. Douceur, J.R.: The Sybil attack. In: Druschel, P., Kaashoek, F., Rowstron, A. (eds.) IPTPS 2002. LNCS, vol. 2429, pp. 251–260. Springer, Heidelberg (2002). doi: 10.1007/3-540-45748-8_24
8. ENISA: Botnets: Detection, Measurement, Disinfection & Defence, European Network and Information Security Agency (ENISA) (2011)
9. Feily, M., Shahrestani, A., Ramadass, S.: A survey of botnet and botnet detection. In: Third International Conference on Emerging Security Information, Systems and Technologies (2009)
10. Garcia, S., Grill, M., Stiborek, J., Zunino, A.: An empirical comparison of botnet detection methods. Comput. Secur. **45**, 100–123 (2014)
11. Garcia, S., Zunino, A., Campo, M.: Survey on network-based botnet detection methods. Secur. Commun. Netw. **7**(5), 878–903 (2014)
12. Goebel, J., Holz, T.: Identify bot contaminated host by IRC nickname evaluation. In: Proceedings of USENIX HotBots 2007 (2007)
13. Gu, G., Zhang, J., Lee, W.: BotSniffer: detecting botnet command and control channels in network traffic. In: Proceedings of the 15th Annual Network and Distributed System Security Symposium (NDSS 2008), February 2008
14. Gu, G., Perdisci, R., Zhang, J., Lee, W.: BotMiner: clustering analysis of network traffic for protocol and structure-independent botnet detection. In: Proceedings of the USENIX Security Symposium (Security) (2008)
15. Honeynet Project and Research Alliance. Know your enemy: Tracking Botnets, March 2005. http://honeynet.org/papers/bots/
16. Ligh, M., Adair, S., Hartstein, B., Richard, M.: Malware Analyst's Cookbook and DVD. Wiley, New York (2011)
17. Lyon, F.: Nmap Network Scanning: The Official Nmap Project Guide to Network Discovery and Security Scanning. Insecure.com (2009)
18. Malwarebytes, Kujawa, A.: You dirty RAT! Part 2 – Blackshades NET, 15 June 2015. https://blog.malwarebytes.com/threat-analysis/2012/06/you-dirty-rat-part-2-blackshades-net/

19. Manasrah, A.M., Hasan, A., Abouabdalla, O.A., Ramadass, S.: Detecting botnet activities based on abnormal DNS traffic. Int. J. Comput. Sci. Inf. Secur. (IJCSIS) (2009)
20. NOVETTA: Elastic Zombie Botnet Report (2015)
21. Provos, N.: A virtual honeypot framework. In: Proceedings of the 13th USENIX Security Symposium, pp. 1–14 (2014)
22. Raghava, N.S., Sahgal, D., Chandna, S.: Classification of botnet detection based on botnet architecture. In: International Conference on Communication System and Network Technologies (2012)
23. Ramachandran, A., Feamster, N., Dagon, D.: Revealing botnet membership using DNSBL counter-intelligence. In: USENIX 2nd Workshop on Steps to Reducing Unwated Traffic on the Internet (SRUTI 2006), June 2006
24. Sayoid, S., Chanthakoummane, Y.: Improving intrusion detection on snort for botnet detection. Software Networking, pp. 191–212, July 2016
25. Sikorski, M., Honig, A.: Practical Malware Analysis. No Strach Press (2012)
26. Silva, S.S., Silva, R.M., Pinto, R.C., Salles, R.M.: Botnets: a survey. Comput. Netw. **57**(2), 378–403 (2013)
27. Strayer, T., Lapsely, D., Walsh, R., Livadas, C.: Botnet detection based on network behavior. In: Lee, W., Wang, C., Dagon, D. (eds.) Botnet Detection, pp. 1–24. Springer, Boston (2008)
28. Stringhini, G., Holz, T., Stone-Gross, B., Kruegel, C., Vigna, G.: BOTMAGNIFIER: locating spambots on the internet. In: Proceedings of the 20th USENIX Conference on Security, SEC 2011, p. 28. USENIX Association, Berkeley (2011)
29. Holz, T., Steiner, M., Dahl, F., Biersack, E., Freiling, F.: Measurements and mitigation of peer-to-peer-based botnets: a case study on storm worm. In: Proceedings of the 1st Usenix Workshop on Large-Scale Exploits and Emergent Threats. USENIX Association, Berkeley (2008)
30. Wang, P., Sparks, S., Zou, C.: An advanced hybrid peer-to-peer botnet. In: USENIX First Workshop on Hot Topics in Understanding Botnets (HotBots 2007), April 2007
31. Yen, T.-F., Reiter, M.K.: Traffic aggregation for malware detection. In: Zamboni, D. (ed.) DIMVA 2008. LNCS, vol. 5137, pp. 207–227. Springer, Heidelberg (2008). doi: 10.1007/978-3-540-70542-0_11

Easy 4G/LTE IMSI Catchers
for Non-Programmers

Stig F. Mjølsnes and Ruxandra F. Olimid[(✉)]

Department of Information Security and Communication Technology, NTNU,
Norwegian University of Science and Technology, Trondheim, Norway
{sfm,ruxandra.olimid}@ntnu.no

Abstract. IMSI Catchers are tracking devices that break the privacy of the subscribers of mobile access networks, with disruptive effects to both the communication services and the trust and credibility of mobile network operators. Recently, we verified that IMSI Catcher attacks are really practical for the state-of-the-art 4G/LTE mobile systems too. Our IMSI Catcher device acquires subscription identities (IMSIs) within an area or location within a few seconds of operation and then denies access of subscribers to the commercial network. Moreover, we demonstrate that these attack devices can be easily built and operated using readily available tools and equipment, and without any programming. We describe our experiments and procedures that are based on commercially available hardware and unmodified open source software.

Keywords: 4G · LTE security · IMSI Catcher · Denial-of-Service

1 Introduction

1.1 IMSI Catchers

IMSI Catchers are active attack devices against the radio link protocols in mobile networks with the main goal of collecting IMSIs (International Mobile Subscriber Identities), the subscribers' identifiers used in the authentication and access control procedures. In particular, these attacks break one of the important security requirements set in the international specifications, namely the privacy and non-traceability of the subscriber. The malicious devices usually act as a man-in-the-middle to fulfil more advanced attacks. IMSI Catchers can be used for mass-surveillance of individuals in a geographical area, or link a real person to his/her identity in the network, trace a person with a known IMSI (check his/her presence in a building or area), eavesdrop on private conversations, all these being privacy issues concerns. IMSI disclosure is a direct consequence of the poor cryptographic mechanism used or its improper usage. On the other hand, DoS (Denial-of-Service) attacks introduce serious financial losses on a targeted operator, as the subscribers cannot access the mobile services; moreover, other services that use the mobile infrastructure are impacted by the network unavailability; these include emergency calls or SMSs containing one-time codes for two-way authentication mechanisms used in the bank sector.

© Springer International Publishing AG 2017
J. Rak et al. (Eds.): MMM-ACNS 2017, LNCS 10446, pp. 235–246, 2017.
DOI: 10.1007/978-3-319-65127-9_19

1.2   Related Work

IMSI Catchers were first built for 2G/GSM, and later extended to 3G/UMTS protocols. Until recently LTE (Long Term Evolution) protocols were considered secure against these privacy attacks due to the stronger authentication and key exchange mechanisms. This claim has now been proved to be incorrect both by ourselves and others. Independently of our work, Shaik et al. showed that IMSI Catchers can be built for LTE mobile networks with similar consequences as for 2G and 3G networks [1]. The vulnerabilities in LTE protocols allow an adversary to trace the location of users with fine granularity, enable DoS attacks, or eavesdropping on the communication [1–5]. General techniques to set up attacks against LTE include traffic capture, jamming and downgrade to 2G. All these academic works implement IMSI Catchers by modifying the code of open-source software projects, such as OpenLTE [6], srsLTE [7,8] or gr-LTE [9]. Rupprecht et al. have very recently used Open Air Interface (OAI) [10] to test compliance of UE (User Equipment) with the LTE standard with respect to encryption and to exemplify a man-in-the-middle attack, but they assume that the UE tries to connect to the rogue base station [5]. Most of the works use OpenLTE code because, according to these researchers, the OpenLTE architecture is easier to modify. We use the unmodified OAI software here for the purpose of building an IMSI Catcher.

1.3   Summary of Results

Our main goal here is to demonstrate that it is easy to build a low-cost LTE IMSI Catcher that requires absolutely no programming skills, but only readily available standard equipment and tools. Although other related works show that an IMSI Catcher for LTE can be built, they all require modification to the source code. We are the first to build an LTE IMSI Catcher using existing "commercial off the shelf" hardware and readily available software only. This result demonstrates that anyone who has basic operational computer skills (installing and running software) can mount an IMSI Catcher attack; in particular, our attack set up requires no programming.

A second, but no less important, result is the ability of the adversary to perform a DoS attack, under the same conditions. The access to the authorised mobile network is controlled by the adversary in time and space: UEs are denied mobile services within the area of the rogue eNodeBs for the time they are active. Again, our attack set up requires no programming skills.

2   LTE Mobile Networks

2.1   LTE Architecture

LTE architecture (see Fig. 1) consists of two parts: EUTRAN (Evolved Universal Terrestrial Radio Access Network) and EPC (Evolved Packet Core), each of them being composed of several components that we briefly described next.

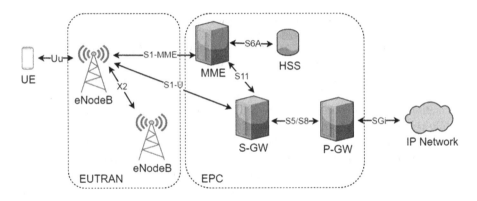

Fig. 1. LTE architecture

UE (User Equipment) refers to the mobile user terminal. It contains a USIM (Universal Subscriber Identity Module), which stores the IMSI (International Mobile Subscriber Identity) and the associated permanent secret key, used to derive temporary keys for authentication and encryption. IMSI is a permanent unique value that globally identifies the subscriber.

eNodeB (evolved NodeB) is the base station that communicates with UEs by radio links and represents the access point to the operator's network.

MME (Mobile Management Entity) is responsible for authentication and resources allocation to UEs. It manages the mobility of UEs in the network when eNodeBs cannot.

HSS (Home Subscriber Server) stores the authentication parameters, private keys and other details about the UEs.

S-GW (Serving Gateway) is an interconnection point between EUTRAN and EPC, being and anchor point for intra-LTE mobility.

P-GW (PDN Gateway) is a routing point to provide connectivity to the external PDN(Packet Data Network).

A mobile network is identified by MCC (Mobile Country Code) and MNC (Mobile Network Code). The MCC and MNC are publicly available online [11]. An eNodeB controls a set of cells running at a specific frequency in an LTE band, or equivalently, on an EARFCN (EUTRA Absolute Radio-Frequency Channel Number) [12,13]. The frequency ranges allocated to the network operators are also public information [14]. Several cells in a geographically region form a TAC (Tracking Area Code), which is managed by a single MME. The eNodeB broadcasts information such as MCC, MNC or TAC via SIB (System Information Block) messages. This allows the UE to identify the operator. To attach to the network, UE then sends an ATTACH_REQUEST message to the eNodeB. If UE moves to a new area, it initiates a TAU_REQUEST and a TRACK-ING_AREA_UPDATE procedure is performed.

We skip other details here, but invite the reader to refer to the specifications for more details [15,16].

2.2   LTE Cell Selection and Reselection

A mobile device that attempts to access the mobile network performs a *cell selection* procedure. This means that the UE searches for a suitable cell and chooses to camp on the one that provides the best service. If later on the UE finds a more suitable cell (according to some reselection criteria), then it performs *cell reselection* and camps onto the new cell. Cell selection and reselection in LTE mobile networks are complex processes involving several steps and different criteria [17,18]. We do not describe the complete processes here, but only highlight the aspects that are further required for the understanding of our work.

When the UE is switched on, it camps on a cell within a PLMN (Public Land Mobile Network) selected accordingly to a list stored locally and some selection criteria. In practice, the selected PLMN corresponds to the last mobile network the UE had successfully connected to before switch off. Note that this is not always the home PLMN (the mobile network the USIM belongs to).

At reselection, the UE monitors intra-frequency, inter-frequency and inter-RAT (Radio Access Technology) cells indicated by the serving cell. In the following, we refer to inter-frequency reselection, as its understanding is a prerequisite for our results. The UE performs inter-frequency reselection when it camps on a cell that runs on a different frequency than the serving cell. First level criterion for reselection is the absolute priority list: the UE always monitors and tries to camp on cells that run on higher priority frequencies. The eNodeB of the serving cell broadcasts in clear the list of absolute priorities (along with other reselection parameters) in SIB messages. For each frequency that is listed, cellReselection-Priority field defines its absolute priority, where 0 indicates the lowest priority and 7 indicates the highest priority. Note that LTE reselection uses the radio link quality as second level criteria, so simply running a rogue eNodeB in the vicinity of the UE does not automatically trigger a reselection.

Operators use the absolute priority frequency criteria to gain robust coverage. They design the network such that within an area coexist multiple cells that run on distinct frequencies with associated priorities. In case of incidents or network congestion on the highest priority frequency, the UE will not lose connectivity, but reselect a cell that runs on the next priority frequency. Deciding the number of frequency levels that should coexist in an area and their associated priorities is a task of the design network engineer.

2.3   Security Requirements and the Adversarial Model

The main goals of the adversary are to collect IMSIs and to deny network availability. The adversary is constrained in both budget and technical skills, so it aims for a low-cost and simple attack that only requires basic computer knowledge. Our adversary will only use commercially available hardware and unmodified open source software.

Furthermore, the adversarial model follows the one of previous work [1,3]. The attacker is active in the sense that it can build up a rogue eNodeB that interacts with the UEs. The model of a passive adversary (an adversary that can only sniff LTE traffic, but cannot actively interfere) is inappropriate both for practical and theoretical reasons. On the practical side, active adversaries have been proved successful, so LTE mobile networks must protect against them, while on the theoretical side TMSIs (Temporary Mobile Subscriber Identities) have been introduced as a security measure starting with 2G. TMSIs are temporary values that replace the IMSIs in the process of subscribers' identification, minimising the transmission of IMSIs through the air and hence drastically decreasing the chances of a passive adversary to collect them.

3   Equipment and Tools

3.1   Hardware

Only Commercial Off-The-Shelf (COTS) devices have been used in our attack setup. The hardware components that we used for our experiments (excluding the mobile phones) are shown in Fig. 2.

Fig. 2. Experimental hardware (excluding UEs)

Computers. We used two different computers: one Intel NUC D54250WYK (i5-4250U CPU@1.30GHz) and one Lenovo ThinkPad T460s (i7-6600U CPU@2,30GHz). Both run 64-bit Kubuntu 14.04 kernel version 3.19.0-61-low latency and have USB3 ports, which are prerequisites for running the OAI software. The Intel NUC computer was attached with standard peripherals (display screen, mouse, keyboard).

USRPs. The B200mini is a USRP (Universal Software Radio Peripheral) from Ettus Research that can be programmed to operate over a wide radio-frequency range (70 MHz–6 GHz), communicating in full duplex. It can be used for all of the LTE frequency bands. The technical specifications of the B200mini are available at [19]. We used two USRP B200mini to set up the eNodeBs.

User Equipment. We used a Samsung Galaxy S4 device to find the LTE channels and TACs used in the targeted area. For testing the IMSI Catcher, we used two LG Nexus 5X phones running Android v6. We used different USIMs from the two biggest Norwegian operators, and the two biggest Romanian operators (see Sect. 5).

The total hardware cost is less than 3000EUR. Any two OAI compatible computers and USRPs can be used to mount the experiments [20]. Also, a single mobile device is sufficient if it can provide the minimal information needed (EARFCN and TAC) for setting up the rogue eNodeBs. So, the minimal kit includes: two computers and two USRPs for the network side and one mobile device with a USIM from the targeted mobile operator for the client side. Keeping the configuration to minimum, cost might be decreased. Also, we expect the costs to be significantly lower in the near future.

3.2 Software

We used open-source freely available software that did not require any modification for our purposes to build and run the 4G/LTE IMSI Catcher.

Service and Testing Modes. Seen as a facility of the operating system and the privilege rights of the user, service or testing modes of mobile devices offer important information about the LTE network. We describe, for comparison, the information displayed by the two types of phones we used during the experiments.

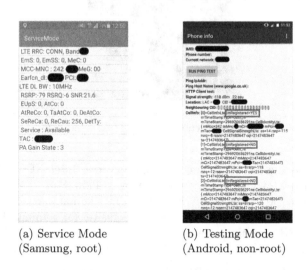

(a) Service Mode
(Samsung, root)

(b) Testing Mode
(Android, non-root)

Fig. 3. Service and testing modes

Samsung phones offer LTE connection details by default [21]. To access Service Mode, call *#0011#. The most important pieces of information are the EARFCN_DL (downlink EARFCN) and the TAC. Other interesting information include the MCC, MNC and Cell ID. Refer to Fig. 3(a) for more details.

Android phones (including Samsung phones) access Testing Mode by calling *#*#4636#*#*. This is a feature available on all Android phones, which does not necessarily display EARFCN_DL by default (it is dependent of the Android version), but displays information about several LTE cells that coexist in the area on which the phone might downgrade to in case the actual cell becomes unavailable. Figure 3(b) shows the Testing Mode of a LG Nexus 5X display. The UE is registered to the first displayed cell (mRegistered=YES), while the others are showed to be accessible. However, last versions of Android or applications such as LTE G-Net Track Lite or NetCell Tracker [22,23] (in root mode) can provide EARFCN_DL and other information in a user-friendly format.

OAI (Open Air Interface). OAI is open source software that implements both the core network (EPC) and access-network (EUTRAN) of 3GPP cellular networks [10,24]. Currently, it provides a standard compliant implementation of Release 10 LTE and establishes generic interfaces with various hardware manufactures (including Ettus Research). Basically, the LTE network is emulated on a computer, and the USRP is used as the radio platform for the eNodeB implementation. It is recommended to run EPC and EUTRAN on different machines, but OAI accepts both on a single computer too. For our tests, keeping in mind the goal of a low-cost IMSI Catcher, we used two machines, one for each of the two rogue eNodeBs that must run concurrently.

OpenBTS. OpenBTS is an open source software development project for GSM mobile networks [25]. OpenRegistration in OpenBTS allows an IMSI that match a given regular expression to access the network. The one-sided authentication protocol of GSM permits the OpenBTS process to accept mobile terminals without proper mutual authentication. Note that we have used OpenBTS for testing purposes only, to make a roaming USIM connect to a masquerade home network, but this is not a prerequisite for setting up the LTE IMSI Catcher (see Sect. 5.4).

4 The LTE IMSI Catcher

We now describe how we built and operated our LTE IMSI Catcher. We ran two rogue eNodeBs using the OAI software, and set up with the proper configuration files. One rogue eNodeB (called eNodeB_Jammer from now on) causes the UE to detach from the serving cell that it is camped on, and to reselect to our rogue cell set up by the second eNodeB (called eNodeB_Collector), which masquerades as an authorized eNodeB but with higher signal power.

The eNodeB_Collector broadcasts the MCC and the MNC of the target network operator to impersonate the real network. The eNodeB_Collector signals a TAC value different from the commercial one, which brings the UE to initiate a TAU_REQUEST message. For simplicity, we configured it to the next available TAC (TAC of the commercial network + 1). We found that the TAC must not be changed for multiple runs of the experiment (assuming the commercial TAC is unchanged), therefore we kept this value constant. Besides the MCC-MNC of the target network, the eNodeB_Collector must run on the LTE EARFCN (the absolute physical radio channel) which corresponds to the highest priority next to the jammed channel. This assures that the UE prefers the eNodeB_Collector prior to any other commercial eNodeB in the area. The eNodeB_Jammer is turned on, using the radio channel of the cell that the UE camps on. This jams the radio interface and decreases the signal of the commercial eNodeB under the specified threshold (see Sect. 2), causing the UE to trigger a new search for available eNodeBs. The UE tries to camp to the cell that runs on the next priority frequency and provides the best signal, namely the rogue eNodeB.

We divide the adversarial actions into two main phases:

Phase 1. Gather the configuration parameters (EARFCN and TAC):

1. Connect a mobile phone to the target network and read the EARFCN_DL and TAC;
2. Configure and run the eNodeB_Jammer, using the MCC and MNC of the target network and the EARFCN_DL from the previous step;
3. Read the new value of EARFCN_DL, after the UE performs reselection.

Phase 2. Configure and run the LTE IMSI Catcher:

1. Configure and run theeNodeB_Collector, using the MCC and MNC of the target network, a different TAC than the one in *Phase 1.1* and the EARFCN_DL set to the value in *Phase 1.3*;
2. Configure and run the eNodeB_Jammer, using the MCC and MNC of the target network and the EARFCN_DL set to the value in *Phase 1.1*.

The channel displayed in *Phase 1.1* is associated with the highest priority (unless the signal power is below the reselection threshold, see Sect. 2.2). The UE connects to it even if the signal power is not so strong. This can be easily seen by comparing the information displayed by the mobile device before and after the eNodeB_Jammer is turned on. The channel in *Phase 1.3* has either the same priority, but lower signal power, or lower priority, regardless the signal power. Once the eNodeB_Jammer is active, this triggers an ATTACH_REQUEST message from the UE to the eNodeB_Collector. Then the UE will reveal its IMSI as a response to an IDENTITY_REQUEST query from our Collector cell.

5   Experiments and Results

5.1   Introduction

All our experiments were run in our wireless security lab at the university. We intend our work to be a motivation for solving the problem of privacy attacks in mobile networks both in existing and emerging systems at the technical specification level, as well as for mobile network operators to use the already existing security mechanisms.

```
77 [MESSAGE] 6 -> 8 0 0103:9902850 NAS_UPLINK_DATA_IND ue_id 0x00000002 len 17
78 [MESSAGE] 8 -> 9 0 0103:9903210 EMMAS_DATA_IND ue id 0x00000002 len 17 tai:  plmn 242.██ tac██
79 [EVENT] 9 0103:990822T3470 stopped UE 0x00000002
80 [MESSAGE] 9 -> 9 0 0103:990956EMMREG_COMMON_PROC_CNF ue id 0x00000002
81 [EVENT] 9 0103:991075EMM state DEREGISTERED UE 0x00000002
82 [MESSAGE] 8 -> 13 0 0103:9911920 S6A_AUTH_INFO_REQ IMSI 242████████ visited_plmn 242.██ re_sync 0
83 [MESSAGE] 13 -> 8 0 0103:9921110 S6A_AUTH_INFO_ANS imsi 242████████ DIAMETER_AUTHENTICATION_DATA_UNAVAILABL
84 [EVENT] 7 0103:9921680 S6A_AUTH_INFO_ANS S6A Failure imsi 242██████
85 [MESSAGE] 8 -> 9 0 0103:9921820 EMMCN_AUTHENTICATION_PARAM_FAIL
```

Fig. 4. IMSI Capture

```
28 56.711592   127.0.0.1    127.0.1.10   S1AP/NAS-EPS   186 id-uplinkNASTransport, Attach request, PDN connectivity request
35 81.793250   127.0.0.1    127.0.1.10   S1AP/NAS-EPS   194 id-initialUEMessage, Attach request, PDN connectivity request
46 106.793796  127.0.0.1    127.0.1.10   S1AP/NAS-EPS   194 id-initialUEMessage, Attach request, PDN connectivity request
47 106.795616  127.0.1.10   127.0.0.1    S1AP/NAS-EPS   110 SACK id-downlinkNASTransport, Identity request
48 106.812750  127.0.0.1    127.0.1.10   S1AP/NAS-EPS   138 SACK id-uplinkNASTransport, Identity response
55 108.816179  127.0.1.10   127.0.0.1    S1AP/NAS-EPS   110 SACK id-downlinkNASTransport, Attach reject
```

```
  NAS-PDU: 074403
v Non-Access-Stratum (NAS)PDU
    0000 .... = Security header type: Plain NAS message, not security protected (0)
    .... 0111 = Protocol discriminator: EPS mobility management messages (0x07)
    NAS EPS Mobility Management Message Type: Attach reject (0x44)
  v EMM cause
      Cause: Illegal UE (3)
```

Fig. 5. ATTACH_REJECT message

5.2 IMSI Catching

We successfully ran experiments with three subscriptions from two mobile operators in Norway, testing two, respectively one USIM card for each. For all, we used the same mobile device, the LG Nexus 5X. To respect privacy of other users, IMSI values were captured from our own USIM cards only.

All the three IMSIs used for tests were successfully captured by the eNodeB_Collector within a few seconds after the eNodeB_Jammer is switched on. Figure 4 shows a portion from the log file that contains a captured IMSI.

Experiments were repeated several times, with different values for Cell ID or eNodeB ID. They were all successful, so we conclude there is no protection mechanism in place (e.g. a list of accepted cells, TACs or timers).

5.3 Denial-of-Service

We observed that running the IMSI Catcher results in a DoS attack because authentication fails after the UE triggers the ATTACH_REQUEST and consequently sends its identity as a response to the IDENTITY_REQUEST. This is normal, as the IMSI is not recognised by the HSS as a valid subscriber and no handover procedures can be accomplished. The eNodeB_Collector responds to the UE with ATTACH_REJECT cause 3 (Illegal UE), making the UE to consider the network unavailable until reboot (Fig. 5) [16].[1]

If the UE is powered off and on again while our rogue eNodeBs are still up, the UE keeps failing to camp on any cell. This turns into a controlled DoS attack against the target network in the area covered. This DoS mode remains active as long as the rogue eNodeBs are up.

---

[1] Depending on the exact software version of OAI being used, UE connectivity to the eRogueB fails in various ways, but all end up with DoS until the reboot of UE.

```
72 [MESSAGE] 8 -> 9 0 0370:7869980 EMMAS_DATA_IND ue id 0x00000002 len 11 tai:    plmn 226.██ tac ███
73 [EVENT] 9 0370:787279T3470 stopped UE 0x00000002
74 [MESSAGE] 9 -> 9 0 0370:787345EMMREG_COMMON_PROC_CNF ue id 0x00000002
75 [EVENT] 9 0370:787404EMM state DEREGISTERED UE 0x0███████
76 [MESSAGE] 8 -> 13 0 0370:7874860 S6A_AUTH_INFO_REQ IMSI 226██ vis ited_plmn 226.██ re_sync 0
77 [MESSAGE] 13 -> 8 0 0370:7889220 S6A_AUTH_INFO_ANS imsi 226█ DIA METER_AUTHENTICATION_DATA_UNAVAILABLE
78 [EVENT] 7 0370:7889830 S6A_AUTH_INFO_ANS S6A Failu re imsi 226█
79 [MESSAGE] 8 -> 9 0 0370:7889920 EMMCN_AUTHENTICATI██████████
80 [EVENT] 9 0370:789185send ATTACH_REJECT to ue id 0x00000002
81 [MESSAGE] 8 -> 6 0 0370:7893480 NAS_DOWNLINK_DATA_REQ ue id 0x00000002 len 0
82 [MESSAGE] 7 -> 7 0 0370:7893890 DOWNLINK NAS TRANSPORT enb_ue_s1ap_id 0xFA3950 ue id 0x00000002
83 [MESSAGE] 6 -> 1 0 0370:7894640 downlinkNASTransport/initiatingMessage ue_id 0x00000002 mme_ue_s1ap_id 0x00000002
```

Fig. 6. IMSI capture in roaming

5.4 Roaming

An even simpler IMSI Catcher is available for USIMs in a roaming situation, in particular under restricted scenarios like airport arrivals. The adversary can now run a single rogue eNodeB with the MCC and MNC of the home network.

We distinguish 2 scenarios: (1) USIMs that are inactive in roaming (roaming was not activated or the user travels to a country without any roaming agreements with the home network) and (2) USIMs that are active in roaming, but did not connect to any network while in roaming. For both cases, the UE reveals its IMSI on power on, if the IMSI Catcher is up and running at that time.

USIMs inactive in roaming. A USIM for which roaming is disabled is directly susceptible to an LTE IMSI Catcher using the same MCC and MNC as the home network. Hence, to setup an IMSI Catcher in this scenario, an adversary simply configures the corresponding MNC and MCC, then runs OAI. The LTE frequency band, EARFCN or any other information are irrelevant in this scenario. If the IMSI Catcher is running when the UE is turned on, then the UE will try to camp on the cell that masquerades the HPLMN and hence, responds to the IDENTITY_REQUEST message with its IMSI.

We carried out this attack using an inactive LTE USIM card from one of the most known Romanian mobile operators. Figure 6 shows the IMSI, as captured by the IMSI Catcher as a response to an IDENTITY_REQUEST message.

USIM active in roaming. A USIM for which roaming is enabled is susceptible to an IMSI Catcher built as previously explained, when the UE is first powered on in roaming. Once connected in roaming, the UE will not search for its home network because in practice, regardless of the specifications, the UE will always try to connect to the most recent network for which the connection was successfully (this is an issue inherited from previous generations, as for example it exists in GPRS also [26]). The scenario could make sense on an airport: the user turns off its device (or equivalently, enable the fly mode) while connected to the home network and later turns it on (or equivalently, disables the fly mode) after landing, in the presence of a rogue eNodeB that simulates the home network. The UE will try to connect to the rogue eNodeB and hence, it will reveal its IMSI as a response to the IDENTITY_REQUEST message. Such an IMSI Catcher might be used by agencies that want to survey the presence of people arriving from specific countries to their own territory in a hidden manner (without revealing their intentions by asking official documents from the border authorities).

Independent work considers this scenario in theory and proposes correctness and completeness of location update trails and geographically plausibility of location updates to address this issue [27]. We have hereby certified this functionality.

We performed the experiment by using an active LTE USIM card belonging to another network operator in Romania. As the USIM had been already active in roaming, we simulated the test case by connecting it to a fictive 2G network that masquerades the home network. For this, we used OpenBTS in OpenRegistration mode. After the UE connected to the GSM network, we switched it to 4G and immediately turned it off. At power on, the UE tried to connect to the rogue eNodeB that simulated the home 4G network and then revealed its IMSI.

6   Conclusion

In conclusion, our experiments have verified, independently of other works, that IMSI-catching indeed can be done for the 4G/LTE system too. We claim that (1) IMSIs can be collected by the eNodeB_Collector, and (2) DoS (Denial-of-Service) is performed automatically after the UE receives an attach rejection message (with a specific cause). The 4G/LTE is vulnerable to active privacy attacks by IMSI Catcher, and we found that these attacks can be done quite easily and therefore can impact the confidence and reliability of commercial mobile networks. We showed that these attacks are not limited to clever programmers with special hardware. We hope that this report, and others, will make the 4G/LTE service providers aware of this threat, and lead to demands for improved privacy and security protocols in the mobile networks.

Acknowledgements. The authors would like to thank master student Fredrik Skretteberg for providing the Samsung phone necessary for some experiments.

References

1. Shaik, A., Seifert, J., Borgaonkar, R., Asokan, N., Niemi, V.: Practical attacks against privacy and availability in 4G/LTE mobile communication systems. In: 23nd Annual Network and Distributed System Security Symposium, NDSS 2016, San Diego, California, USA, February 21–24, 2016 (2016)
2. Jover, R.P.: Security attacks against the availability of LTE mobility networks: overview and research directions. In: 2013 16th International Symposium on Wireless Personal Multimedia Communications (WPMC), pp. 1–9. IEEE (2013)
3. Jover, R.P.: LTE security, protocol exploits and location tracking experimentation with low-cost software radio. CoRR abs/1607.05171 (2016)
4. Lichtman, M., Jover, R.P., Labib, M., Rao, R., Marojevic, V., Reed, J.H.: LTE/LTE-a jamming, spoofing, and sniffing: threat assessment and mitigation. IEEE Commun. Mag. **54**(4), 54–61 (2016)
5. Rupprecht, D., Jansen, K., Pöpper, C.: Putting LTE security functions to the test: a framework to evaluate implementation correctness. In: 10th USENIX Workshop on Offensive Technologies (WOOT 2016) (2016)
6. OpenLTE: An open source 3GPP LTE implementation. https://sourceforge.net/projects/openlte/

246   S.F. Mjølsnes and R.F. Olimid

7. srsLTE: Open source 3GPP LTE library. https://github.com/srsLTE/srsLTE
8. Gomez-Miguelez, I., Garcia-Saavedra, A., Sutton, P.D., Serrano, P., Cano, C., Leith, D.J.: srsLTE: an open-source platform for LTE evolution and experimentation. arXiv preprint arXiv:1602.04629 (2016)
9. gr-LTE: GNU Radio LTE receiver. https://github.com/kit-cel/gr-lte
10. Open Air Interface: 5G software alliance for democratising wireless innovation. http://www.openairinterface.org
11. SMScarrier.EU: Mobile Country Codes (MCC) and Mobile Network Codes (MNC). http://mcc-mnc.com
12. Wikipedia: LTE frequency band. https://en.wikipedia.org/wiki/LTE_frequency_bands
13. Niviuk: LTE frequency band calculator. http://niviuk.free.fr/lte_band.php
14. Europen Communication Office: ECO Frequency Information System. http://www.efis.dk
15. ETSI TS 136 331 V13.0.0 (2016–01): LTE; Evolved Universal Terrestrial Radio Access (E-UTRA); Radio Resource Control (RRC); Protocol specification (3GPP TS 36.331 version 13.0.0 Release 13) (2016). http://www.etsi.org/deliver/etsi_ts/136300_136399/136331/13.00.00_60/ts_136331v130000p.pdf
16. ETSI TS 124 301 V12.6.0 (2014–10): Universal Mobile Telecommunications System (UMTS); LTE; Non-Access-Stratum (NAS) protocol for Evolved Packet System (EPS); Stage 3 (3GPP TS 24.301 version 12.6.0 Release 12) (2014). http://www.etsi.org/deliver/etsi_ts/124300_124399/124301/12.06.00_60/ts_124301v120600p.pdf
17. ETSI TS 136 304 V12.2.0 (2014–09): LTE; Evolved Universal Terrestrial Radio Access (E-UTRA); User Equipment (UE) procedures in idle mode (3GPP TS 36.304 version 12.2.0 Release 12) (2014). http://www.etsi.org/deliver/etsi_ts/136300_136399/136304/12.02.00_60/ts_136304v120200p.pdf
18. ETSI TS 136 133 V12.7.0 (2015–06): LTE; Evolved Universal Terrestrial Radio Access (E-UTRA); Requirements for support of radio resource management (3GPP TS 36.133 version 12.7.0 Release 12) (2015). http://www.etsi.org/deliver/etsi_ts/136100_136199/136133/12.07.00_60/ts_136133v120700p.pdf
19. Research, E.: USRP B200mini (Board only). https://www.ettus.com/product/details/USRP-B200mini
20. Open Air Interface: Hardware Requirements. https://gitlab.eurecom.fr/oai/openairinterface5g/wikis/OpenAirSystemRequirements
21. Samsung: Samsung Service Mode. http://samsungservicemode.blogspot.no
22. Solutions, G.: G-NetTrack Lite. https://play.google.com/store/apps/details?id=com.gyokovsolutions.gnettracklite&hl=en
23. Cell Mapper.net: Cell Mapper. https://play.google.com/store/apps/details?id=cellmapper.net.cellmapper&hl=en
24. Nikaein, N., Knopp, R., Kaltenberger, F., Gauthier, L., Bonnet, C., Nussbaum, D., Ghaddab, R.: OpenAirInterface 4G: an open LTE network in a PC. In: International Conference on Mobile Computing and Networking (2014)
25. RangeNetworks: OpenBTS. http://openbts.org
26. McGuiggan, P.: GPRS in Practice: A Companion to the Specifications. Wiley, New York (2005)
27. Dabrowski, A., Petzl, G., Weippl, E.R.: The messenger shoots back: network operator based IMSI catcher detection. In: Monrose, F., Dacier, M., Blanc, G., Garcia-Alfaro, J. (eds.) RAID 2016. LNCS, vol. 9854, pp. 279–302. Springer, Cham (2016). doi:10.1007/978-3-319-45719-2_13

Anomaly Detection in Cognitive Radio Networks Exploiting Singular Spectrum Analysis

Qi Dong[1]([envelope]), Zekun Yang[1], Yu Chen[1], Xiaohua Li[1], and Kai Zeng[2]

[1] Department of Electrical and Computer Engineering, Binghamton University, Binghamton, NY 13902, USA
{qdong3,zyang26,ychen,xli}@binghamton.edu
[2] Volgenau School of Engineering, George Mason University, Fairfax, VA 22030, USA
kzeng2@gmu.edu

Abstract. Cognitive radio networks (CRNs) is a promising technology that allows secondary users (SUs) extensively explore spectrum resource usage efficiency, while not introducing interference to licensed users. Due to the unregulated wireless network environment, CRNs are susceptible to various malicious entities. Thus, it is critical to detect anomalies in the first place. However, from the perspective of intrinsic features of CRNs, there is hardly in existence of an universal applicable anomaly detection scheme. Singular Spectrum Analysis (SSA) has been theoretically proven an optimal approach for accurate and quick detection of changes in the characteristics of a running (random) process. In addition, SSA is a model-free method and no parametric models have to be assumed for different types of anomalies, which makes it a universal anomaly detection scheme. In this paper, we introduce an adaptive parameter and component selection mechanism based on coherence for basic SSA method, upon which we built up a sliding window based anomaly detector in CRNs. Our experimental results indicate great accuracy of the SSA-based anomaly detector for multiple anomalies.

Keywords: Cognitive radio networks · Anomaly detection · Singular spectrum analysis

1 Introduction

The rigid spectrum allocation scheme regulated by governmental agencies leads to great deficit on spectrum band resources utility. The emergence of new intelligent spectrum allocation/re-allocation scheme, especially cognitive radio network (CRN), is studied elaborately in the last decade, due to the ever-increasing wireless applications. CRNs allow secondary wireless devices (unlicensed users) access spectrum resources dynamically without introducing major interference to licensed primary users (PUs). Because of the great difficulty and high complexity in dynamic spectrum access (DSA), and many open issues on security deployment, CRN study still stays in tentative phase and needs all-round improvements despite a large quantity of research. A well-designed CRN aims to serve for two

© Springer International Publishing AG 2017
J. Rak et al. (Eds.): MMM-ACNS 2017, LNCS 10446, pp. 247–259, 2017.
DOI: 10.1007/978-3-319-65127-9_20

purposes: to maximize the usage of spare spectrum resource as well as to protect the incumbent primary system from secondary network interference [1].

Due to the uncertainties in PU behaviours and unavoidable interloper including many malicious entities, it is extremely hard to maintain a stable cognitive radio system. Existence of anomaly behaviours, which include traditional anomaly security threats and newly emerged CRN-specific security threats, such as jamming, primary user emulation (PUE) attacks, spectrum sensing data falsification (SSDF), common control channel jamming, selfish users, intruding nodes and more [2], make the situation worse.

In CRNs, "anomaly situation" can be introduced by various malicious activities as well as by versatile unpredictable PU activities, both of which can cause degradation on link quality of CRNs. Sometimes, it is necessary to detect those anomaly situations without introduce much overhead to cognitive entities. This task belongs to change-point detection, which concerns the design and analysis of procedures for "on-the-go" detection of possible changes in the characteristics of a running (random) process. Specifically, the process is assumed to be continuously monitored through sequentially made observations (e.g., measurements), whose behaviors should suggest the process may have statistically changed. The aim is to conclude so within the fewest observations possible, subject to a tolerable level of the risk of false detection [3,4]. The time instance at which the state of the process changes is referred to as the change-point, which is not known in advance.

In this work, we exploit the Singular Spectrum Analysis (SSA) theory to solve the anomaly detection problem in CRNs. The key contribution lies in an adaptive parameter and component selection mechanism that enables the SSA cope with the complexity in anomaly detection in CRNs. For the convenience of discussion, we assume an ON/OFF Markov PU activity model and PUE attacks anomaly model.

The rest of this paper is organized as the following. Section 2 provides background and some most closely related work. Section 3 describes the system model with interference to SU activities. Section 4 explores a study of SSA on CRNs anomaly detection. Then Sect. 5 reports our experimental results. Section 6 concludes this paper.

2   Background and Related Work

To date, there are significant amount of works have been presented to address various CRN seciruty issues. For instance, the counter-measures to SSDF attacks include deploying reputation metric to denote the scale of trustworthy of each user [5], or reporting continuous sensing result to minimal attacks [6]. Game theory and Q-learning algorithm are often utilized to discuss attacker-SU action patterns [7] and against selfish users [8]. In confront of common control channel jamming attack, traditional communication technique of channel hopping is proved efficient for SUs exchanging channel information via multiple common control channels stochastically [9]. From the perspective of intrinsic features of CRNs, there is hardly in existence of an universal anomaly detection scheme.

SSA is introduced by Broomhead and King in 1986 [10]. Since then, it has shown its significant ability in a wide field of time series processing, such as finding data structure, extracting periodic pattern and complex trends, smoothing and change point detection [11,12]. Wu *et al.* applied SSA for data preprocessing, associating with ANN, to predict daily rainfall-runoff transformation [13]. Oropeza and Sacchi presented multichannel singular spectrum analysis (MSSA) as a tool for simultaneously denoising and reconstructing seismic data [14]. Moskvina and Zhigljavsky developed an algorithm of change-point detection in time series, based on sequential application of SSA [15].

A PUE attack is that malicious entities mimic PU signals in order to either occupy spectrum resource selfishly or conduct Denial of Service (DoS) attacks. PUE attacks can be easily implemented in CRNs and introduce great overhead on cognitive radio communication and cause chaos in dynamic spectrum sensing. Many detection techniques are based on geometrical information of the PU transmitter. In [16], the authors claimed that in order to achieve a better attack result, attackers intend to adjust transmission power according to PU activities. By implementing a variable detection method that can measure the received power at SUs, it achieved a good detection result. However, it requires priori knowledge of distances among the nodes in the wireless environment. On the other hand, it is not accurate to identify PU signal by measuring the RSS. Not only because signal strength may vary by a large magnitude over small area, but also the attackers can constantly change the transmitter position and transmission power to disguise themselves. Thus, researchers have tried to eliminate noisy from received signals by constructing a sensor network [17], which introduces overhead to CRNs.

Comparing to all discussed PUE attack counter-measures, we do not aim at sifting adversaries' signal from PU signal. Instead, our method is able to detect abnormal activities without acquiring any priori information of PUs or malicious entities, and neither is there any overhead to PUs.

3   System Model

Let us consider a typical centralized CRN. Due to the opportunistic nature of cognitive radio spectrum access methods and intricate wireless channel traffic model, a method for detecting abnormal activities in CRNs is not always universally applicable to all situations. In an environment of non-deterministic PU traffic pattern, it is difficult to precisely predict channel idle periods. In a distributed CRN, all cognitive nodes share the spectrum resource with incumbent users, thus a single cognitive node can hardly be aware of an anomaly at system level. Therefore, a smart attacker can take advantage of the nature that channel idle period could fluctuate dramatically, and disguise as the PU to occupy spectrum resource selfishly. In our system model, an online detection technique is designed to fit many wireless environments regardless of channel fluctuation, by simply inspecting cognitive nodes' activities.

3.1 Assumptions

We made the following assumptions for our model:

- The CRN consists of several cognitive nodes that can dynamically access spectrum resource, and a fusion center (FC) that collects cognitive nodes' data flow information, and detects abnormal activates;
- The total available spectrum resource is composed by multiple PU channels. The channels are independent to each other on traffic pattern. The traffic model for each channel is non-deterministic with fluctuation in both busy and idle periods;
- The spectrum resource is intensively used by CRNs in which the cognitive node stores the sensed channel state at local and will transmit data when the channel is not used by other cognitive nodes, while a minimal transmission spectrum opportunity time slot T_{min_tx} is required;
- Every cognitive node will broadcast a packet P_{num} to FC after a transmission period T_{period} via an idle channel. P_{num} contains information of the number of received data packets in last T_{period}. The overhead to each cognitive node is minimal for only one extra packet is required for every T_{period};
- It is always feasible for each cognitive node to find an idle channel to broadcast P_{num}, because $T_{period} \gg T_{busy}$. (T_{period} is in the order of second, while T_{busy} is always in order of millisecond [18]);
- Attackers are smart enough to mimic PUs' signals, and they can conduct secret attack without introducing great fluctuation to the entire CRN;
- The FC can perform online anomaly detection based on the integrated statistics from all cognitive nodes.

3.2 Wireless Traffic Model and Analysis

Dynamic spectrum access (DSA) allows a cognitive radio to assign SUs some licensed bands temporarily, in an opportunistic and non-interfering manner. Therefore, the information about the spectrum occupancy pattern of the PUs is necessary. Because PU channels are independent with each other, it is feasible to analyze the model of an individual wireless channel. At a particular time point and a geographical location, a primary radio channel is either busy or idle. As illustrated in Fig. 1, T_{busy}^i denotes PU busy time slot on the i-th channel, which indicates there is PU activity exist in such channel. T_{idle}^i stands for PU idle time slot on i-th channel, which means no primary user is occupying this channel. Hence, the primary radio channel's spectrum occupancy pattern, which is also the PU's traffic pattern, describes the distribution of the durations of the busy and idle time slots.

Basically, there are two classes of traffic patterns in wireless environment: (1) Deterministic patterns, where the duration of either idle time (T_{idle}) or busy time (T_{busy}), if not both, is fixed; and (2) Stochastic patterns, where the start time and duration of both states are random and be modeled with statistical properties [19]. For the former, the appearance of an attack will certainly change

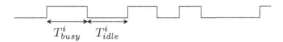

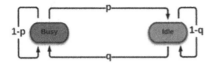

Fig. 1. Channel model of idle & busy time.

the deterministic patterns, making it easy to detect. For the later, which is more likely in real world situation, since the state exchanges randomly, it is hard to determine if the change of the occupancy pattern is related to an attack. Therefore, considering a continuous-time model, the channel remains in one state for a random period before switching to the other state. It is proven to be efficient that the PU activity can be modeled as continuous-time, alternating ON/OFF two-state Markov Renewal Process (MRP) [20], as shown in Fig. 2.

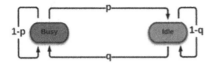

Fig. 2. PU channel ON/OFF two-state Markov Renewal Model.

In this model, both T_{idle}^i and T_{busy}^i can be regarded as independent and identically distributed (i.i.d.) process, where the PU activity arrival follows Poisson distribution. The continuous time span, i.e. T_{idle}^i and T_{busy}^i, follows exponential distribution, if PU activity arrival is a Poisson process [21].

The length of T_{idle}^i is critical for CRNs when exploiting the spectrum resource. A high time resolution of PU activity pattern may cause futile spectrum resource. For example, a successful packet transmission in CRNs requires a minimal transmission time span T_{min_tx}. In some intermittent PU activity channel, T_{idle}^i is usually too small for a complete transmission by SU, where $T_{idle}^i < T_{min\_tx}$. A valid idle transmission slot requires $T_{idle}^i > T_{min\_tx}$.

With a stable PU transmission pattern, there is a corresponding stable spectrum resource pool for CRNs. Any anomaly behaviour introduced either by malicious entities or PU itself, will cause variation on rate parameters λ_{idle} and λ_{busy}, and afterwards the available SU transmission time span T_{tx}. In addition, a certain external symptom will show at FC as a change of the integrated packet flow P_{num}.

In this paper, we implement anomaly detection based on the channel information P_{num} from all cognitive nodes, without knowing prior information λ_{idle} and λ_{busy}.

4   SSA-based Anomaly Detection

When the channel fluctuation is not considered, it is straightforward to attribute a deterioration of CRN channel quality to an anomaly in certain category. From the viewpoint of the FC, an anomaly results in the decrease of the overall receiving packets rate of all the SUs. Therefore, SSA algorithm is introduced to detect the change of the overall packets rate. The basic algorithm of SSA is described as following.

Assume $\mathbb{X} = (x_1, x_2, \cdots, x_N)$ is a real-value time series with the length of N. A sliding window, with a fixed window length of M, is adopted to truncate $\mathbb{X}$ and get a series of lagged vectors, and then, transform these vectors to a trajectory matrix X. The trajectory matrix X includes the whole information of the original time series $\mathbb{X}$. The columns X_j of the trajectory matrix X can be considered as vectors in an M-dimensional space $\mathbf{R}_M$. A particular combination of a certain number l of the Singular Value Decomposition (SVD) eigenvectors determines an l-dimensional subspace $\mathcal{L}_l$ in $\mathbf{R}_M$, $l < M$. The M-dimensional data $X_1, \cdots, X_K$ is then projected onto the subspace $\mathcal{L}_l$.

In our system model, FC gets the packets rate in every T_{period} from each single SU, and calculates the whole network's packets rate $\mathbb{X} = (x_1, x_2, \cdots, x_N)$, which is the object of the SSA processing. The SSA processing of $\mathbb{X}$ includes the following steps.

Step 1: Embedding

Map the vector $\mathbb{X}$ into an $M \times K$ matrix X,

$$X = \left[\overrightarrow{X_1}, \overrightarrow{X_2}, \cdots, \overrightarrow{X_K} \right] = (x_{i,j})_{i,j=1}^{M,K} \tag{1}$$

$$\overrightarrow{X_i} = (x_i, \cdots, x_{M+i-1})', i = 1, \cdots, K \tag{2}$$

where $K = N - M + 1$. The matrix X is called trajectory matrix and the vectors $\overrightarrow{X_i}$ are called lagged vectors. Note that X is a Hankel matrix, which has the equal elements on it's skew-diagonals $i + j = const$.

Step 2: Singular Value Decomposition

Apply SVD procedure on the trajectory matrix X and obtain M singular values $\sqrt{\lambda_1}, \sqrt{\lambda_2}, \cdots, \sqrt{\lambda_M}$ (in decreasing order) and the corresponding left singular vectors $U_1, U_2, \cdots, U_M$, and right singular vectors $V_1, V_2, \cdots, V_M$. The collection $(\sqrt{\lambda_i}, U_i, V_i)$, $i = 1, 2, \cdots, M$ is called the i-th eigentriple of the SVD. According to the standard SVD terminology, λ_i and U_i are the eigenvalues and eigenvectors of matrix $R = XX'$, respectively, while V_i are the eigenvectors of matrix $R' = X'X$, V_i also are called the principal components. The eigentriple satisfies $V_i = X'U_i/\sqrt{\lambda_i}$. Note that the rank of X is d, which is also the rank of R, then $\lambda_i = 0$, where $i > d$. So the trajectory matrix X will be:

$$X = X_1 + X_2 + \cdots + X_d \tag{3}$$

where $X_i = \sqrt{\lambda_i}U_iV_i'$ are rank-one biorthogonal matrices, $i = 1, \cdots, d$.

Step 3: Grouping

Select a subset indices I of $\{1, 2, \cdots, d\}$, with l elements

$$I = \{i_1, i_2, \cdots, i_l\} \tag{4}$$

such that

$$\bar{I} = \{1, 2, \cdots, d\}/I \tag{5}$$

Then the representation turns to

$$X = X_{i_1} + X_{i_2} + \cdots + X_{i_l} + X_{\bar{I}} \tag{6}$$

where $X_{\bar{I}} = \sum_{i \notin I} X_i$.

Step 4: Diagonal Averaging

Diagonal Averaging is used to transfer matrix $X_I = \sum_{i \in I} X_i$ into a time series (reconstruction). According to mathematic deduction, it is the component-sum of the original series $\mathbb{X}$.

$$x_i = \begin{cases} \frac{1}{i} \sum_{j=1}^{i} x_{j,i-j+1} & for \ 1 \leq i < M \\ \frac{1}{M} \sum_{j=1}^{M} x_{j,i-j+1} & for \ M \leq i \leq K \\ \frac{1}{N-i+1} \sum_{j=i-K+1}^{N-K+1} x_{j,i-j+1} & for \ K < i \leq N \end{cases} \tag{7}$$

That is, the reconstructed series element x_i equals to the average of the corresponding matrix elements sharing the same location with that x_i appears in the trajectory matrix X. The main purpose of SSA is to decompose the original time series into several additive components, based on the assumption that this series is a sum of several simpler series. Specifically, a general descriptive model of the series that we use in SSA methodology is an additive model in which the components are trends, oscillations and noise. Figure 3 shows a SSA decomposition of a section of CRN packet rate flow. The conception of "trend" depicts a components that is (i) not stationary and (ii) 'slowly varies' during the whole period of time that the series is being observed, as the first and second components shown in Fig. 3. Meanwhile, the 'oscillation' components can be divided into periodic and quasi-periodic, like the third and forth components

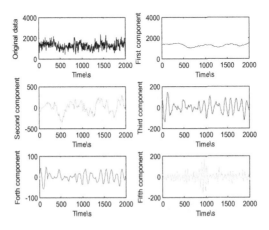

Fig. 3. SSA decomposition example.

shown in Fig. 3. Compared to them, the 'noise' component doesn't have a certain boundary with others. But generally speaking, 'noise' are aperiodic series and contribute less to the original series than others, like the fifth component.

Figure 4 shows the differences among the three kinds of components in frequency domain. In general, the trend converge its energy at the low frequency region, shown by the first and second components. The oscillation corresponds to a peak at particular frequency, and always occur in pairs, shown by the forth and fifth component. Separating the whole series into these components and analyzing the LRRs for interpretable components are helpful to obtain reliable and meaningful SSA results. In our case, only the general variation trend of channel traffic flow are considered, so that the gentle periodical fluctuation and random channel error are ignored.

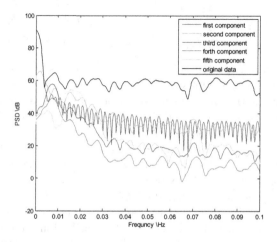

Fig. 4. Frequency domain analysis example.

Table 1. Network setting

Simulation time	10000 s
Number of PUs	5
Number of SUs	10
Number of tranmission channles	5
SU spectrum sensing duration	10 ms
Transmission cycle of PUs	40 ms to 50 ms ($not\ fixed$)
Idle cycle of PUs	50 ms to 70 ms ($not\ fixed$)
Data packet size	2000 bytes
SU data channel rate	1.00 Mbps
SU transmission period T_{period}	5 s
Attacker hopping	Yes

5   Experimental Results

This paper reports a preliminary study, where the SSA method is employed to off-line anomaly detection problem. It illustrates the capability of SSA on capturing the operating trend of random packet rate.

5.1   Experimental Setup

Network Setting: A CRN is constructed using OMNET++ 4.6. In our implementation, SUs are randomly distributed in the environment and they can access to all channels in an opportunistic spectrum sensing manner. Each channel is legally allocated to a PU, whose duty cycle and idle cycle are stochastically distributed in a range. All SUs know neither geometry information of PUs, nor their broadcasting patterns. We test our detection method via introducing PUE attacks in experiment scenarios.

Table 2. Off-line detector setting

SSA setting	Widow length	2000 *samples*
	Trajectory matrix size M	300 *samples*
	Grouping element I	$\{1, 2\}$
Differentiation setting	Interval	4 *samples*
Detector setting	Threshold	15.12

Scenario Setting: This anomaly detector is applied to a PUE attack specified environment as the following. A malicious party is a smart attacker can start PUE attack at a randomly chosen time, and stop after accomplished sufficient attacks. For disguise purpose, the attacker hops among all spectrum channels randomly and implement secret PUE attacks. In this simulation, we applied 20 different seeds to construct 20 different CRN scenarios for anomaly detection. Among all scenarios, the attacker conduct PUE attack at 1500 s, 5000 s, 8000 s respectively, and end at 3000 s, 7000 s, 9300 s respectively. Specific parameter setting can be referred to Table 1.

Detector Setting: An efficient detector requires a sufficiently long sliding window N in order to catch the principal system features, and the row size of trajectory matrix M should be restricted to $M < N/2$. In this off-line detection, since a long window is preferred, N can be pre-set as large as 2000 samples, and M can be pre-set as 300 samples. The detection threshold setting is critical in our detector. It can be generated by history observation data in normal non-attacking scenarios with proper guarding pad. Table 2 presents all detector parameters.

5.2   Anomaly Detection Experimental Results

We present detection results with and without PUE attack respectively. In Fig. 5, the left-top subfigure shows an original packet flow synthesized by FC, which consists of oscillations and spikes. The right-top subfigure shows the data sequence reconstructed by the SSA process. Based on the features carried by principal components of the original data, the first and the second principal components, which are shown by the two subfigures in the bottom of Fig. 5, are selected for reconstruction due to the great oscillations in other components. The reconstructed data sequence shows clear changes around the time points: 1500 s, 3000 s, 5000 s, 7000 s, 8000 s, and 9300 s, when the PUE attacks started or ended. In contrast, Fig. 6 shows an original packet flow without PUE attack and the reconstructed data sequence from SSA. The reconstructed data indicates a smooth and steady CRN behavior. Besides the reconstruction process, our detection model contains a differential detector. Figures 7 and 8 show the outputs of the differential detector corresponding to cases with and without PUE attack respectively. While the detector output in Fig. 7 also shows spikes at those six

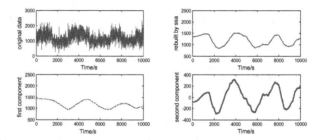

Fig. 5. Original data flow, SSA reconstructed data flow, and the first and the second principal components with attack.

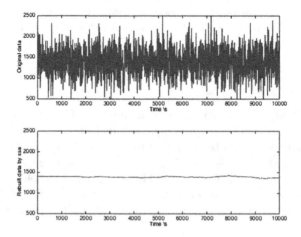

Fig. 6. Original data flow and SSA reconstructed data flow without attack.

anomaly points, the output in Fig. 8 presents only small fluctuations. Threshold configuration in differential detector is critical. Thus, a training session is required to find threshold properly.

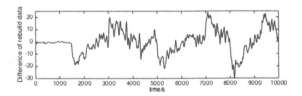

Fig. 7. Differential detector result with attack.

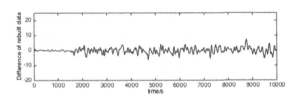

Fig. 8. Differential detector result without attack.

Based on our detection method, with respective history data training, our SSA based detection method achieved a detection rate of 84%, with false alarm rate of 8%, as shown in Table 3. However, we suffered an average delay of 45.96 s, which may be resulted from two factors. The results show the applicability of SSA based anomaly detection in CRN.

Table 3. Simulation study result

Detection rate	84%
False alarm	8%
Average delay	45.96 s

6   Discussions and Conclusions

From the experiment result, our SSA based anomaly detection method show high detection rate and low false alarm rate, even when encountered with subtle PUE attack. Although the simulation environment only considered two anomalies:

PUE attack and PU abnormality, our proposed method can be used for many other anomaly detections, such as spectrum sensing data falsification (SSDF), jamming, because those anomaly activities will inevitably deteriorate communication condition of CRNs. However, our detection method suffers from relatively high detection delay. The delay is generally caused by two factors: (1) our light-weighted anomaly detector requires SUs report their transmission quality every several seconds, this relative low report time resolution will bring small amount of detection delay; (2) our detection method is built upon transportation-layer-based data flow, which is not very sensitive to physical layer anomaly activities (most common in CRNs).

In comparison to traditional attack-specified security insurance techniques, our SSA based anomaly detection method is applicable to most anomaly environment in CRNs. However, this method is no more than a detector. Due to its lightweight and ease of use, this method can be used as a rudimentary CRN network monitor and anomaly detector; once anomaly is detected, further action is needed to eliminate the anomaly.

Singular Spectrum Analysis (SSA) method possesses attractive features such as parametric model free that enables it to detect different categories of anomalies. The SSA algorithm is suitable for off-line batch data processing. Our experimental results verified the effectiveness of the SSA detector. While this algorithm can detect subtle changes with high accuracy, it suffers relatively long delays.

As our on-going effort, we are exploring to extend SSA to handle online anomaly detection problem. An adaptive parameter and component selection mechanism is being introduced to enable real time operation. In addition, we will also focus on the delay issue and aiming at an efficient anomaly detection scheme with both satisfactory accuracy and acceptable delays.

References

1. Adelantado, F., Verikoukis, C.: Detection of malicious users in cognitive radio ad hoc networks: a non-parametric statistical approach. Ad Hoc Netw. 11(8), 2367–2380 (2013)
2. Esch, J.: A survey of security challenges in cognitive radio networks: solutions and future research directions. Proc. IEEE 12(100), 3170–3171 (2012)
3. Basseville, M., Nikiforov, I.V., et al.: Theory and Application, vol. 104. Prentice Hall, Englewood Cliffs (1993)
4. Poor, H.V.: Hadjiliadis O Quickest detection, vol. 40. Cambridge University Press, Cambridge (2009)
5. Rawat, A.S., Anand, P., Chen, H., Varshney, P.K.: Countering byzantine attacks in cognitive radio networks. In: IEEE (2010)
6. Min, A.W., Shin, K.G., Hu, X.: Attack-tolerant distributed sensing for dynamic spectrum access networks. In: IEEE (2009)
7. Wang, B., Wu, Y., Liu, K.R., Clancy, T.C.: An anti-jamming stochastic game for cognitive radio networks. IEEE J. Sel. Areas Commun. 29(4), 877–889 (2011)
8. Attar, A., Nakhai, M.R., Aghvami, A.H.: Cognitive radio game for secondary spectrum access problem. IEEE Trans. Wireless Commun. 8(4), 2121–2131 (2009)

9. Cormio, C., Chowdhury, K.R.: Common control channel design for cognitive radio wireless ad hoc networks using adaptive frequency hopping. Ad Hoc Netw. **8**(4), 430–438 (2010)

10. Broomhead, D.S., King, G.P.: Extracting qualitative dynamics from experimental data. Physica D **20**(2–3), 217–236 (1986)

11. Rukhin, A.L.: Analysis of time series structure ssa and related techniques. Technometrics **44**(3), 290–290 (2002)

12. Yang, Z., Zhou, N., Polunchenko, A., Chen, Y.: Quick online detection of start time of disturbance in power grid. The IEEE GlobeCom 2015. Selected Areas in Communications Symposium, Smart Grid Communications Track, pp. 1–6. IEEE (2015)

13. Wu, C., Chau, K.: Rainfall-runoff modeling using artificial neural network coupled with singular spectrum analysis. J. Hydrol. **399**(3), 394–409 (2011)

14. Oropeza, V., Sacchi, M.: Simultaneous seismic data denoising and reconstruction via multichannel singular spectrum analysis. Geophysics **76**(3), V25–V32 (2011)

15. Moskvina, V., Zhigljavsky, A.: An algorithm based on singular spectrum analysis for change-point detection. Commun. Stat. Simul. Comput. **32**(2), 319–352 (2003)

16. Chen, Z., Cooklev, T., Chen, C., Pomalaza-Ráez, C.: Modeling primary user emulation attacks and defenses in cognitive radio networks. IEEE (2009)

17. Chen, R., Park, J.M., Reed, J.H.: Defense against primary user emulation attacks in cognitive radio networks. IEEE J. Sel. Areas Commun. **26**(1), 25–37 (2008)

18. Mahamuni, S., Mishra, V.: Performance evaluation of spectrum detection in cognitive radio network. Int. J. Commun. Netw. Syst. Sci. **7**(11), 485 (2014)

19. Marko Hoyhtya, S.P., Mammela, A.: Improving the performance of cognitive radios through classification, learning, and predictive channel selection. In: Advances in Electronics and Telecommunications (2011)

20. Rehmani, M.H., Viana, A.C., Khalife, H., Fdida, S.: Surf: a distributed channel selection strategy for data dissemination in multi-hop cognitive radio networks. Comput. Commun. **36**(10), 1172–1185 (2013)

21. Sriram, K., Whitt, W.: Characterizing superposition arrival processes in packet multiplexers for voice and data. IEEE J. Sel. Areas Commun. **4**(6), 833–846 (1986)

HEPPA: Highly Efficient Privacy Preserving Authentication for ITS

An Braeken[1], Sergey Bezzateev[2], Abdellah Touhafi[1], and Natalia Voloshina[2(✉)]

[1] INDI and ETRO Department, Vrije Universiteit Brussel, Anderlecht, Belgium
[2] ITMO University, Saint Petersburg, Russia
nataliv@yandex.ru

Abstract. Intelligent Transport Systems (ITS) play a very important role to increase the safety and to decrease road congestions. These systems require secure communication between both infrastructure and vehicles.

In this paper, we construct a three-factor highly efficient privacy preserving authentication (HEPPA) protocol between vehicles and road side units (RSUs) using a telematics device enabling biometric operations, bonded to the vehicle. Broadcast messages sent by the vehicles only contain symmetric key cryptographic operations. Elliptic curve cryptographic operations are used for the key establishment and renewal between the vehicles and RSUs. Due to the clever construction of the pseudonyms, the RSU listening the broadcast messages is able to directly detect malicious behaviour and to alert the neighbouring vehicles.

Moreover, no certificate revocation lists need to be stored at the vehicles and no list of key material is required at the RSUs. The real identity of malicious behaving vehicles and corresponding drivers can be revealed by a cooperation among RSU and certificate authority (CA). Consequently, attacking an RSU will not leak privacy related information. What is more, the tamper resistant hardware in the telematics device only stores user specific and temporary key related information, so no global system security parameters.

1 Introduction

Intelligent Traffic Systems (ITS) offer innovative services in order to inform the traffic users about the road status, resulting in a decrease of traffic congestions, a reduction of air pollution and an increase of safety. To do so, the ITS needs to receive information from infrastructural sensors (eg. traffic light) and traffic users as for instance vehicles equipped with wireless communication capabilities. Vehicular ad hoc networks (VANETs), representing an important part of such an ITS, are able to realize both vehicle-to-vehicle (V2V) and vehicle-to-road side unit (V2R) communication using dedicated short range communications DSRC [1]. In the context of road safety applications, vehicles need to continuously broadcast traffic messages, including the vehicle's location, speed, etc. It can warn a driver that a collision is likely, or alert a driver to a vehicle that is

© Springer International Publishing AG 2017
J. Rak et al. (Eds.): MMM-ACNS 2017, LNCS 10446, pp. 260–271, 2017.
DOI: 10.1007/978-3-319-65127-9_21

braking hard but is hidden from view. Consequently, an essential requirement for establishing successful and safe services is that the participants of the system are honest and trustworthy, which can only be realized when there is a sufficient degree of security and privacy. Note that we assume the vehicle is bonded to a telematics device provided with biometric technology [4], similar as in the 2FLIP protocol description [5]. This device allows monitoring of an individual vehicle's movements and is able to record the speed, location and mass of a vehicle, which can be used as a regulatory tool, for purposes such as road user charging, compliance and enforcement. Besides security requirements, also a good performance is critical due to the high speed of the vehicles and the need for realtime analysis of the information (especially in the case of safety applications). For instance, following [6], the frequency of safety messages is on average around 300 ms, dropping to 100 ms in case of dense environments. Thus, if a vehicle has 50–200 vehicles in its communication range, it needs to analyze approximately 200–2000 messages per second. Moreover, in order to offer resilience against DoS, authentication operations should be lightweight both with respect to storage and computation.

In this paper, we present a system that is able to offer all of the above mentioned security characteristics in a very efficient way. Three-factor authentication between the driver and the telematics device is first required. The three factors correspond with the possession of the telematics device and biometrics and knowledge of the password. Next, the vehicle remotely requests the group key and the individual shared key of the region from the local RSU using temporary approved credentials of the central registration unit of the CA. This key is used in the broadcast messages, sent among the vehicles of the region. The RSU has the responsibility to check the validity of the identity in the broadcast messages, while the vehicles can check the integrity and authentication. The proposed system is based on ideas from a recently proposed anonymous multi-server authentication protocol [7]. We show how HEPPA can offer a more user friendly alternative with respect to maintenance and key update, compared to the 2FLIP [5] protocol, which has been recently proposed and shown to be the most efficient and secure protocol in the state of the art.

The rest of the paper is organized as follows. Section 2 presents related work. In Sect. 3 we describe some background. Section 4 is dedicated to the description of our proposed system. The security and performance analysis is explained in Sects. 5 and 6 respectively. Finally, Sect. 7 ends with conclusions.

2   Related Work

The main issue to solve is the establishment of a privacy preserving system. For this purpose, the two most often used mechanisms in the literature of VANETs are pseudonyms and group signatures.

Pseudonym-based schemes [6] use anonymous certificates, issued by the CA, which are related to some pseudo-identity. The messages are signed with the private keys and the associated certificates are presented to proof the validity of the signature. The main disadvantage in this approach is the huge storage requirement of the different certificates, the enormous length of the certificate revocation list (CRL) stored in each vehicle, and thus also the significant time to check this list before verifying the signature. Proposals in literature have been made to either reduce the length of the CRL or even to avoid its usage. In [8], a mechanism based on hash chains allowed the reduction of the CRL. Identity-based verification schemes, requiring costly pairing operations [9], were able to remove the need for CRLs. Also in [10], CRLs could be removed by using two levels of pseudonyms, acquired from CA and RSU. However, this system requires pervasive deployment of infrastructure.

In group based systems [11,12], anonymity is obtained by creating a group of vehicles with hidden identities. The message is signed with the private key of a group member and verified by means of the public group key [13]. Although the CRL only grows linearly in this approach, the group based systems suffer from the huge overhead of the creation of the groups, which are frequently changing.

Besides the pseudonym and group based approaches, also symmetric key based solutions [5,14,15] have been proposed for VANETs. Both [14,15] propose schemes where the vehicles are able to send a message to the RSU using symmetric key mechanisms after a Diffie Hellman key agreement exchange. The RSU then collects all the info and forwards this info to the other vehicles, signing it with its private key to guarantee authenticity. The system of [15] can be seen as an improvement of [14], where issues are solved of neighbouring RSUs and where the Diffie Hellmann key exchange is organized by means of a pseudo identity, determined by the CA.

In [5], 2FLIP allows symmetric key based mechanisms for both the sending and receiving of broadcast messages directly among the vehicles. This protocol is the most efficient one presented in literature. However, the main disadvantage of the protocol is that it heavily depends on the tamper resistant device storing the secret key of the total system. This key needs to be physically preloaded by the CA, and especially for the key renewal this is not an evident process as it all needs to be changed at the same time. Note that a public key approach of 2FLIP, where also the long term security of the broadcast messages depends of key material stored in a tamper resistant device, is presented in [16]. The broadcast messages in this scheme contain public key operations.

To compare, we propose a system with similar performance as 2FLIP [5] for the message broadcast among the vehicles. Nevertheless, we do not require the existence of a tamper resistant device for the storage of the long term key, requiring a very inefficient installation and renewal procedure as in [5]. Instead, we propose a remote process to exchange a frequently changing group key with each of the RSUs in the vehicle's communication range, using ideas presented in [7].

3   Background

The scheme is based on Elliptic Curve Cryptography (ECC), since it offers light-weight public key cryptographic (PKC) solutions. We denote by G the base point generator of the elliptic curve (EC) of prime order p, defined in the finite field $\mathbb{F}_p$.

The main entities in the system are as follows.

- A vehicle possesses an electronic identity VID_i, which is installed into the onboard unit (OBU) of the vehicle by a vehicle registration authority. The vehicle can be controlled by different users with identity UID_i, each carrying their own portable telematics device with unique serial number (DID_i) bonded to the vehicle's OBU. The telematics device possesses a secure tamper resistant module TRM_i to store user specific, temporary key material. This is a reasonable assumption, as tamper resistant packaging modules are nowadays mature in industry (eg. IBM 4758 cryptographic coprocessor). The OBU is used to regularly communicate traffic information, emergency warnings, etc., and to interpret incoming valid messages.
- The RSUs are stationary beacons, responsible for the local management of the information in their communication range. This mainly includes key management and authentication verification of the broadcasted messages. It has large storage and powerful communication capabilities of 1 Km to 3 km.
- The central authority (CA) consists of two separated entities, being the general central authority (GCA) and the registration center (RC). The GCA checks the request of the user by verifying the identity of itself, its telematics device and its vehicle to get access to the communication infrastructure. The RC derives the required security material in case a valid certificate of the GCA can be shown.
- A law enforcement agency (LEA) has the right to request the identity of the driver and the vehicle after the declaration of malicious behaviour. Based on this information, it can exclude a particular user or vehicle to further participate by contacting the RC and GCA.

We assume that the required cryptograhic functions and the EC parameters, together with the EC operations, are implemented in each entity participating the scheme. We further assume that all OBUs on the vehicles, RSUs, GCA, and RC possess a GPS receiver, and thus are time synchronized, since timestamps are used in our protocol to avoid replay attacks.

3.1 Notations

Each entity in the system has a unique electronic identity and private and public key pair. In addition, the user also has password PW_i and biometric template Bio_i. Table 1 summarizes the most common abbreviations and parameters in this paper.

4 Protocol HEPPA

Six main phases are distinguished in the protocol: registration to GCA, registration to RC, authentication and session key establishment with RSU, communication between vehicle and RSU, broadcast communication among vehicles, and renewal of user's password.

Table 1. Overview of most common abbreviations

G	Base point EC generator
VID_i, UID_i, DID_i	Identity of vehicle, user and telematics device
PID_i	Pseudo identity of the user, derived by the RSU
TRM_i	Tamper resistant module of DID_i
SID_i	Identity of the RSU
$(x, T_i)_{cert_y}$	Certificate on x, generated by y with expiration time T_i
$sig_x(y)$	Signature of x on y
(d_i, Q_i)	Private-public key pair of user
(d_S, Q_S)	Private-public key pair of RSU
(d_R, Q_R)	Private-public key pair of RC
y	Master key of RC
GK	Secret group key, shared between RC and RSUs
k_i	Secret session key, shared between RSU and user

4.1 Registration to GCA

First, the user needs to generate its own key pair (d_i, Q_i). Next, the user contacts the GCA to obtain a certificate on the combination of its identity together with the identities of the telematics device and the vehicle (UID_i, DID_i, VID_i) and the public key Q_i. Note that we need a secure channel for this process. These actions are detailed below.

– Public-private key definition of the user:
  The user enters its identity UID_i, password PW and biometrics Bio into its telematics device with identity DID_i, bonded to the vehicle with identity VID_i. Using the preloaded identities VID_i, DID_i on the device, together with a randomly chosen variable rb stored in the memory of the device, the private key $d_i = H(UID_i \| DID_i \| VID_i \| H(PW) \oplus rb \| H(Bio))$ is computed. Next, the corresponding public key $Q_i = d_i G$ is derived for it. The values UID_i, DID_i, VID_i, Q_i are sent to the CA through a secure channel.
– Response of GCA:
  The CA checks the request of the user by contacting the national vehicle management department. After a positive check, it validates the link between the identities and the corresponding public key Q_i by generating a certificate on $\{H(UID_i, VID_i, DID_i), Q_i, T_i\}$, where T_i represents the expiration time of the certificate. Finally, the GCA stores $\{(UID_i, VID_i, DID_i), Q_i, T_i\}$.

The device first computes $E_i = H(H(PW) \oplus rb \| H(Bio) \oplus rb \| UID_i \| DID_i \| VID_i)$. Then it stores the parameters rb, Q_i, T_i and E_i, together with the received certificate $cert_i = \{H(UID_i \| VID_i \| DID_i), Q_i, T_i; T_i\}_{cert_{GCA}}$. The parameters d_i, UID_i, DID_i, VID_i are stored in the TRM_i of DID_i.

4.2 Registration to RC

Actions to Be Performed by the RSUs. The RSU generates its own secret key d_S and public key $Q_S = d_S G$ and publishes its public key Q_S, together with its corresponding certificate generated by the GCA. The RC shares with all registered RSUs a group key GK through a well known multicast group key mechanism, like eg. [17]. This key is regularly updated. Note that the previous versions of the group key, together with the period of their life time, are stored at the RSUs until their expiration date.

Actions to Be Performed by the User. Using the certificate $cert_i$ of GCA, the user is now able to register with the RC without the need of a secure channel by performing the following operations. We assume that the public key of the RC can be consulted through secure publicly available repositories. The visualization of this process after user login step is depicted in Fig. 1.

User login: The identity of the driver should be verified. As a first step, the driver needs to plug the telematics device into the vehicle. Then, the user logs in with password and biometrics on the telematics device. Based on this input and the stored values, the device computes $H(H(PW) \oplus rb \| H(Bio) \oplus$

UID, DID, VID	RC
$Q_i, T_i, cert_i, rb, E_i$	$d_R, Q_R, GK, y,$ Public key of GCA
d_i, UID_i, DID_i, VID_i	
Q_R	

$F_i = H(d_i \| UID_i \| DID_i \| VID_i)$
$d_i = H(UID_i \| DID_i \| VID_i \| H(PW) \oplus rb \| H(Bio))$
$l \leftarrow_R \mathbb{F}_p, L = lG$
$P_{lR} = lQ_R$
$P_{iR} = d_i Q_R$
$k_1 = H(P_{iR} \| T_1 \| H(UID_i \| DID_i \| VID_i))$
$k_{lR} = H(P_{lR} \| T_1)$
$C_1 = E_{k_{lR}}(k_1 \| F_i \| H(UID_i \| DID_i \| VID_i) \| Q_i \| T_i \| cert_i)$

$\xrightarrow{C_1 \| T_1 \| L}$

$T_2 - T_1 \leq \epsilon$
$P_{Rl} = d_R L$
$k_{Rl} = H(P_{Rl} \| T_1)$
$k_1 \| F_i \| H(UID_i \| DID_i \| VID_i) \| Q_i \| T_i \| cert_i \| Q_r = D_{k_{Rl}}(C_1)$
$P_{Ri} = d_R Q_i$
Check $cert_i, k_1$

$A_i = H(H(UID_i \| DID_i \| VID_i) \| GK \| y \| n)$
$B_i = A_i \oplus GK$
$C_i = H(A_i) \oplus H(F_i \| Q_i \| H(UID_i \| DID_i \| VID_i))$
$k_2 = H(k_{Rl} \| T_1 \| T_2 \| H(UID_i \| DID_i \| VID_i))$
$sig = sig_{RC}(H(T_2 \| GK \| B_i \| Q_i))$
$C_2 = E_{k_2}(B_i \| C_i \| T_2 \| sig)$
Store $H(UID_i \| DID_i \| VID_i), n$

$\xleftarrow{C_2 \| T_2}$

$T_3 - T_2 \leq \epsilon$
$k_2 = H(k_{lR} \| T_1 \| T_2 \| H(UID_i \| DID_i \| VID_i))$
$B_i \| C_i \| T_2 \| sig = D_{k_2}(C_2)$
Check T_2
Store B_i, C_i, T_2, sig

Fig. 1. Steps during the registration request of user with RC after successful user login

$rb\|UID_i\|DID_i\|VID_i)$. If this value corresponds with the stored E_i, the user is authenticated and can further proceed. The telematics device is now activated until it is unplugged or reached a certain period.

Note that each variable in the derivation of RSU has a specific meaning. The parameter A_i is only constructible by RC (knowledge of y) and the variable C_i by the device (knowledge of F_i). Also, a valid relation between A_i and B_i can only be defined by the RC and checked by the RSUs (knowledge of GK), taking into account that the device can only determine $H(A_i)$ from C_i. We also make attention to the fact that the device is not able to verify the signature sig, as it does not know the group key GK. Instead, the signature verification will be performed later by the RSUs.

4.3   Authentication and Session Key Establishment with RSU

For this step, we suppose that the user has successfully logged in and the telematics device is activated. If the vehicle enters a new RSU communication area, it requests the public key and corresponding certificate $(SID_i, Q_S)_{cert_{GCA}}$ of this RSU. After successful verification, the authentication and session key establishment with this RSU can start. The steps of the process are shown in Fig. 2.

As a result of the protocol, the vehicle and RSU possess a common shared secret key k_i, a set of m pseudonyms and a group key k_g, which are all stored in the TRM_i of the device. Also $H(A_i)$ is stored in TRM_i.

4.4   Communication Between Vehicle and RSU

We consider here both the transmission and reception of messages by the vehicle with the RSU.

– Transmission from vehicle to RSU: As the RSU is in the possession of a shared symmetric key k_i, the vehicle will send the message M in the following way

$$t\|PID_i\|H(H(A_i)\|T_5)\|M\|T_5\|H(k_i\|t\|PID_i\|H(H(A_i)\|T_5)\|M\|T_5)$$

where t is a random value between 1 and m, and T_5 the current timestamp.
– Reception of message by RSU: First the timestamp is checked. From $t\|PID_i$, the RSU can compute $A_i = PID_i \oplus H(d_S\|k_g\|t)$ and also $H(H(A_i)\|T_5)$ to verify the validity of the vehicle's message. Next, the RSU is able to derive $k_i = H(A_i\|d_S\|k_g)$ and to check the second hash value.

4.5   Broadcast Communication Among Vehicles

In order to submit a broadcast message M at timestamp T_6, the vehicle will send the following message.

$$t\|PID_i\|H(H(A_i)\|T_6)\|M\|T_6\|H(k_g\|t\|PID_i\|H(H(A_i)\|T_6)\|M\|T_6)$$

This message is verified by the other vehicles and the RSU.

User – Vehicle	RSU
$T_i, Q_i, cert_i, rb, E_i, B_i, C_i, T_2, sig, Q_S, Q_R$ d_i, UID_i, DID_i, VID_i	d_S, Q_S, Q_R, GK, y

$E_i? = H(H(PW) \oplus rb \| H(Bio) \oplus rb \| UID_i \| DID_i \| VID_i)$
$F_i = H(d_i \| UID_i \| DID_i \| VID_i)$
$f \leftarrow_R \mathbb{F}_p, F = fG$
$P_{fS} = fQ_S$
$P_{iR} = d_iQ_R$
$H(A_i) = C_i \oplus H(F_i \| Q_i \| H(UID_i \| DID_i \| VID_i))$
$CID_i = B_i \oplus H(P_{fS} \| T_3)$
$k_3 = H(T_3 \| P_{fS}) \oplus H(A_i)$
$C_3 = E_{k_3}(sig \| Q_i \| T_2)$

$$\xrightarrow{\quad C_3 \| CID_i \| F \| T_3 \quad}$$

 $T_4 - T_3 \leq \epsilon$
 $P_{Sf} = d_S F$
 $B_i = CID_i \oplus H(P_{Sf} \| T_3)$
 $A_i = B_i \oplus GK$
 $k_3 = H(T_3 \| P_{Sf}) \oplus H(A_i)$
 $sig \| Q_i \| T_2 = D_{k_3}(C_3)$
 $M = H(T_2 \| GK \| B_i \| Q_i)$
 Check sig

 $b \leftarrow_R \mathbb{F}_p, B = bG, P_{bi} = bQ_i, P_{bf} = bF$
 $k_g = H(d_S \| T_s)$
 $k_i^* = H(P_{bf} \| P_{bi} \| P_{Sf} \| T_3 \| T_4)$
 $k_i = H(A_i \| d_S \| k_g)$
 $Off_i = k_i \oplus k_i^*$
 $\{t \| PID_i\}_{t \in \{1,...,m\}} = \{t \| A_i \oplus H(d_S \| k_g \| t)\}_{t \in \{1,...,m\}}$
 $H_4 = H(k_g \| \{t \| PID_i\}_{t \in \{1,...,m\}} \| B \| Off_i \| T_4)$
 $C_4 = E_{i_i}(k_g \| \{t \| PID_i\}_{t \in \{1,...,m\}})$

$$\xleftarrow{\quad C_4 \| B \| Off_i \| T_4 \| H_4 \quad}$$

$T_5 - T_4 \leq \epsilon$
$P_{ib} = d_i B, P_{fb} = fB$
$k_i^* = H(P_{fb} \| P_{ib} \| P_{fS} \| T_3 \| T_4)$
$k_i = k_i^* \oplus Off_i$
$k_g \| \{t \| PID_i\}_{t \in \{1,...,m\}} = D_{k_i}(C_4)$
Check $H(k_g \| \{t \| PID_i\}_{t \in \{1,...,m\}} \| B \| Off_i \| T_4)? = H_4$
Store $H(A_i), k_g, k_i, \{t \| PID_i\}_{t \in \{1,...,m\}}$ in TPM_i

Fig. 2. Steps during the user login and authentication and key agreement phase

- The other vehicles in the communication range possess the group key k_g and are able to check the hash value.
  However, in order to determine the authentication of the message, they depend on the RSU. Therefore, after the verification of a valid message, they send an acknowledge to the RSU of reception of the message, using the communication mechanism as described before. To refer to this message, the serial number $H(H(A_i) \| T_6)_{23}$ (message cropped after 23 bits) is taken.
- The RSU is responsible for checking the existence and authenticated usage of the pseudonym PID_i in the message with serial number $H(H(A_i) \| T_6)_{23}$. Therefore, it first derives $A_i = PID_i \oplus H(d_S \| k_g \| t)$. If $H(H(A_i) \| T_6)$ is included in the transmitted message, no further actions are needed.
  However, suppose $H(H(A_i) \| T_6)$ is not valid, then all vehicles that have sent an acknowledge of reception of this message, are responded in unicast mode by

$$M \| T_7 \| H(k_i \| M \| H(H(A_i) \| T_7) \| M \| T_7))$$

with k_i the key of the infected vehicle and $M = 0\|H(H(A_i)\|T_6)_{23}$, meaning that the message with serial number $H(H(A_i)\|T_6)_{23}$ was invalid.

4.6   Password Change Phase

If the user wants to change its password, it can complete the procedure without involvement of the RC, the GCA or the RSU. The user first logs in with identity and password. The device checks the entered information with E_i. If the user is authentic, the device prompts the user for a new password PW^* and computes

$$rb^* = PW \oplus PW^* \oplus rb$$
$$d_i^* = H(UID_i\|DID_i\|VID_i\|PW^* \oplus rb^*\|Bio) = d_i$$
$$Q_i^* = d_i \cdot G = Q_i$$
$$E_i^* = H(PW^* \oplus rb^*\|Bio \oplus rb^*\|UID_i\|DID_i\|VID_i)$$
$$= H(PW \oplus rb\|Bio \oplus rb^*\|UID_i\|DID_i\|VID_i)$$

Finally, the values of E_i, rb are updated by E_i^*, rb^*.

5   Security Analysis

Below is a list of different required security features, whose definition is explained in the context of VANETs [2,3].

- Data integrity: The content of the data cannot be changed during transmission without being noticed by the receiver. Consequently no false image of the traffic status can be sent to the system.
- Mutual authentication: Both the traffic user and the RSU authenticate each other as registered entities by the CA, and contribute to the construction of the secret key.
- Anonymity or referred as privacy preserving: Identity related information of the driver (name, age, etc.) and vehicle (licence plate, speed, model, vehicle identification number, etc.) is not leaked from the transmitted messages for any outsider, RSU, and even CA.
- Conditional cooperative traceability: Only authorized parties should be able to request the identity of the driver and vehicle. If so, the CA and the RC need to collaborate with the RSU to reveal this information. Consequently, attacking a RSU does not lead to leakage of privacy related information.
- Unlinkability: Different messages cannot be linked to the same user by any outsider collecting the transmitted messages in order to monitor a user or vehicle's path.
- Lost or stolen devices: Even if the car is stolen or lost, an attacker is not able to use the information eventually derived from the telematics device. Consequently, the identity of the user cannot be stolen.

- Non-repudiation and strong non-repudiation: A vehicle and even the driver of the vehicle cannot deny its involvement in the communication of a certain message.
- Resistance against impersonation attacks: No attacks are possible such that a malicious user would be able to insert fake information into the system. A malicious or selfish user could for instance send false info about the traffic status, allowing a congestion free route for him/herself or even causing accidents. Note that a malicious user can be from inside and outside the system.
- Resistance against replay attacks: The system makes it impossible to collect data and then reuse this data in a valid way for the same purposes as in an impersonation attack.
- Resistance against denial of service attacks (DoS) are meant to make the network unavailable and thus the users uninformed.

In the full version of the paper, we informally show that the proposed scheme satisfies all the required security features, similar as the 2FLIP [5] protocol. In addition, we also provide a formal proof on the mutual authentication of the entities and the secrecy of the generated session keys using the tool AVISPA.

To conclude, the main difference between HEPPA and 2FLIP is in the storage of the long term key material. In 2FLIP, the TRM of the device is used to store the system key. If this key is leaked somehow, the whole system is broken. The update of this key is highly inefficient and unpractical, as the system key needs to be replaced in the TRM of all vehicles at the same time.

Since the key agreement is through remote communication in HEPPA, the key management is much more flexible. Moreover, HEPPA does not include one potential security breach.

6 Performance Analysis

We restrict the comparison of HEPPA to the 2FLIP protocol [5]. This last one has been shown to outperform the latest state of the art with more than 55%–85% for communication and computation overhead, by comparing it witj GIS [11] and VAST, VAST* [18]).

The communication overhead and computation effort of a broadcast message sent by the vehicles will now be discussed, as it is the most frequently used operation. Note that we use the timings for EC point multiplication, tate pairing, SHA1, HMAC, and AES-128 encryption on a machine equipped with an Intel Core (TM) 2 Duo CPU 2.4 GHz, which are approximately equal to respectively 5.4 ms, 40.7 ms, 6 μs, 16.7 μs, and 40.7 μs. These numbers are computed in [5], and thus facilitate the comparison.

6.1 Communication Overhead

We assume that the timestamps are 4 bytes, the parameter t in the pseudonym computation 1 byte, the outputs of the hash operations 20 bytes, and the message to be sent 3 bytes. Than, 2FLIP broadcast messages consist of 47 bytes, while in HEPPA 67 bytes are required. The additional 20 bytes follows from the inclusion of $H(H(A_i)\|T)$ in the message, such that the vehicle can prove its identity to the RSU.

6.2   Computation Efforts

The submission of a broadcast message requires from the sending entity in HEPPA two hashes, while in 2FLIP seven hashes and one MAC operation are needed. This follows from the fact that in HEPPA some identity related information is stored in the TRM of the device, while in 2FLIP a new pseudonym needs to be derived all the time on the spot. Consequently, the construction of a broadcast message corresponds with timings of $12\,\mu s$ for HEPPA and $54.5\,\mu s$ for 2FLIP, or a total of 83 333 and 18 382 messages, which can be sent in one second by HEPPA and 2FLIP respectively.

On the other hand, the message verification requires only one MAC operation in 2FLIP, while in HEPPA one hash operation is needed, together with one additional acknowledge message to be sent in which another 2 hashes are required. In the worst case when the message is revoked by the RSU, another hash needs to be computed.

Consequently, the computational effort for the message verification in HEPPA equals to $16.2\,\mu s$ best case or $21.7\,\mu s$ in worst case. For 2FLIP, this effort is approximately similar to the best case of HEPPA and equals to $16.4\,\mu s$. These numbers correspond with a total of (61728–46829) and 60 976 messages to be verified per second in HEPPA (best case, worst case) and 2FLIP respectively.

From these numbers, we can clearly conclude that both 2FLIP and HEPPA can easily handle 2000 messages in one second, as in the case of a very dense environment (approximately 200 vehicles in its neighbourhood).

7   Conclusion

This paper presents HEPPA, a three-factor based authentication protocol for VANETs. Thanks to an elegant construction of the security material shared among vehicles and RSUs, symmetric key operations can be used in the broadcast communication among the vehicles, both for transmission and verification. As a consequence, the efficiency of the protocol for regular broadcast communication is in the same line as the efficiency of the recently proposed 2FLIP protocol, which was already outperforming the other systems in literature between 55% and 85% for both communication overload and computation costs.

HEPPA has the main advantage above 2FLIP that it does not depend of one global system parameter stored in the tamper resistant part of the telematics device. Consequently, no global key update process needs to be organized in which all vehicles are involved at the same time. Instead, regular key establishments need to be made with the local RSUs, requiring.

We show that HEPPA satisfies all the required security features of a highly secure VANET, including anonymity, unlinkability, mutual authentication, and resistance against well-known security attacks.

References

1. Armstrong, L.: Dedicated short range communications (DSRC) home (2002)
2. Parno, B., Perrig, A.: Challenges in securing vehicular networks. Workshop on Hot Topics in Networks (HotNets-IV), pp. 1–6 (2005)
3. Raya, M., Hubaux, J.P.: Securing vehicular ad hoc networks. J. Comput. Secur. **15**(1), 39–68 (2007)
4. Brown, L., Stallings, W.: User Authentication, Computer Security Principles and Practice, 2nd edn, pp. 71–105. Pearson, Upper Saddle River (2012)
5. Wang, F., Xu, Y., Zhang, H., Zhang, Y., Zhu, L.: 2FLIP: a two-factor lightweight privacy preserving authentication scheme for VANET. IEEE Trans. Veh. Technol. **65**(2), 896–911 (2015)
6. Raya, M., Hubaux, J.: The security of vehicular ad hoc networks. In: 3rd ACM Workshop on Security of Ad hoc and Sensor Networks, pp. 11–21 (2005)
7. Braeken, A., Porambage, P.: Efficient anonym smart card based authentication scheme for multi-server. Architecture **9**(9), 177–184 (2015)
8. Sun, Y., Lu, R., Lin, X., Shen, X.S.: An efficient pseudonymous authentication scheme with strong privacy preservation for vehicular communications. IEEE Trans. Veh. Technol. **59**(1), 3589–3603 (2010)
9. Zhang, C., Lu, R., Lin, X., Ho, P., Shen, X.S.: An efficient identity based batch verification scheme for vehicular sensor networks. In: IEEE INFOCOM, pp. 246–250 (2008)
10. Rajput, U., Abbas, F., Eun, H., Hussain, R., Oh, H.: Two level privacy preserving pseudonymous authentication protocol for VANET. In: IEEE 11th International Conference on Wireless and Mobile Computing, Networking and Communications (WiMob), pp. 643–650 (2015)
11. Lin, X., Sun, X., Ho, P.-H., Shen, X.: GSIS: a secure and privacy-preserving protocol for vehicular communications. IEEE Trans. Veh. Technol. **56**(6), 3442–3456 (2007)
12. Zhang, L., Wu, Q., Solanas, A., Domingo, F.J.: A scalable robust authentication protocol for secure vehicular communications. IEEE Trans. Veh. Technol. **59**(1), 1606–1617 (2010)
13. Chaum, D., Heyst, E.: Group Signatures. In: Davies, D.W. (ed.) EUROCRYPT 1991. LNCS, vol. 547, pp. 257–265. Springer, Heidelberg (1991). doi:10.1007/3-540-46416-6_22
14. Wu, H.-T., Hsieh, W.-S.: RSU-based message authentication for vehicular ad-hoc networks. Springer- Multimed Tools Appl. **35**, 1–13 (2011)
15. IEEE Trial-Use Standard for Wireless Access in Vehicular Environments, IEEE Standard 1609.2 Std. (2006)
16. Xie, Y., Wu, L., Shen, J., Alelaiwi, A.: EIAS-CP: new efficient identity-based authentication scheme with conditional privacy-preserving for VANETs. Telecommun. Syst. pp. 1–12 (2016)
17. Porambage, P., Braeken, A., Schmitt, C., Gurtov, A.V., Ylianttila, M., Stiller, B.: Group key establishment for enabling secure multicast communication in wireless sensor networks deployed for IoT applications. IEEE Access **3**, 1503–1511 (2015)
18. Studer, A., Bai, F., Bellur, B., Perrig, A.: Flexible, extensible, and efficient VANET authentication. J. Commun. Netw. **11**, 589–598 (2009)

Applied Cryptography

Automated Cryptographic Analysis
of the Pedersen Commitment Scheme

Roberto Metere$^{(\boxtimes)}$ and Changyu Dong

Newcastle University, Newcastle upon Tyne, UK
{r.metere2,changyu.dong}@ncl.ac.uk

Abstract. Aiming for strong security assurance, recently there has been an increasing interest in formal verification of cryptographic constructions. This paper presents a mechanised formal verification of the popular Pedersen commitment protocol, proving its security properties of correctness, perfect hiding, and computational binding. To formally verify the protocol, we extended the theory of EasyCrypt, a framework which allows for reasoning in the computational model, to support the discrete logarithm and an abstraction of commitment protocols. Commitments are building blocks of many cryptographic constructions, for example, verifiable secret sharing, zero-knowledge proofs, and e-voting. Our work paves the way for the verification of those more complex constructions.

Keywords: Formal verification · Cryptography · Commitment · EasyCrypt

1 Introduction

The high and increasing volume of communication exchanged through insecure channels, e.g. the Internet, confers increasing significance on security guarantees of cryptographic protocols. However, the increasing complexity in the design of such protocols leads to more complex and long proofs, making them error-prone and difficult to check. In fact, it happened that protocols believed to be secure, even for years, were found to be vulnerable to attacks after further investigation [2,16,25,34]. As a result, it is highly desirable to have tools that can formally and automatically verify cryptographic protocols. Recently, many tools have been developed based on different approaches for this purpose [3,9, 18,22,26,27] and have been proven to be effective in verifying security properties and finding both known and new attacks.

Most of the automatic tools aiming to aid proofs for cryptographic protocols [5,6,15,17,20,24,28,29,32–34,36,37] work in the symbolic model, some providing computational soundness for special cases [7], while only few support the computational model [4,11,12,14]. The symbolic model [19] describes the real world cryptographic protocols abstractly. Messages are literals, therefore it is difficult to model partial leakage. Cryptographic primitives are assumed to be perfect and used as black boxes, which is not realistic. The adversaries strategies are often predefined and limited to the inference rules provided, therefore

© Springer International Publishing AG 2017
J. Rak et al. (Eds.): MMM-ACNS 2017, LNCS 10446, pp. 275–287, 2017.
DOI: 10.1007/978-3-319-65127-9_22

the proofs are limited to case-by-case reasoning [8]. This overly simplistic way can capture errors in the logic of the design, but cannot fully describe situations in which the cryptographic primitives cannot be treated as black boxes and when the security properties are defined computationally, which is often true in cryptographic protocols and other fields of cryptography. On the contrary, the computational model is more realistic when modelling cryptographic protocols and can capture many low level details which are needed in proofs. Cryptographic primitives are secure in the sense that computationally bounded adversaries can break the security properties with only a negligible probability, if certain assumptions hold. Messages are bit strings and adversaries can be any polynomial time probabilistic Turing machine. Therefore, it allows for reasoning with probabilities and cryptographic assumptions. This allows for rigorous proofs that cannot be obtained in the symbolic model.

In this paper we focus on proving properties of commitment schemes. Commitment schemes are a cryptographic primitive that have been widely used by its own or as a building block in other protocols, for example, verifiable secret sharing, zero-knowledge proofs, and e-voting [21,30,35]. The high level concept behind commitment protocol is intuitively simple, a committer wants to commit to a message, while keeping it secret from a receiver until a later time when the committer reveals the message to the receiver. In this paper we prove the security properties of the popular Pedersen commitment scheme [31]. The source code is available on github at the address: https://github.com/nitrogl/easycrypt, theories and examples. To the best of our knowledge, this is the first mechanised formalisation of this protocol.

Despite being a basic primitive in secure computation, to formalise it and have a computer generated proof is far from trivial. In the security proof generated by humans, many small gaps are left by the prover as they are easy to prove. However, for a machine the gaps can be huge and extra efforts need to be spent to let the machine complete the proof. In particular, to prove the perfect hiding property, we created a sequence of games that vary slightly to allow the machine to carry on the proof. This additional construction is totally absent from proofs in the original paper and textbooks. In addition, to prove computational binding, we constructed a discrete logarithm game to allow for reduction.

The paper is organised as the following: in Sect. 2 we review the related work. In Sect. 3, we introduce the preliminaries. We then describe the formal proofs in relation to the constructions, in Sect. 4. In Sect. 5 we conclude and discuss possible future work.

2 Related Work

To avoid the limitations of symbolic model tools and capture all the properties of the cryptographic primitive, we used a tool allowing for reasoning in the computational model. Some frameworks are available to work in such a model. CryptoVerif [14] is based on concurrent probabilistic process calculus. Although it is highly automatic, it is limited to prove properties related to secrecy and authenticity. The tool gga$^\infty$ [4] specialises in reasoning in the generic group model and seems promising when attackers have access to random oracles, which does not apply to our setting. Certicrypt is a fully machine-checked language-based framework built on top of the Coq proof assistant [12]. However it is no longer maintained. EasyCrypt [11] follows the same approach as CertiCrypt and supports automated proofs as well as interactive proofs that allow for interleaving both program verification and formalisation of mathematical theories. This is desirable because they are intimately intertwined when formalising cryptographic proofs, and can leave the tedious parts of proofs to machines.

Recently, a machine-checked formalisation of Σ-protocols to prove statements about discrete logarithms has been developed in CertiCrypt [13]. A commonality between the work in [13] and our work is that the Schnorr protocol proved in [13] is also based on the discrete logarithm assumption.

3   Background

3.1   Commitment Protocols

Commitment protocols are two-party schemes between a committer C and a receiver R, and run in two phases. Let M be the space of messages to commit to. The first phase is called *commitment phase*, where the party C sends R its commitment for a private message $m \in M$ and secretly holds an opening value. The second phase is called *verification phase*, where the party C sends R the original message m along with the opening value, so that R can verify that the message committed in the first phase was indeed m.

Commitment protocols involve three efficient algorithms: (i) $\mathcal{G}(1^n)$ which outputs a public value h, (ii) $\mathcal{C}(h, m)$ which takes as input the public value h and the message m, and outputs (c, d) where c is the commitment to send in the first phase and d is the opening value to be send in the second phase, and (iii) $\mathcal{V}(h, m, c, d)$ which takes as input the public value h, the message m, the commitment c and the opening value d, and outputs *true* if verification succeeds or *false* otherwise. Let $\pi = (\mathcal{G}, \mathcal{C}, \mathcal{V})$ be a commitment scheme, its security properties are (i) correctness, i.e. for every message the commitment generated is valid, (ii) computational or perfect hiding, where any attacker cannot learn information from the commitment c about the message m with any advantage (perfect), or with a negligible advantage (computational), and (iii) computational or perfect binding, where the message m is uniquely bound to c (perfect) or finding another message with the same commitment has negligible probability of success (computational). We defer the formal definitions of these properties to Sect. 4.

3.2   Reasoning in EasyCrypt

We present a brief overview of EasyCrypt. More information about Easycrypt and the syntax of its language can be found in [1,10]. Those who are familiar with EasyCrypt can skip the rest of this section.

EasyCrypt handles the computational model, in which adversaries are probabilistic algorithms. To capture this, we have modules that are containers of global variables and procedures. Procedures capture the idea of algorithm, and one can reason about procedures running in a memory (as an execution environment). In the computational model, one has to reason about the probability of adversaries returning some specific results. EasyCrypt captures this idea as the probability of running a procedure $M.c$ in a memory m with post-condition Q evaluating true, where M is the module containing the procedure c, written as

$$\texttt{Pr[}M.c\texttt{(...)} \texttt{ @ \&}m \texttt{ :}Q\texttt{]}$$

To express and to prove properties, in EasyCrypt we use judgements (assertions) in (i) basic higher-order logic for implemented theories, (ii) Hoare logic (HL), (iii) probabilistic Hoare logic (pHL), and (iv) probabilistic relational Hoare logic (pRHL). For the last three of them, there are concepts of pre-condition P and post-condition Q, as well as procedures $M.c$, $M.c_1$, $N.c_2$, ..., inside modules M, N, running in some memory m.

HL hoare$[M.c \ :P \Rightarrow Q]$ - When P is true relating to some memory m and $M.c$ terminates in m, then after running $M.c$, Q always evaluates to true in the (modified) memory.

pHL phoare $[M.c \ :P \Rightarrow Q]$ < r - When P is true relating to some memory m and $M.c$ terminates in m, then after running $M.c$, Q evaluates to true in the (modified) memory with probability less than $r \in [0,1] \subset \mathbb{R}$. Other supported relations are the common relations $=$, $>$, $\geq$, and $\leq$.

pRHL equiv$[M.c_1 \sim N.c_2 \ :P \Rightarrow Q]$ - When P is true relating to some memory m and $M.c_1$ and $N.c_2$ terminate in m, then after running them in two separate copies of m, Q always evaluates to true in the corresponding memories.

In cryptography, security is usually defined by requiring certain properties to hold for all adversaries. To capture the *for all* quantifier, in EasyCrypt, adversaries are defined with abstract procedures, which means the adversaries can do anything without any prescribed strategies. Working with abstract procedures may require to assume their termination. In Easycrypt, the idea of termination is modelled by the keyword islossless. We can declare a procedure to be *lossless* using the following syntax:

islossless $M.c$

The statement is defined as a pHL judgement phoare$[M.c \ : \ \texttt{T} \Rightarrow \texttt{T}]$ = 1%r, which means the procedure M.c always returns and terminates with a probability 1 (1%r means real number 1).

All the above constructions are useful for our formalised proof. In particular, to prove the correctness we used a HL judgement, to prove perfect hiding we used both pRHL to compare the hiding experiment with an artificial experiment and a pHL to finalise the proof, and to prove computational binding we used a pHL judgement to compare the binding experiment to the discrete logarithm experiment.

4 Formal Verification of Pedersen Commitment Scheme

In this section we show how we modelled the generic commitment scheme, its security experiments, and the Pedersen commitment scheme. Finally, we prove its correctness, perfect hiding, and computational binding.

4.1 Modelling the Scheme

The abstract commitment scheme is modelled by the following few lines, proto-typing the algorithms introduced in Sect. 3:

```
module type CScheme = { (* Abstract commitment scheme *)
  proc gen() : value
  proc commit(h: value, m: message) : commitment * openingkey
  proc verify(h: value, m: message, c: commitment, d: openingkey) : bool
}.
```

The Pedersen commitment protocol runs between a committer C, holding a secret message $m \in \mathbb{Z}_q$ to commit to, and a receiver R who agrees on the group $(\mathbb{G}, q, g)$, where q is the order of $\mathbb{G}$ and g is its generator, and is defined as the following:

Commitment phase
  – R samples a value $h \in_R \mathbb{G}$ and sends h to C.
  – C samples an opening value $d \in_R \mathbb{Z}_q$, computes the commitment $c = g^d h^m$, and sends c to R.
Verification phase
  – C sends the pair (m, d) to R.
  – R checks whether $g^d h^m$ matches to the previously received commitment c, and either *accepts* if they match or *reject* if the do not.

We modelled the protocol in EasyCrypt as the following three procedures inside the module `module Ped : CScheme`:

```
module Ped : CScheme = { (* Implements a CScheme *)
  proc gen() : value = {
    var x, h;
    x =$ FDistr.dt; (* This randomly samples an element in Z_q *)
    h = g^x; (* g is globally defined from the cyclic group theory *)
    return h;
  }

  proc commit(h: value, m: message) : commitment * openingkey = {
    var c, d;
    d =$ FDistr.dt;
    c = (g^d) * (h^m);
    return (c, d);
  }
```

```
proc verify(h: value, m: message, c: commitment, d: openingkey)
    : bool = {
  var c';
  c' = (g^d) * (h^m);
  return (c = c');
}
}.
```

4.2 Formalising Security Properties

The security properties we want to prove are correctness, hiding and binding. The properties are captured by experiments, which are formally defined below and modelled as in Fig. 1.

Definition 1 (Correctness). *A commitment protocol π defined by the triplet $(\mathcal{G}, \mathcal{C}, \mathcal{V})$ is correct if for all messages $m \in M$ to commit, let $h = \mathcal{G}(1^n)$ and $(c, d) = \mathcal{C}(h, m)$, then $\mathcal{V}(h, m, c, d) = 1$.*

Loosely speaking, the verification done by the algorithm $\mathcal{V}$ of any message m committed using the algorithm $\mathcal{C}$ will always succeed.

For hiding and binding, we have two different adversaries: (i) the *unhider* $\mathcal{U}$, which plays the hiding experiment and has two abstract procedures, one to choose a pair of messages, and another to guess which of the two messages corresponds to a given commitment; (ii) the *binder* $\mathcal{B}$, which plays the binding experiment and has only a procedure to output two different pairs (message, opening value) that bind to the same commitment.

Definition 2 (Hiding). *Let $\pi = (\mathcal{G}, \mathcal{C}, \mathcal{V})$ be a commitment protocol. Then we can define the hiding properties for each polynomial time adversary $\mathcal{U}$.*

$$\text{(perfect hiding)} \quad \Pr\left[\text{HExp}_{\mathcal{U},\pi}(n) = 1\right] = \frac{1}{2}$$

$$\text{(computational hiding)} \quad \exists \mu(n). \Pr\left[\text{HExp}_{\mathcal{U},\pi}(n) = 1\right] \leq \frac{1}{2} + \mu(n)$$

where $\mu(n)$ is a negligible function.

Hiding experiment. The hiding experiment $\text{HExp}_{\mathcal{U},\pi}$ runs as follows:

- The adversary is given the output of $\mathcal{G}$ and asked to *choose* two messages,
- the experiment randomly selects one of them and calls $\mathcal{C}$ to compute its commitment,
- the adversary is asked to *guess* which one of the two messages the commitment corresponds to, and finally
- the experiments outputs 1 if the guess of the adversary is correct.

A commitment protocol satisfies the hiding security property if no adversary exist such that the probability of winning the hiding experiment is (significantly) better than a blind guess. If this is true, the committer is guaranteed that no information can be inferred by the commitment itself.

Definition 3 (Binding). *Let $\pi = (\mathcal{G}, \mathcal{C}, \mathcal{V})$ be a commitment protocol. Then we can define the binding properties for each polynomial time adversary $\mathcal{B}$.*

$$(\textit{perfect binding}) \quad \exists \mu(n) \cdot \Pr\left[\text{BExp}_{\mathcal{B},\pi}(n) = 1\right] = 0$$

$$(\textit{computational binding}) \quad \exists \mu(n) \cdot \Pr\left[\text{BExp}_{\mathcal{B},\pi}(n) = 1\right] \leq \mu(n)$$

where $\mu(n)$ is a negligible function.

Binding experiment. The binding experiment $\text{BExp}_{\mathcal{B},\pi}$ runs as follows:

- The adversary is given the output of $\mathcal{G}$ and asked to *bind* two messages to the same commitment value, then
- the experiment outputs 1 if the two messages differ and the commitment is valid for both the messages, that is if both can be verified by calling $\mathcal{V}$.

A commitment protocol satisfies the binding security property if no adversary exist such that the probability of winning the binding experiment is higher than negligible. If this is true, the receiver is guaranteed that the value committed cannot be changed.

```
module Corr (S:CScheme)={
  proc main(m: message) : bool = {
    var h, c, d, b;
    h = S.gen();
    (c, d) = S.commit(h, m);
    b = S.verify(h, m, c, d);
    return b;
  }
}.
```

```
module HExp(S:CScheme,U:Unhider)={
  proc main() : bool = {
    var b, b', m0, m1, h, c, d;

    h = S.gen();
    (m0, m1) = U.choose(h);
    b =$ {0,1};
    (c, d) = S.commit(h, b?m1:m0);
    b' = U.guess(c);

    return (b = b');
  }
}.
```

```
module BExp(S:CScheme,B:Binder)={
  proc main() : bool = {
    var h, c, m, m', d, d', v, v';

    h = S.gen();
    (c, m, d, m', d') = B.bind(h);
    v  = S.verify(h, m , c, d );
    v' = S.verify(h, m', c, d');

    return v /\ v' /\ (m <> m');
  }
}.
```

Fig. 1. Commitment scheme properties. Correctness (top), hiding experiment (left) and binding experiment (right) modelled in EasyCrypt.

4.3   Proofs

Relating to the properties modelled in Sect. 4.1, the Pedersen commitment scheme security properties we prove are correctness, perfect hiding, and computational binding. These security properties rely on the existence of a group $(\mathbb{G}, q, g)$ in which the discrete logarithm is *hard* to compute (discrete logarithm assumption).

Correctness. Correctness in EasyCrypt is formalised with a HL judgement: `hoare[ Corr(Ped).main : T ⇒ res]`. Its proof is straightforward. The first step is to unfolding the definition of `Corr(Ped).main`, which is the correctness algorithm described in Fig. 1 instantiated with `Ped` illustrated in Sect. 4.1. Then we have $c = g^d h^m$ and $c' = g^d h^m$ which are always equal.

Perfect hiding. In the Pedersen protocol we prove the perfect hiding:

$$\forall \mathcal{U}. \quad \Pr\left[\mathrm{HExp}_{\mathcal{U},\mathrm{Ped}}\left(\mathbb{G}, q, g\right) = 1\right] = \frac{1}{2} \tag{1}$$

In EasyCrypt, we modelled it with the following lemma:

```
lemma perfect_hiding: forall (U <: Unhider) &m,
  islossless U.choose ⇒ islossless U.guess ⇒
  Pr[HExp(Ped, U).main() @ &m : res] = 1
```

Where `U <: Unhider` is the adversary $\mathcal{U}$ with abstract procedures `choose` and `guess`, of which we needed to assume they terminate `islossless U.choose` and `islossless U.guess`.

Perfect hiding can be proved by comparing the hiding experiment to an intermediate experiment in which the commitment is replaced by g^d which contains no information about m_b. The experiment is described in Fig. 2.

$\mathrm{HInterm}_{\mathcal{U},\,\mathrm{Ped}}\left(\mathbb{G}, q, g\right)$
- $h \in_R \mathbb{G}$;
- $(m_0, m_1) \leftarrow \mathcal{U}.choose\,(h)$;
- $b \in_R \{0,1\}$;
- $d \in_R \mathbb{Z}_q$;
- $c \leftarrow g^d;$ // msg independent
- $b' \leftarrow \mathcal{U}.guess\,(c)$;
- return $b = b'$;

```
module HInterm(U:Unhider) = {
  proc main() : bool = {
    var b, b', x, h, c, d, m0, m1;

    x =$ FDistr.dt;
    h = g^x;
    (m0, m1) = U.choose(h);
    b =$ {0,1};
    d =$ FDistr.dt;
    c = g^d; (* message independent *)
    b' = U.guess(c);

    return (b = b');
  }
}.
```

Fig. 2. The intermediate hiding experiment is almost equal to the hiding experiment, but the commitment is replaced by a random group element.

We prove it by first showing that for all adversaries, the probability of winning the hiding experiment is exactly the same as winning the intermediate experiment.

$$\forall \mathcal{U}. \quad \Pr\left[\mathrm{HExp}_{\mathcal{U},\mathrm{Ped}}\left(\mathbb{G}, q, g\right) = 1\right] = \Pr\left[\mathrm{HInterm}_{\mathcal{U},\mathrm{Ped}}\left(\mathbb{G}, q, g\right) = 1\right]$$

In code,

```
lemma phi_hinterm (U<:Unhider) &m:
  Pr[HExp(Ped,U).main() @ &m : res] = Pr[HInterm(U).main() @ &m : res].
```

To prove that, we unfold the two experiments in a pRHL judgement. The first experiment is automatically instantiated by EasyCrypt as follows:

HExp $_{\mathcal{U},\ \mathbf{Ped}}$ $(\mathbb{G}, q, g)$
$\quad h \in_R \mathbb{G};$
$\quad (m_0, m_1) \leftarrow \mathcal{U}.choose\,(h);$
$\quad b \in_R \{0, 1\};$
$\quad d \in_R \mathbb{Z}_q;$
$\quad c \leftarrow g^d h^{m_b};$
$\quad b' \leftarrow \mathcal{U}.guess\,(c);$
$\quad \mathrm{return}\ b = b';$

The proof is done by comparing the execution of the two experiments and is based on the fact that the distribution of $h^{m_b} g^d$ is taken over g^d.

Then, we prove that for all adversaries, the probability of winning the intermediate experiment is exactly a half.

$$\forall \mathcal{U}. \quad \Pr\left[\mathrm{HInterm}_{\mathcal{U},\mathrm{Ped}}\left(\mathbb{G}, q, g\right) = 1\right] = \frac{1}{2}$$

In EasyCrypt, we have:

```
lemma hinterm_half (U<:Unhider) &m:
  islossless U.choose ⇒ islossless U.guess ⇒
  Pr[HInterm(U).main() @ &m : res] = 1
```

Combining the two lemmas, by transitivity, we prove perfect hiding for Pedersen commitment protocol as in Eq. (1).

Computational binding. For the Pedersen protocol, we prove the computational binding property.

$$\forall \mathcal{B}. \exists \mu\,(n). \quad \Pr\left[\mathrm{BExp}_{\mathcal{B},\mathrm{Ped}}\left(\mathbb{G}, q, g\right) = 1\right] \le \mu\,(n) \tag{2}$$

where $\mu\,(n)$ is a negligible function. The proof is done by a reduction to the discrete logarithm assumption. In cryptography, proof by reduction usually means to show how to transform an efficient adversary that is able to *break* the construction into an algorithm that efficiently solves a problem that is assumed to be hard. In this proof, the problem assumed to be hard is the discrete logarithm problem [23, p. 320]. We show that if an adversary can break the binding property, then it can output (m, d) and (m', d') such that $g^d h^m = g^{d'} h^{m'}$. If this is true then the discrete logarithm of $h = g^x$ can be computed by

$$x = \frac{d - d'}{m' - m}.$$

DLog $_A$ $(\mathbb{G}, q, g)$
> $x \in_R \mathbb{Z}_q;$
> $x' \leftarrow A.guess\,(g^x);$
> if $x' = \bot$ then
> > $b \leftarrow$ false;
>
> else
> > $b \leftarrow (x' = x);$
>
> return $b;$

$A\,(B)$ .guess(h)
> $(c, m, d, m', d') \leftarrow B.bind\,(h);$
> if $c = g^d h^m = g^{d'} h^{m'} \wedge m \neq m'$ then
> > $x \leftarrow \dfrac{d - d'}{m' - m};$
>
> else
> > $x \leftarrow \bot;$
>
> return $x;$

```
module DLog(A:Adversary)={
  proc main () : bool = {
    var x, x', b;

    x =$ FDistr.dt;
    x' = A.guess(g^x);
    if (x' = None)
      b = false;
    else
      b = (x'= Some x);

    return b;
  }
}.
```

```
module DLogAttacker(B:Binder):Adversary={
  proc guess(h: group) : F.t option = {

    var x, c, m, m', d, d';
    (c, m, d, m', d') = B.bind(h);
    if ((c = g^d * h^m) /\
        (c = g^d' * h^m') /\ (m <> m'))
      x = Some((d - d') * inv (m' - m));
    else
      x = None;

    return x;
  }
}.
```

Fig. 3. The discrete logarithm experiment (left) and an adversary reducing the binding experiment with the Pedersen protocol to the discrete logarithm experiment (right), where DLogAttacker(B).guess models $A\,(B)$.guess.

We capture the reduction by two modules in EasyCrypt (Fig. 3). A small technical subtlety is that since the adversary is abstractly defined, it can return $m = m'$ with some probability. This can cause division by zero. Therefore, we check the output from the adversary to avoid it. Formally, the adversary assumed to break the binding experiment is B and we construct an adversary A to break the discrete logarithm experiment with equal probability of success:

$$\forall B. \quad \Pr\left[\text{BExp}_{B,\text{Ped}}\,(\mathbb{G}, q, g) = 1\right] = \Pr\left[\text{DLog}_{A(B)}\,(\mathbb{G}, q, g) = 1\right]$$

The above is captured in EasyCrypt by the lemma:

```
lemma computational_binding: forall (B <: Binder) &m,
  Pr[BExp(Ped, B).main() @ &m : res] =
  Pr[DLog(DLogAttacker(B)).main() @ &m : res].
```

To prove the lemma, we unfolded the experiments as much as possible, i.e. up to abstractions, in a pRHL judgement which created an equivalence of the two experiments in the sense illustrated in Sect. 3.2. The binding experiment is automatically unfolded to the following.

$$\mathbf{BExp}_{\mathcal{B},\,\mathbf{Ped}}\,(\mathbb{G}, q, g)$$
$$\left\lfloor\ \begin{array}{l} h \in_{\mathrm{R}} \mathbb{G}; \\ (c, m, d, m', d') \leftarrow \mathcal{B}.bind\,(h); \\ v \leftarrow c = g^d h^m \\ v' \leftarrow c = g^{d'} h^{m'} \\ \text{return } v \wedge v' \wedge m \neq m'; \end{array}\right.$$

The automatic tactics could not automatically prove the lemma, as the expression $(d - d') / (m' - m)$ used by the attacker $\mathcal{A}$ (modelled as `DLogAttacker`) in the DLog experiment was too complex to be automatically used by the prover into the binding experiments and needed to be manually guided.

Assuming that the discrete logarithm is hard, then the probability of the experiment $\mathrm{BExp}_{\mathcal{B},\mathrm{Ped}}\,(\mathbb{G}, q, g)$ returning 1 must be negligible. Finally,

$$\forall \mathcal{B}.\ \exists\,\mu\,(n)\,.\quad \Pr\left[\mathrm{BExp}_{\mathcal{B},\mathrm{Ped}}\,(\mathbb{G}, q, g) = 1\right] \leq \mu\,(n)$$

which is the definition of computational binding we gave in Eq. (2).

5   Conclusion and Future Work

In this paper, we showed how EasyCrypt can be used for formally verifying practical cryptographic primitives and automatising mechanised proofs. With a game based approach, we could construct fully mechanised proofs of the security properties of the Pedersen commitment protocol, a building block primitive for many cryptographic protocols.

Composability is a desirable property of cryptographic protocols. When designing a protocol, we often want to guarantee that the composition of the protocol does not break the required security properties. In cryptography, advanced theories like Universal Composability have been proposed. As a future work, we will investigate how to enable machine-aided proofs for composability.

Acknowledgments. This work was partly supported by the EPSRC under grant EP/M013561/2.

References

1. EasyCrypt   Reference   Manual.   https://www.easycrypt.info/documentation/refman.pdf. Accessed Feb 2017
2. Abadi, M.: Explicit communication revisited: two new attacks on authentication protocols. IEEE Trans. Software Eng. **23**(3), 185–186 (1997)
3. Abadi, M., Blanchet, B.: Computer-assisted verification of a protocol for certified email. Sci. Comput. Program. **58**(1–2), 3–27 (2005)

4. Ambrona, M., Barthe, G., Schmidt, B.: Automated unbounded analysis of cryptographic constructions in the generic group model. In: Fischlin, M., Coron, J.-S. (eds.) EUROCRYPT 2016. LNCS, vol. 9666, pp. 822–851. Springer, Heidelberg (2016). doi:10.1007/978-3-662-49896-5_29

5. Armando, A., et al.: The AVANTSSAR platform for the automated validation of trust and security of service-oriented architectures. In: Flanagan, C., König, B. (eds.) TACAS 2012. LNCS, vol. 7214, pp. 267–282. Springer, Heidelberg (2012). doi:10.1007/978-3-642-28756-5_19

6. Armando, A., Compagna, L.: SATMC: a SAT-based model checker for security protocols. In: Alferes, J.J., Leite, J. (eds.) JELIA 2004. LNCS, vol. 3229, pp. 730–733. Springer, Heidelberg (2004). doi:10.1007/978-3-540-30227-8_68

7. Backes, M., Pfitzmann, B., Waidner, M.: A composable cryptographic library with nested operations. In: Proceedings of the 10th ACM Conference on Computer and Communications Security (CCS), pp. 220–230. ACM (2003)

8. Bana, G., Comon-Lundh, H.: A computationally complete symbolic attacker for equivalence properties. In: Proceedings of the 21st ACM SIGSAC Conference on Computer and Communications Security (CCS), pp. 609–620. ACM (2014)

9. Barthe, G., Danezis, G., Grégoire, B., Kunz, C., Zanella-Beguelin, S.: Verified computational differential privacy with applications to smart metering. In: 2013 IEEE 26th Computer Security Foundations Symposium, pp. 287–301. IEEE (2013)

10. Barthe, G., Dupressoir, F., Grégoire, B., Kunz, C., Schmidt, B., Strub, P.-Y.: EasyCrypt: a tutorial. In: Aldini, A., Lopez, J., Martinelli, F. (eds.) FOSAD 2012-2013. LNCS, vol. 8604, pp. 146–166. Springer, Cham (2014). doi:10.1007/978-3-319-10082-1_6

11. Barthe, G., Grégoire, B., Heraud, S., Béguelin, S.Z.: Computer-aided security proofs for the working cryptographer. In: Rogaway, P. (ed.) CRYPTO 2011. LNCS, vol. 6841, pp. 71–90. Springer, Heidelberg (2011). doi:10.1007/978-3-642-22792-9_5

12. Barthe, G., Grégoire, B., Zanella Béguelin, S.: Formal certification of code-based cryptographic proofs. ACM SIGPLAN Not. 44(1), 90–101 (2009)

13. Barthe, G., Hedin, D., Béguelin, S.Z., Grégoire, B., Heraud, S.: A machine-checked formalization of Sigma-protocols. In: 2010 23rd IEEE Computer Security Foundations Symposium (CSF), pp. 246–260. IEEE (2010)

14. Blanchet, B.: A computationally sound mechanized prover for security protocols. IEEE Trans. Dependable Secure Comput. 5(4), 193–207 (2008)

15. Blanchet, B., et al.: An efficient cryptographic protocol verifier based on Prolog rules. In: CSFW, vol. 1, pp. 82–96 (2001)

16. Bouillaguet, C., Derbez, P., Fouque, P.-A.: Automatic search of attacks on round-reduced AES and applications. In: Rogaway, P. (ed.) CRYPTO 2011. LNCS, vol. 6841, pp. 169–187. Springer, Heidelberg (2011). doi:10.1007/978-3-642-22792-9_10

17. Corin, R., Etalle, S.: An improved constraint-based system for the verification of security protocols. In: Hermenegildo, M.V., Puebla, G. (eds.) SAS 2002. LNCS, vol. 2477, pp. 326–341. Springer, Heidelberg (2002). doi:10.1007/3-540-45789-5_24

18. Cremers, C., Horvat, M., Scott, S., van der Merwe, T.: Automated analysis and verification of TLS 1.3: 0-RTT, resumption and delayed authentication. In: 2016 IEEE Symposium on Security and Privacy (SP), pp. 470–485. IEEE (2016)

19. Dolev, D., Yao, A.: On the security of public key protocols. IEEE Trans. Inf. Theory 29(2), 198–208 (1983)

20. Escobar, S., Hendrix, J., Meadows, C., Meseguer, J.: Diffie-Hellman cryptographic reasoning in the Maude-NRL protocol analyzer. In: Proceeding of SecRet 2007 (2007)

21. Goldreich, O., Krawczyk, H.: On the composition of zero-knowledge proof systems. SIAM J. Comput. **25**(1), 169–192 (1996)
22. Goubault-Larrecq, J.: A method for automatic cryptographic protocol verification. In: Rolim, J. (ed.) IPDPS 2000. LNCS, vol. 1800, pp. 977–984. Springer, Heidelberg (2000). doi:10.1007/3-540-45591-4_134
23. Katz, J., Lindell, Y.: Introduction to Modern Cryptography. CRC Press, Boca Raton (2014)
24. Kemmerer, R.A.: Analyzing encryption protocols using formal verification techniques. IEEE J. Sel. Areas Commun. **7**(4), 448–457 (1989)
25. Lowe, G.: An attack on the Needham-Schroeder public-key authentication protocol. Inform. Process. Lett. **56**(3), 131–133 (1995)
26. Lowe, G.: Breaking and fixing the Needham-Schroeder public-key protocol using FDR. In: Margaria, T., Steffen, B. (eds.) TACAS 1996. LNCS, vol. 1055, pp. 147–166. Springer, Heidelberg (1996). doi:10.1007/3-540-61042-1_43
27. Meadows, C.: The NRL protocol analyzer: an overview. J. Logic Programm. **26**(2), 113–131 (1996)
28. Meier, S., Cremers, C., Basin, D.: Strong invariants for the efficient construction of machine-checked protocol security proofs. In: 2010 23rd IEEE Computer Security Foundations Symposium (CSF), pp. 231–245. IEEE (2010)
29. Mitchell, J.C., Mitchell, M., Stern, U.: Automated analysis of cryptographic protocols using Murφ. In: 1997 IEEE Symposium on Security and Privacy, Proceedings, pp. 141–151. IEEE (1997)
30. Naor, M.: Bit commitment using pseudorandomness. J. Cryptology **4**(2), 151–158 (1991)
31. Pedersen, T.P.: Non-interactive and information-theoretic secure verifiable secret sharing. In: Feigenbaum, J. (ed.) CRYPTO 1991. LNCS, vol. 576, pp. 129–140. Springer, Heidelberg (1992). doi:10.1007/3-540-46766-1_9
32. Ramsdell, J.D., Guttman, J.D.: CPSA: A cryptographic protocol shapes analyzer. In: Hackage. The MITRE Corporation, vol. 2(009) (2009)
33. Ryan, P., Schneider, S.A.: The Modelling and Analysis of Security Protocols: The CSP Approach. Addison-Wesley Professional, Reading (2001)
34. Schmidt, B., Meier, S., Cremers, C., Basin, D.: Automated analysis of Diffie-Hellman protocols and advanced security properties. In: 2012 IEEE 25th Computer Security Foundations Symposium (CSF), pp. 78–94. IEEE (2012)
35. Schoenmakers, B.: A simple publicly verifiable secret sharing scheme and its application to electronic voting. In: Wiener, M. (ed.) CRYPTO 1999. LNCS, vol. 1666, pp. 148–164. Springer, Heidelberg (1999). doi:10.1007/3-540-48405-1_10
36. Song, D.X., Berezin, S., Perrig, A.: Athena: a novel approach to efficient automatic security protocol analysis. J. Comput. Secur. **9**(1–2), 47–74 (2001)
37. Turuani, M.: The CL-Atse protocol analyser. In: Pfenning, F. (ed.) RTA 2006. LNCS, vol. 4098, pp. 277–286. Springer, Heidelberg (2006). doi:10.1007/11805618_21

Steganalysis Based on Statistical Properties of the Encrypted Messages

Valery Korzhik[1,2], Ivan Fedyanin[1,2], Artur Godlewski[1],
and Guillermo Morales-Luna[2(✉)]

[1] Department of Protected Communication Systems, The Bonch-Bruevich
Saint-Petersburg State University of Telecommunications, St. Petersburg, Russia
val-korzhik@yandex.ru, ivan.a.fedyanin@gmail.com, artigodl@gmail.com
[2] Computer Science, CINVESTAV-IPN, Mexico City, Mexico
gmorales@cs.cinvestav.mx

Abstract. It is introduced a new steganalytic method based on investigation of statistical properties of the extracted encrypted messages. It is assumed that the message is encrypted before embedding by some sufficiently strong cipher. The extracted messages are exposed to the testing on pseudorandomness, namely to NIST-tests. When passing these tests, the tested objects are assumed stego-objects, otherwise as cover objects. Support vector machine methodology is used to improve the testing process. Experiments demonstrate that the proposed algorithm is able to detect stegosystems as LSB-based embedding (both replacing and matching), with pseudorandom walks given by stego-keys, and with matrix embedding based on Hamming codes with reasonable reliability.

Keywords: Stegosystem · Steganalysis · NIST-tests · Suport vector machine · Embedding into LSB

1 Introduction

Steganalysis is a complementary task of steganography. It is well known [1] that the main goal of steganalysis (SGA) is to distinguish between cover objects (CO) and stego objects (SG) with probability better than random guessing. It is common to consider steganography in digital media where the CO are digital motionless or video images or signals like speech and music. For simplicity reasons, our experiments will be restricted to motionless grey scale images only. (In the future our proposals can be extended to other types of CO without significant difficulties.)

Steganalysis is very important on two reasons. Firstly it is used as a notion that should be taken into account during design of any steganographic algorithm because such algorithm is useless if it can be easily detected by some known steganalytic method. Secondly, SGA has its own rights. In fact, it is very important to prevent a leakage of sensitive information outside of some areas because this can be arranged by steganographic methods. (It is well known the

J. Rak et al. (Eds.): MMM-ACNS 2017, LNCS 10446, pp. 288–298, 2017.
DOI: 10.1007/978-3-319-65127-9_23

system *"Digital Leakage Prevention"* (DLP) whose goal is to render impossible the transmission of sensitive information outside some company area. But without steganalysis it fails to work fine.)

All stegosystems known previously were intrinsically restricted by the methods of SGA. One of the first papers devoted to SGA was [2] but in a more complete form SGA has been presented in a monograph due to Fridrich [1]. After this book, the SGA methods may be divided into two main areas: *targeted SGA* and *blind SGA*. For the first area the features in SGA are constructed for a specific embedding method. The goal of blind staganalysis is to detect any steganographic method irrespectively to its embedding mechanism. It seems today that the best method of blind SGA is to use *Support Vector Machines* (SVM) which are realized in two stages [1]. The first one is training on both CO and SG databases. (It is worth to note that although the embedding mechanism may be unknown to the staganalyst, it is possible to test many SG using embedding algorithms as black boxes.) During the first stage some features must be extracted from both the CO and the SG. At the second stage these features are used to recognize some new test objects belonging to one of either two classes: CO or SG. The algorithm of such classification is detailed in [1], and there it was remarked that an important problem is the selection of appropriate features.

Kerckhoffs's principle in cryptography [3] can be extended to steganography as well. This means that an "attacker" (say steganalyst) may know all about the embedding and the extraction algorithm but ignores the crypto and the stego keys. The stego key usually determines a pseudo-random walk through the CO where the message bits are embedded. A weak stego key may create a detectability flaw that can be used by an attacker to extract the embedded "message" and to decide whether a SG occurs if the extracted "message" is meaningful (see Algorithm 10.2 in [1]). Moreover it is highly risked to hide the embedded message content only with the use of a stego key [4]. Therefore, as a rule it is required to use also very strong ciphers for message encryption. On the other hand each strong cipher provides a ciphertext close to a perfect pseudo-random bit sequence satisfying to so called *NIST-tests* [5].

Then the following idea arises to build a *new steganalytic algorithm*:

1. Extract the sequence of "message" bits from the tested object following the known (or expected) algorithm.
2. Apply the NIST tests to this sequence.
3. If all NIST tests are fully satisfied then decide that the tested object is a SG, otherwise decide that it is a CO.

A generalization of this procedure consists in comparing the number of passed tests with some chosen threshold, and then to assume that the tested object is a SG if the threshold is exceeded, otherwise that it is a CO. (In fact, it is unlikely that a "clear" CO satisfies all pseudo-random tests. It is well known that truly random generators are designed with the use of additional deterministic transforms like transpositions and summation. So we can assume the following motto: "strong ciphers compromise stegosystems".

This steganalytic algorithm and its experimental verification constitute our main contributions.

We note that although there exists a stego key that makes impossible to extract the embedded message correctly it does not prevent SGA, in fact it makes SGA harder and requires more time to break it.

The remainder of this paper is organized as follows. In Sect. 2 there are presented some results of experiment on stegosystems with the *least significant bits* (LSB) replacing and matching using the above given algorithm based on the NIST-tests. In Sect. 3 there are given results of similar experiment but with additional use of the SVM technique. Section 4 presents the results of the proposed steganalysis with matrix embedding based on Hamming code. Section 5 concludes the paper.

2   Experimental Results of Steganalysis Based on Pseudo-random Properties of the Extracted Messages for LSB-Based Stegosystems

Let us briefly recall the steganalysis algorithm in frames of the LSB-embedding method. For full embedding, the least significant bits from all pixels of the image are extracted and they are subject to pseudo-randomness tests taken from a list of the NIST. If SG with encryption of the embedded messages with strong cipher occurs, then we expect that the extracted bits pass all tests, whereas if CO occurs then test successes are rather unlikely.

In the case of non full embedding when it was embedding into a part of pixels according to the secret stego key, we keep the same detection algorithm but we set some threshold in the decision process. (Of course in the worst case, because if an attacker would be able to find somewhat the stego key then the situation with partial embedding is reduced to the case of full embedding.) Since both LSB-replacing and LSB-matching have the same decoding algorithms, namely extraction of LSB, then the stego-analytic algorithm described above can be applied to both embedding methods without changing. (It is worth to note that detection of LSB-matching (or ±1-LSB) is a harder problem than detection of LSB-replacing and it requires the application of more sophisticated methods, which are not very effective so far [6].)

As a list of tests on pseudo-randomness we use the well known 15 NIST tests whose titles are displayed in Table 1. A detailed description of these tests can be found in [5].

In Table 2 there are presented the testing results for LSB-based stegosystems with full embedding of meaningful text encrypted with GOST-28147-89 [7] for 15 different digital grey-scale images (in reality much more images were tested with similar results but just a selection of only 15 images is explained due to paper space limitation). We see from this table that all image SG's have passed these tests (similar results were obtained for other block ciphers, as DES and AES). It does not wonder because these strong ciphers were designed in such a way to pass these tests for cryptographic unbreakability.

Table 1. Titles of NIST tests on pseudo-randomness.

N	Title of test
1	The frequency test
2	Frequency test within a block
3	The runs test
4	Tests for the longest-run-of-ones in a block
5	The binary matrix rank test
6	The discrete Fourier transform (spectral) test
7	The non-overlapping template matching test
8	The overlapping template matching test
9	Maurer's "Universal Statistical" test
10	The linear complexity test
11	The serial test
12	The approximate entropy test
13	The cumulative sums (cusums) test
14	The random excursion teat
15	The random excursions variant test

Table 2. Results of stegoanalytic testing by NIST criteria for full LSB-based embedding stegosystem with encryption of messages with cipher GOST-28147-89. (Grey color means that test is passed, otherwise test is marked by white color.)

Images / Test	1	2	3	4	5	6	7	8	9	10	11	12	13	14	15
1															
2															
3															
4															
5															
6															
7															
8															
9															
10															
11															
12															
13															
14															
15															

Table 3. Results of NIST testing for 15 different covers.

Test \ Images	1	2	3	4	5	6	7	8	9	10	11	12	13	14	15
1											■		■		■
2											■		■		■
3		■													
4		■													
5		■			■	■	■	■			■				
6	■	■			■		■								
7															
8															
9															
10	■	■			■	■	■		■	■	■		■		■
11															
12		■										■	■		■
13		■										■	■		
14															
15															

Table 3 presents the results of NIST tests for 15 different cover images (without embedding). All images without embedding fail to pass many tests, hence it is very easy to distinguish full LSB-based stego systems against cover images.

In the case of non-full LSB-based embedding, the problem of SG detection is complicated. In Table 4 there are presented the results of NIST tests for LSB-based embedding with the probability 0.6 in each pixel. We see that, in contrast

Table 4. Results of testing by NIST criteria for LSB-based embedding in the pixels of every image with the probability 0.6 for 15 different covers.

Test \ Images	1	2	3	4	5	6	7	8	9	10	11	12	13	14	15
1											■		■		■
2											■		■		■
3		■									■				
4		■									■				
5		■			■	■		■	■		■				■
6	■	■				■		■			■				
7															
8		■													
9		■													
10	■	■			■	■	■	■	■	■	■				■
11		■													
12		■									■		■		
13		■											■		
14															
15															

with Table 2, not all images pass all tests, hence it is not so easy to distinguish stego-systems with partial pixel embedding from cover images.

In order to improve SG detection based on the NIST tests and especially to simplify the choice of thresholds for a decision taking, we propose to use SVM technique as considered in the next section.

3   The Use of SVM Technique for an Improvement of NIST-Based Steganalytic Method

SVM gained popularity due to its efficiency in a solution of classification problems and its relative use easiness. According to the notations and terminology in [4], let us denote by X the input space and by Y the set of signs $\{-1, +1\}$. In our case $X = \mathbb{R}^n$ and it is a set of training examples $(\overline{x}_i)_{i=1}^{\ell}$ with associated labels $(\overline{y}[i])_{i=1}^{\ell}$, namely $(\overline{x}_1, \overline{y}[1], \ldots, \overline{x}_\ell, \overline{y}[\ell])$. We will also assume that each $\overline{x}_i$ is a vector realization consisting of p-value coordinates after the procedures of the NIST-testing of the i-th image, while the corresponding binary label $\overline{y}[i]$ is either a cover or a stego image.

The goal is to use the training examples to build a decision map $f : X \to Y$, while minimizing the number of errors. We note that the p-values in NIST-tests mean the probabilities of the test statistics being at least as extreme as the one observed given that the null hypothesis holds. A small p-value is an indication that the null hypothesis is false.

We use the most effective version of SVM known as *nonlinear kernelized weighted SVM*, where the kernel function is Gaussian:

$$(x, x') \mapsto k(x, x') = \exp\left(-\gamma \|\overline{x} - \overline{x}'\|^2\right)$$

with $\gamma > 0$ being a parameter controlling the kernel width and $\| \cdot \|$ is the Euclidean norm in $\mathbb{R}^n$. The penalization coefficient introduced in order to provide a trade off between accuracy of classification on the training set and accuracy of the classification on previously unknown testing set. An overtrained classifier is tight to the training set and might perform poorly on the testing set.

The number of covers and SG (with different probabilities of LSB-based embedding at training stage) has been taken about 500 for each class. Next we use a support vector machine in order to present the probability of error $P_e = \frac{1}{2}(P_m + P_{fa})$ as a function of both γ and C, where P_m is the probability of SG missing and P_{fa} is the probability of false detection of SG. The number of chosen objects for testing was taken as 500. In Figs. 1(a)–(c) there are presented the results of steganalysis based on the NIST-test associated with SVM for different probabilities of LSB-based embedding $p = 0.9, 0.8$ and 0.6 respectively. We see from these figures that it is possible to select such parameters γ and C giving minimal probabilities of error detection $P_e = \frac{1}{2}(P_m + P_{fa})$ as presented in Table 5.

We see from this table that the new steganalysis is rather inferior to the best known target steganalytic methods in [4] for LSB-replacing embedding but it is

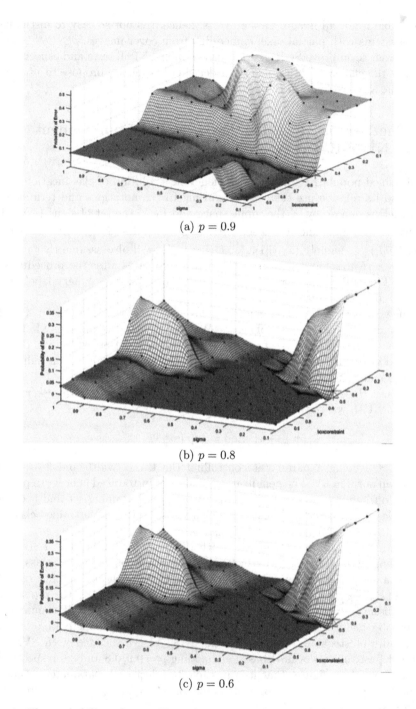

(a) $p = 0.9$

(b) $p = 0.8$

(c) $p = 0.6$

Fig. 1. The probability of error P_e against parameters γ and C of SVM-NIST steganalysis for the LSB based embedding with the indicated probabilities.

Table 5. The minimal error probabilities on parameters γ and C for SVM-NIST steganalysis with LSB-based embedding and different probabilities p.

p	P_{fa}	P_m	P_e	γ	C
0.9	0	0	0	0.1	0.5
0.8	0	0	0	0.1	0.5
0.6	0.3253	0	0.10714	0.1	0.5

superior to ±1-LSB embedding. In fact in Fig. 2 there are presented the results of steganalysis for LSB embedding based on two-dimensional Fourier transform of image histogram obtained in [6]

We can see from this figure that in the case of full embedding this steganalytic method provides for $P_{fa} = 0.2$, the probability $P_m = 0.4$, that is much worser than $P_m = 0$, $P_{fa} = 0$ for the proposed steganalytic method.

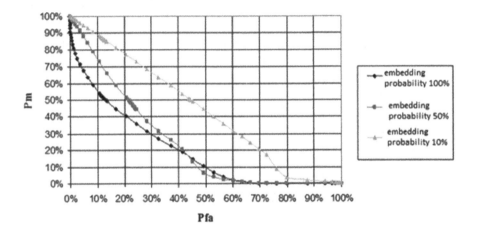

Fig. 2. The probability of SG missing P_m against the probability of P_{fa} for the case steganalysis of ±1 LSB based on the use of two-dimensional Fourier transform from coincident matrix.

4 Results of Steganalysis Based on NIST Tests for Matrix Embedding

Let us consider now detection of stegosystems with matrix embedding based on the use of Hamming codes. The binary Hamming codes can be determined uniquely by their $p \times (2^p - 1)$-parity check matrix, consisting of all possible nonzero binary columns of length p [8]. In order to embed some given message into the grey scale digital image it is necessary to extract from this image all LSBs, divide the obtained binary string on blocks of length $2^p - 1$ and "embed" p bits of the message into each block changing only one symbol on the opposite one performing the following steps [1]:

1. Compute the vector

$$\mathbf{z} = \mathbf{x}H^T \oplus \mathbf{m},$$

where $\mathbf{x}$ is a LSB vector of length $2^p - 1$, $\mathbf{m}$ is the part of the message vector of length p, and is T is the symbol of matrix transposition.

Table 6. Results of the NIST testing criteria for 20 covers under the assumption that they could be Hamming-based stegosystems, with different parameter p values.

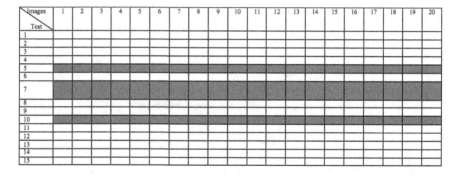

(a) $p = 3$

(b) $p = 5$

(c) $p = 12$

Table 7. Results of NIST-testing for ciphertext obtained by encryption of meaningful English text with cipher GOST.

Number of NIST test	1	2	3	4	5	6	7	8	9	10	11	12	13	14	15
Results of testing															

2. Find the number i corresponding to the column of matrix H that equals vector $\mathbf{z}$.
3. Invert the i-th symbol of $\mathbf{x}$ to the opposite one that results in block $\mathbf{y}$ with embedding of the first p message symbols.

In a similar manner, the following p bits of the message should be embedded into the next block of length $2^p - 1$ and so on, up to the end of the full message sequence. In order to extract the message bits $\mathbf{m}$ from each block $\mathbf{y}$ it is necessary to do the following:

$$\mathbf{m} = H\mathbf{y} \tag{1}$$

The detection algorithm presented in Sect. 2 was used for the stegosystem with matrix embedding by three types of Hamming codes with the parameter $p = 3, 5$ and 12. This means that initially LSB were extracted from grey scale images, next the LSB blocks of the length $2^p - 1$ are subject by the transform in (1) and the resulting sequences have been tested by NIST criteria. In Tables 6(a), (b) and (c), there are presented the results of NIST tests for covers but under the assumption that they are matrix embedded stego systems based on Hamming codes with parameters $p = 3, 5$ and 12, respectively.

In Table 7 there are presented the result of NIST-tests for stego image. But since it is assumed that the parameter p is known (or found by an exhaustive steganalysis) it results in a fact that regardless of image, it is extracted the encrypted sequence. Therefore it is sufficiently in our experiment to test only one sequence of the encrypted meaningful text independently on type of image. (It is worth to note that if the embedding rate is very lower then the length of the encrypted sequence occurs very short and it may result in breaking of good statistics even for strong ciphers). Comparing Tables 6(a), (b) and (c) with Table 7 we can see that it is very easy to distinguish covers against stegosystem based on matrix embedding for Hamming codes with parameter even equal to 12. Then we do not need to use SVM classification for improvement of SG detection because covers pass not all tests whereas stego passes all NIST tests.

5 Conclusion

In this paper, a new steganalytic algorithm is proposed. The main idea of our approach is to investigate the pseudorandom properties of the extracted messages if they were encrypted by some strong cipher before embedding. Then the extracted sequence of message should satisfy the main pseudorandom properties determined by NIST criteria. If the extracted sequence belongs to cover then it is unlikely that it satisfies all NIST tests. Our experiments show that the proposed method works at least for LSB (both matching and replacing) stegosystems and matrix stegosystems based on Hamming codes with parameter $p \geq 14$. (The last SG has the embedding rate about 8.5×10^{-4} and nevertheless it can be reliably detected.) The proposed steganalytic method can be significantly improved with the use of SVM technique. Moreover no selection of specific stegosystem features for SVM is required in contrast with common assumptions on conventional blind steganalysis.

Of course, a stegosystem can be especially modified to be more robust against the proposed method. So, the encryption of messages can be made artificially "worse" from the point of view pseudorandomness property keeping a good protection against cipher breaking. Next improvement can be connected with secrecy of message extraction algorithm.

In the future we are going to investigate the proposed method with such stegosystem as a model based, perturbed steganography and embedding with the use of trellis code and Viterbi algorithm (HUGO project [9]).

Acknowledgments. Authors thank Mr. M. Tokareva for assistance in some calculations.

References

1. Fridrich, J.: Steganography in Digital Media: Principles, Algorithms, and Applications, 1st edn. Cambridge University Press, New York (2009)
2. Johnson, N.F., Jajodia, S.: Steganalysis: the investigation of hidden information. In: 1998 IEEE Information Technology Conference, Information Environment for the Future (Cat. No.98EX228), pp. 113–116, September 1998
3. Menezes, A.J., van Oorschot, P.C., Vanstone, S.A.: Handbook of Applied Cryptography. The CRC Press Series on Discrete Mathematics and Its Applications, pp. 33431–9868. CRC Press, 2000 N.W. Corporate Blvd, Boca Raton (1997)
4. Fridrich, J., Goljan, M., Soukal, D., Holotyak, T.: Forensic steganalysis: determining the stego key in spatial domain steganography (2005)
5. Bassham III, L.E., Rukhin, A.L., Soto, J., Nechvatal, J.R., Smid, M.E., Barker, E.B., Leigh, S.D., Levenson, M., Vangel, M., Banks, D.L., Heckert, N.A., Dray, J.F., Vo, S.: Spp. 800-22 rev. 1a. a statistical test suite for random and pseudorandom number generators for cryptographic applications. Technical report, Gaithersburg, MD, United States (2010)
6. Ker, A.D.: Steganalysis of LSB matching in grayscale images. IEEE Signal Process. Lett. **12**, 441–444 (2005)
7. Schneier, B.: The GOST encryption algorithm. Dr. Dobb's J. **20**, 123–124 (1995)
8. MacWilliams, F., Sloane, N.: The Theory of Error-Correcting Codes. North-Holland (1977)
9. Pevný, T., Filler, T., Bas, P.: Using high-dimensional image models to perform highly undetectable steganography. In: Böhme, R., Fong, P.W.L., Safavi-Naini, R. (eds.) IH 2010. LNCS, vol. 6387, pp. 161–177. Springer, Heidelberg (2010). doi:10.1007/978-3-642-16435-4_13

Security Assessment of Cryptographic Algorithms

Marcin Niemiec[✉] and Maciej Francikiewicz

AGH University of Science and Technology, Department of Telecommunications,
Mickiewicza 30, 30-059 Krakow, Poland
niemiec@kt.agh.edu.pl

Abstract. This article presents a way to assess security of block cryptographic algorithms in universal manner. We presented implementation of test methods that analyse input and corresponding output of a cryptography algorithm and assign a metric for evaluation how strong is the encryption scheme. The methods – inspired by NIST test suit – are based on specified threshold for accepting the test result (P-value). The methods were validated in practise using several experiments. We checked behaviours of secure and unsecure cryptographic algorithms: AES, DES and Ceasar cipher, as well as idealized encryption scheme as a reference. The methods were packed in a framework that can be used as a cryptographic assessment tool for cryptographers, requiring only a slight knowledge of programming language from them. As experiments has shown, test suit proposed in this paper can be used to check whether encryption scheme has some properties or features which are expected from a good cryptographic algorithm.

Keywords: Cryptography · Security assessment · Encryption · Cryptanalysis

1 Introduction

Cryptography is a very wide topic. It plays important role in many nowadays solutions – from privacy of cloud-based services [1] to Internet of Things security [2]. We would like to think about it as a field of study that deals with the task of making our data and communication secure from eavesdropping. There are many concepts that applies numerous different encryption techniques in order to achieve cryptographic goal. Most commonly they can be simplified to some kind of transformation of a raw information, called message, into a string of data called ciphertext. The way of doing it is defined in encryption scheme which is used by specific cryptographic algorithm. The transformation should be reversible, meaning that we are able to derive message from ciphertext, but complex enough to make this process so hard, it is not possible to perform it in effective way, without knowing the secret recipe (essentially a secret key). Very often cryptographic algorithms are crucial elements of security architecture for

© Springer International Publishing AG 2017
J. Rak et al. (Eds.): MMM-ACNS 2017, LNCS 10446, pp. 299–312, 2017.
DOI: 10.1007/978-3-319-65127-9_24

telecommunication systems [3]. A vast majority of modern encryption schemes is a public knowledge, along with the algorithms needed for decryption, and quite often the same implementation is used for both encrypting and decrypting. In those cases the strength of cryptographic algorithm comes from the secrecy of the key.

Cryptographic system should prevent an adversary from acquiring a secret information being transmitted between two nodes of that system. Figure 1 presents a schematic of general secrecy system proposed by Shannon [4]. In symmetric cryptography, the source sends some message m which is encrypted and decrypted using the same key, known both for sender and receiver [5]. Encryption process is done by applying a family of transformations denoted as E_k to the message m. Transformation E_k uniquely corresponds to the key k being used. As a result cryptogram c is produced. Potential adversary might get an access to the ciphertext c, so it cannot reveal any information about the message m. At the receiver side cryptogram is decrypted using reversed transformation $D_k = E_k^{-1}$, in order to acquire message m.

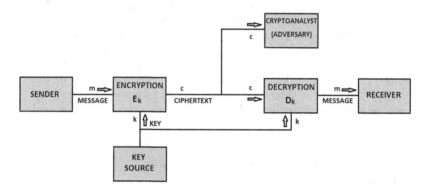

Fig. 1. Schematic of general secrecy system

In order to create secure system, cryptographic algorithm designer must assure that the operation E_k of specific encryption scheme is safe [6]. It means that adversary cannot be able to reproduce exact steps that have been performed to transform a plaintext message m into ciphertext c. He must not acquire key and he must not read any part of the message based on cryptogram c.

2   Cryptoanalytic Assessment Framework

Finding out a set of universal features that a secure cipher should have is not an easy task. Each cryptographic algorithm is different, which means it can have various strengths and weaknesses. During designing process, the creator should think ahead of vulnerabilities to specific attacks, but it is hard or even impossible to predict all the threats.

In order to test and assess the security of block ciphers, we present cryptoanalytic framework, that is capable of basic security assessment of any block cryptographic algorithm provided as an input. It utilizes such features of cryptographic algorithms as: randomness, nonlinearity, diffusion, inter-symbol dependence, completeness, strict avalanche criterion, and others [7]. Motivation was to provide universal way of security estimation of encryption schemes. Using this framework, cryptographer is able to define or include various cryptographic algorithms as an input to the assessment methods. The framework has been implemented in *.NET* using *C♯* programming language. All framework elements are presented in a schematic on Fig. 2.

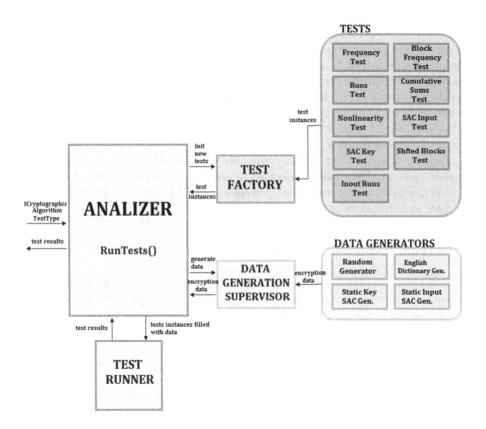

Fig. 2. Architecture of Crass framework.

From the user point of view only a few elements of the framework are important:

- **ICryptographicAlgorithm** interface which is used as a wrapper of cryptographic algorithm defined by user,
- **Analizer** main class delivering RunTest() method for triggering test suit execution and harvesting results,

- **TestType** enum containing all implemented test method names, which is used as argument in Run method to specify which tests should be executed,
- **TestResult** class representing result of single test method, run on concrete class instance implementing ICryptographicAlgorithm interface,
- **Configuration** class defining configuration of test suit execution.

The methods implemented in this framework are designed to provide information whether the cryptographic algorithm being tested generates output that has features that are expected from a good encryption scheme. All of them use a collection of plaintext-ciphertext pairs generated by the algorithm in order to perform their task. First pack of methods concentrates its effort to check if ciphertexts are indistinguishable from a truly random sequence. Next few tests are meant to detect whether there are no linear relations between bits, whether avalanche and propagation criterions are satisfied, and if the correlation between the input and output is not too strong. A vast number of presented methods makes use of solutions proposed in NIST test suit [8]. The threshold for accepting the test result – in a form of P_{value} – was set to 0.05 (except for frequency, nonlinearity and runs tests, where threshold value was set to 0.01). In NIST test suite [8] threshold value is equal to 0.01, although [9] claimed 0.05 is enough and our tests has confirmed it.

Because of space limit of this article, we were not able to present all implemented method. Therefore, we decided to show one selected – Strict Avalanche Criterion (SAC). Additionally, we presented tests results of experiments based on SAC and frequency method.

3   Strict Avalanche Criterion Method

This method was developed in order to check whether algorithm being tested satisfies strict avalanche criterion with k-degree. This principle was found to standardize property that is expected from an encryption scheme, that any change of k input bits should result in change of around half of the bits in output [10]. The idea is to generate a set of plaintexts that in each adjacent row they differ exactly in one bit position. In this way we can check the number of changes in considered ciphertexts corresponding to the selected plaintexts. If we would like to check 1-SAC property we would compare adjacent rows from ciphertexts matrix. If we would like to try k-SAC we should take every i-th and (k + i)-th row in that matrix. The comparison proposed here consist of bitwise addition modulo 2 of selected ciphertexts, and calculation of number of ones in resulting sequence. The value acquired in this way, represents the number of positions at which a change occurred. The expected number of changes in a large test set should be around half of the ciphertext length. If the result differ significantly from this value, we can reject the hypothesis that tested algorithm satisfies strict avalanche criterion.

In this section k is reserved to define degree of strict avalanche criterion (k-SAC). Therefore, key will be represented by letter p (instead of k).

3.1 Input Preparation

As an input for strict avalanche criterion test, we must provide a set of plaintexts and corresponding ciphertexts (encrypted by the same key). This set will be called a key set. In order to get significant results, SAC method should be run with different key sets and results of each calculation should be combined. Key set is defined as matrix C^p acquired from M plaintext matrix:

$$M = \begin{bmatrix} m_{11} & m_{12} & m_{13} & \dots & m_{1n} \\ m_{21} & m_{22} & m_{23} & \dots & m_{2n} \\ \vdots & \vdots & \vdots & \ddots & \vdots \\ m_{l1} & m_{l2} & m_{l3} & \dots & m_{ln} \end{bmatrix} = \begin{bmatrix} 0 & 0 & 0 & \dots & 0 \\ 1 & 0 & 0 & \dots & 0 \\ 1 & 1 & 0 & \dots & 0 \\ 1 & 1 & 1 & \dots & 0 \\ \vdots & \vdots & \vdots & \ddots & \vdots \\ 1 & 1 & 1 & \dots & 1 \end{bmatrix} \xrightarrow{k=const} C^p = \begin{bmatrix} c_{11}^p & c_{12}^p & c_{13}^p & \dots & c_{1n}^p \\ c_{21}^p & c_{22}^p & c_{23}^p & \dots & c_{2n}^p \\ \vdots & \vdots & \vdots & \ddots & \vdots \\ c_{l1}^p & c_{l2}^p & c_{l3}^p & \dots & c_{ln}^p \end{bmatrix}$$

where $C_i = (c_{i1}^p, c_{i2}^p, \dots, c_{in}^p)$ denotes a bit sequence ($c_{ij}^p \in \{0,1\}$) generated by tested cryptographic algorithm E, using pre-specified constant key:

$$C_i = E(M_i \xleftarrow{R} \{0,1\}^n, p = const)$$

3.2 SAC Test

For n-bit input we can define up to n degrees of strict avalanche criterion. This method is constructed to provide result for all possible values of SAC degree k. However, 10 degrees is enough to acquire proper results, so it was chosen to check only from 1-SAC to 10-SAC. For each $k \in \{1, \cdots, 10\}$ we use data defined in key set for key p to calculate SAC indexes $\Pi_{i(i+k)}^p$ representing the proportion of bits that has changed to overall number of bits within a sequence, assuming that k bits of plaintext has changed. The procedure is as follows:

$$\forall i \in \{1, \cdots, n-k\} : \Pi_{i(i+k)}^p = \frac{\left| 2 \cdot \sum_{j=1}^{n-k} (c_{ij}^p \otimes c_{(i+k)j}^p) - n \right|}{n}$$

Then we can calculate mean value and standard deviation of sac index for k-SAC in order to get overall SAC result SAC_k^p for this key set p.

$$\mu_k^p = \frac{\sum_{i=1}^{n-k} \Pi_{i(i+k)}^p}{n-k}, \sigma_k^p = \sqrt{\frac{1}{n-k} \sum_{i=1}^{n-k} (\Pi_{i(i+k)}^p - \mu_k^p)^2}$$

$$SAC_k^p = \mu_k^p - \sigma_k^p$$

The next step is to combine results of k-SAC calculated for each key p in a set of provided keys K.

$$\mu_k = \frac{\sum_{i=1}^{|K|} SAC_k^i}{|K|}, \sigma_k = \sqrt{\frac{1}{|K|}\sum_{i=1}^{|K|}(SAC_k^i - \mu_k)^2}$$

$$SAC_k = \mu_k - \sigma_k$$

Finally for each k-SAC we can calculate p-value to evaluate whether observed SAC_k value is what we expect from an algorithm that satisfies strict avalanche criterion.

$$P_k = erfc(\frac{SAC_k}{\sqrt{2}})$$

Result of the test is returned in a manner:

$$\begin{cases} \forall j \in \{1, \cdots, 10\} : P_j \geq 0.05 \rightarrow passed \\ \exists j \in \{1, \cdots, 10\} : P_j < 0.05 \rightarrow failed \end{cases}$$

3.3   SAC Test Verification

For experiments with strict avalanche criterion method we have used encryption schemes accepting 64-bit input and generating 64-bit output. Plaintexts were encrypted using 20 different, randomly generated keys. That gave 20 key sets C, each containing 64 ciphertexts.

* Ideal Cipher

Firstly we have tested ideal case [11], with algorithm working in analogous way to encryption scheme E_{ideal}:

$$E_{ideal}(P) = \{c_1, \cdots, c_n\} : \forall i \in \{1, \cdots, n\} : Pr(c_i = 1) = 0.5 \wedge Pr(m_i = c_i) = 0.5$$

This encryption scheme generates random output, no matter what we put as the input of the algorithm. As our experiments shown for all k degrees of strict avalanche criterion this cipher passed SAC test, having in worst case result of P_{value} equal to 0.889.

* Encryption Schemes Not Satisfying Strict Avalanche Criterion

As the next step we performed experiments with encryption schemes that did not perfectly satisfy strict avalanche criterion. For this we defined encryption scheme as follows:

$$K = k_1, \cdots, k_n$$

K is a n-bit sequence representing a key used in encryption process.

$$E_x^K(P = (p_1, \cdots, p_n)) = \{c_1, \cdots, c_n\} : \begin{cases} \forall i \in \{1, \cdots, x\} : c_i = p_i \otimes k_i \\ \forall i \in \{x+1, \cdots, n\} : P(p_i = c_i) = 0.5 \end{cases}$$

E_x^K works in such a way that for x first plaintext P bits it just add them modulo 2 with the corresponding key K bits, and all the remaining bits values are randomly chosen.

We have used this encryption scheme with various values of x. Obviously the ideal case is when $x = 0$. For better intuition we have presented results using percentage of x to n ratio:

$$V = \frac{x}{n} \cdot 100\%$$

for example if we take $x = 32$ it means that $V = 50\%$ of the ciphertext is random and 50% is generated by adding modulo 2 plaintext with key bits (Fig. 3).

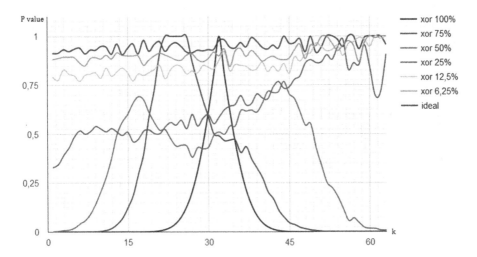

Fig. 3. Plot of strict avalanche criterion test P_{value} in a function of k-SAC degree for encryption schemes E_x^K where $x \in \{0, 8, 16, 32, 48, 64\}$.

As we can see in Fig. 3, for ideal cipher and encryption schemes with high percentage of random output bits (V = 6,25%, V = 12,5%), P_{value} is quite constant and higher then 0.75. For example with V = 0.25% result increases along with k. Higher k degree means comparing sequences with more input changes. For encryption scheme E_x^K ciphertext changes are proportional to plaintext changes and V rate. That means more 'distant' sequences we are comparing (greater k value) the more likely they satisfy strict avalanche criterion. For the worst case when V = 100% whole sequence is added modulo 2 with key we can observe a peak P_{value} for $k = 32$. This is because in order to check 32-SAC we are comparing ciphertexts created by plaintext encryption that differs on 32 positions. This difference is proportional for E_x^K, so we get exactly 32 bit changes between first and 32-th ciphertext. The probability of change is 0.5, so the value we are expecting to ideally pass SAC criterion. Analogously we can see similar P_{value} peaks for V = 50% at $k = 16$ and $k = 48$, and for V = 75% at $k = 24$.

Additionally, Fig. 3 confirms our assumption that 10 degrees is enough to acquire proper results to test SAC. To determine whether we are dealing with a large number of dependencies, it is sufficient to just check the initial k values (i.e. check only from 1-SAC to 10-SAC).

* Ceasar Cipher

A good example of a cipher that does not satisfy strict avalanche criterion at all is Ceasar cipher. It simply encodes a letter by choosing another letter that is a particular number of positions further in the alphabet. So for example if we choose shift to be equal to 3, the encryption of letter A would be letter C. The encryption scheme presented here works in the exactly same way using ASCII code for letters and symbols. Each symbol is represented by one byte so in order to create adaptation of Ceasar cipher we only need to use cryptographic algorithm that would accept as input 64-bits of data, so 8 symbols, and produce ciphertexts by adding shift to the ASCII representation of a symbol:

$$M = \{m_1, \cdots, m_8\} C = \{c_1, \cdots, c_8\}$$

$$E_{ceasar}(M, s) = C : \forall i \in \{1, \cdots, 8\} : c_1 = m_i + s$$

where m_i is a symbol coded in ASCII represented by one byte of data, c_i represents one byte of ciphertext, and s is a shift of Ceasar cipher. Plot in Fig. 4 presents results of strict avalanche criterion test for $E_{ceasar}(M, 3)$. As we can see P_{values} for all k are pretty small.

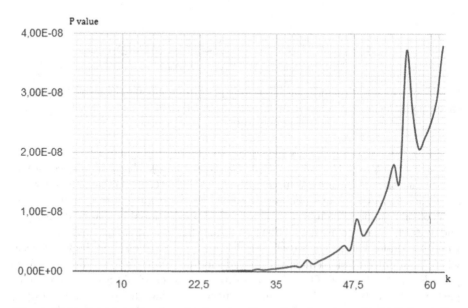

Fig. 4. Plot of strict avalanche criterion test P_{value} in a function of k-SAC degree for encryption scheme $E_{M,3}^{ceasar}$.

4   Frequency Test

Frequency method is the simple test for randomness hypothesis. A good cryptographic algorithm should produce the output in such a way, that adversary cannot tell the difference between the ciphertext and a truly random sequence. Frequency test makes use of obvious assumption that a truly random bit generator should have the probability of returning a bit of value 1 equal to the probability of returning 0. So if the bit sequence generated by the algorithm is going to be classified as random-like (meaning indistinguishable from truly random string of bits) the number of ones within that sequence should be close to the number of all bits divided by 2. Method presented in this section calculates the difference between number of ones and zeros (called overload), normalize it and outputs sufficient p-value describing probability that for the value observed randomness hypothesis is true. Very small p-value indicates that sequences generated have too many zeroes or ones to be described as random-like.

* The Ideal Case

The first encryption scheme considered is:

$$E_1(M) = \{c_1, \cdots, c_n\} : \forall i \in \{1, \cdots, n\} : P(c_i = 1) = \frac{1}{2} \wedge P(c_i = 0) = \frac{1}{2}$$

Definition proposed here describes encryption scheme that on any input message M produces ciphertext $\{c_1, \cdots, c_n\}$, such as for all bits within this ciphertext, the probability of ones and the probability of zeros are equal to $\frac{1}{2}$. This is the ideal case. With sufficient number of samples (in our case 1000) we should be able to reach the overall number of ones within the sequence to be very close to the analogous number of zeroes.

Overload simply inform about the number of ones (bits that have the value equal to one) minus the number zeros within all considered sequences. In our experiments we considered a test set of $k = 1000$ plaintext-ciphertext pairs, each one containing $n = 64$ bits. Ideally we would like to have overload equal to 0, so in out test case the number of ones and zeroes should be both equal to 32000.

We have performed experiment with E_1 encryption scheme 10 times in order to get meaningful results. The subject of our frequency test was the algorithm that was generating random ciphertexts satisfying the requirements specified in E_1 definition. During all runs of the experiment overload did not hold larger values then 486. In the worst case P_{value} calculated was around 0.05. On average P_{value} was equal to 0.52. As we can see frequency method correctly classified a good scheme in all ten cases, even though there were some rare cases when test returned high overload values.

* Slight Bias from Ideal Frequency

The next step was to check encryption scheme that was slightly worse in case of frequency. Consider encryption scheme E_2:

$$E_2(M) = \{c_1, \cdots, c_n\} : \forall i \in \{1, \cdots, n\} : P(c_i = 1) = 0.51 \wedge P(c_i = 0) = 0.49$$

Probability of ones is only a little bit larger then the probability of zeros. Although it has a very strong impact on the frequency method results. We have performed experiment 10 times with similar algorithm as in previous section generating random ciphertext, but with different probabilities (as defined in E_2). In this case overload held values between 884 and 1728, which drastically lowered P_{value}. The results of the method hold between $4.8 \cdot 10^{-4}$ and $8.5 \cdot 10^{-12}$. This is a serious drop of P_{value}, but it is expected behaviour. Cryptographic algorithm should generate ciphertexts that are indistinguishable from random. A large set of random-like sequences should level out any anomalies, ending up with similar number of ones and zeros. If it does not happen and frequency fluctuation is still detectable, there is a grave problem with encryption scheme. In case of E_2 this fluctuation is amplified across 1000 sequences, since it makes the offset value even larger.

* Strong Bias from Ideal Frequency

There were two more experiments performed to see how this method behaves given even worse encryption schemes:

$$E_3(M) = \{c_1, \cdots, c_n\} : \forall i \in \{1, \cdots, n\} : P(c_i = 1) = 0.55 \land P(c_i = 0) = 0.45$$

$$E_4(M) = \{c_1, \cdots, c_n\} : \forall i \in \{1, \cdots, n\} : P(c_i = 1) = 0.67 \land P(c_i = 0) = 0.33$$

For E_3 overload was around 10000, thus P_{value} was equal to $1 \cdot 10^{-347}$. In case of E_4 overload was around 17000, so $P_{value} = 6 \cdot 10^{-981}$.

* Overload Acceptance Limits

The value of overload that is acceptable differs depending on the number of samples. The limit proposed in frequency method is when P_{value} reaches value that is lesser then 0.01. P_{value} is calculated considering the number of samples in test set. The larger is this set, the larger offset value is feasible.

Figure 5 presents P_{value} in a function of overload for different sizes of test sets (all containing 64-bit ciphertexts). We can see that P_{value} decreases along with incrementation of overload. Slope of those functions depends on the number of samples. Function for a 1-element test set decreases the most rapidly. For 1000-element set P_{value} decrementation is much slower.

The table in Fig. 6 presents the lowest overload values that are accepted by the frequency method (for each set). Third column describes the percentage of overload bits comparing to the number of all the bits considered. We can see that for larger sets, acceptable percentage value is smaller. That is exactly what we want – for small number of considered sequences we should tolerate more frequency fluctuations, and for larger those fluctuations should be levelled out.

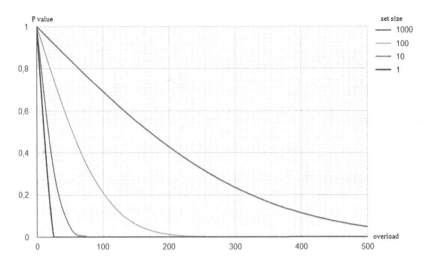

Fig. 5. Frequency test P_{value} in a function of overload for different set sizes.

number of samples	overload	overload bits percentage
100000	4958	0,08%
10000	1567	0,24%
1000	495	0,77%
100	156	2,43%
10	49	7,66%
1	15	23,43%

Fig. 6. Table of lowest overload values with percentage of their values compared to the number of all considered bits in frequency method for different set sizes.

5 Crypographic Algorithms Assesment

In this section we concentrated on application of the test suit proposed in order to assess some popular encryption algorithms. We used idealized (ideal cipher) encryption scheme as a reference. It generates random outputs with equal probability of each bit to have zero or one value, no matter what plaintext it was given on input. Then we tested DES and AES cryptographic algorithms to check their properties. Finally we tested Ceasar cipher as a example of a weak encryption scheme. It simply shifts ASCII codes corresponding to input symbols by some pre-specified value. We have run our test suite ten times with 10 000 randomly generated samples (words from English Dictionary). The results are presented in tables Figs. 7, 8, 9 and 10.

Each entry represents a result (for all tests except nonlinearity test it is P_{value}) for a test described in the first column. Each row contains results for one corresponding test run 10 times (10 columns).

	Run 1	Run 2	Run 3	Run 4	Run 5	Run 6	Run 7	Run 8	Run 9	Run 10
Frequency	0.16	0.82	0.05	0.92	0.45	0.66	0.09	0.53	0.96	0.05
Block Frequency	0.79	0.79	0.79	0.79	0.79	0.80	0.79	0.79	0.79	0.79
Runs	0.75	0.53	0.05	0.39	0.20	0.83	0.39	0.47	0.18	0.48
Cumulative Sums Upper	0.95	0.95	0.95	0.95	0.95	0.95	0.95	0.95	0.95	0.95
Cumulative Sums Lower	0.19	0.19	0.19	0.19	0.19	0.19	0.19	0.19	0.19	0.19
Nonlinearity	100%	100%	100%	100%	100%	100%	100%	100%	100%	100%
Sac Input	0.89	0.89	0.89	0.88	0.88	0.89	0.89	0.89	0.89	0.89
Sac Key	0.89	0.88	0.88	0.89	0.89	0.88	0.89	0.88	0.89	0.89
Shifted Blocks	0.90	0.91	0.91	0.91	0.90	0.91	0.90	0.90	0.91	0.90
Inout Runs	0.72	0.71	0.70	0.72	0.72	0.72	0.71	0.72	0.71	0.71

Fig. 7. Test suit results for ideal cipher.

	Run 1	Run 2	Run 3	Run 4	Run 5	Run 6	Run 7	Run 8	Run 9	Run 10
Frequency	0.30	0.12	0.85	0.56	0.40	0.07	0.85	0.04	0.93	0.66
Block Frequency	0.79	0.79	0.79	0.79	0.79	0.79	0.79	0.78	0.79	0.79
Runs	0.45	0.88	0.89	0.40	0.60	0.38	0.74	0.99	0.10	0.86
Cumulative Sums Upper	0,89	0,89	0,89	0,89	0,89	0,89	0,89	0,89	0,89	0,89
Cumulative Sums Lower	0.19	0.19	0.19	0.19	0.19	0.19	0.19	0.19	0.19	0.19
Nonlinearity	100%	100%	100%	100%	100%	100%	100%	100%	100%	100%
Sac Input	0.89	0.89	0.89	0.88	0.89	0.89	0.90	0.91	0.90	0.91
Sac Key	0.90	0.88	0.89	0.89	0.89	0.88	0.92	0.90	0.91	0.89
Shifted Blocks	0.90	0.91	0.91	0.90	0.90	0.90	0.90	0.90	0.91	0.89
Inout Runs	0.71	0.70	0.71	0.71	0.70	0.71	0.71	0.71	0.70	0.71

Fig. 8. Test suit results for DES encryption scheme.

	Run 1	Run 2	Run 3	Run 4	Run 5	Run 6	Run 7	Run 8	Run 9	Run 10
Frequency	0.75	0.63	0.15	0.76	0.89	0.17	0.86	0.18	0.42	0.07
Block Frequency	0.79	0.79	0.79	0.79	0.79	0.79	0.79	0.79	0.79	0.79
Runs	0.89	0.81	0.24	0.69	0.75	0.31	0.27	0.62	0.11	0.37
Cumulative Sums Upper	0.95	0.95	0.95	0.95	0.95	0.95	0.95	0.95	0.95	0.95
Cumulative Sums Lower	0.19	0.19	0.19	0.19	0.19	0.19	0.19	0.19	0.19	0.19
Nonlinearity	100%	100%	100%	100%	100%	100%	100%	100%	100%	100%
Sac Input	0.87	0.88	0.87	0.88	0.88	0.88	0.87	0.88	0.89	0.89
Sac Key	0.88	0.89	0.87	0.87	0.88	0.90	0.89	0.87	0.87	0.87
Shifted Blocks	0.90	0.91	0.91	0.90	0.90	0.90	0.90	0.90	0.91	0.89
Inout Runs	0.71	0.70	0.71	0.71	0.70	0.71	0.71	0.71	0.70	0.71

Fig. 9. Test suit results for AES encryption scheme.

	Run 1	Run 2	Run 3	Run 4	Run 5	Run 6	Run 7	Run 8	Run 9	Run 10
Frequency	0	0	0	0	0	0	0	0	0	0
Block Frequency	0.92	0.92	0.92	0.92	0.92	0.92	0.92	0.92	0.92	0.92
Runs	0	0	0	0	0	0	0	0	0	0
Cumulative Sums Upper	0.95	0.95	0.95	0.95	0.95	0.95	0.95	0.95	0.95	0.95
Cumulative Sums Lower	0.22	0.22	0.22	0.22	0.22	0.22	0.22	0.22	0.22	0.22
Nonlinearity	53%	53%	53%	53%	53%	53%	53%	53%	53%	53%
Sac Input	0	0	0	0	0	0	0	0	0	0
Sac Key	0	0	0	0	0	0	0	0	0	0
Shifted Blocks	0	0	0	0	0	0	0	0	0	0
Inout Runs	0.20	0.20	0.20	0.20	0.20	0.20	0.20	0.20	0.20	0.20

Fig. 10. Test suit results for Ceasar cipher.

In case of nonlinearity test the result is presented in a different manner. This test considers a huge amount of sequence fragments that are compared to each other. For each fragment P_{value} is calculated independently. The nonlinearity results in a table shows percentage of fragments that passed the test (P_{value} calculated was higher than 0.01) to the number of all examined fragments. For Ideal, DES and Ceasar encryption schemes we used 64-bit inputs, so the number of fragments analized by nonlinearity test was equal to 32768. In case of AES since input was 128 bit long, 131072 fragments were examined. For strict avalanche criterion, shifted blocks, input-output runs tests worst P_{value} cases were put in the table.

As experiments has shown, test suit proposed in this paper can be used to check whether encryption scheme has some properties or features which are expected from a good cryptographic algorithm. Frequency test detects if bits of some value significantly dominates in sequences being generated by encryption scheme (detects problems with bit balance). Block frequency test should verify some issues with bit oscillation (frequency of switches between ones and zeros in a bit string). Nonlinearity and shifted blocks test are created in order to find relations between input and output bits (similarity to affine transformation). Input-output runs test detects whether related plaintext-ciphertext bits keep appearing in some significantly numerous groups. Finally we could check that DES and AES are indeed good encryption schemes. The results of test methods were very similar to the ideal cipher (generating completely random output) in all test categories. As the example of weak cryptographic algorithm we proposed a Ceasar cipher. In this case methods were able to find numerous problems with this encryption scheme including bit balance, oscillation, strong ciphertext-plaintext relation, strict avalanche criterion issues.

6   Conclusion

In this article a way for assessment of block cryptographic algorithms was presented. The main motivation of this research was investigation whether there is a way to assess security of block cryptographic algorithms in some universal manner. We wanted to check if regardless the details of encryption scheme used, cryptographer is able to detect weaknesses and bugs within considered algorithm. Therefore, we presented selected test methods that analyse input and corresponding output of the algorithm and assign a metric for evaluation how strong is the encryption scheme. Having those features is necessary (however not sufficient to certainly classify considered cryptographic algorithm to be safe).

The methods were implemented using .NET C♯ and packed in a framework that can be used as a cryptographic assessment tool for cryptographers, requiring only a slight knowledge of programming language from them. Those methods were validated in practise using several experiments and also test results were compared for known encryption schemes including DES, AES with ideal cases. Applied test suit would be a very good starting point in a process of proving security of encryption scheme. Cryptographic algorithm designer can use this tool to speed up testing process and verify security level of algorithms at the early stages of design, in order to get rid of basic mistakes.

Acknowledgments. This work was funded by the Polish National Centre for Research and Development under "SDNRoute: integrated system supporting routing in Software Defined Networks", project number LIDER/30/0006/L-7/15/NCBR/2016.

References

1. Kurek, T., Lason, A., Niemiec, M.: First step towards preserving the privacy of cloud-based IDS security policies. Secur. Commun. Netw. **8**(18), 3481–3491 (2015)
2. Zhao, K., Ge, L.: A survey on the Internet of Things security. In: IX International Conference on Computational Intelligence and Security, Leshan (2013)
3. Stoianov, N., Uruena, M., Niemiec, M., Machnik, P., Maestro, G.: Security infrastructures: towards the INDECT system security. Multimed. Commun. Serv. Secur. **287**, 304–315 (2012)
4. Shannon, C.: Communication theory of secrecy systems. Bell Syst. Tech. J. **28**, 656–715 (1949)
5. Stallings, W.: Cryptography and Network Security: Principles and Practices. Prentice Hall, Upper Saddle River (2005)
6. Niemiec M., Machowski.: A new symmetric block cipher based on key-dependent S-boxes. In: IV International Congress on Ultra Modern Telecommunications and Control Systems, St. Petersburg (2012)
7. Sadowski, A.: Wybrane zagadnienia kryptologii i ochrony informacji. Helion (1999)
8. NIST SP-800-22: A statistical test suite for random and pseudorandom number generators for cryptographic applications. National Institute of Standards and Technology (NIST) (2000)
9. McCaffrey, J.: Test Run - Implementing the National Institute of Standards and Technology Tests of Randomness Using C (2013). https://msdn.microsoft.com/enus/magazine/dn520240.aspx
10. Gustafson, H., Dawson, E., Pettitt, A.N.: Strict key avalanche criterion. Aust. J. Comb. **6**, 147–153 (1992)
11. Dodis, Y., Puniya, P.: On the relation between the ideal cipher and the random oracle models. In: Halevi, S., Rabin, T. (eds.) TCC 2006. LNCS, vol. 3876, pp. 184–206. Springer, Heidelberg (2006). doi:10.1007/11681878_10

Quick Response Code Secure: A Cryptographically Secure Anti-Phishing Tool for QR Code Attacks

Vasileios Mavroeidis[1(✉)] and Mathew Nicho[2(✉)]

[1] University of Oslo, Oslo, Norway
vasileim@ifi.uio.no
[2] Robert Gordon University, Aberdeen, Scotland
m.nicho1@rgu.ac.uk

Abstract. The two-dimensional quick response (QR) codes can be misleading due to the difficulty in differentiating a genuine QR code from a malicious one. Since the vulnerability is practically part of their design, scanning a malicious QR code can direct the user to cloned malicious sites resulting in revealing sensitive information. In order to evaluate the vulnerabilities and propose subsequent countermeasures, we demonstrate this type of attack through a simulated experiment, where a malicious QR code directs a user to a phishing site. For our experiment, we cloned Google's web page providing access to their email service (Gmail). Since the URL is masqueraded into the QR code, the unsuspecting user who opens the URL is directed to the malicious site. Our results proved that hackers could easily leverage QR codes into phishing attack vectors targeted at smartphone users, even bypassing web browsers' safe browsing feature. In addition, the second part of our paper presents adequate countermeasures and introduces QRCS (Quick Response Code Secure). QRCS is a universal efficient and effective solution focusing exclusively on the authenticity of the originator and consequently the integrity of QR code by using digital signatures.

Keywords: Quick response (QR) codes · 2D codes · Smartphone security · Mobile phishing attacks · Cryptography · Digital signatures

1 Introduction

Quick response (QR) code has become one of the more popular two-dimensional barcodes due to its inherent data capacity and higher damage resistance [1]. With smartphone security and privacy becoming a major concern [2], a hijacked QR code can be a dangerous attack vector for smartphone users. With millions of QR codes displayed by companies in public places, it's not difficult for a malicious author to replace or modify them. The rapid pace of smartphone adoption and usage [3] has not only enhanced QR code popularity and usage over a much wider range of applications [4], but also introduced newer QR code

© Springer International Publishing AG 2017
J. Rak et al. (Eds.): MMM-ACNS 2017, LNCS 10446, pp. 313–324, 2017.
DOI: 10.1007/978-3-319-65127-9_25

attack vectors for malicious users [5] thus posing a serious threat to unsuspecting smartphone users. With mobile phone usage crossing the two billion mark in 2016, outnumbering personal computers [6], this threat assumes greater significance. Compared to the infamous 376 bytes Slammer worm that destroyed millions of computers in the year 2003 [4], the maximum binary data that a QR code can hold is roughly 2.9 KB which can be a threat vector for malicious payloads. QR codes can be used in several different types of attacks such as social engineering and automated processes attacks. Automated processes attacks are executed by exploiting SQL injection vulnerabilities, command injection, as well as Cross-Site Scripting (XSS) attacks [7].

In this article, we ethically simulate a QR code phishing attack to demonstrate the attack methodology and the bypass method that can be employed by hackers to counter safe browsing. In addition, we propose Quick Response Code Secure (QRCS), a secure framework that makes use of digitally signed QR codes to verify their genuineness.

Our paper is structured as follows. In Sect. 2, we explain smart phone vulnerabilities with respect to QR codes. Section 3 provides an overview of QR codes and how it has been leveraged as an attack vector. Thereafter, Sect. 4 details the simulated attack using malicious QR codes, which demonstrates how it can be leveraged as a phishing attack vector, including the identified vulnerable points. In Sect. 5, we present our QRCS solution, which details the components, and the subsequent process used to authenticate genuine QR codes by users. Section 6 provides a conclusion along with future directions.

2   Smartphone Vulnerability

Phishing is a difficult unresolved problem [8]. Since, phishing attacks can be made more convincing on smartphones than on a desktop browser, users can expect to see more phishing attacks on mobile malware in the future [8]. Attackers create different kinds of malware to exploit devices for financial gain, utilization of resources, information and data theft, search engine optimization, spam messages, access private networks, or even damaging devices for amusement. Generally, such malware are attached to popular legitimate applications or in new applications having some functionality to trick the user.

Mobile users put mobile devices in their everyday life using them for several reasons like making phone calls, sending text messages and emails, online transactions, accessing social networks, accessing corporate data, portable storage, saving information (notes) and many more. These make mobile devices a valuable asset to target for malicious attacks. Moreover, in US only 14% of the mobile users have antivirus installed while 34% of the users don't use any form of technical protection, let alone the four-digit screen lock PIN [9]. In addition, the lack of security in legitimate mobile applications makes them vulnerable to traditional attacks like SQL injection, cross site scripting (XSS), and man in the middle attacks (MITM).

Several smartphone antivirus applications do not handle malware adequately due to the limitations imposed by Android's security system [10]. Hence, not all antivirus applications are effective at preventing malware and spyware from infecting an Android phone [11]. Furthermore, most of the antivirus software for smartphone devices are signature based, thus making it impossible to protect the devices from zero day attacks and sophisticated (complex) polymorphic malware. The subsequent sections explain QR codes and how it can be leveraged by phishers, the simulated attack we conducted, the vulnerabilities we detected, subsequent countermeasures, and our proposed solution to secure QR codes.

3   QR Codes as Attack Vector

QR codes, developed by a subsidiary of Toyota named Denso Wave in Japan in 1994, consist of black square dots arranged in a square pattern (matrix code) on a white background. It can store 7,089 numeric characters or 4,296 alphanumeric characters, 2,953 bytes of binary, and 1,817 Japanese Kanji/Kana symbols [12]. QR code has six desirable features namely high capacity encoding of data, small printout size, Chinese/Japanese (kanji and kana) capability, dirt and damage resistance, readability from any direction in 360°, and a structure append feature [13].

3.1   Leveraging QR Codes for Malicious Purpose

QR codes are being increasingly used as an attack vector, facilitating phishing attacks and redirecting users to malicious websites that host malware [5]. Even though people might fall for QR code leveraged phishing attacks, there are other possible weaknesses that QR codes can possibly exploit [7]. Specifically, QR codes can be used for SQL injection and command injection attacks in automated readers-programs that extract information from QR-codes. Moreover, depending upon the type of data recognized and the nature of the application, the decoding of QR codes can result in a phone number being automatically dialed, a short text message being sent, a web page corresponding to the decoded URL displayed in a mobile browser, or a different application executed [14]. In addition, the Unstructured Supplementary Service Data (USSD) codes encoded in 2D barcodes can be used to wipe a phone, execute other system functions, generate premium rate SMS messages, trigger vulnerabilities in the reader software, the operating system, or a remote site, such as SQL injections [15].

3.2   Leveraging QR Codes for Phishing

The most prevalent attacks employing QR codes are phishing and drive by downloads [3] that trick users to disclose confidential information. QR codes enable users to open web pages via scanning, without typing the URL. Furthermore, to improve usability some browsers in mobile devices hide the URL and even if the browser shows the URL, due to limitations in smartphone screen size users won't be able to notice it clearly thus making QR codes a very attractive vector for phishers. In addition, some attackers use URL shortening mechanisms to hide the true URL, thus tricking naive users. Regarding the possibility of exploited sites, attackers can also direct users to malicious sites that can initiate 'drive by downloads' based on the fingerprint of the device. As the fingerprint information is included in the HTTP header when a user requests a site (GET Request) [16], the exploit kit retrieves the information about the device and sends the relevant malicious code.

QR codes have been misused as attack vectors by social engineers via encoded malicious links that enable phishing sites to execute fraudulent codes [17]. Kharraz, Kirda, Robertson, Balzarotti and Francillon conducted an empirical analysis across 14 million web pages to discover the extent to which QR codes are leveraged by attackers in the wild. Their results showed that QR codes are being abused by attackers to distribute malware or direct to phishing sites on the public web [3]. The results not only revealed the malicious use of QR codes, but also identified 145 malicious QR codes out of 94,770 QR codes. However, this experiment was limited to QR codes found only on the Web, and not in public places. To demonstrate that QR codes can be used for conducting phishing attacks, Vidas, Owusu, Wang, Zeng, Cranor and Christin [18] deployed QR code posters across 139 different location where they found that most users (75%) scanned the QR code out of curiosity or for fun, with very few scanned to solicit more information within the context surrounding the QR code. The results indicate that most users who scan a QR code will subsequently visit the related URL, even if the domain is unfamiliar and uses shortened style URL. A similar experiment was conducted where the researcher placed QR coded stickers in high traffic areas around a target town. When users scanned the QR code, they were redirected to a WordPress site that informed them about the experiment, and the dangers that QR codes can hide [19].

However, our research not only simulates leveraging QR codes for phishing, but also proposes a cryptographic methodology to counter the attack vector.

4   Experiment

In this part, we demonstrate and analyse how QR codes can be used in phishing attacks, making them a potent attack vector. Particularly, we start by creating a malicious QR code and a phishing Gmail page, followed by the demonstration of the attack. Finally, we bypass Google safe browsing to keep the malicious QR codes alive even in case they are flagged malicious.

To support our experiment, we captured a photo of a QR code at a bus stop in a city in United Kingdom (Fig. 1) that we use in a way to simulate a phishing attack. We can clearly see that the bus stop has an NFC chip, and a QR code attached for commuters to check time table electronically. In this regard, attackers do not need any special-purpose tools to launch a phishing attack neither sophisticated methods to trick unaware commuters to scan the malicious QR codes.

Fig. 1. QR code at a bus stop in UK

4.1   Create a QR Code

The first step in our experiment was to create a QR code with a malicious URL attached directing the user to a phishing site.

The requirement of a successful phishing attack is a domain name similar to the original website for deceiving users including a link management platform to hide (masquerade) our domain name. The latter is a common method to deceive users in case a domain name is not similar to the original to keep the malicious QR codes operational. In our simulation, we used Bitly which has the following structure http://bit.ly/... Bitly is a link-management platform service allowing users to shorten a URL making it more attractive and practical. Attackers normally use such services as a masquerading method to trick people to visit the malicious site. Since the shortened link replaces the original, users are unable to find out the destination without first visiting the website.

Furthermore, some QR code readers allow users to see the human readable QR code content (e.g. URL), before performing the action, while other code readers redirect without this intermediate action. We have to make clear that this is not a flaw of the mobile device, but a limitation of the application software itself. For this demonstration, we created a cloned Gmail page to demonstrate the attack.

4.2   Create a Phishing Gmail Page

In this scenario, we copied the official Gmail page people use to access their email accounts. Furthermore, we deployed a web server to host our phishing website and a database to store the credentials retrieved. In addition, we added a descriptive logo of the public transport service company in the city where the experiment was conducted (Fig. 2 with name of the bus company blurred for anonymity).

4.3   Launch the Attack

We simulated the attack on ourselves (unlike a normal QR code phishing attack scenario conducted at a public place). The browser will open and direct the user to the phishing site. The unsuspected user adds the requested credentials and when taps the subsequent button, will be redirected to the official Gmail page without noticing anything suspicious. The simulated credentials are stored into our created database.

Fig. 2. Phishing Gmail page

4.4   Bypassing Google Safe Browsing

Google has web crawlers searching for malicious sites making the job of attackers difficult, or not that difficult. Two days later, our page was flagged as deceptive by 'Google safe browsing' feature. We hereby demonstrate how with only one line of code, even this countermeasure can be bypassed.

The bypass method that can be employed by hackers is to change the name of the phishing page. However, in reality, it is not convenient because the attacker would have to change the URL in the malicious QR code. The warning pop-up window alerts that "This web page at (url) has been reported as deceptive and has been blocked based on your security preferences" which actually means that Google flagged only the actual phishing page (file) as malicious, and not the domain name. This practice helps web developers to identify the compromised page; otherwise, the domain name would be flagged malicious. Worthy to note is that it is not considered best practice to blacklist domain names because malicious domain names today may be benign after a period of time. In reality, the phishing page should be the first page someone sees when directed to the site. A malicious actor can automatically redirect a victim from a blank main page to the malicious phishing page with one line of PHP. Therefore, we use the main page (for example index.php), only to redirect users to a phishing subpage. The victim will still see it as the main page because of the following PHP code (header("location: test.azurewebsites.net/test.php")) which redirects the victim automatically to the phishing page without Google's warning message popping up anymore.

5   Secure QR Code Solution

This section of the paper deals with the security of QR codes where our universal QR Code Secure tool is presented which ensures that users get redirected only to the intended sites. Since, QRCS authenticates the originator by using digital signatures, our solution is a safe way to certify that the QR code a user scan is genuine and not tampered with.

5.1   Related Work-Security of QR Codes

Chuang, Hu and Ko [20] proposed a technique that improves data security for data transmission during QR code communication. The secret sharing technique divides the "secret" data (QR code) into shadows (several QR codes) that are distributed to "n" participants where some parts or all of them are needed to reconstruct the message. However, this secret sharing technique for QR codes focuses primarily on confidentiality of data rather than prevent phishing.

Gao, Kulkarni, Ranavat, Chang and Mei [21] proposed a 2D barcode based mobile payment system, which uses QR codes to conduct secure and reliable payment transactions using mobile devices. While this solution secure QR code based transactions, it doesn't audit the integrity of the initial QR code the user scans.

In addition, Narayanan [22] describes several non-technical solutions to raise awareness of the security of QR codes that should not be overlooked. Interesting is his suggestion of using descriptive features such as logos into the QR codes that will raise the difficulty for the hackers to design similar QR codes, as well as using distinctive colors. Our opinion regarding the former is that this solution should be avoided as hackers or even everyday users can use online tools to add logos or change the colors of the traditional QR codes easily. As a result, a QR code with distinctive properties can be used to easier trick people believing that this code is coming from a legitimate source. Regarding the use of colors, Krombholz, Frhwirt, Kieseberg, Kapsalis, Huber and Weippl [17] believe that the more complex the color theme, the harder it is for an attacker to replicate such QR codes, where they proposed the extension of these complex color schemes to the whole advertising campaign hosting the QR code. Futhermore, they point out the relevance of digital signatures to verify the originator of a QR code.

Two encryption schemes for QR codes have been proposed that make use of symmetric and asymmetric cryptography respectively [23]. For symmetric QR codes, the use of a shared secret key between the reader and the writer is used with AES as the recommended cryptographic algorithm. The asymmetric solution makes use of the RSA algorithm to encrypt the symmetric key that can be appended next to the message. Worthy to note is that Peng et al. [24] proposed the use of digital signatures for verification of the source before any action is performed. Their idea to use a number of bits to identify the signers public key can be used to QRCS. However, the solution occupies a considerable amount of space in a QR code that makes it appropriate only for specific purposes. In this regard, we emphasize that the RSA algorithm may not be an efficient algorithm that can be used in mobile devices. Hence, to minimize the computational overhead, we suggest to use only small public keys (exponent e).

Accordingly, we differentiate our research by creating a universal solution that can be used for the integrity and authenticity of any QR code for information or transaction purpose.

5.2   Secure QR Code Solution (QRCS)

Our proposed solution adopts the traditional server-client architecture using digital signatures. The server side controls and authenticates the entities that wish to access our platform to create QR codes under their company's profile (can be verified by the users that scan the codes), while the client is an application available (like the traditional QR readers) for public use. Our proposed solution makes use of the popular hash functions and digital signatures to provide integrity and authenticity to the QR codes.

Hash Functions: QRCS makes use of the cryptographically secure hash function SHA-2 (SHA-3 can be used too) to generate a digest message of 256 bit, which is currently resistant to brute force attacks. A hash function or better a hash algorithm is a mechanism that can be fed with arbitrary length input to generate a fixed length output. This property is not only significant for the use of digital signatures if the plaintext is large enough, but it also overcomes storage limitations in the QR code.

Digital Signatures: Our solution makes use of digital signatures, which is a way to prove that a certain entity generated the message we observe, such as the plaintext into the QR code. The cryptographic primitive is achieved through the public key cryptography, which actually makes use of the difficulty to factorize large prime numbers or the discrete logarithm problem. Since smartphones have limited resources for doing heavy calculations we propose the ECDSA (elliptic curve digital signature algorithm) for signing the hash functions. The entity that generated the plaintext and the hash will digitally sign the hash by making use of a private key and an ephemeral key (the ephemeral key is different every time we want to sign a new QR code). The solution we propose does the above mentioned automatically to generate the QR code. Consequently, a user that scans the code needs a reader specialized in decoding, decrypting, and verifying the signature.

Server-Side Platform. On the server side, we propose a platform that can host our certificate authority (to generate digital certificates) and the registration system. Since companies, organizations, or even small businesses can apply for an approved profile on our platform, to illustrate the process, we use a fictional company named ABC. Company ABC can get access to our platform by applying and submitting the requested documents that actually prove their claimed identity. The approved entity will get authorized access, a unique digital certificate, and can generate digitally signed QR codes (Fig. 3).

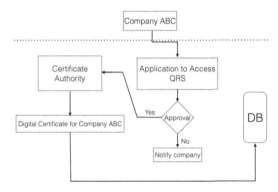

Fig. 3. Server-side platform (QRCS)

In summary, at the server side, company ABC has to include only the plaintext needed to be encoded and QRCS will calculate the hash function and digitally sign it (encryption with the private key and a unique ephemeral key). In addition, we make use of Peng et al. [24] concept of using a number of bits to uniquely identify the signer's public key. As a result, when a code is scanned, the application identifies the public key that is used to verify whether the QR code is genuine or not.

Client-Side Application. Once we have a QR code created by QRCS it contains the plaintext, the unique number which specifies the public key of the signer, and the digitally signed hash. Figure 4 presents the client-side QRCS.

The application can access the public keys of the entities online, stored into our database or they can be downloaded to the application for offline access in case a network connection is not available. When a code is scanned, the application will check with the use of the public key and the signature if the verification condition is satisfied. If it is satisfied, then the application will perform the intended action; otherwise the QR code is classified as non-verified. In case of a non-verified QR code, the application will alert the user and the QR code will be blocked from action. In addition, the user is able to submit a report for the non-genuine QR code with details.

This option is available only for registered users who have proved their identity with an OTP (one time password) sent to their submitted mobile number when they first registered. For example, if the QR code is available on the Internet, then the user can submit the URL targeting the non-verified code. The user also has the option to specify the geographic location of the non-genuine code by tapping a button and choosing from a list the organization that the QR code claims. These options are available only after a code has been flagged as non-verified. These options are completely optional and a user can use the application without registering.

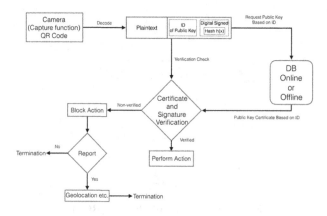

Fig. 4. Client software (QRCS)

6   Conclusion

In this paper, we went through the process commonly deployed by hackers to leverage QR codes for phishing attacks and subsequently proposed a client-server based solution using digital signatures to authenticate benign QR codes from malicious ones. Considering the rate at which QR codes are being deployed by the industry targeting the mobile phone users, we believe that hackers are increasingly leveraging QR codes as attack vectors putting companies and users at risk. In this regard, our simulated attack using a compromised QR code revealed vulnerabilities that can lead to unintentional disclosure of sensitive personal information. Subsequently, we conceptually demonstrated our client-server based QRCS cryptographic solution using digital signatures that can successfully thwart malicious QR code attacks at the initial scanning phase itself by digitally verifying the genuine QR code. Security analysis of our model shows that apart from preventing users from redirection to malicious sites by the malicious QR codes, our model is also effective against man in the middle and replay attacks as well. This model is straightforward to implement as it requires less modification from a QR code deployment perspective.

Our future work focuses on making QRCS convenient to use for both companies and everyday users by separating the application in security levels needed by the interested party. Unlike companies, everyday users normally won't go through a formal checking process. In this regard, our future work targets the lower trust level zone in the application layer where user access is provided through a unique email, username, password, and mobile number.

References

1. Lin, P.Y., Chen, Y.H.: High payload secret hiding technology for QR codes. EURASIP J. Image Video Process. 2017(1), 14 (2017)

2. Zhou, Y., Jiang, X.: Dissecting android malware: characterization and evolution. In: 2012 IEEE Symposium on Security and Privacy (SP), pp. 95–109. IEEE (2012)

3. Kharraz, A., Kirda, E., Robertson, W., Balzarotti, D., Francillon, A.: Optical delusions: a study of malicious QR codes in the wild. In: 2014 44th Annual IEEE/IFIP International Conference on Dependable Systems and Networks (DSN), pp. 192–203. IEEE (2014)

4. Sharma, V.: A study of malicious QR codes. Int. J. Comput. Intell. Inf. Secur. **3**(5), 21–26 (2012)

5. Jain, A.K., Shanbhag, D.: Addressing security and privacy risks in mobile applications. IT Prof. **14**(5), 28–33 (2012)

6. Chaffey, D.: Mobile marketing statistics compilation. http://www.smartinsights.com/mobile-marketing/mobile-marketing-analytics/mobile-marketing-statistics/

7. Kieseberg, P., Leithner, M., Mulazzani, M., Munroe, L., Schrittwieser, S., Sinha, M., Weippl, E.: QR code security. In: Proceedings of the 8th International Conference on Advances in Mobile Computing and Multimedia, pp. 430–435. ACM (2010)

8. Felt, A.P., Finifter, M., Chin, E., Hanna, S., Wagner, D.: A survey of mobile malware in the wild. In: Proceedings of the 1st ACM Workshop on Security and Privacy in Smartphones and Mobile Devices, pp. 3–14. ACM (2011)

9. Tapellini, D.: Smart phone thefts rose to 3.1 million in 2013 industry solution falls short, while legislative efforts to curb theft continue. http://www.consumerreports.org/cro/news/2014/04/smart-phone-thefts-rose-to-3-1-million-last-year/index.htm

10. Fedler, R., Schütte, J., Kulicke, M.: On the effectiveness of malware protection on android. In: Fraunhofer AISEC, vol. 45 (2013)

11. Ramachandran, R., Oh, T., Stackpole, W.: Android anti-virus analysis. In: Annual Symposium on Information Assurance & Secure Knowledge Management, pp. 35–40. Citeseer (2012)

12. Rouillard, J.: Contextual QR codes. In: The Third International Multi-conference on Computing in the Global Information Technology (ICCGI 2008), pp. 50–55. IEEE (2008)

13. Chen, W.Y., Wang, J.W.: Nested image steganography scheme using QR-barcode technique. Opt. Eng. **48**(5), 057004 (2009)

14. Liao, K.C., Lee, W.H.: A novel user authentication scheme based on QR-code. JNW **5**(8), 937–941 (2010)

15. Dabrowski, A., Krombholz, K., Ullrich, J., Weippl, E.R.: QR inception: barcode-in-barcode attacks. In: Proceedings of the 4th ACM Workshop on Security and Privacy in Smartphones & Mobile Devices, pp. 3–10. ACM (2014)

16. Penning, N., Hoffman, M., Nikolai, J., Wang, Y.: Mobile malware security challeges and cloud-based detection. In: 2014 International Conference on Collaboration Technologies and Systems (CTS), pp. 181–188. IEEE (2014)

17. Krombholz, K., Frühwirt, P., Kieseberg, P., Kapsalis, I., Huber, M., Weippl, E.: QR code security: a survey of attacks and challenges for usable security. In: Tryfonas, T., Askoxylakis, I. (eds.) HAS 2014. LNCS, vol. 8533, pp. 79–90. Springer, Cham (2014). doi:10.1007/978-3-319-07620-1_8

18. Vidas, T., Owusu, E., Wang, S., Zeng, C., Cranor, L.F., Christin, N.: QRishing: the susceptibility of smartphone users to QR code phishing attacks. In: Adams, A.A., Brenner, M., Smith, M. (eds.) FC 2013. LNCS, vol. 7862, pp. 52–69. Springer, Heidelberg (2013). doi:10.1007/978-3-642-41320-9_4

19. Deborah, M.: Security expert warns smartphone users of the risks in scanning cybercoding. http://www.post-gazette.com/business/businessnews/2012/06/01/ Security-expert-warns-smartphone-users-of-the-risks-in-scanning-cybercoding/ stories/201206010228

20. Chuang, J.C., Hu, Y.C., Ko, H.J.: A novel secret sharing technique using QR code. Int. J. Image Process. (IJIP) 4(5), 468–475 (2010)

21. Gao, J., Kulkarni, V., Ranavat, H., Chang, L., Mei, H.: A 2D barcode-based mobile payment system. In: Third International Conference on Multimedia and Ubiquitous Engineering (MUE 2009), pp. 320–329. IEEE (2009)

22. Narayanan, A.S.: QR codes and security solutions. Int. J. Comput. Sci. Telecommun. 3(7), 69–71 (2012)

23. Paar, C., Pelzl, J.: Understanding Cryptography: A Textbook for Students and Practitioners. Springer, Heidelberg (2009). doi:10.1007/978-3-642-04101-3

24. Peng, K., Sanabria, H., Wu, D., Zhu, C.: Security overview of QR codes. Student project in the MIT course 6.857,'14 (2014)

New Ideas and Paradigms for Security

A Novel and Unifying View of Trustworthiness in Cyberphysical Systems

Steven Drager[1] and Janusz Zalewski[2(✉)]

[1] Air Force Research Laboratory, Rome, NY 13441, USA
steven.drager@us.af.mil
[2] Department of Software Engineering, Florida Gulf Coast University, Ft. Myers, FL 33965, USA
zalewski@fgcu.edu

Abstract. The objective of this work was to study how to assess trustworthiness of computer systems and software used in cyberphysical applications, by developing a multifaceted assessment method and building models based on theories, which rely on non-probabilistic methods and have not been used for such purposes before: (1) Bayesian belief networks, (2) rough sets, (3) Dempster–Shafer theory of evidence, and (4) particle filters. The project objective was accomplished by assuming that trustworthiness is related to the confidence in the results with which related system parameters are evaluated, and then addressing the issue from the perspective of each of the four theories, using a computational model of a cyberphysical system and applying these theories in simple case studies, which can be extended for use in practice.

Keywords: Cyberphysical systems · Security · Safety · Trustworthiness

1 Introduction

The critical issue in most cyberphysical systems, especially those used in the military, is that they operate under significant degrees of uncertainty, with unknown probability distributions of major parameters, which makes it difficult to predict and assess their behavior. Estimation of respective system properties, such as safety, security, reliability, resiliency, trustworthiness, and others, is crucial in evaluating system's response to unpredictable circumstances that may negatively affect its operation and hurt accomplishing its mission. This paper addresses the situation by studying how to evaluate trustworthiness of cyberphysical systems to shed a new light on its usage, to help in evaluation of existing and building new such systems.

The approach is based on the previous work of the authors in the area of assessment of system properties, which makes two essential assumptions. First, a distinction is made between system property and system's state, to filter out the views and notions unrelated to the measurement of properties. On this basis, the second assumption is to adopt the

---

© Springer International Publishing AG 2017 (outside the US)
J. Rak et al. (Eds.): MMM-ACNS 2017, LNCS 10446, pp. 327–338, 2017.
DOI: 10.1007/978-3-319-65127-9_26

previously proposed view how to measure these properties. In this regard, we follow an earlier study, in which the following characteristics of the measurement process have been identified [1]:

- Clearly and uniquely select the property to be measured.
- Establish a metric to quantitatively characterize the property.
- Develop a measure (instrument, formula, or any other physical or mental device), which would apply the metric to related objects under investigation to obtain a value.
- Design the measurement process, using the model of the property and a measure.
- In each measurement obtain a result composed of the value of the measurement and the estimate of its accuracy (an error), to establish a confidence in the results.

It is our view that confidence in the results of the measurement determines the trustworthiness. It may involve error, accuracy, variance, standard deviation, dispersion, confidence interval, etc. Thus, it can be loosely viewed as inversely proportional to the uncertainty of the result. The rest of the paper is structured as follows. Section 2 explains the problem in more detail. Section 3 presents the applied methodology, Sect. 4 discusses initial results of the study, and Sect. 5 formulates some conclusions.

2 Model of a Cyberphysical System

The objective of this research is to investigate how to assess trustworthiness of computer systems and software used in cyberphysical applications, by developing a multifaceted assessment method based on several new theories, which rely on non-probabilistic methods and have not been used for this purpose before. Consequently, a crucial consideration has been made to look for theories, which account for uncertainty in their view of the models they allow and reason about. One essential aspect to consider is that this kind of uncertainty can rarely be described in terms of probability distributions, since such distributions simply cannot be applied due to the significant statistical irregularities of system behaviors. In this regard, the following four theories have been selected, each addressing the issue of uncertainty in its own way:

- Bayesian belief networks, which allow evaluating a hypothesis based on the incomplete information;
- rough sets, which let characterize objects in terms of insufficient knowledge about possibilities;
- Dempster–Shafer theory of evidence, which models the hypotheses according to a special calculus proposed by the method inventors;
- particle filters, which allow reasoning based on hidden Markov models, primarily designed for and known from modeling the time series.

The essential model of a cyberphysical system assumed in this study, that was used earlier [2], captures the system interaction with the physical environment and system's susceptibility to external disturbances. Its interfaces to the external world form an attack surface, as illustrated in Fig. 1. The disturbances are an abstraction of all undesired effects, in response to which the controller has to adjust to perform the required functions. The next section describes the methodology used to reach the project objective.

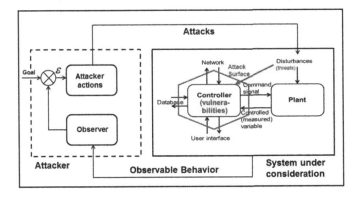

Fig. 1. Generic model of a cyberphysical system with defined attack surface.

3   Methodology

The way the problem of trustworthiness assessment is approached here is to determine, first, what trustworthiness is and how to build its model. To accomplish this, we examine some common ways of understanding trustworthiness in selected technical literature and, then, propose our own approach. Next, we elaborate on possible mechanisms, which could be used in formulas assessing trustworthiness. Finally we discuss major factors in the theories used, to prepare for experiments.

3.1   Selected Views of Trustworthiness

There is an extensive number of papers published on trustworthiness assessment in technical systems. Due to the limited space, it is only possible to discuss a handful, which are believed to be the most important due to their origin from the standards institutions [3, 4], or their widespread coverage [5].

The NIST report [3] views trustworthiness of software as composed of multiple factors, including accuracy, availability, conformance, and others, a dozen overall, as shown in Fig. 2. The BSI standard [4] takes a similar approach and considers trustworthiness as composed of five facets: availability, reliability, resilience, safety, and security (Fig. 3).

These two views do not differ, applying the same principle, making trustworthiness composed of other properties, except that the British report restricts consideration to only five components of trustworthiness. A relatively large industrial study published in 2011 [5], surveying 151 stakeholders in open source software, indicated that two primary factors determined users' trustworthiness: functionality and reliability of software. The same study stated, though, that "the notion of trustworthiness might be inherently subjective".

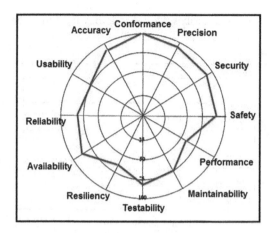

Fig. 2. NIST view of software trustworthiness [3].

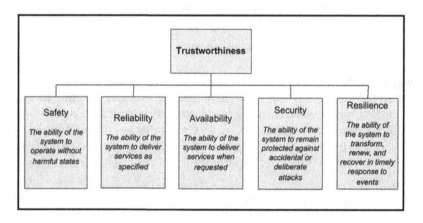

Fig. 3. View of trustworthiness from the BSI report [4].

The presented approaches to trustworthiness, and others like this in the literature, suffer from two basic deficiencies: subjectivity and incompleteness. Subjectivity is discussed in [5], and incompleteness can be explained taking a closer look at Fig. 2 and asking a question: how many potential factors can trustworthiness be composed of, using this type of "composability"? Since various authors give various numbers and factors contributing to trustworthiness, it is in fact not possible to determine what factors would form a complete notion of trustworthiness. It is our position that this view of trustworthiness confuses this property with software quality. One might think that high quality of software, as documented by high values of the component factors, gives a reason to believe that this software is trustworthy, but in fact, it is only software of high quality and may have little to do with trustworthiness.

A very recent report from NIST [6], addresses trustworthiness in a completely different manner, which coincides with our views. The word "trustworthy" is used as an adverb, in combination with an adjective related to a system property, saying that a system may be "trustworthy secure". Such usage implies that trustworthiness is not treated as a separate property of a system, in its own right, possibly composed of other properties, as in [3, 5], but shall be viewed as a complementary factor, expressing how much trust can be placed in a specific value of a given property. What follows is that we propose a different view of trustworthiness, considering it as being inversely related to uncertainty. That is, the less uncertainty there is in a value of a system property (such as security, safety, resiliency, etc.) the more trustworthy the value is and the more trustworthy the system is.

Thus, trustworthiness could be assessed using concepts similar to those normally applied in evaluating results, especially in statistics, such as measurement error (or result accuracy), standard deviation (or variance), confidence interval, etc. Applying those concepts, one must remember, however, that in this research we are not talking about statistical processes, since the studied phenomena have no known probability distributions. In the following subsections, we discuss how some of the non-statistical theories, which are often applied to describe uncertainties in system behavior, could be used to help in assessing trustworthiness understood as above. Some of these descriptions can be skipped by a reader already familiar with the specific theory, but we present them all for completeness.

3.2   Rough Sets

Rough set theory was invented by Zdzisław Pawlak to cope with limited perception of the surrounding world. The theory is helpful in dealing with vagueness and uncertainty in decision situations. Its main purpose is the "automated transformation of data into knowledge" [7]. The data are perceived in terms of objects and their features, i.e., values of the attributes characterizing the objects. The knowledge deduced from these data is expressed in terms of "surely" and "possibly" meeting certain statements.

Intuitively a concept of a rough set can be compared to an ordinary set and a fuzzy set, in a single dimension (Fig. 4). For an ordinary set, the interval [A, B], numbers from this interval have values of their membership function equal to 1.0. For a fuzzy set, elements on the set boundaries, in the intervals [A, C] and [D, B], have values of membership functions equal to a number from the interval [0.0, 1.0]. So these elements only partially belong to the set, to the extent specified by the membership function.

In contrast to the traditional concepts of a set, whether ordinary or fuzzy, for a rough set one cannot determine, even partially, the membership of the elements on the set boundary. Therefore, the value of the membership function for boundary elements of a set is undefined. A rough set can only be described by its approximations, as illustrated in the lower part of Fig. 4.

To introduce it more formally, let B be a subset of the condition attributes and let $[v]_B$ stand for an equivalence class, i.e., a set of objects u in U with identical description (narrowed to the set B) as the object v. The subset X of U can be characterized using information contained in B by means of so-called B-*lower* and B-*upper* approximations defined, correspondingly, as:

$$B(X)_* = \left\{ u \in U \middle| [u]_B \subseteq X \right\}$$

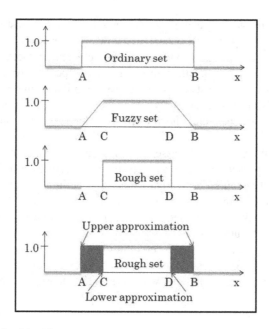

Fig. 4. Intuitive illustration of a rough set vs. an ordinary and a fuzzy set.

$$B(X)^* = \left\{ u \in U \middle| [u]_B \cap X \neq \varnothing \right\}$$

The lower approximation of X is the collection of objects which can be viewed *surely* as members of the set X, while the upper approximation of X is the collection of objects that *possibly* are members of X. The set $BN_B = B(X)^* - B(X)_*$ is called a *B-boundary* region; it specifies the objects that cannot be classified with certainty to be either inside X, or outside X. In relation to the model of a cyberphysical system in Fig. 1, the value of a regular property, such as security, can be assessed in terms of a vague description of vulnerabilities mapped on a rough set.

3.3 Bayesian Belief Networks

Bayesian Belief Networks (BBN's) are widely known and have been widely described and used since 1996 [8, 9]. One can think of BBN as a model for evaluating certain hypotheses based on the available evidence. Its basis is the popular inversion formula for belief updating from evidence (E) about a hypothesis (H) using probability measurements of the prior truth of the statement updated by posterior evidence

$$P(H|E) = (P(E|H) * P(H))/P(E)$$

where H is the hypothesis, E is the evidence, and $P(x|y)$ is the conditional probability of x given y. It is derived by the use of the joint probability definition

$$P(x,y) = P(x|y) * P(y) = P(y|x) * P(x)$$

where x = H and y = E. Even though the concept itself is illustrated using the notion of probability, actual applications of Bayesian networks use the idea of likelihood instead, because the available models are not probabilistic. Complex models with multiple hypotheses and evidence sources can be constructed usually in a graph form relating cause to effect.

BBN is defined by a directed acyclic graph of nodes representing variables and arcs representing probabilistic dependency relations among the variables. If there is an arc from A to B, then variable B depends directly on A. If the variable represented by a node has a known value then the node is said to be observed as an evidence node. A node can represent any kind of variable, be it a measured parameter or a hypothesis. Figure 5 shows examples of a network that is structured as converging and diverging.

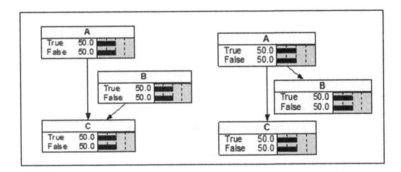

Fig. 5. Examples of three-node Bayesian networks: converging (left) and diverging (right).

The examples are causal BBN's where the directed arcs represent causal relations in some domain with prior information. Knowledge about causal relations is often used as a guide in drawing BBN graphs, thus resulting in cause and effect networks. In the converging model, A is conditionally independent of B and both cause C, while in the diverging model, A causes both B and C. In each case an effect is observed at node C illustrating the update of the joint probabilities when new information is added. The applicability of the BBN model to evaluate a regular property, such as security, in relation to a cyberphysical system in Fig. 1, relies on estimating a contribution of specific vulnerabilities, possibly using a hierarchy of dependencies, and collectively assessing their overall impact on the aggregate value of security.

3.4 Dempster-Shafer Theory of Evidence

Dempster-Shafer theory of evidence has been broadly described, since its inception in the late 1960's [10]. For this research, one can think of it as a model for evaluating certain hypotheses based on the available evidence. There are several basic concepts of the theory that are important:

- Data Sources, which may involve results of experimental studies, expert's statements, etc.;

- Evidence, which is composed of a description of symptoms of behavior, concrete events, etc.;
- Hypotheses to be proved by the reasoning process, and the reasoning process itself.

A typical example of using Dempster-Shafer theory would be the reasoning on what has caused a system malfunction? Thus, evidence in the form of failures and/or breaches could be used to reason about a set of hypotheses, which specific faults may have caused a malfunction. A typical case study would involve failure of a system, for which only outputs Y (evidence) are known and hypotheses information on system state, S, which may have caused the failure is collected from the experts who are system operators.

With these data, the first step in Dempster-Shafer theory is to produce a formal mapping, called Basic Assignments, of all the hypotheses (potential faults) onto the collected evidence $ev_i \in [0, 1]$:

$$m: 2^\Omega => [0, 1]$$

where Ω is a universe of discourse, that is, a set of all the hypotheses. With the Basic Assignments on hand, a Belief function can be calculated, as sum of all Basic Assignments for all its subsets:

$$Bel(A) = \Sigma_{A \supseteq B} \, m(B) \quad \text{for all A}$$

Similarly, a Plausibility function, calculated as sum of all Basic Assignments for all statements, which have at least one hypothesis in common, is defined as follows:

$$Pl(A) = \Sigma_{B \cap A \neq 0} \, m(B) \quad \text{for all A}$$

In addition, two complementary functions are defined in Dempster-Shafer theory:

$$Doubt(A) = 1 - Bel(A) \quad \text{and} \quad Disbelief(A) = 1 - Pl(A)$$

The interpretation of these four functions is shown in Fig. 6, with an important conjecture defining uncertainty as Plausibility minus Belief.

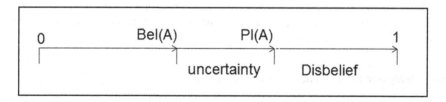

Fig. 6. Simple interpretation of Dempster-Shafer functions.

The Dempster-Shafer theory can be applied directly to assessment of regular properties, such as safety or security of a cyberphysical system from Fig. 1, by associating the evidence of failures with faults as potential causes (for safety) and, by analogy, associating evidence of breaches with potential vulnerabilities (for security).

3.5 Particle Filters

In contrast to the previous methods, the original concept of a particle filter is probabilistic, based on a hidden Markov model, as illustrated in Fig. 7. Each system state S_t and its observable output Y_t, at discrete time t, can be represented by a node. Nodes S_t are not observable, they represent a random variable S_t that can take any value labeled $1 <= t <= K$. The arrows represent state transition probabilities and output probabilities, correspondingly. In other words, S_t is a state of the (latent) process hidden from the observer that generates an observation at time t.

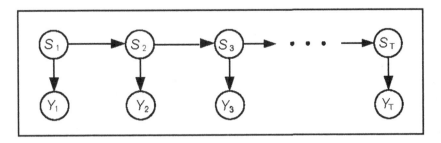

Fig. 7. Illustration of conditional relations for a hidden Markov model.

The states of a hidden process satisfy the Markov property, that is, given the previous state, S_{t-1}, the current state, S_t, is independent of all states prior to $(t-1)$, which is known as first-order Markov property. More formally, assuming the following notation:

- t – time of observation (measurement), sampled at discrete, equally spaced intervals;
- Y_t – discrete variable representing the value of observation at time t; can take L values, $1, ..., L$;
- $S_{1:T}$ – a sequence $S_1, S_2, ..., S_T$ of hidden states;
- $Y_{1:T}$ – a sequence $Y_1, Y_2, ..., Y_T$ of observations.

the joint distribution of a sequence of states S_t and observations Y_t can be the likelihood function [11]:

$$P(S_{1:T}, Y_{1:T}) = P(S_1)P(Y_1|S_1) \prod_{t=2}^{T} P(S_t|S_{t-1}) \, P(Y_t|S_t)$$

$$\text{or} \quad P(S_{1:T}) = P(S_1) \prod_{t=2}^{T} P(S_t|S_{t-1}) \text{ and } P(Y_{1:T}|S_{1:T}) = \prod_{t=1}^{T} P(Y_t|S_t)$$

Particle filters are a group of simulation based methods, which provide samples approximately distributed according to posterior distributions of the form P(S1:T | Y1:T) and facilitate the approximate calculation of P(S1:T). They are useful in solving optimal estimation problems for non-linear non-Gaussian state-space models, which have no analytical solution in general. Thus, their value for security assessment lies in avoiding the assumption of any specific probability distribution of state variables, which can rarely be assumed in case of threats for a cyberphysical system model in Fig. 1.

4   Preliminary Results

The application of theories to the data sets requires extensive data collection, which was not possible during the course of this work, so here only preliminary results are presented, based on simulated data. Additionally, in presenting and discussing the results, we focus on the quantification of the *trustworthiness* itself, rather than on the estimation process to assess a property, such as security.

Rough sets theory has a concept to evaluate the quality of approximation of a value of property. To get a numerical characterization of the "roughness" of a set X one introduces so-called *accuracy of approximation*:

$$\alpha_{B(X)} = |B(X)_*| / |B(X)^*|$$

where the symbol $|Y|$ stands for the cardinality of the set Y. X is said to be crisp (or precise) with respect to the set of attributes B, if and only if $\alpha_{B(X)} = 1$, otherwise X is said to be rough (vague) with respect to B. Trustworthiness is based on the crispiness of a rough set, accuracy of approximation. The more vague the concept, the less trustworthy it is. Given the data set is validated, trustworthiness is related to the reasoning (evaluation), not to the data set (model) itself. For numerical data taken from [12], the accuracy is very low, at the order of 50%, so uncertainty is high and trustworthiness tends to be low. When the cardinality of a data set increases, more data items are added and the accuracy tends to increase, given the new data fall into a lower approximation of a set, so trustworthiness can increase.

The approach taken by the Dempster-Shafer theory is very similar, as explained in Fig. 6. Calculations for the example taken from [13] are illustrated in Fig. 8. Based on the evidence, the Probability column suggests adopting hypotheses h1 (.711), but values of Belief functions are comparable for {h1 & h2} and {h1 & h3} combinations (.895 and .789, respectively), so what to choose? The notion of uncertainty comes into play (Plausibility, marked UDP in the last column, minus Belief), which is the smallest for {h1 & h2}. Thus, this combination is the least uncertain and the respective decision the most trustworthy.

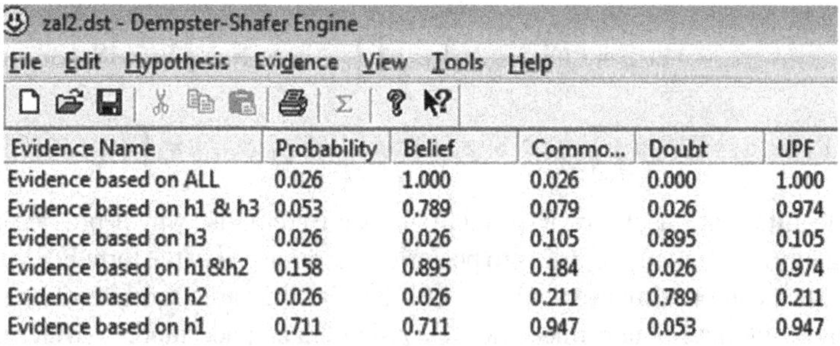

Evidence Name	Probability	Belief	Commo...	Doubt	UPF
Evidence based on ALL	0.026	1.000	0.026	0.000	1.000
Evidence based on h1 & h3	0.053	0.789	0.079	0.026	0.974
Evidence based on h3	0.026	0.026	0.105	0.895	0.105
Evidence based on h1&h2	0.158	0.895	0.184	0.026	0.974
Evidence based on h2	0.026	0.026	0.211	0.789	0.211
Evidence based on h1	0.711	0.711	0.947	0.053	0.947

Fig. 8. Illustration of the Dempster-Shafer model.

The selection of a decision with highest trustworthiness is truly an issue. Just as it turned out with rough sets and Dempster-Shafer theory that the newly available data not necessarily contribute to lowering the overall uncertainty, Bayesian networks confirm it from another end.

Experiments conducted for data sets from [14] affirm this conjecture. The computational results presented in Fig. 9 show that, in a certain range of a variable, the posterior variance exceeds the prior variance of 1, so decisions based on posterior probabilities can be less accurate as more information comes in, thus, lowering decision trustworthiness.

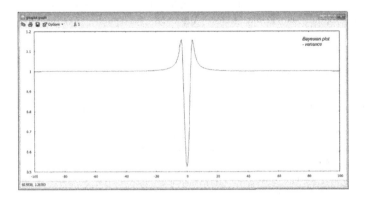

Fig. 9. Posterior variance computed for Bayesian reasoning.

Since the particle filter is designed for a hidden Markov model, to make decisions on values of the hidden variable based on observations (Fig. 7), its quality is also of paramount importance. However, being essentially a statistical tool, the particle filter relies on probabilistic information, which is rarely available for the systems considered and the reasoning can only be based on experiments deriving the true distributions. To counteract this lack of full knowledge, one can use a mixed technique combining a particle filter with a theory that does not rely on probability distributions. One such possibility [15] involves the use of Dempster-Shafer theory to use the basic assignments $m(.)$, as outlined in Sect. 3.4, in the particle filter prediction phase to determine the value of the state variable, S_t, in the next step t (Fig. 7), replacing $P(S_t \mid S_{t-1})$. This conjecture has not been confirmed in the current work and requires a more extensive study.

5 Conclusion

In conclusion, the project objective was accomplished by building a new model of trustworthiness and addressing the issue of trustworthiness assessment from the perspective of four theories. They were successfully applied in simple case studies, showing a significant promise for use in practice. The essential conceptual result of this study is the conjecture that all individual system properties combined, security, safety, reliability, etc., are an indication of quality, not of trustworthiness. Trustworthiness itself is viewed as an indication how much confidence can be placed in a specific value of system property. Not only good news can be trustworthy, but bad news can be trustworthy, as well. A system can be trustworthy secure or trustworthy insecure. Additionally, one may be less or more certain (uncertain) about values of system properties after the new information comes.

In practice, the overall assessment of trustworthiness can hardly be achieved by a single formula or method. Thus, it is very likely that a combination of multiple methods should be used for evaluation purposes. More work is needed to develop tools assessing trustworthiness, especially for using Bayesian networks and particle filters.

Acknowledgment. This project was supported in part by the AFOSR 2016 Summer Faculty Fellowship Program at Rome Labs. Approved for public release, Case Number 88ABW-2017-1078. Distribution unlimited.

References

1. Zalewski, J., Drager, S., McKeever, W., Kornecki, A.: Measuring security: a challenge for the generation. Ann. Comput. Sci. Inf. Syst. **3**, 131–140 (2014)
2. Kornecki, A., Zalewski, J.: Aviation software: safety and security. In: Webster, J. (ed.) Wiley Encyclopedia of Electrical and Electronics Engineering. Wiley (2015)
3. Boland, T., Cleraux, C., Fong, E.: Toward a preliminary framework for assisting the trustworthiness of software, report NIST I.A. 7755, National Institute of Standards and Technology, Gaithersburg, November 2010
4. PAS 754:2014 Software Trustworthiness – Governance and Management – Specification. British Standards Institution, June 2014
5. Bianco, V., et al.: A survey on open source software trustworthiness. IEEE Softw. **28**(5), 67–75 (2011)
6. Ross, R., McEvilley, M., Oren, J.C.: Systems security engineering: considerations for multidisciplinary approach in the engineering of trustworthy secure systems, NIST S.P. 800-160 – Second Public Draft, National Institute of Standards and Technology, Gaithersburg, May 2016
7. Pawlak, Z.: Rough sets. Int. J. Comput. Inform. Sci. **11**(5), 341–356 (1982)
8. Pearl, J.: Probabilistic Reasoning in Intelligent Systems: Networks of Plausible Inference. Morgan Kaufmann, San Mateo (1988)
9. Jensen, F.V.: An Introduction to Bayesian Networks. Springer, Heidelberg (1996). doi: 10.1007/978-3-540-85066-3
10. Dempster, A.P.: A generalization of Bayesian inference. J. R. Stat. Soc. Ser. B **30**, 205–247 (1968)
11. Doucet, A., Johansen, A.M.: A tutorial on particle filtering and smoothing: fifteen years later. In: Crisan, D., Rozovsky, B. (eds.) The Oxford Handbook of Nonlinear Filtering, pp. 656–704. Oxford University Press, Oxford (2011)
12. Kornecki, A.J., Wierzchon, S.T., Zalewski, J.: Reasoning under uncertainty with Bayesian belief networks enhanced with rough sets. Int. J. Comput. **12**(1), 16–31 (2013)
13. Rakowsky, U.K.: Fundamentals of the Dempster-Shafer theory and its applications to system safety and reliability modelling. Reliab. Theor. Appl. **2**(3–4), 173–185 (2007)
14. Al-Saleh, M.F., Masoud, F.A.: A note on the posterior expected loss as a measure of accuracy in Bayesian methods. Appl. Math. Comput. **134**, 507–514 (2003)
15. Reineking, T.: Particle filtering in the Dempster-Shafer theory. Int. J. Approx. Reason. **52**, 1124–1135 (2011)

Information Security of SDN on the Basis of Meta Data

Alexander Grusho[✉][iD], Nick Grusho, Michael Zabezhailo,
Alexander Zatsarinny, and Elena Timonina[iD]

Institute of Informatics Problems of Federal Research Center,
"Informatics and Control" of the Russian Academy of Sciences,
Vavilova 44-2, 119333 Moscow, Russia
{grusho,m.zabezhailo,eltimon}@yandex.ru, info@itake.ru,
AZatsarinny@ipiran.ru

Abstract. Information security of SDN (Software Defined Network) is a part of support of information security in service-oriented architectures and clouds. These services can be presented in the form of tasks and the sets of subtasks and/or tasks represented by schedule diagrams of subtasks. Therefore it is necessary to consider the integrated information security system of such services.

The model of security of cloud computing on the basis of interaction between level of tasks and level of SDN is constructed. It is shown that meta data about solvable tasks can be used for effective control of information flows at a network and can reduce the level of network threats. The constructed protocols allow different strength of a security.

Keywords: Information security · Software Defined Network · Meta data · Hierarchical decomposition

1 Introduction

The information security of SDN (Software Defined Network) is a part of support of information security in service-oriented architectures and clouds. These services can be presented in the form of tasks and the sets of subtasks and/or tasks represented by schedule diagrams of subtasks. Therefore it is necessary to consider the integrated information security system of such services.

In the paper we consider construction of information security on the basis of two-level representation of services (tasks - network) in the distributed systems. In [1] the idea of controlling of information flows by means of graphs of admissible interactions of tasks expressed.

In this paper this idea is developed and the description of protocols of interaction between levels in two-level model is built. The aim is to compensate a set of threats by means of such protocol. It is necessary to note that some threats for networks aren't compensated by the developed protocol. However the protocol allows to achieve effective counteraction to remaining threats by additional measures.

© Springer International Publishing AG 2017
J. Rak et al. (Eds.): MMM-ACNS 2017, LNCS 10446, pp. 339–347, 2017.
DOI: 10.1007/978-3-319-65127-9_27

The detailed review of SDN threats and methods of counteraction to these threats at the network layer can be found in [2]. Some methods of SDN security, which are close to our approach, are found in scientific literature. In [3] it is noted the neediness of consideration of context of services for the organization of the next generation network on the basis of SDN. However an accounting of context is used only for optimization of data transfer at the network layer.

Approach in [4] offers to consider hierarchies of flow tables (FT) for separation and the accounting of hierarchies of policies in SDN. This approach is close to ours since it suggests to consider semantic characteristics of policies for processing of packets. In our paper the simplified diagram of semantic interactions for the accounting of tasks dependencies is used.

In [5] a computation of additional characteristics for information collection and analysis is offered. This information allows to reveal and localize failures in SDN.

The idea of usage of the graph theory in the description of routes of SDN is described in [6].

One of the major information security problems in SDN is incorrect reconfiguration of a network. The secure protocol of such reconfiguration is constructed in [7]. There are many other papers devoted to this problem ([8], etc.).

In [9] the method of Galois closures is used for acceleration of search in sets of flow tables (FT) of additional signs.

It is necessary to note the papers on security of SDN [10, 11].

The paper has the following structure. The Sect. 2 presents the main information for SDN understanding. In Sect. 3 the two-level hierarchical decomposition is defined. Section 4 is devoted to the description of the protocol of secure interactions in two-level system. Analysis of security of two-level system is in Sect. 5. In Sect. 6 the reinforced protocol of secure interactions in two-level system is considered. Conclusion is devoted to the unsolved problems.

2   Structure of SDN

Usually SDN is presented in the form of three planes. The plane of data (Data Flow Level) consists of hosts and switches. Each switch has FT. In this table there are rules for the switch for forwarding data. The order of number of such rules can be more 1000. Rules of the table contain three fields:

- action;
- counter;
- example.

The packet arriving on the switch is being processed as follows. The switch looks for data in FT, after finding of the rule the counter increases its value, and there is an action intended for such packet. If the rule isn't found, then the packet header comes to the controller or the packet is discarded at all.

Rules are created by the controller. The plane of the controller is described as follows. Host of the controller is connected to switches either via the common channel, or via the special channel. The controller creates routes for connection of hosts.

On the third plane there are applications which support the functions of the controller.

From the information security point of view an usage of hosts for the organization of connections on a network isn't always secure. So, the malicious code can be the initiator of connection. Therefore on a network it is necessary to use fire-walls, IDS and other security features. However, if interactions of hosts are defined only by necessary interactions of legal tasks, then problems with information security become less. The controller has task of formation of routes for interaction of legal tasks, then the filtering of flows by means of fire-walls and IDS isn't necessary. The main thing, that a necessity of the appeal to the controller of hosts and switches disappears.

3   Two-Level Model "Tasks – Network"

Let SDN be network level for the distributed information system (service-oriented system or cloudy system). However the network is necessary not for itself, but for tasks interactions in service-oriented systems or in cloudy information systems. It means that above the level of network there is the level of tasks. The level of tasks can be also divided into sublevels. The task is defined by input data, information transform, and output data.

Information transform is carried out in computers. Let it be that in any computer one or several tasks at the same time can be solved.

For the solution of a task the network helps for receiving input data from other tasks functioning on other computers.

Let's consider in more detail the level of tasks. Complex tasks are, as a rule, representable in the form of the subtasks described by means of a reduction [12]. The sequence of subtasks is described by the oriented graph which nodes are subtasks, and arcs define the sequence of their solution.

Often complex tasks are described by schedule diagrams [13]. These diagrams are the oriented circuit-free graphs and define the sequence of interactions of tasks at the level of tasks. At the level of tasks it is possible to define correctly decomposition and an order of interactions of tasks among themselves, and this order we will present in the form of an oriented graph.

Let's consider interaction of level of tasks and level of network. Interaction of tasks functioning on different computers which are also network hosts requires a network interaction. Consider the transfer protocol for two-level system. At the high level there is a need of interactions of tasks A and A_1, which at the network layer are executed in hosts $H(A)$ and $H(A_1)$. Information on tasks, their order and layout on hosts we will define as meta data for SDN. The initiator of interaction at the top level is the task A having a process status in the computer. For its execution the task A can need an information which is a result of execution of task A_1. At the same time the task A_1 can require additional interactions with other tasks A_2, A_3, ... Results of decision of these tasks are also necessary for decision of task A.

The knowledge of the need for interactions of tasks is based on contents of these tasks. However for control of interactions of hosts $H(A)$ and $H(A_1)$ informative information isn't necessary, it is necessary to only define where is the task A_1, and to give the chance to the host $H(A_1)$ to initiate a network interaction between $H(A)$ and $H(A_1)$, i.e. to open a communication session between $H(A)$ and $H(A_1)$.

The route of an information flow between $H(A)$ and $H(A_1)$ via switches is defined by the controller. Therefore the controller needs to obtain information on necessity of the connection $H(A)$ and $H(A_1)$. And it is unimportant how this information comes to the controller from A via $H(A)$, or from some process $\mathcal{N}$ on the host $H(\mathcal{N})$, which on the basis of meta data creates permission for interaction of A and A_1 on hosts $H(A)$ and $H(A_1)$. For example, host $H(\mathcal{N})$ transfers this information directly to the controller.

Let's consider a problem of information security of the two-level system described above. Information security is ensured by a subsystem of controlling of information flows [10]. In the offered model this controlling is implemented via schedule of tasks. If all tasks legally solved by system are launched by the owner of system or from his name, then graphs of necessary tasks and subtasks or graphs of tasks which fulfill legal requirements of the owner are set. Violation of information security arises only when the system begins to solve illegal tasks connected to information theft, functioning of a malicious code or other harmful influences. It means that in graphs of tasks there can be illegal tasks and illegal interactions.

The security policy for the level of tasks consists in forbidding the start of illegal tasks and illegal interactions. In this paper the tasks functioning on different computers are considered and we exclude intracomputer interactions from reviewing.

Security mechanisms are necessary for implementation of a security policy. It is clear, that legal interactions between tasks on different computers are implemented through a network level. From this it follows that in interactions of hosts it is possible to select a set of the admissible interactions which realize necessary interactions of tasks. We will consider all non permitted interactions of hosts as non admissible interactions.

Unfortunately, such security policy at the network layer doesn't solve all problems of information security. At the network layer there can be additional threats (see, for example, [2]).

In this paper we consider questions of counteraction to non admissible interactions through a network. Any interaction through a network is a set of information flows. Non admissible interactions generate forbidden information flows. Thus, the basis of a security policy of a system is created at the level of tasks, and security mechanisms for detection and blocking of forbidden information flows are implemented at the level of network.

All permitted information flows need to have a possibility of implementation through the network. All forbidden information flows should be absent. If there is a failure at a network, then there should exist mechanisms of its detection and bypass.

Counteraction to additional threats at the network layer [2] can demand addition to the described security policy which have to be implemented by additional security mechanisms. Additional requirements and mechanisms should not contradict the main security policy.

4   The Protocol of Secure Interactions in Two-Level System

Let the task $\mathcal{N}$ be permanently functioning on host $H(\mathcal{N})$ which possesses meta data and on demand defines an admissibility of interactions of the tasks located on different hosts. Let all requests for host-to-host connections (sessions) be passing via the task $\mathcal{N}$. The task $\mathcal{N}$ is connected to the SDN controller which performs function of creation of a route (main and reserve) for connection of hosts with admissible interactions of tasks.

Free packets (UDP, etc.) and other connections (except permanent connections of the launched tasks) with $\mathcal{N}$ are absent. Switches don't forward information of packets to the controller. But the controller can modify FT on any switch. If in FT there is no information on forwarding of a packet, then the packet is dropped. Any failures of transmission are identified by end hosts, and information is transferred to the task $\mathcal{N}$.

Modifying architecture of SDN a little, we will construct the simplest protocol for implementation of the considered security policy. Let the executing task A demand to obtain information from the task A_1. These data are stored in meta data in task $\mathcal{N}$. Then task A generates the identifier $Id(A, A_1)$, and the host $H(A)$ sends the message to host $H(\mathcal{N})$ with information on the executing task A, $Id(A, A_1)$ and the need of interaction with the task A_1. The task $\mathcal{N}$ under meta data checks the need of an interaction A and A_1. If this interaction is admissible then the host $H(\mathcal{N})$ sends:

- to the host $H(A_1)$ the necessity of a session with $H(A)$, $Id(A, A_1)$, time stamp, the address and the port number in $H(A)$ via which interaction with $H(A)$ can be organized;
- to the host $H(A)$ the identifier $Id(A, A_1)$, the address and the port number of host $H(A_1)$ for communication with the task A_1, time stamp;
- to the SDN controller an information on the forthcoming session of $H(A)$ and $H(A_1)$, identifier $Id(A, A_1)$, time stamp.

This information allows to create the main and reserve routes for a session of $H(A)$ and $H(A_1)$. At the same time in FT of switches $Id(A, A_1)$ is built in. After that hosts of $H(A)$ and $H(A_1)$ will organize a session for the solution of the task A_1 on the instructions of the task A.

For the task A_1 an additional information which can be provided by other task A_2 on other host can be required. Then A_1 initiates the appropriate permission at the task $\mathcal{N}$, and it is an initiator of interaction with other host. This session in A_1 has the identifier $Id(A_1, A_2)$. At the same time the return of results to the task A goes with the identifier $Id(A, A_1)$. After execution of the task A_1 which was solved according to the job for A the session is finished. Information about it is transmitted via the task $\mathcal{N}$ to the controller. The controller liquidates $Id(A, A_1)$ from FT and by that destroys a possibility of interaction of hosts $H(A)$ and $H(A_1)$ with using of $Id(A, A_1)$. Therefore a usage of $Id(A, A_1)$ for the transmission of illegal messages via a network becomes impossible. Thus, there are only routes of the admissible interactions at the network. It also helps to reduce a number of information flows.

A switch FT has a disjunction of formulas with the description of identifiers of tasks which use it for forwarding. If this expression is empty, then this row in commutation table is deleted. Thus, at a network there is the fixed set of routes.

One of the most important tasks of the controller of traditional SDN is detection of overloads of switches and balancing of loadings. As in our model of a network there are only allowed routes, then an overload will come to light through deceleration of communication of the end's hosts. Information about it is transferred to the task $\mathcal{N}$ which transfers it to the controller. If there are several such decelerations, then the controller calculates the congested switch, and changes routes, bypassing the congested switch. If deceleration happens only for couple of hosts, then the controller includes a reserve route for this pair of tasks.

5 Analysis of Security of Two-Level System

The provided protocol is the least secure in a series of protocols which have additional security support. According to [2] the following network attacks should be considered as most important.

5.1 Man-in-the-Middle Attack

If one or several communication links are listened, then an adversary can transfer the intercepted information through its own channels outside of network. However, if the adversary has no channels outside of network, then transmission of the intercepted information is impossible because in the switch there is no allowed route to a hostile host with legally solvable task. But man-in-the-middle attack can lead to distortion of information.

5.2 Capture of a Switch

This attack allows to solve many problems for an adversary. In traditional SDN there is a possibility of duplicating of a traffic. However in our model of transmission through a network of a duplication of traffic is possible only in case the captured switch is directly connected to a hostile host. In remaining cases transmission are impossible. The captured switch gives more opportunities for distortion of transit data. However it is equivalent that a part of sessions is locked. Therefore hosts easily reveal such attacks. As it is described above the attack with distortion of data is possible to consider as failures, and for restoration of sessions it is possible to use reserve routes.

5.3   Capture of the Controller

Capture of a switch in traditional SDN can initiate an attack on the controller. For this purpose in traditional SDN an overflowing of input buffers of a switch is imitated. In this case together with heads of packets the whole packets are sent to the controller. Thus, it is possible to increase a traffic in the channel between the controller and the switch. Thus, denial-of-service attack on the controller is built. In our model such attack is impossible since all routes are fixed and the appeal to the controller from switches is forbidden.

5.4   Direct Capture of the Controller or $H(\mathcal{N})$

Physical capture of the controller or a host $H(\mathcal{N})$ completely compromises network functioning and information security at the level of tasks.

5.5   Capture of Hosts $H(A)$ or $H(A_1)$

Capture of $H(A)$ or $H(A_1)$ can create a possibility of distribution of malicious code or harmful influence into network hosts, and also attack the controller or $H(\mathcal{N})$. This attack is based on implementation in a captured host of malicious code and means of its implementation into other hosts.

Summarizing results of the short analysis of security of the elementary protocol, it is possible to claim that the considerable part of threats connected to redirection and duplicating of information flows is liquidated, the possibility of start of illegal tasks is reduced, and the possibility of interaction of illegal tasks is restricted. However some attacks to a network are staying actual.

6   The Reinforced Protocol of Secure Interactions in Two-Level System

For lowering a danger of other leaks it is possible to strengthen the protocol in SDN. At the same time all "pluses" of the feeble protocol remain. Gain of the protocol is connected to reliability augmentation and security of interactions of the level of tasks and the level of a network.

Let's assume that on each host H there is an agent $\mathcal{N}(H)$ for implementation of the encoded communication with host $H(\mathcal{N})$. I.e. each host has cryptographical facilities and a personal key for fast symmetric enciphering, providing a secure interaction of the agent $\mathcal{N}(H)$ with the task $\mathcal{N}$. Then the feeble protocol may be strengthened by opportunities of a secure communication and monitoring of integrity of interactions of hosts $H(A)$ and $H(A_1)$.

When enciphering communication of $H(A)$ and $H(A_1)$ with the secret key $k(H(A), H(A_1))$ which is received from $\mathcal{N}$ a threat "Man-in-the-middle" and, therefore, a threat of interception of information or distortion of information disappear.

Capture of the switch can input a chaos to transit of the information via the captured switch that is equivalent to failure of this switch. In case of capture of the switch each information flow for any pair of tasks is isolated by means of the identifiers of tasks which are protected by integrity controlling. Protection of integrity of the identifiers won't allow to change this parameter on the captured switch, and traffic confusing will be locked directly on other switches. However usage of integrity control will demand a complication of technology:

– introduction of certificates of public keys;
– check of monitoring of identifiers integrity will demand on each switch of computation of cryptographic algorithms with asymmetric keys.

Unlike the feeble protocol an existence of cryptography in switches won't allow to create false switches and controllers.

7   Conclusion

In the paper the model of security of cloud computing on the basis of interaction on level of tasks and architecture of SDN is constructed. It is shown that meta data about solvable tasks can be used for effective control of information flows on a network and reduction of risks. The constructed protocols allow different strength of a security.

The main idea consists in the control of all connections through meta data. Such approach allows to exclude any initializations of connections of hosts and switches with the controller. All safety features are carried out under the control of meta data.

The explained approach requires a further in-depth study. It is necessary to evaluate delay period in the offered organization of data communication. Preliminary experiments show the positive result.

It is necessary to develop algorithms of creation of meta data on the basis of a business process model and basic services.

Acknowledgements. The research is supported by Russian Foundation for Basic Research (project 15-29-07981, project 15-07-02053).

References

1. Grusho, A.A., Abaev, P.O., Shorgin, S.Y., Timonina, E.E.: Graphs for information security control in software defined networks. In: AIP Conference Proceedings (2017). (to be published)

2. Shu, Z., Wan, J., Li, D., Lin, J., Vasilakos, A.V., Imran, M.: Security in software-defined networking: threats and countermeasures. J. Mob. Netw. Appl. **21**(5), 764–776 (2016). doi:10.1007/s11036-016-0676-x

3. Luo, S., Wu, J., Li, J., Guo, L., Pei, B.: Context-aware traffic forwarding service for applications in SDN. In: IEEE International Conference on Smart City/SocialCom/SustainCom, pp. 557–561. IEEE Press, New York (2015). doi:10.1109/SmartCity.2015.128

4. Fergusson, A.D., Guha, A., Liang, C., Fonseca, R., Krishnamurthi, S.: Hierarchical policies for software defined networks. In: HotSDN 2012, 13 August, Helsinki, pp. 37–41. ACM (2012). doi:10.1145/2342441.2342450

5. Sokolov, V., Alekseev, I., Mazilov, D., Nikitinskiy, M.: A network analytics system in the SDN. In: SDN and NFV: The Next Generation of Computational Infrastructure: 2014 International Science and Technology Conference Modern Networking Technologies (MoNeTec), pp. 160–162. MAKS Press, Moscow (2014)

6. Pantuza, G., Sampaio, F., Viera, L., Guedes, D., Viera, M.: Network management through graphs in software defined network. In: 10th CNSM and Workshop, pp. 400–405. IFIP (2014)

7. McGeer, R.: A safe, efficient update protocol for OpenFlow networks. In: HotSDN 2012, August 13, Helsinki, pp. 61–66. ACM (2012)

8. Grusho, A.A., Zabezhailo, M.I., Zatsarinny, A.A., Piskovski, V.O.: Secure automatic reconfiguration of cloudy computing. J. Syst. Means Inform. **26**(3), 83–92 (2016). doi:10.14357/08696527160306

9. Grusho, A.A., Zabezhailo, M.I., Zatsarinny, A.A.: On the advanced procedure to reduce calculation of Galois closures. J. Inform. Appl. **10**(4), 97–106 (2016). doi:10.14357/19922264160410

10. Grusho, A.A., Zabezhailo, M.I., Zatsarinny, A.A.: Information flow monitoring and control in cloud computing environment. J. Inform. Appl. **9**(4), 95–101 (2015). doi:10.14357/1992264150410

11. Grusho, A., Grusho, N., Piskovski, V., Timonina, E.: Five SDN-oriented directions in information security. In: SDN and NFV: The Next Generation of Computational Infrastructure: 2014 International Science and Technology Conference Modern Networking Technologies (MoNeTec), pp. 68–71. MAKS Press, Moscow (2014). doi:10.1109/MoNeTeC.2014.6995586

12. Nilsson, N.J.: Problem-Solving Methods in Artificial Intelligence. McGraw-Hill Pub. Co., New York (1971)

13. Lazarev, A.A., Gafarov, E.R.: Scheduling Theory. Tasks and Algorithms. Publ. House MSU, Moscow (2011)

Toward Third-Party Immune Applications

Omar Iraqi[1,2(⊠)] and Hanan El Bakkali[1]

[1] Information Security Research Team, ENSIAS,
Mohammed V University, Rabat, Morocco
o.iraqi@aui.ma, h.elbakkali@um5s.net.ma
[2] School of Science and Engineering,
Al Akhawayn University, Ifrane, Morocco

Abstract. Component reuse has become a trend in software engineering. How-ever, third-party components have the potential to introduce vulnerabilities into software applications and become the weakest link in the security chain. In this paper, we discuss the limitations of traditional security practices and controls against vulnerable components. As a solution, we present a software design and development approach, combined with a collaborative, cloud-based vulnerability and threat management system. This combination aims at enabling applications to gain "artificial immunity" to third-party components by dynamically identifying and controlling related security risks. It also strives to promote the automatic discovery of, and near real-time information dissemination about emerging threats and zero-day vulnerabilities. At the heart of our solution, we use application-level API sandboxing, as well as adaptive signature-based and anomaly-based API intrusion detection and prevention. The need-to-know, cost-effectiveness, and user acceptance through separation of concerns have been our guiding security engineering principles.

Keywords: Third-party components · Artificial immunity · Collaborative · Cloud-based vulnerability and threat management · Component sandboxing · Adaptive intrusion detection and prevention · Separation of concerns

1 Introduction

In this digital era, information systems have become an intrinsic element of corporates daily activities and people's lives. From Enterprise Resource Planning (ERP) to social networking, use cases are permanently expanding, while system boundaries are con-tinually falling. However, the increasing system ubiquity has led to more frequent and highly damaging security incidents, as confirmed by recent surveys [1–3].

Information security threats exercise a large spectrum of flaws throughout the information system lifecycle. More specifically, OWASP 2013 Top 10 Report [4] identifies using known vulnerable components as one of top application security risks.

In fact, component reuse has become a trend in software engineering as it promotes developer productivity, but it has also the potential to introduce security vulnerabilities into applications. One of the most significant examples in recent years has been the Heartbleed bug. A buffer overread attack against OpenSSL tls1_process_heartbeat method, caused the leakage of encryption key material of millions of websites [5].

© Springer International Publishing AG 2017
J. Rak et al. (Eds.): MMM-ACNS 2017, LNCS 10446, pp. 348–359, 2017.
DOI: 10.1007/978-3-319-65127-9_28

Secure software development methodologies such as Microsoft Security Development Lifecycle (SDL) [6] and OWASP Software Assurance Maturity Model (SAMM) [7] help reduce such a risk via a set of practices throughout the development lifecycle. These include developer training, unsafe APIs deprecation, code review, penetration testing, and software certification. They also include operational controls such as vulnerability management, intrusion detection and prevention, and incident response. The benefits are straightforward, but the residual risk may still be unacceptable. While trained developers would avoid using deprecated APIs, this does not guarantee that all used APIs are and will remain safe. Even code verification and penetration testing may miss identifying serious bugs in application code and used APIs. Moreover, we will show how operational controls as well as other specific controls such as application sandboxing and partitioning become ineffective against vulnerable APIs.

As a solution to these limitations, we propose a software design and development approach that promotes and supports building applications that are capable of monitoring, identifying, assessing and dynamically controlling the security risks pertaining to third-party components. Along with this approach, we propose a collaborative, cloud-based system that promotes and supports the automatic discovery of, and information dissemination about, emerging threats and zero-day vulnerabilities.

The remainder of this paper is organized as follows. Section 2 gives the background of secure software development and security solutions pertaining to third-party APIs. It also discusses their limitations and outlines the building blocks of our envisioned solution. Section 3 reviews and compares the relevant state of the art initiatives. Section 4 describes in details the building blocks identified in Sect. 2 and integrates them in a holistic and coherent solution. Section 5 gives an implementation example. Finally, we conclude in Sect. 6 by giving future work and direction.

2 Secure Software Development: Background and Limitations

2.1 Relevant Information Security Principles

Information security principles are the intrinsic security expectations that must be met by an information system regardless of its size, type or owner [8]. The need-to- know is one of these principles. It refers to the restriction of the subject to access only the objects that are necessary to perform legitimate and justified duties. This can be enforced through practices such as the least privilege and security domains [9]. Other relevant information security principles include cost-effectiveness, user acceptance/ease of use, security by design and security in depth [9].

In the next sections, we will show how current practices fail to meet these principles in protecting applications from vulnerable third-party components.

2.2 Application Sandboxing and Partitioning

Application sandboxing is an isolation technique that draws a boundary between the application or mobile code such as an applet, and its runtime environment. The boundary enforces a well-defined sandboxing policy. In contrast, application partitioning refers to isolating the application trusted code from the untrusted code. However, for a sandboxed or a partitioned application to work correctly, the confined code shall be granted at least the sum of access rights required by each of its third-party APIs. Such a policy would then allow each API to have higher privileges than it really needs. This leads to the violation of the need-to-know principle. In contrast, confining each third-party API in its own sandbox governed by its own policy shall enforce the need-to-know principle. Indeed, each API will be granted the least privilege that it requires to access legitimate, justified and authorized resources only. We call this technique API sandboxing, as described in Sect. 4 of this paper.

2.3   Intrusion Detection and Prevention, and Application Firewalling

While API sandboxing as proposed above promises an enhanced security, it does not prevent the API from performing unauthorized operations on authorized resources. This is why we think that an additional application-level, API-specific intrusion detection and prevention layer is needed. We will show how this same layer can also serve for the systematic identification of potential API vulnerabilities. But first, why wouldn't traditional intrusion detection and prevention solutions be enough? This family of operational security controls range from general network intrusion detection and prevention, to host intrusion detection and prevention, to the more specialized application firewalling. Intrusion detection techniques can be categorized as signature-based, anomaly-based or hybrid [10]. Threat-specific frameworks such as XSS-Guard [11] are also available and can act as an additional protection layer.

While these solutions can be more or less effective in detecting and stopping threats, they don't allow a systematic identification of the potential vulnerability being targeted. Let's consider the case of a web application sitting behind a web application firewall. Let's assume that the application is vulnerable to SQL injection and XSS attacks. The firewall may successfully stop them, but without the administrator analyzing the alerts, it is impossible to link threats to their corresponding vulnerabilities. Because of the large number of log entries and false alerts, administrators would rarely dig more. Under these conditions, if the vulnerabilities in question had never been discovered, then we would have missed the opportunity to unravel them.

In the example above, web application firewalls can at least intercept and analyze the problematic I/O. However, application firewalls have no access to intermediary data that is processed and passed from one module to another inside the application. Indeed, while application I/O may be genuine, intermediary data can intentionally or unintentionally become problematic during the request processing lifecycle.

For all these reasons, we suggest to go one step further and add another layer of defense consisting of intrusion detection and prevention inside the application, i.e. at the API level. This would allow detecting and stopping known threats, as well as systematically discovering emerging threats and zero-day vulnerabilities at the method level, e.g. OpenSSL tls1_process_heartbeat method. However, detection techniques applied at the network or host levels need to be reinvented. For example, what are the most significant features for analyzing a method behavior? What is normal vs. abnormal behavior for a method? We will provide more details in Sects. 4 and 5 below.

2.4 Vulnerability Management

Vulnerability management is the process of identifying, classifying, and mitigating vulnerabilities [12]. Vulnerability identification is performed by the API provider, the security community, as well as hackers. Depending on who finds the vulnerability first and how it is disclosed and treated, multiple critical windows are created during which the affected applications can be compromised. These critical windows include the time between the vulnerability discovery and the API patch release, the time between the API patch release and the affected applications patch release, and finally the time before the upgrade of the affected applications in their production environments. In Sect. 4, we will show how the suggested API intrusion detection and prevention addresses these issues systematically.

3 Related Work

To the best of our knowledge, no work has been conducted on systems that support the automatic discovery of emerging threats or zero-day vulnerabilities related to third-party components. Similarly, no research has been conducted on applications that are capable of dynamically managing the security risks pertaining to third-party components. Therefore, we will consider state of the art research projects in the closest field to our envisioned solution, namely application partitioning and sandboxing.

Privman is a library that makes privilege separation easy by providing a reusable framework and library for developing partitioned applications [13]. Programs that use Privman split into two processes that communicate via IPC: a privilege server running security-specific code and the main application running non-security-specific code. Privman configuration-based policy may give a broad amount of privilege to an attacker, while the extension framework adds development overhead.

In Android environment, as the sandboxing technique is process-based, native libraries enjoy all the permissions granted by the end user to the application. Native-Guard addresses this issue by splitting an application into a client application, which holds pure Java code in addition to resource and user-interface files; and the service application, which holds native libraries [14]. NativeGuard confines all native libraries in the same sandbox. This leads to the violation of the need-to-know principle.

As opposed to NativeGuard, AppCage creates its own in-app sandboxes. The first one, dex sandbox, confines (pure Java) sensitive APIs, while the second one, native sandbox, targets native libraries. Dex sandbox uses API hooking at the level of the Dalvik virtual machine to inject a reference monitor into the application. In contrast, the native sandbox uses software fault isolation (SFI) to prevent native libraries from tampering with the application and the dex sandbox [15]. AppCage violates the need-to-know principle as all sensitive APIs are confined in the same sandbox.

NativeProtector is a solution that is inspired from NativeGuard. However, and in order to support the need-to-know principle, NativeProtector enhances NativeGuard and AppCage, by intercepting the native libraries and applying a fine-grained policy. However, the incurred performance overhead may not be acceptable when the number of native calls increases. Indeed, it can reach 80% in some cases [16].

Boxify is another user-level sandboxing technique for Android applications. Boxify virtualizes applications within a reference monitor, rather than injecting the monitor inside applications [17]. The monitor is split into a shim monitor hosting the target application, and a privileged broker that is isolated from the application. As Boxify does not support application partitioning, the nee- to-know principle is violated.

LibCage is the closest solution to our proposed API sandboxing. First, LibCage strives to adhere to the need-to-know principle by isolating each third-party library in its own sandbox. Secondly, LibCage involves application developers in API sandboxing through a library that they use with minimum development overhead [18].

We will show next how our solution transcends application sandboxing and partitioning. It goes much beyond and includes adaptive API intrusion detection and prevention, as well as collaborative, cloud-based vulnerability and threat management.

4   Third-Party Security-Aware Solution (3SAS)

4.1   Solution Overview

Threat Model. We consider attacks that try to jeopardize the security of software applications by exploiting the vulnerabilities of third-party components. These attacks may be local or remote. They may have well-defined signatures and target known vulnerabilities, or be emerging threats trying to exercise zero-day vulnerabilities. A known vulnerability may already have a patch, or may not.

Solution Objectives. 3SAS aims at enabling applications to gain *artificial immunity* to attacks under the threat model defined above. In the case of known threats, 3SAS strives to automatically stop the attacks based on their signature (Objective 1). However, if the targeted vulnerability has been unknown so far, 3SAS will try to detect the emerging threat and seize the opportunity to unravel the potential zero-day vulnerability (Objective 2). This information shall be shared with the security community, and particularly with other concerned applications for dynamic adjustment of their security posture, while the vulnerability is being fixed (Objective 3).

Solution Overview and Requirements. To achieve the objectives defined above, we propose a third-party security-aware software design and development approach (Sect. 4.2), along with a collaborative, cloud-based third-party vulnerability and threat management system (Sect. 4.3). The combination of the proposed approach and system shall:

1. Empower applications to become aware of third-party components and capable of monitoring, identifying, assessing and dynamically controlling related risks;
2. Promote and support the automatic discovery of, and information dissemination about, emerging threats and zero-day vulnerabilities related to third-party APIs;
3. Minimize the implementation overhead on both the component provider and the application provider;
4. Minimize the operational cost in terms of performance overhead.

4.2   Third-Party Security-Aware Software Design and Development Approach

Assumptions. To minimize the implementation overhead (3rd requirement), our proposed software design and development approach assumes that the adopted technology supports separation of concerns and declarative development. The cross-cutting concern that we are interested in here is third-party component security monitoring and control. This can be achieved by leveraging aspect oriented programming (AOP) techniques and the interceptor design pattern. These assumptions are verified with most modern software frameworks and in many popular languages. For example, JEE and Spring (Java) frameworks support proxy-based AOP and the interceptor design pattern through inversion of control (IoC) and dependency injection. They also support declarative development through Java annotations and/or xml configuration files.

To minimize the operational overhead (4th requirement), the logic of anomaly-based intrusion detection can be moved off the application to a remote, trusted module. Moreover, since the aim of anomaly-based intrusion detection is not to stop attacks, but rather to discover emerging threats (Sect. 4.1, objective 2), the remote module can be invoked asynchronously. Concerning signature-based intrusion detection and prevention, the incurred overhead is reduced by having the application dynamically deactivate the signature(s) as soon as it gets patched against the vulnerable component.

Roles and Responsibilities. Our design and development approach defines different roles and maps them to one of three SDL phases: design, development and operation. Moreover, each role corresponds to one of three providers: third-party component provider, security provider, and application provider. Table 1 summarizes these roles and responsibilities, according to these two dimensions: provider and SDL phase.

Table 1. Proposed software design & development approach – roles and responsibilities

Provider/SDL phase	Design	Development	Operation
Component provider	**Third-party component designer:** Specifies components whose method calls may be intercepted	**Third-party component developer:** Marks the specified component methods for eventual call interception	–
Security provider	–	**Security Developer:** Develops security monitoring interceptors	–
Application provider	**Application Architect:** Selects the components whose method calls shall actually be intercepted	**Application Developer:** Applies security monitoring interceptors on method calls of selected components	**Application Admin:** Makes sure the application is well integrated with the system, described in Sect. 4.3

Process. As shown in Fig. 1, the third-party component designer specifies the components whose method calls may be intercepted by the application runtime (1). Then, the component developer builds and marks these components for eventual interception, using inline annotations or external (xml) configuration (2). This task can be automated using a code enhancer. The newly developed components are non-vulnerable so far, but are enabled for the automatic discovery of potential vulnerabilities in the future. The application architect decides about the components that shall actually be intercepted for monitoring and control (3.1). The application architect also describes how the application will be integrated with the proposed vulnerability and threat management system (3.2). Finally, the application developer uses dependency injection to inject the third-party components that have been selected by the application architect for monitoring, and specifies the interceptors to apply (4). Accordingly, the application runtime applies security monitoring and control interceptors at the injection points (5). Independently, these interceptors are provided by the security developer (0) and ensure both anomaly-based and signature-based intrusion detection. Anomaly-based intrusion detection is used to detect emerging threats and inform the third-party vulnerability and threat management system, proposed in Sect. 4.3, about potential zero-day vulnerabilities. Signature-based intrusion detection gets feedback from the proposed system about confirmed vulnerabilities along with their corresponding attack signatures. These are automatically applied to raise the security bar of the application dynamically and stop such attacks. This adaptive signature-based intrusion detection acts as a compensating control while the component provider is releasing the updated version of the affected component. Once this version is released and the application is patched, the security interceptors shall dynamically return the application security posture to its previous state, by deactivating the so called attack signatures.

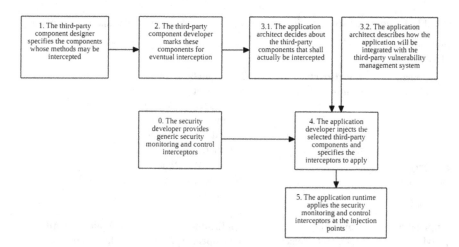

Fig. 1. Third-party security-aware software design & development approach – flowchart

4.3   Collaborative Cloud-Based Third-Party Vulnerability and Threat Management System

Popular third-party APIs, such as Apache Commons and GNU APIs, are used by millions of applications. This makes them an appealing target, but creates a promising collaboration opportunity. Indeed, applications can continuously exchange information about detected anomalies. This would enhance both security effectiveness and efficiency. On one hand, aggregating alarms from millions of applications would reduce false positives/negatives. On the other hand, an application doesn't need to monitor every API it uses. It can get related information from other applications.

System Stakeholders

- *Vulnerability and Threat Management Authority (VTMA):* This is an authoritative, public or private organization that orchestrates third-party vulnerability and threat management. It also establishes the link with the security community. There could be many of such authorities, and they may exchange their findings about threats and vulnerabilities.
- *Application Owner:* This is an organization that runs applications, and is interested in the cloud-based vulnerability and threat management. It may decide to contribute to the system by allowing its applications to report anomalies to one or more authorities.
- *Security Community:* Analyzes and confirms or disconfirms the published anomalies. At this level, research teams such as IBM X-Force [19] could be very helpful.
- *OVDR Owner:* This is an OVAL (Open Vulnerability and Assessment Language) Definitions Repository owner such as MITRE, NIST, IT Security DB, etc.

System Architecture. As shown in Fig. 2, the proposed system is made of:

- *Vulnerability and Threat Management Broker (VTMB):* The VTMB is managed by the application owner. It keeps sending/receiving security alerts to/from one or more VTMO(s) on behalf of managed applications.
- *Vulnerability and Threat Management Orchestrator (VTMO):* The VTMO is a cloud-based service that is managed by the VTMA. It gathers and correlates security alerts from VTMBs to compute an aggregate score per component. When a component score exceeds a threshold, the VTMO publishes a security alert on the VTMP. If the alert is confirmed, the VTMO sends a notification to VTMBs.
- *Vulnerability and Threat Management Portal (VTMP):* The VTMP is managed by the VTMA to communicate with the security community.
- *Open Vulnerability Sync Agent (OVSA):* The OVSA is managed by the vulnerability and threat management authority. It allows the system to submit confirmed vulnerabilities to the OVDR. It also fetches the definitions of vulnerabilities discovered independently of this system, for the VTMO to feed concerned VTMBs.
- *Open Vulnerability Definitions Registry (OVDR):* The OVDR keeps track of confirmed vulnerabilities.

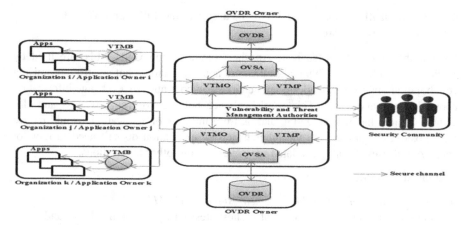

Fig. 2. Cloud-based third-party vulnerability and threat management system – architecture

Trust-Based Collaboration. Score aggregation and computation performed by the VTMO may be poisoned by false alarms sent by rogue or weak VTMBs. This can lead to overwhelming the security community with false positives, which undermines the proposed collaboration. To address this issue, score aggregation shall take into consideration the reputation of every VTMB, and be weighted accordingly. This reputation/weight shall be dynamically assessed and updated based on the accuracy of its alerts. A security alert is considered accurate if and only if it has been confirmed by the security community. The initial reputation/weight assigned to an unknown VTMB should be very low. VTMBs reporting anomalies accurately will see their reputation/weight growing. In contrast, rogue or weak VTMBs, will see their reputation/weight decreasing as they send fake alarms. Ultimately, they will be kicked out of the system and blacklisted, as soon as their score reaches a predefined threshold.

5 Implementation Example

5.1 Example Overview

In this example, we illustrate signature and anomaly-based API intrusion detection and prevention. Other aspects, such as trust-based collaboration, are out of the scope of this example. We consider a JEE application that uses a class called JOpenSSL, a Java version of OpenSSL, marked for eventual interception. We also consider a security monitoring interceptor called SimpleInterceptor that we apply on JOpenSSL. We leverage Weka data mining library [20] for anomaly-based intrusion detection using algorithms such as Naïve Bayes, Decision Trees and K-Nearest Neighbors (KNN), as well as their combination. The extracted and analyzed features are the serialized parameter(s) of the intercepted methods, their metadata such as the length of a string or the size of an array, returned values, thrown exceptions, call stack and execution time. We train and evaluate the interceptor based on two classes: genuine requests generated through Apache JMeter [21] and malicious requests generated through ZAP [22].

5.2   Code Snippets

```
org.ssl.JOpenSSL riskySSL;
```

/* Thanks to this injection, riskySSL will be an intercepted version/instance of JOpenSSL, with minimum overhead on the application developer. */

```
public void thirdPartyAwareMethod(SSL s){
     //some code
     result = riskySSL.tls1ProcessHeartbeat(s);
     //more code
 }
}
```

/* Here the application developer creates an interceptor by simply extending SimpleInterceptor, and binds it to classes annotated with @Monitored, i.e. JOpenSSL. */

```
package com.example.thirdpartyawareapp.interceptors;
@javax.interceptor.Interceptor
@org.ssl.Monitored
public class ThirdPartyAPIMonitoringInterceptor
     extends org.thirdpartymonitoring.SimpleInterceptor {}
```

/* Here the security community provides the interceptor */

```
package org.thirdpartymonitoring;
import javax.interceptor.*;
public class SimpleInterceptor {
  @AroundInvoke
  public Object aroundInvoke(InvocationContext ctx)
  throws Exception {
```

/* Extract invocation metadata; check for intrusion signatures using a synchronous call to VTMB; iff no match, proceed to intercepted method; then send method parameter(s), result or exception, execution time and call stack asynchronously to VTMB for anomaly-based intrusion detection. */

```
}
```

In this example, we illustrated how it is easy for both the third-party developer and the application developer to use our proposed approach. Indeed, the overhead on both actors is negligible thanks to the technology support. We also illustrated how performance overhead can be reduced by moving the security monitoring logic off the application, and using non-blocking calls for anomaly-based intrusion detection.

6 Conclusion and Future Work

In this paper, we presented 3SAS: a third-party security-aware solution that aims at enabling software applications to acquire *artificial immunity* to third-party components. 3SAS also strives to promote the automatic discovery of, and information dissemination about emerging threats and zero-day vulnerabilities. It consists of a third-party security-aware software design and development approach, along with a collaborative, cloud-based third-party vulnerability and threat management system. At the heart of our solution, we use application-level API sandboxing, as well as adaptive signature-based and anomaly-based API intrusion detection and prevention. The need-to-know, cost-effectiveness, user acceptance, and defense in depth have been our guiding security engineering principles.

We already started experimenting with our solution. To this end, we used the proposed third-party security-aware software design and development approach to build sample third-party components, sample security monitoring interceptors, and sample applications as shown in the implementation example above. We started testing and evaluating anomaly-based intrusion detection using different data mining techniques such as Naïve Bayes, Decision Trees and K-Nearest Neighbors, as well as statistical methods such as standard deviation. We are also intending to implement and test signature-based intrusion detection. We will develop a code enhancer that automatically instruments components for interception. In addition, we will implement and test a prototype of our proposed collaborative, cloud-based third-party vulnerability and threat management system. We have started designing and comparing different reputation management strategies. Moreover, we are thinking about an integrated test environment along with significant test scenarios on popular components to evaluate the security improvements of the whole solution. Finally, we will work on system scalability beyond traditional scale-up and scale-out practices.

References

1. Information Security Breaches Survey (2015). pwc.co.uk/assets/pdf/2015-isbs-technical-report-blue-03.pdf
2. Forbes & IBM. The Reputational Impact of IT Risk (2014). www-935.ibm.com/services/multimedia/RLL12363USEN_2014_Forbes_Insights.pdf
3. Kaspersky Security Bulletin 2015, Overall statistics for 2015. securelist.com/files/2015/12/KSB_2015_Statistics_FINAL_EN.pdf
4. OWASP 2013 Top 10 Application Security Report. owasptop10.googlecode.com/files/OWASP_Top_10-2013.pdf
5. The Heartbleed Bug. heartbleed.com
6. Microsoft Security Development Lifecycle. microsoft.com/en-us/sdl/
7. OWASP Software Assurance Maturity Model. owasp.org/index.php/Category:Software_Assurance_Maturity_Model
8. Swanson, M., Guttman, B.: Generally Accepted Principles and Practices for Securing Information Technology Systems (1996)

9. Stoneburner, G., Hayden, C., Feringa, A.: Engineering Principles for Information Technology Security (A Baseline for Achieving Security) (2001)
10. Chang, J., Venkatasubramanian, K.K., West, A.G., Lee, I.: Analyzing and defending against web-based malware. ACM Comput. Surv. **45**, 49:1–49:35 (2013)
11. Bisht, P., Venkatakrishnan, V.N.: XSS-GUARD: precise dynamic prevention of cross-site scripting attacks. In: Zamboni, D. (ed.) Detection of Intrusions and Malware, and Vulnerability Assessment, pp. 23–43. Springer, Berlin Heidelberg (2008)
12. Foreman, P.: Vulnerability Management. CRC Press, Boca Raton (2009)
13. Kilpatrick, D.: Privman: a library for partitioning applications. In: USENIX Annual Technical Conference, FREENIX Track, pp. 273–284 (2003)
14. Sun, M., Tan, G.: NativeGuard: protecting android applications from third-party native libraries. In: Proceedings of the 2014 ACM Conference on Security and Privacy in Wireless & Mobile Networks, pp. 165–176. ACM, New York (2014)
15. Zhou, Y., Patel, K., Wu, L., Wang, Z., Jiang, X.: Hybrid user-level sandboxing of third-party android apps. In: Proceedings of the 10th ACM Symposium on Information, Computer and Communications Security, pp. 19–30. ACM, New York (2015)
16. Hong, Y.-Y., Wang, Y.-P., Yin, J.: NativeProtector: protecting android applications by isolating and intercepting third-party native libraries. In: Hoepman, J.-H., Katzenbeisser, S. (eds.) SEC 2016. IAICT, vol. 471, pp. 337–351. Springer, Cham (2016). doi:10.1007/978-3-319-33630-5_23
17. Backes, M., Bugiel, S., Hammer, C., Schranz, O., von Styp-Rekowsky, P.: Boxify: full-fledged app sandboxing for stock android. In: 24th USENIX Security Symposium (USENIX Security 2015), pp. 691–706. USENIX Association, Washington, D.C. (2015)
18. Wang, F., Zhang, Y., Wang, K., Liu, P., Wang, W.: Stay in your cage! A sound sandbox for third-party libraries on android. In: Askoxylakis, I., Ioannidis, S., Katsikas, S., Meadows, C. (eds.) ESORICS 2016. LNCS, vol. 9878, pp. 458–476. Springer, Cham (2016). doi:10.1007/978-3-319-45744-4_23
19. IBM X-Force Research. www-03.ibm.com/security/xforce/
20. Weka 3: Data Mining Software in Java. cs.waikato.ac.nz/ml/weka/
21. Apache JMeter. jmeter.apache.org
22. Zed Attack Proxy. owasp.org/index.php/OWASP_Zed_Attack_Proxy_Project

Author Index

Antkiewicz, Ryszard 223

Bezzateev, Sergey 260
Biernat, Jay 104
Braeken, An 260
Branitskiy, Alexander 143

Chechulin, Andrey 75
Chen, Yu 247

Davis, Matthew 62, 185
De Decker, Bart 37
Debar, Hervé 75
Dolgikh, Andrey 62, 91, 185
Dong, Changyu 275
Dong, Qi 247
Doynikova, Elena 75
Drager, Steven 327

El Bakkali, Hanan 348

Fedyanin, Ivan 288
Francikiewicz, Maciej 299

Gkioulos, Vasileios 115
Godlewski, Artur 288
Gonzalez-Granadillo, Gustavo 75
Górski, Janusz 3
Grusho, Alexander 28, 339
Grusho, Nick 339

Hutchison, Andrew 16

Iraqi, Omar 348
Isoaho, Jouni 171

Kolomeec, Maxim 75
Konorski, Jerzy 131
Kopeikin, Anton 195, 211
Korkmaz, Emrah 62, 185
Korzhik, Valery 288
Kotenko, Igor 75, 143
Kotulski, Zbigniew 158

Lemaire, Laurens 37
Li, Xiaohua 247
Łukasiewicz, Katarzyna 3

Mavroeidis, Vasileios 313
Metere, Roberto 275
Mjølsnes, Stig F. 235
Morales-Luna, Guillermo 288
Murenin, Ivan 50

Naessens, Vincent 37
Nagothu, Deeraj 91
Nicho, Mathew 313
Niemiec, Marcin 299
Nigussie, Ethiopia 171
Novikova, Evgenia 50

Olimid, Ruxandra F. 235
Ostap, Hubert 223

Popyack, Leonard 104

Rydzewski, Karol 131

Satybaldina, Dina 195, 211
Sitek, Albert 158
Skormin, Victor 62, 185

Tashatov, Nurlan 195, 211
Thanigaivelan, Nanda Kumar 171
Timonina, Elena 339
Tokhtabayev, Arnur 195, 211
Touhafi, Abdellah 260

Virtanen, Seppo 171
Voloshina, Natalia 260
Vossaert, Jan 37

Wolthusen, Stephen D. 115

Yang, Zekun 247

Zabezhailo, Michael   339
Zalewski, Janusz   327

Zatsarinny, Alexander   339
Zeng, Kai   247